Caught in the Crossfire

Caught in the Crossfire

Revolutions, Repression,
and the Rational Peasant

T. David Mason

ROWMAN & LITTLEFIELD PUBLISHERS, INC.
Lanham • Boulder • New York • Toronto • Oxford

ROWMAN & LITTLEFIELD PUBLISHERS, INC.

Published in the United States of America
by Rowman & Littlefield Publishers, Inc.
A Member of the Rowman & Littlefield Publishing Group
4501 Forbes Boulevard, Suite 200, Lanham, Maryland 20706
www.rowmanlittlefield.com

PO Box 317, Oxford, OX2 9RU, UK

British Library Cataloguing in Publication Information Available

Library of Congress Cataloging-in-Publication Data

Mason, T. David (Thomas David), 1950–
    Caught in the crossfire : revolutions, repression, and the rational peasant /
    T. David Mason.
        p. cm.
Includes bibliographical references and index.
    ISBN 0-7425-2538-4 (cloth : alk. paper) — ISBN 0-7425-2539-2 (pbk. : alk. paper)
1. Peasantry—Developing countries—History.   2. Peasantry—Developing countries—
Political activity.   3. Revolutions—Developing countries.   I. Title.
    HD1542.M37 2004
    305.5'633'091724—dc22
                                                            2003018141

Printed in the United States of America

Contents

Preface

This is a book about revolutions in the countryside. Why would an otherwise ordinary person embark upon such an extraordinary course of action as taking up arms (with other like-minded ordinary people) against his or her own government? This question has puzzled me for most of my adult life. Of course, I am not alone in this concern. Fortunately, I have been able to make a living in academia by wrestling with this and related questions. This book represents my first opportunity to report on my intellectual journey to date. As the reader will see, however, I am no closer to an answer, only more acutely aware of the breadth and depth of my ignorance on the subject. I hope that exploring these newly identified realms of ignorance will keep me intellectually engaged and gainfully employed for some time to come.

Unfortunately, part of the reason I and many others in academia are able to make careers out of the study of revolution and other forms of political violence is that our fellow human beings continue to provide us with new material to study. There have been well over one hundred instances of civil war during my lifetime. These conflicts have inflicted over 15 million battle deaths. More than twenty new civil wars erupted while I was writing this book. Since I completed this manuscript, new research on civil wars has added new dimensions to our understanding of the destructiveness of large-scale organized political violence. Besides the battle casualties, civil wars have been implicated as a cause of famine in such places as Ethiopia and Somalia. Recent studies have documented the short- and long-term economic costs of civil war as well as its impact on postwar rates of death and disease among populations caught in the crossfire. A recent report of the State Failure Project at the University of Maryland has documented the impact of civil war on the chronic incapacity of states and their occasional collapse into the chaos of "statelessness." This erosion of state capacity makes those nations even more susceptible to the recurrence of civil war, a subject that I am presently researching. Barbara Harff has recently reported that most of the nearly fifty instances of genocide and political mass murder that have taken place over the last half century have occurred in conjunction with civil wars. In the aftermath of the September 11th terrorist attacks on the United States, it should come as no surprise that the terrorist organizations that perpetrate such acts often find safe haven in nations torn by civil wars. The annual reports from the Peace Research Institute of Oslo (PRIO) offer us little reason to expect any significant decline in these human costs, because there appears to be no significant decline in the frequency with which ordinary people feel motivated to take up arms against their government.

Writing this book has taken me far longer than it should have. Indeed, most civil wars do not last as long as it took me to complete this manuscript. Along the way, a number of people have played a significant role in making it possible for me to complete this project. I am deeply indebted to Charles Tilly, who invited me to contribute this volume to a series he was editing. For someone of his stature to invite someone of my humble standing to undertake such a project was gratifying, to say the least. The patience he showed in awaiting the completion of a draft manuscript was more than anyone should expect. I am further indebted to him for reviewing in great detail the first draft of the manuscript and compelling me, through the force of his arguments, to return to the drawing board and undertake a near total rewrite of the manuscript. Two chapters were dropped from that first draft, and a new chapter (chapter 10) was added. Chapters 2, 4, and 7 were so substantially revised as to bear scant resemblance to the originals. The reader will have to take my word that the new draft is a substantial improvement over the original (and perhaps shudder at the thought of how turgid that original must have been). Without Charles Tilly's critique, I fear I would have submitted a manuscript that would have served neither me nor the students for whom this book is intended.

Others have been equally generous with their time and their comments. Will Moore read early drafts of most of the chapters and was kind enough to offer detailed comments and suggestions that significantly improved the arguments and the style of the manuscript. His own work on the subject continues to define the contours of research on political violence, and I would owe him an intellectual debt even if he had never taken the time to review the manuscript. Joe Weingarten pored through early drafts of a number of chapters. His keen eye and sharp editorial pen helped me to hone the logic of the arguments and sharpen the language of the presentation. Alas, there is only so much that even a Joe Weingarten can do, so I must assume responsibility for the state of the prose that follows. It is a blessing to have a friend like Joe who actually enjoys providing a sounding board for ideas, picking them apart and forcing me to rethink them (and rewrite them) until they pass muster with his exacting standards. That he could do that without discouraging me—indeed, encouraging me with his enthusiasm for a subject that is only marginally relevant to his own expertise in economics—is greatly appreciated. Doug Imig did much the same for me during some difficult times in this project. When the problems with the first draft left me wondering whether I should abandon the project altogether, it was Doug who encouraged me to rethink the organization and content of the book, and it was Doug who guided me through aspects of the contentious politics literature that I had ignored because it did not deal directly with revolutionary collective action. He showed me that the line separating violent from nonviolent collective action is often a thin and rather permeable one. Doug's ability to revive my enthusiasm for the project made it possible for me to complete the manuscript.

A number of other people have played less direct but no less important roles in making it possible for me to complete this book. Paul Hagner was chair of the Department of Political Science at the University of Memphis while I was completing this project. I have never served under a chair who was better able to lead a department in the accomplishment of collective goals while simultaneously making it possible for faculty to fulfill their personal research goals. His good humor and effective leadership made it possible for me to concentrate on this project. He also served as my role model when I was asked to assume the chair's position upon his departure. Gary Carman and Timitrial Pettis made my job as department chair far easier than it should have been. Their competence, efficiency, initiative, and good humor allowed me to continue working on this project while serving as chair. Likewise, David Madlock, Bill Marty, and Nanette Graddy took on a number of administrative tasks that otherwise would have landed on my desk and further postponed the completion of this manuscript. In addition to their competence and commitment to the department and its students, their friendship and support made the job of department chair much more palatable and manageable.

I have also had the pleasure of working with a number of graduate students during the course of this project. Several of them have contributed to this project through their research assistance and the challenges they posed to me with their own insightful research. I apologize to them for doing nothing more than listing their names here, but they know how much I appreciate the intellectual stimulation and spiritual energy I derived from my time working with them. Among those people (and in no particular order) are Jon Stevenson, David Galbreath, Jason Quinn, Chris Campany, Maria Trif, Thomas Neeley, Perry Miller, Nana Bellerud, Ronnie Lindström, and Connie Oxford. I have had the good fortune to teach a number of classes in which parts of this book were the subject matter of the course. I have had the further good fortune of having excellent students in those classes, many of whom (too numerous to list here) have contributed to this book by raising questions about revolutions and forcing me to rethink parts of my argument.

Although I completed the manuscript before I moved to the University of North Texas, I am indebted to my new colleagues here for providing me with the opportunity—and the intellectual stimulation—to return to this work and begin the next stage in this research program. Steve Poe and John Booth in particular have inspired me to pursue new directions in this research. The Johnie Christian Family Peace Professor Endowment has provided me with the resources to undertake some new projects that, hopefully, will bring to the analysis of revolutions, their causes, and their consequences the expertise and creativity of colleagues here and at other universities.

Once the manuscript was completed, I learned that other people play important roles in transforming the typed manuscript into a published volume. Dean Birkenkamp was the editor who offered me the original contract for this book. His encouragement and guidance helped me get the project off the ground. Although the series it was initially intended for was cancelled, Dean had by that time moved to Rowman & Littlefield and he was kind enough to offer me a new contract. He has since left Rowman & Littlefield, but he turned the project over to Alden Perkins, whose patient professionalism in guiding me through the editorial production process is truly laudable.

Finally, I would not have undertaken this project, much less completed it, without the support and encouragement of my family. My parents, to whom this book is dedicated, inspired me to pursue a career as a scholar. I don't think they realize how much the way they conducted themselves in their lives and their careers—with honesty, dignity, and the courage to take a stand for what they thought was right—inspired me in my career and influenced my choice of contentious politics as the subject of my scholarly endeavors. My wife, Tyffany Mason, has been my partner throughout this project, and her contribution to its success has been immeasurable, far beyond the conventional spousal role. She is the one person whose sharp intellect was unfettered by the strictures of that body of often arcane social science theory that can confine our thinking to narrowly defined intellectual niches. As such her responses to my theorizing always brought a good dose of common sense to my thinking. She and my two sons, Tom and Ben, were patient with me beyond belief as I took time away from them to devote to this book. They loved me anyway. For that I am more grateful than the three of them will ever realize.

I hope that this book will be of some use to students of revolutionary conflict. I will add that part of my motivation for writing it was selfish: I tried to write the book that I would want to use in my courses on revolution and political violence. I hope that students and teachers interested in this subject find it to be of some use to them. The subject, unfortunately, will be with us for some time to come.

Chapter One

The Puzzle of Revolution
in the Third World

On the night of May 17, 1980, the eve of Peru's first presidential election in seventeen years, groups of armed youths attacked a number of polling places in the southern Andean department of Ayacucho. The guerrillas dragged voter lists and ballot boxes into the town square, where they burned them in a public display of opposition to the elections (Degregori 1992: 33). This marked the beginning of the Shining Path's (Sendero Luminoso) revolutionary uprising against the government of Peru. Initially the Peruvian government paid little attention to these assaults, viewing them as a police problem rather than a revolutionary threat. However, as the newly elected president Fernando Belaundé Terry prepared to assume office, the guerrillas expanded their targets to include bridges, rail lines, power stations, and telecommunications facilities.[1] Soon there were reports of "people's trials" being staged in remote villages of Ayacucho: Abusive landlords, corrupt local officials, greedy local merchants, and money lenders were being put on trial and punished by armed guerrillas claiming the mandate to dispense the people's justice. In the first three months of 1981, Shining Path guerrillas carried out between 300 and 400 separate attacks. Despite the restoration of democracy in Peru, the newly elected government could no longer ignore the fact of a viable revolutionary movement in their midst.[2]

Why would an armed insurrection erupt on the very day that Peru's military returned to the barracks and turned over the reins of government to elected civilians for the first time in twelve years? And why would a rural insurgency, relying on peasants as its initial base of support, emerge just a few years after a military junta had redistributed over 8.6 million hectares of land to over 370,000 families in what was to date the most extensive land reform program in Latin American history (Alberts 1983: 141–42)?

1

In January 1981 the Faribundo Martí National Liberation Front (FMLN) launched what it proclaimed would be the "final offensive" in its revolutionary war against the government of El Salvador. The FMLN had been formed a few months earlier to coordinate the separate armed insurgencies being waged by a number of leftist groups in El Salvador.[3] Those groups, most of which were affiliated with legal political parties, had adopted a strategy of armed revolt in response to the escalating program of state-sanctioned violence against legal opposition organizations. During the late 1970s political leaders who advocated reforms of any sort became targets of death squad violence perpetrated by paramilitaries and, increasingly, by uniformed troops of the Salvadoran government. The death toll came to include the attorney general of El Salvador, the archbishop of San Salvador, and even reform-minded officers of the military. In November of 1980 security forces murdered almost all the leaders of the nonviolent left just a few hours before a press conference at which those leaders were to announce that they had agreed to negotiate with the government over a possible solution to El Salvador's conflict (Stanley 1996: 2). By late 1980 the death toll from state-sanctioned violence had escalated to a thousand a month, including large numbers of anonymous civilian nonelites. It was in this environment that the FMLN launched its final offensive.

What makes this sequence of events all the more puzzling is that on October 15, 1979, a group of young military officers had seized power in a coup that they proclaimed was necessary because the incumbent regime had "violated the Human Rights of the population," "fomented and tolerated corruption," and "created a veritable economic and social disaster."[4] To remedy this situation—and, they hoped, to preempt civil war—they announced the formation of a civilian-military junta that would include leaders from the major opposition parties, elections for a constituent assembly that would write a new democratic constitution, and a full transition to civilian democracy by 1984. In addition they announced a three-phased land reform program that would provide impoverished peasants with land and, it was hoped, persuade them to withhold their support from the guerrilla armies. Why would armed forces escalate their violence against the population in the aftermath of a reformist coup? Why would guerrilla armies form a coalition to mount a "final offensive" against a government that had just announced a sweeping agrarian reform program?

These are just two examples of the puzzle of revolutionary violence in the Third World that has confronted students of conflict processes since the end of World War II. Other examples abound. In 1959 Fidel Castro led a guerrilla insurgency that succeeded in deposing the regime of Fulgencio Batista. In 1975 the Khmer Rouge guerrillas overthrew the government of General Lon Nol in

Cambodia, and in 1979 the Frente Sandinista de Liberación Nacional (FSLN) guerrillas overthrew the government of Anastasio Somoza in Nicaragua. In Vietnam Vietcong guerrillas waged a protracted insurgency against the government of South Vietnam and the United States. In the Philippines the Huk rebellion was defeated in the 1950s, but in 1973 the New People's Army (NPA) launched a revolutionary insurgency that by 1990 claimed an estimated 25,000 full-time guerrillas operating in sixty-three Philippine provinces (Hawes 1990: 262; on the Huk rebellion, see Kerkvliet 1977). Since the democratically elected President Jacobo Arbenz was overthrown in a right-wing military coup in Guatemala in 1954, that nation has experienced a series of guerrilla insurgencies that waxed and waned periodically during the 1960s, 1970s, and 1980s, before finally ending with a settlement agreement in 1995. All told, the Correlates of War Project (COW) lists over 100 civil wars that have occurred in the Third World since 1945 (see appendix).

Just as revolution in the Third World has become the dominant conflict modality over the last half of the twentieth century, so finding the causes of these conflicts has become one of the most salient issues confronting students of comparative politics. Since the end of World War II, there has not been a single day in which there was not a war of some sort going on somewhere in the world. Of course noting the persistence and pervasiveness of war in the international system is hardly a novel observation, nor is it a feature unique to the post–World War II era.

What is different about the last half of the twentieth century is that, first, the dominant form of armed conflict since 1945 has not been interstate war between two sovereign nations but civil war within nations. Revolutions, secessionist movements, ethnic conflicts, communal violence, and other forms of war within nations have replaced war between nations as the dominant form of conflict in the post–World War II nation-state system. Second, until 1989 these wars occurred almost exclusively in the Third World. For at least three centuries prior to World War II, interstate wars involving the central system states of Europe and North America dominated the patterns of armed conflict in the world.[5] Summarizing the findings from their Correlates of War project, Melvin Small and David Singer (1982: 180) note that

> most of the war in the [international] system [between 1816 and 1945] has been accounted for by a small fraction of the nations, most of which would be found near the top of any hierarchy based on diplomatic status, military-industrial capability, or related indicators. It is not surprising that every one of the nations cited so far was a member of what we defined as the central system.

As the end of World War II ushered in the Cold War nuclear standoff between East and West, armed conflict among central system members became all but unthinkable. Kal Holsti (1992: 37) notes that from 1945 until 1989 there were only four instances of the use of armed force by European states against each other on European soil: the British intervention in the Greek civil war (1945–1948), the Soviet intervention in Hungary (1956), the Warsaw Treaty Organization (WTO) intervention in Czechoslovakia (1968), and the Turkish invasion of Cyprus (1974). These conflicts resulted in 176,000 deaths, which represents less than 1 percent of the 22 million battle deaths that occurred worldwide during that same forty-five-year period. The remaining battle casualties occurred on the soil of Third World nations.

If an event as momentous as the end of World War II could be followed by such a dramatic change in the dominant patterns of armed conflict in the world, then we might expect an equally dramatic change in the patterns of conflict to accompany the end of the Cold War. Unfortunately the waning of U.S.–Soviet rivalry has not brought an end to the epidemic of civil war.

Three features of the post–Cold War environment are noteworthy. First, the end of the Cold War and the disintegration of the Soviet Union have ended Europe's forty-year immunity to armed conflict. Secessionist conflicts in Slovenia, Croatia, Bosnia, and Kosovo have resulted in the dismantling of the Yugoslav federation. The former Soviet republics of Georgia and Azerbaijan have been torn by armed secessionist movements as well. And even the Russian Republic has been confronted with a secessionist war in Chechnya.

A second, more hopeful trend in the post–Cold War environment has been the successful mediation of peaceful settlements to a number of protracted civil wars in the Third World. Negotiated settlements, many mediated by the United Nations, brought an end to hostilities in Cambodia, El Salvador, Nicaragua, and Angola, to name but a few. To some degree these settlements are a direct result of the waning of Cold War tensions and the subsequent withdrawal of Soviet and U.S. support for one or the other parties to these conflicts. Unfortunately not all of these settlements have held; witness the resumption of hostility in Angola and Sierra Leone. However, even flawed and fragile peace agreements arguably would not have been feasible as long as these conflicts were entangled in Cold War hostilities.

This leads us to the discouraging third trend in the post-Cold War era: Overall there has been no significant decline in the frequency or destructiveness of civil wars. Indeed quite the opposite appears to be the case. According to the Stockholm International Peace Research Institute (SIPRI) Yearbook, there were 47 armed conflicts underway in thirty-seven nations around the world in 1989 (supposedly the last year of the Cold War). Thirty-two of these were severe enough to have resulted in at least a thousand battle deaths (Wallensteen and Sollenberg 1998: 622–23). Three years later (1992), there were still 55 conflicts underway in forty-one nations, and 32 of them had resulted

Table 1.1. Number of Armed Conflicts, 1989–1997

Level of conflict	1989	1990	1991	1992	1993	1994	1995	1996	1997	All years
Minor[a]	15	16	18	23	15	16	12	17	12	46
Intermediate[b]	14	14	13	12	17	19	17	13	14	15
War[c]	18	19	20	20	14	7	6	6	7	42
All conflicts	47	49	51	55	46	42	35	36	33	103
All locations	37	39	38	41	33	32	30	29	26	69

Source: Wallensteen and Sollenberg (1998: 622).
[a]Fewer than 1,000 battle-related deaths during course of conflict.
[b]More than 1,000 battle-related deaths during course of conflict but fewer than 1,000 in any given year.
[c]More than 1,000 battle-related deaths in any given year.

in more than a thousand battle deaths. Altogether 103 different armed conflicts occurred between 1989 and 1997, and 57 of them resulted in at least a thousand battle deaths (see table 1.1). Only 6 of these conflicts were interstate wars (see table 1.2); the other 97 were some form of civil war.[6]

THE PUZZLE OF REVOLUTIONARY CONFLICT

Arguably civil war remains the least understood and most intractable form of conflict with which governments and scholars alike must concern themselves. Rarely have governments succeeded in formulating reform programs or counterinsurgency strategies that could defeat, preempt, or prevent civil war. In the aftermath of World War II, the European powers were unable to subdue or prevent anticolonial revolts in their Asian and African colonies. The United States became entangled in failed counterinsurgency efforts in Vietnam, El Salvador, and elsewhere. The Soviet Union's inability to defeat the Afghan *mujahideen* and Vietnam's failure to suppress armed resistance to the government it installed in Cambodia in 1979 suggest that liberal democracies are not alone

Table 1.2. Types of Armed Conflicts, 1989–1997

Level of conflict	1989	1990	1991	1992	1993	1994	1995	1996	1997	All years
Civil war	43	44	49	52	42	42	34	33	29	88
Civil war with foreign intervention	1	2	1	2	4	0	0	1	3	9
Interstate	3	3	1	1	0	0	1	2	1	6
All armed conflicts	47	49	51	55	46	42	35	36	33	103

Source: Wallensteen and Sollenberg (1998: 623)

in their inability to anticipate, prevent, or defeat revolutions in the country-side. Even victorious revolutionaries in Nicaragua, Cambodia, and Ethiopia could not prevent a recurrence of the very kinds of armed opposition that brought them to power in the first place.

What, then, do we know about civil wars in the Third World? There is much that we think we might know about the subject, but there is much more about such conflicts that perplexes and bewilders us. What we can agree upon is that there is a great deal of revolutionary violence going on in the world, and that until recently virtually all of it was concentrated in the Third World. Although our ability to document the frequency, destructiveness, and other dimensions of civil wars in the Third World has grown substantially in recent decades, one could question whether our understanding of the causes and dynamics of revolutions in the countryside has advanced in proportion to our experience in dealing with their deadly consequences.

Our puzzlement over civil wars in the Third World certainly cannot be attributed to a lack of scholarly effort. The vast proliferation of case studies, theoretical and empirical inquiries, and strategic analyses on the subject attests to its salience as a concern for policy makers and social scientists alike. Indeed, when confronted with the profusion of studies on the subject, one is tempted to conclude that our failure to translate rigorous analysis into effective policy may be less a matter of government analysts misapprehending the phenomenon than of policy makers becoming confused when confronted with a cacophony of widely disparate analyses, findings, and recommendations emanating from the scholarly community.

This book by no means presumes to resolve this confusion. Instead it is intended to draw on the insights derived from several diverse research traditions to present a reasonably coherent analytical essay on the social, economic, and political roots of Third World revolutions. Specifically it is an effort to explain how, why, and under what circumstances one of the more common forms of Third World revolt—the revolutionary insurgency in the countryside—comes about. Examples of this type of conflict abound, from the Chinese Communist revolt of the 1930s and 1940s, through the Vietminh uprising against the French that evolved into the Vietcong insurgency against the government of South Vietnam and the United States. It also includes the Huk Rebellion and the New People's Army insurgencies in the Philippines, the Khmer Rouge revolution in Cambodia, and the anti-Khmer Rouge insurgencies that arose after they took power. Latin America has witnessed the Shining Path and Tupac Amaru insurgencies in Peru, the Castro-led revolution in Cuba, the Sandinista revolution in Nicaragua, the Faribundo Martí Liberation Front (FMLN) revolt in El Salvador, and the several insurgencies in Guatemala, to name but a few. A number of rural-based revolts have the added element of ethnic divisions within society exacerbating the tensions that led to civil war. We have witnessed such conflicts in Ethiopia, Angola, Sudan, Mozambique, Zimbabwe (Rhodesia), Sri Lanka, Burundi, and Rwanda.

All these revolts have some common elements. First, they are rural-based, with peasant farmers and landless rural laborers providing the primary base of popular support and source of recruits for the rebel movement.[7] Second, the issues that gave rise to these revolutions—the sources of the grievances that motivated peasants and other nonelites to support the revolutionary movement—originated in the rural economy. They involve issues of land use and land tenure arising from the displacement of peasant cultivators from the land and the lack of occupational alternatives for the landless and land-poor.[8]

Third, conflict between the state and society escalates to the point of armed conflict because, first, dissident leaders emerge to mobilize aggrieved peasants for various forms of collective action aimed at remedying their economic distress, and second, the state responds to dissident collective action with repression rather than accommodation. In other words, these movements do not usually start out as revolutionary insurgencies. They begin as legal and nonviolent opposition movements that succeed in mobilizing a significant bloc of popular support for their agenda of reform.[9] That support can take the form of voting for opposition candidates in elections, participating in dissident activities such as strikes and demonstrations, or simply contributing time and money to opposition organizations. Whether or not the struggle between regime and opposition escalates to civil war depends in large part upon whether the state responds to the opposition challenge with repression or accommodation. Civil war occurs when the state's response is predominantly repressive. In this circumstance the opposition is forced to either withdraw from the political arena in defeat or shift to a strategy of violence of its own. When the latter occurs, the cycle of violence between regime and rebels can quickly escalate to civil war.

This, then, is the purpose of this book: to explain how, why, and under what circumstances revolutions in the countryside arise in Third World nations. Even confining ourselves to peasant-based revolutions in the Third World does not measurably simplify our task. We still must choose from an extensive menu of political, economic, sociological, and psychological theories on the causes of revolutions and peasant participation in them. How, then, does one synthesize the insights of such a widely divergent set of research traditions into a logically consistent and conceptually coherent explanation of this form of conflict?

At the risk of falling into a reductionist trap, I approach this task by arguing that the fundamental question we must ask ourselves is the following: What syndrome of social, economic, and political dynamics would induce an otherwise politically inert peasant to risk violent death by joining an armed uprising intent upon overthrowing the incumbent regime?

The individual peasant provides us with a useful common denominator with which to integrate theories as diverse as relative deprivation, resource mobilization, and rational choice. There is a vast and complex array of forces at work in the eruption of revolutionary violence in the Third World. Ultimately, however, revolutions are fought by collections of individuals who join the movement for their own reasons. If we are to make any sense out of the otherwise baffling array of theories that offer explanations for the inception of revolutionary violence, it seems reasonable and prudent to do so by asking how the dynamics depicted by each theory affect the life conditions and behavioral calculus of ordinary citizens in Third World societies.

THE ARGUMENT: WHY PEASANTS REVOLT

Before addressing directly the question of why an individual would participate in an armed revolt against an entrenched regime, I first document the patterns of civil conflict in the Third World and the common experiences that have made those nations especially susceptible to civil war. The remainder of this chapter presents a series of observations concerning the patterns of civil war in the contemporary world. Specifically I consider why such conflicts have been so frequent in the post–World War II era, why they have been so deadly, and why the epidemic of civil war has been concentrated in the Third World.

Chapter 2 presents an overview of some of the major research traditions that offer important insights into the origins and dynamics of Third World revolution. Review essays on these works are numerous, and there is no reason to add yet another review of this literature.[10] Instead the purpose of chapter 2 is to distill from some of the most influential works on revolution the critical questions concerning the social and economic antecedents of revolutionary violence, the developmental processes that have generated these conditions in Third World nations, the motives that inspire revolutionary leaders to rise up from these conditions and initiate a challenge to the incumbent regime, the strategies those leaders use to mobilize supporters for their cause, and the role of the state, through its response to opposition challenges, in determining whether opposition will take the form of peaceful political activism or violent revolutionary conflict.

Chapter 3 addresses the question of why the Third World (but not other regions of the world) has been the site of almost all of the revolutionary violence that has occurred over the past half century. The answer lies in the ways in which Third World regions were integrated into the global economy as suppliers of raw materials and agricultural goods for the industrial economies of Europe and North America. Adapting to this role required a drastic change in land use and land tenure patterns in many Third World nations. Land ownership became more concentrated, and land use was shifted from food crop production by peasant cultivators to export crop production by large commercial estates. The resulting transformation of the agrarian political economy disrupted traditional patterns of rural social organization, leaving large numbers of peasants devoid of any protections against the ever-present threat of subsistence crisis. In this manner, they became available for mobilization by aspiring opposition leaders.

But the mere existence of an aggrieved population is not sufficient for revolution to erupt. Even people facing severe economic distress will not necessarily join a revolutionary movement because, first, revolution is itself a dangerous enterprise, and second, many of the benefits that would result from revolutionary victory are, by nature, public goods: Everyone will be able to enjoy the benefits of the postrevolutionary order, regardless of whether or not they participated in the revolution. Given this collective action problem, how do revolutionary leaders ever manage to mobilize enough support to succeed in overthrowing an entrenched and well-defended government? In chapter 4 I examine the mobilization strategies that opposition leaders use to overcome the collective action problem and build a movement with sufficient popular support to challenge an incumbent regime.

Two points are salient here. First, rarely do peasants spontaneously organize for revolutionary violence against the incumbent regime. Spontaneous peasant revolts, when they do occur, are usually short-lived and focused on remedying specific local grievances over such matters as land tenure and land use, tenancy terms and tenant rights, taxes, and other elite claims on peasant production. They are not explicitly revolutionary movements in the sense that their goals fall short of what Theda Skocpol (1979: 4–5) depicts as the defining characteristics of a social revolution: They do not seek to overthrow the incumbent regime and replace it with a fundamentally different configuration of state institutions and elites, nor do they seek to transform patterns of social organization, class structures, or institutions of social authority.[11] Left to their own devices, peasants may join forces to seize lands from landlords (land invasion). They may even attack the landlord and loot his estate. But such movements stop short of abolishing the landlord class or overthrowing the state that sustains landlords as a class. For such action to become revolutionary requires the intervention of outside actors: specifically, dissident leaders who can harness peasant support for their challenge to the incumbent regime. More often than not, these revolutionary leaders are drawn not from the peasantry but from among white-collar urban classes, including intellectuals, students, civil servants, and frustrated politicians.[12]

Second, peasant-based insurgencies do not usually start out as explicitly revolutionary movements. Instead they begin as nonviolent movements aimed at remedying specific grievances. It is easier for dissident leaders to mobilize peasants for nonviolent collective action than for violent collective action because the risks are so much less. However, once the mobilizing structures are in place to induce peasant participation in nonviolent collective action, it is much easier to persuade them to take the next step of supporting revolutionary collective action.[13] Goodwin and Skocpol (1989: 491) observe that the converse is true as well: "During the 1960s a number of Latin American revolutionary groups . . . including the Sandinistas in Nicaragua—failed to make headway, largely because they were too quick to engage incumbent regimes in armed struggle, well before they had solidified broad popular support through the provision of collective goods."

Chapter 5 explores the critical role of the state in determining whether opposition politics focuses on peaceful reform or degenerates into political violence. The state can respond to nonviolent collective action by accommodating dissident demands through reforms, or it can repress the opposition leadership and intimidate their followers into withdrawing from the political arena. Many Third World states lack the institutional capacity and the redistributable resources to respond to opposition challenges with reformist policies. This condition has been referred to as the "weak state syndrome" (Migdal 1988; Job 1992; Holsti 1992; Ayoob 1992). Weak states often resort to violent repression of peaceful opposition because that is the response for which they are best equipped. This tendency is reinforced by factional politics within the regime. The military has an institutional interest in pursuing repression rather than reform. The agro-export elite have an interest in maintaining an ample supply of cheap labor. Repressing peasant associations, labor unions, opposition parties, and other opposition organizations serves the immediate interests of both factions in the state. Thus the interests of the military and the agro-export elite converge in what William Stanley (1996) and Charles Tilly (1985) have referred to as a "protection racket state." The result is not only that repression wins out over reform, but that the level of repression often vastly exceeds what is required to quell the opposition challenge.

Chapter 6 addresses the question of whether (and under what conditions) repressive violence by the state deters or enhances popular support for the revolutionary opposition. When the state responds to reform movements by violently repressing the reformers, opposition leaders abandon nonviolent tactics in favor of a program of revolutionary violence intended to force the regime to undertake reforms or face the prospect of being overthrown. Violence begets violence, and repression breeds revolution. A government faced with a revolutionary challenge is soon confronted with the counterinsurgency dilemma. To find and defeat the insurgents, government forces must be able to distinguish the guerrilla irregular and his or her civilian supporter from the uninvolved peasant. All too often, counterinsurgent units in the field err on the side of overkill. As a result, even politically neutral peasants soon realize that simply refraining from supporting the rebels no longer guarantees them immunity from state-sanctioned repressive violence. As the level of violence escalates, uninvolved peasants get caught in the crossfire between rebels and regime. The option of remaining neutral is foreclosed, and many peasants join the rebels if for no other reason than to secure protection from the indiscriminate repressive violence perpetrated by the state. In this manner, state repression can actually enhance popular support for the revolution and hasten the eventual collapse of the regime itself.

On the positive side of the ledger, a number of protracted civil wars have been brought to a peaceful conclusion through negotiated settlement. U.N.–mediated peace accords brought an end to civil wars in El Salvador, Mozambique, Nicaragua, Angola, Guatemala, and Cambodia. This trend has spawned a new body of research into the factors that determine the outcome of a civil war: whether the rebels win, the government wins, or they reach a negotiated settlement. In chapter 7 I look at how civil wars end, by focusing on the choice that rebels and government face between continuing to fight in hopes of eventually winning or bringing an end to the war by working out a negotiated settlement.

Chapters 8 and 9 present a comparative case study analysis of two recent revolutions: Peru and El Salvador. Both these nations fit the patterns of development described in chapters 3 through 6: the displacement of large numbers of peasant cultivators from the land, the mobilization of those peasants by opposition organizations, and the escalation to revolutionary violence when the state responded to nonviolent opposition with repressive violence. What makes these two cases especially noteworthy is that, in both nations, the state attempted to preempt revolution by implementing major land reform programs. In Peru land reform was initiated in 1968. Yet, twelve years later, the Shining Path guerrillas were able to build a support base among peasants that was sufficient to sustain their insurgency for over a decade. In El Salvador a reformist junta launched a land reform program in 1980 in an effort to quell an escalating spiral of violence between the old regime and the opposition. Yet the years immediately following the initiation of land reform in El Salvador turned out to be the bloodiest in that nation's twelve years of civil war. Why did land reform fail to preempt revolution in Peru or end it in El Salvador? I address this question through a comparative analysis of the politics of land reform, repression, and revolution in these two nations.

The epidemic of civil wars over the last half of the twentieth century was in part a product of domestic political and economic dynamics in nations of the

Third World and in part a product of the international politics of decolonization and Cold War bipolarity. With the end of the Cold War, what are the prospects for the future trends in civil war? Will revolution in the countryside dissipate or persist? Chapter 10 looks at the impact of two trends on the prospects for revolution in the countryside: the "third wave" of democracy and the growing integration of the global economy. Will the diffusion of democracy to Asia, Africa, and Latin America make revolutionary violence less likely there? And will globalization bring to the Third World occupational alternatives to agriculture and, more generally, a level of prosperity that will diminish the likelihood of peasant-based revolution in those regions that have been plagued by such conflict for the past half century? Chapter 10 offers some speculative remarks on these trends.

DEFINITIONS: CIVIL WAR, REVOLUTION, AND SECESSION

The remainder of this chapter present some evidence on the questions of (1) why civil war has replaced interstate war as the most common form of conflict in the international system, (2) why such conflicts have become so frequent and destructive, and (3) why, until 1989, they were confined to the Third World. First, however, I should define what types of conflicts are (and are not) the subject matter of this book. I use the term *civil war* as a generic concept to include all forms of armed conflict within a nation. As such, civil wars are distinct from interstate wars, which involve armed conflict between two or more sovereign nation states. This book is not concerned with interstate wars.

Within the category of civil wars, we can distinguish two subcategories: revolutions and secessionist revolts.[14] In a revolution, the rebels seek to overthrow the existing government and take its place as the new government of the nation. Civil wars in Nicaragua (1978–1979), El Salvador (1979–1992), Peru (1980–present), Cambodia (1970–1975; 1979–1991), Colombia (1984–present), Philippines (1972–present), and Guatemala (1978–1995) are examples of revolutionary civil wars.[15] In a secessionist revolt, the rebels seek not to overthrow the existing government but to gain independence from it. In other words, they seek to create a second sovereign nation state out of some portion of the territory and population of an existing nation state. The Tamil revolt in Sri Lanka (1983–present), the Eritrean revolt against Ethiopia (1974–1990), the efforts of the Ibo minority in Nigeria to secede and form the new nation of Biafra (1967–1970), and the Muslim-led Moro National Liberation Front in the Philippines (1972–1989) are a few examples of secessionist revolts.

A number of scholars draw a further distinction between ethnic civil wars and ideological civil wars.[16] This distinction applies mainly to revolutions; all secessionist revolts are ethnically based. In an ideological revolution, the issues that divide rebels from government concern matters such as inequality of land ownership, wealth, income, and political power. The goal of the rebels is still to overthrow the existing government and establish a new state in that nation. The civil wars in El Salvador, Nicaragua, Peru, Cambodia, and Guatemala are examples of ideological revolutions. In ethnic revolutions, the same issues of inequality and repression generate the grievances that motivate rebels and their supporters. However, ethnicity adds another dimension to the conflict between state and society. First, in ethnic revolutions, ethnicity and inequality coincide: Those who are victims of various forms of inequality are from one ethnic group, while those who enjoy a disproportionate share of the advantages available in the nation are from another ethnic group. Second, ethnic divisions add further issues to the fuel of conflict. Members of the subordinate ethnic group fear the suppression of their culture, language, religion, and heritage at the hands of a regime dominated by a rival ethnic group. The civil wars in Angola and Rwanda are examples of ethnically based revolutions. Thus, ethnic revolutions differ from ethnic separatist revolts in terms of the goals of the rebels, and they differ from ideological revolutions in terms of the cultural division that distinguishes the rebels and their supporters from the state and its supporters.

FORMS AND FREQUENCY OF CIVIL WAR

In its various manifestations, civil war has become the most frequent, pervasive, and deadly form of armed conflict in the post–World War II era. The Correlates of War, which is the most widely used database on wars of all kinds, lists 80 civil wars that took place between 1945 and 1992, while only 23 interstate and 24 "extra-systemic" wars occurred during that same period (Singer and Small, 1993; see appendix). Twelve of Singer and Small's post-1945 extra-systemic wars are largely secessionist revolts, consisting of armed rebellions by a regional minority seeking independence as a sovereign nation state. As such, they fall under the definition of civil war used in this book. By that definition, then, 92 of the 127 post-1945 conflicts that were deadly enough to make it into Singer and Small's data set were in fact some form of civil war.[17] Similarly, Kal Holsti (1996: 21) found that, of the 164 wars he identified in the post-1945 era, "almost 77 percent . . . were internal [wars], where armed combat was not against another state but against the authorities within the state or between armed communities." Only 30 of the 164 conflicts (18 percent) were purely state-versus-state wars. Comparing this to earlier eras, he found that "there have been on average only 0.005 interstate wars and armed interventions per state per year since 1945," whereas the figure is almost four times higher for the eighteenth century (0.019), three times higher for the nineteenth century (0.014), and over seven times higher for the period between the two world wars of the twentieth century (0.036).

Why has civil war in the Third World replaced interstate war among central system members as the dominant conflict modality in the post-1945 era? Two factors come to mind. First, the incidence of interstate war has declined dramatically, especially among the central system states of Europe, North America, China, and Japan. This development is largely a function of the nuclear standoff between the United States and the Soviet Union, which made war between the two superpower-led alliances unacceptable. Second, the dismantling of European colonial empires after World War II resulted in the creation of well over a hundred new nation states. The governments in many of these newly independent states were especially susceptible to revolutionary challenges because they often lacked the institutional capacity and resources to build an adequate base of popular legitimacy among their citizens. I discuss the latter issue later in this chapter. For now I turn to the question of why interstate war, especially among the major powers, has been so rare in the last half of the twentieth century.

CIVIL WAR VERSUS INTERSTATE WAR

For most of the 300 years prior to the end of World War II, Europe had been the most war-prone region of the world. Kal Holsti (1992: 38) observes that: "Indeed, the history of international relations between 1648 and 1945 is primarily the history of conflicts and peace arrangements of great powers. . . . Great powers are substantially more war prone than their smaller counterparts." Holsti cites figures from Jack Levy's (1983) work on wars among great powers: "Of the approximately 120 wars since the year 1500 involving great powers and other states, about half were wars exclusively between the great powers. Ten of them were general wars involving all or nearly all of the great powers; these ten wars account for nearly 90 percent of the casualties of the total great-power war list."

By contrast, the period since 1945 has been the longest sustained era of peace in Europe since the Treaty of Westphalia in 1648 (Holsti 1992: 38).[18] Thus civil wars have become more prevalent than interstate wars in part because of the absence of interstate war in Europe. How do we account for the absence of war between states, especially between European states?

The obvious reason, alluded to earlier, is that the nuclear standoff between the United States and the Soviet Union made war among the European powers unacceptable. When the atomic bombs were dropped on the Japanese cities of Hiroshima and Nagasaki in August of 1945, the major powers entered a nuclear age that fundamentally altered the strategic calculus surrounding war as a mode of interaction among them. Within a decade, Europe had polarized into two rival alliances: the North Atlantic Treaty Organization (NATO) and the Warsaw Treaty Organization (WTO). Each alliance was led by one of the two emerging nuclear superpowers: the United States and the Soviet Union. Each alliance relied on the threat of nuclear annihilation to deter attack by its rivals. By the end of the 1960s, both the United States and the Soviet Union had enough nuclear warheads and delivery systems (missiles and bombers) to annihilate each other several times over. Under those circumstances, war of any form between the two alliances was unacceptable because of the risk that it might escalate into an all-out nuclear conflagration. The result has been the "long peace" that prevailed on the European continent from 1945 until the breakup of the Soviet Union in 1991.[19]

The nuclear stalemate did not prevent the superpowers from pursuing their rivalry through less direct means: by intervening, directly or indirectly, in conflicts occurring in the Third World, on the periphery of the major power system. Usually intervention involved one superpower supporting one side in a Third World conflict in which the rival superpower was supporting the opposing side. Thus, the United States supported the Somoza regime in Nicaragua, while the Soviet Union and Cuba provided aid to the Sandinista rebels (the FSLN). Later the United States supported the Contra rebels in Nicaragua while the Soviet Union and Cuba supported the Sandinista government. In Angola the United States and South Africa funneled support to the UNITA rebels, while the Soviet Union and Cuba supported the government led by the MPLA (the People's Movement for the Liberation of Angola). In Afghanistan the Soviet Union supported the government against a coalition of Muslim *mujahideen,* while the United States provided covert support to the rebels.

These are not just isolated events. Of the 80 post-1945 civil wars listed in the Correlates of War, at least 23 were "internationalized" by another nation intervening militarily. Patrick Regan (1996) identifies 138 post-1945 civil wars, of which 85 experienced intervention by at least one other nation. Intervention took a variety of forms, from direct intervention with troops and equipment (as the United States did in Vietnam and Cuba did in Angola) to the provision of military and economic assistance to one side or the other. Thus, while the nuclear stalemate precluded direct conflict between the major powers, it did not prevent them from intervening in, subsidizing, and occasionally instigating conflicts within Third World nations.

CIVIL WAR AS A THIRD WORLD PHENOMENON

While the nuclear standoff might explain the absence of wars among European powers, we are still left with the questions of why the nations of Asia, Africa, and Latin America have been the victims of this epidemic of internal conflict. What common experience would make such a diverse array of nations—differing from each other in terms of their culture, religion, ethnic composition, and form of government—so uniformly susceptible to civil war?

One factor contributing to the rise of armed conflict in the Third World has been simply the proliferation of newly independent nation states in the Third World. There were 51 original members of the United Nations. Today there are over 200. The vast majority of these new nations are in the Third World, and their creation as sovereign entities is largely a consequence of the collapse of European colonial empires after World War II. Thus, there simply are more nation-states in which revolutions *can* occur.

More important, new regimes in newly independent nation-states are more susceptible to civil war than are long-established regimes. Almost all these nations were at one time colonial territories, dominated by one or more European powers. Colonial powers exploited Asia, Africa, and Latin America by harnessing the local economy to serve the demands of U.S. and European markets. In so doing, they disrupted the existing patterns of social organization in those societies. Because the colonial powers' motives were largely commercial, they devoted little attention and even less resources to the task of establishing new patterns of social organization that would restore survival strategies for the indigenous people of their colonies. Consequently, large numbers of those peoples had their lives, their livelihoods, and their communities disrupted by colonial rule.

Gaining independence did not automatically resolve the problems of poverty and social dislocations that were part of the colonial legacy. The post-colonial state often lacked the institutional capacities to provide peace, order, and a reasonable level of material well-being for its citizens. Lacking the legitimacy that comes from a history of effective performance, new regimes frequently felt threatened by the prospect of any challenges—peaceful or otherwise—emanating from society. State leaders viewed opposition challenges not as mere policy debates but as challenges to the very legitimacy of their own continued rule. To preserve themselves against such challenges the incumbent leaders often armed the state and repressed all challengers. Repression forced challengers to resort to violence of their own in order to advance their claims and defend themselves against the state. Thus, the cycle of violence begetting violence often escalated to civil war. The fact that newly independent regimes in the former Soviet Union have likewise been plagued by civil war in the early years of their existence indicates that the susceptibility of new regimes to civil war is not unique to the Third World or to economically less developed nations.

THE DESTRUCTIVENESS OF CIVIL WARS

Not only have civil wars been more frequent than interstate wars, they have also been more deadly. Kal Holsti found that, of the 22 million casualties that resulted from armed conflicts between 1945 and 1989, only 8 million were victims of combat between organized armies of two or more states. The remainder were victims of wars of national liberation or internationalized civil wars (1992: 41). In the Correlates of War data, civil wars accounted for 64 percent of the total battle deaths between 1945 and 1992, for an average of 170,000 battle deaths per year during this period.[20]

Civil wars have become so deadly because their destruction is not confined to conventional battles between organized armies. Inevitably they draw the civilian population into the crossfire between government and rebels, resulting in alarming levels of human casualties. Most civil wars begin as low-intensity insurgencies fought by guerrilla irregulars using unconventional tactics. Guerrilla insurgency brings the civilian population directly into the crossfire between government and rebels. In the words of Mao Zedong, the leader of the Chinese Communist revolution, "The people are like water and the army is like fish."[21] In other words, a revolutionary insurgency has to be sustained by a base of civilian supporters, who provide the rebels with supplies, information, and protection against government troops. In so doing, however, these civilians risk reprisals at the hands of government forces. Government counterinsurgency tactics are often based on the principle of "draining the sea": That is, the government strives to deny the guerrillas their civilian support base by killing or intimidating civilians suspected of providing aid and comfort to the rebels. In many cases, unarmed civilians are targeted by the combatants.

The result has often been near genocidal casualty levels among the civilian populations of nations torn by civil war. Indeed, one of the most tragic features of contemporary civil wars is that civilians make up the overwhelming majority of the casualties. Holsti (1996: 37) reports that there were approximately 921,000 deaths from armed combat during the 1970s. Almost 90 percent of these (820,000) were killed in civil wars, and 90 percent of civil war casualties were civilians. Civil wars in Sudan, Ethiopia, Angola, Mozambique, and Uganda produced between 100,000 (in Angola) and a million (in Uganda) deaths, and most of them were civilians. The 1994 conflict in Rwanda resulted in the death of over 800,000 civilians in less than a year. This made it one of the most intensely deadly incidents of civil war in the post–World War II era (Human Rights Watch 1995: 13–32; Prunier 1995). When the Khmer Rouge seized power in Cambodia in 1975, they embarked on an extermination campaign directed against their suspected enemies in the civilian population. The result was the death of over one million civilians out of a total population of only six million. In Burundi over 100,000 civilians were killed in one year (1972) as a result of clashes between Hutus and Tutsis. Military casualties from this conflict amounted to only about 10,000. In its nine-year war (1961–1970) to suppress Kurdish secessionist efforts, the government of Iraq killed an estimated 100,000 civilians, while military casualties amounted to only about 5,000 troops. Between 1946 and 1948, 800,000 civilians died in communal violence between Hindus and Muslims in India. Half a million civilians died in the Sudanese civil war, while military casualties amounted to only about 6,000. The Eritrean secessionist revolt against the government of Ethiopia resulted in over half a million civilian casualties.[22]

REVOLUTION IN THE COUNTRYSIDE

This brief survey of the pervasiveness and destructiveness of civil wars in the Third World brings us back to the central puzzle of this book: Why would a peasant, otherwise preoccupied with the rigors of subsistence, take up arms in support of a revolutionary challenge to the government? The most widely cited works on revolution have focused on what some view as the more historically momentous social revolutions of the past two and a half centuries: the American, French, Russian, and Chinese revolutions. These events provide the raw material for classic works by Crane Brinton (1965), Barrington Moore (1966), Charles Tilly (1978), Theda Skocpol (1979), and Jack Goldstone (1991). Those revolts occurred in nations that were members of the major power system, and they all began and ended before the midpoint of the twentieth century.

This book is concerned with a different set of civil wars: those that have occurred since 1945 in the periphery of the major power system. These conflicts, which I refer to as "revolutions in the countryside," are the subject of works by Joel Migdal (1974), Jeffery Paige (1975), James Scott (1976), Samuel Popkin (1979), Chalmers Johnson (1982), John Walton (1984), and Timothy Wickham-Crowley (1992), to name but a few.

When we compare these two bodies of research, it is clear that there are profound differences between the "classic" revolutions of the early modern era and "revolutions in the countryside" of the contemporary Third World. First, contemporary revolutions in the Third World are catalyzed by international forces and dynamics that are not of their own making and over which they have little or no control. They occur in a global political economy that has been dominated from the beginning by the industrial powers of Europe, North America, and Japan. John Walton (1984: 19) notes that "international forces affected the early revolutions in European societies, but they are far more constraining" on contemporary revolutions in the Third World. In his view, revolutions in the countryside "are shaped decisively by conflicts over the aims of development policy, the fate of displaced segments of the population, and struggles within the political leadership over nationalist versus dependent paths of development—conflicts that arise mainly in the nexus of penetration and incorporation by the world system."

Revolutions in the countryside also differ from classic social revolutions in that they originate as guerrilla insurgencies in rural areas. They are not primarily urban-based in their origins, their base of popular support, or their strategy and tactics.[23] As such, their political genealogy traces back to Mao Zedong rather than to Lenin or Robespierre. Of course, peasants played a role in classic revolutions as well. Unrest in the countryside helped to overwhelm or undermine the coercive capacity of the state and thereby made it possible for the urban core of the revolution to challenge the state's authority and seize power. In the absence of the revolution's urban vanguard, peasant unrest in France, Russia, and China would likely have followed the more traditional trajectory of premodern peasant rebellions: sporadic, loosely organized, focused on local issues, and restorative in character rather than revolutionary (Desai and Eckstein 1990: 445–46).[24] They consisted of land invasions, food riots, or other spontaneous acts of collective violence intended to restore a more just (to the peasants) distribution of resources between landed elites and peasant cultivators. Rebellious peasants did not seek to create a new social order but to restore a traditional order that had eroded at the hands of neglectful, greedy, or unjust authorities. They sought not to abolish the existing elites as a class or to radically alter the institutional configuration of the state. Instead their fight was over how to distribute both the fruits of peasant production and the burdens of elite extractions (Magagna 1991: 28). Indeed, even when premodern rebellions succeeded, more often than not the victorious leader would proclaim himself king and award large pieces of land to family members and major lieutenants, thereby forming a new landed elite and laying the basis for a new cycle of land concentration (White 1974: 72–73).

By contrast, contemporary revolutions in the countryside have been from their inception truly revolutionary in their goals, their organization, and their scope. They have sought not to restore the stability of the old order but to destroy it and replace it with a new order. In part their revolutionary character derives from the fact that the Third World's integration into the global economy as colonies of European powers had already destroyed the traditional rural social order. Thus the choice between revolution and restorative rebellion is not available to either dissident leaders or their peasant supporters in the Third World. The old order has long since disappeared, whether forcefully through colonialism (as in Africa and Asia) or gradually as a result of national elites' decisions to shift to export agriculture (as in Latin America).

NOTES

1. Fernando Belaundé Terry was the president in 1968, when a military coup removed him from power and installed the junta that governed Peru for the next twelve years.

2. The Shining Path movement is the subject of a number of works, including McClintock 1983, 1984, 1989, 1998; McCormick 1990, 1992; Palmer 1985, 1986, 1992. It is also the subject of chapter 9 of this volume.

3. The FMLN was a coalition of the Fuerzas Populares de Liberación (FPL, the Popular Forces of Liberation), the Ejército Revolucionario del Pueblo (ERP, the People's Revolutionary Army), the Fuerzas Armadas de Resistencia Nacional (FARN, the Armed Forces of National Resistance), the Partido Comunista Salvadoreño (PCS, the Salvadoran Communist Party) and the Partido Revolucionario de Trabajadores Centroamericanos (PRTC, the Central American Revolutionary Worker's Party). See Byrne 1996, McClintock 1998, Leiken 1984, and chapter 8 of this volume for a discussion of these groups, their origins, and the politics of forming and sustaining the FMLN coalition.

4. *Proclamation of the Armed Forces of the Republic of El Salvador, 15 October 1979*, reprinted in Stanley 1996: 267.

5. The Correlates of War Project codes a particular subset of nations as having "major power" and "central system member" status. The coding is based on "scholarly consensus." See Small and Singer 1982: 45 for a listing of the major powers and for a discussion of the criteria used to determine major power status. On the categorization of nations by major power status and central system membership, see Geller and Singer 1998: 162, 175; Small and Singer 1973; Singer 1988.

6. These data are from a joint program on conflict at the Department of Peace and Conflict Research at Uppsala University and the International Peace Research Institute, Oslo (PRIO). The data can be obtained from www.peace.uu.se. See also Sollenberg and Wallensteen 1995, 1996; Wallensteen and Axell 1994.

7. Some scholars contend that, despite the participation of peasants in these conflicts and despite their reliance on the tactics of guerrilla insurgency, postcolonial revolutions are essentially urban in origin and character. See, for instance, Gugler 1982 and Dix 1983. Dix (1983: 282) argues that the Cuban and Nicaraguan revolutions represent a new "type" of revolution (distinct from the peasant-based insurgencies of Asia and the early modern revolutions of Europe) because the revolutionaries did not mobilize the peasantry until after the complete victory of the revolution. Instead the rev-

olution relied on support from urban classes, including the urban middle class. By contrast, Skocpol (1994: 16) observes that, "with the sole exception of the Iranian Revolution, all modern social revolutions from the French Revolution onward have involved *either* widespread, autonomous revolutions by peasant villages (as in France, Russia, Mexico, and Bolivia) *or* the mobilization of peasants by professional revolutionaries operating as armed guerrilla movements in the countryside (as in China, Vietnam, Cuba, and the revolutions against Portuguese colonialism in Africa)" (emphasis in the original).

8. A household is land-poor if it has access to arable land but not enough to fulfill the family's subsistence needs. The household is compelled to supplement their production with off-farm employment.

9. One exception to this is the Shining Path insurgency in Peru during the 1980s (see chapter 9).

10. See, for instance, Goodwin and Skocpol 1989, Aya 1979, Goldstone 1980.

11. Skocpol (1979: 4) defines social revolutions as "rapid, basic transformations of society's state and class structures; and they are accompanied and in part carried through by class-based revolts from below. Social revolutions are set apart from other sorts of conflicts and transformative processes . . . by the combination of two coincidences: the coincidence of societal structural change with class upheaval; and the coincidence of political with social transformation."

12. Forrest Colburn (1994) highlights the role of urban intellectuals as leaders and instigators of contemporary revolutions. He contends that one source of commonality between contemporary revolutions in such a diverse collection of nations is that the leaders of those movements share a common experience of Western education, which exposed them to a common set of revolutionary doctrines that they adopt as the ideological foundation of their revolutionary programs.

13. Samuel Popkin (1979: 262) argues that peasants can be mobilized for relatively low-cost collective action aimed at remedying local grievances and supplying local benefits. Then revolutionary entrepreneurs can coordinate a collection of local movements into a national revolutionary movement, despite the fact that revolution was not the goal that motivated peasant participation in the first place.

14. This classification differs from that used by Singer and Small in the Correlates of War data set. They classify wars into one of three types: interstate wars, extrasystemic wars, and civil wars. They define an interstate war as a conflict "in which a nation that qualifies as a member of the interstate system engages in a war with another member of the interstate system" (1993: 5). In short, it is a war between two sovereign nation-states. (This type of war is not the concern of this book.) Singer and Small also define civil wars differently from the way I do. They classify as civil wars any internal war in which "(a) military action was involved, (b) the national government at the time was actively involved, (c) effective resistance (as measured by the ratio of fatalities of the weaker to the stronger forces) occurred on both sides, and (d) at least 1,000 battle deaths resulted during the civil war" (24). In simpler terms, their definition of civil war is what I have defined as a revolution. It involves conflict within a nation state between the incumbent regime and a rebel force that seeks to overthrow the incumbents and replace them as the sovereign authority in that nation state. As such, their

definition of civil war does not include secessionist wars, which I do include under the generic term *civil war.*

To find their secessionist wars, one must turn to the third type of conflict in the Correlates of War: the extra-systemic war, which is defined as one "in which a nation that qualifies as an interstate system member engages in a war with a political entity that is not an interstate system member" (Singer and Small 1993: 5–6). They further subdivide extra-systemic wars into two subtypes: the imperial war and the colonial war. What they term an imperial war is the same as what I define as a secessionist revolt. The other type of extra-systemic war is what they term a colonial war. This type of conflict occurs when the people of a colonial territory take up arms to gain independence from the colonial power that rules them. The colonial power is a member of the nation-state system, while the rebels (and the colonial territory itself) are not. The rebels' target is the European colonial power that rules them from afar. As such, colonial wars more nearly approximate interstate war. For this reason, these wars are not addressed in this book. The Vietnamese revolt against the French (1945–1954), the Algerian movement for independence from France (1954–1962), and the Mau Mau rebellion against the British in Kenya (1952–1963) are examples of Singer and Small's "colonial war."

15. Guatemala's civil war waxed and waned periodically, and one can treat it as a case of several distinct revolutions or one movement that lapses into dormancy periodically, only to recur later in a new location with, sometimes, new groups of supporters in its coalition. Thus the Correlates of War lists separate revolutions in Guatemala for 1978–1984 and 1966–1972. Most analysts do not regard the Guatemalan revolt as having ended until the peace accords of 1995. The revolution in the Philippines refers to the New People's Army insurgency (see Hawes 1990). The Peruvian civil war refers to the Shining Path insurgency that, as of this writing, is still ongoing, although the rebels' strength has been so dissipated that, for now, they pose no significant threat to the regime (see chapter 9; see also McClintock 1998).

16. Patrick Regan (1996: 338), in his study of third-party intervention in civil wars, distinguishes between ethnically based conflicts, religious conflicts, and ideological conflicts. Roy Licklider (1995) uses a similar distinction in his analysis of factors that contribute to the stability of negotiated settlements to such conflicts.

17. Indeed one could even argue that some of the COW interstate wars come close to qualifying as internal wars. For instance, the conflict between Armenia and Azerbaijan over the disputed enclave of Nagorno-Karabakh is listed as an interstate war after 1991. However, it would have qualified as an internal war prior to the disintegration of the Soviet Union because it was then a conflict between regional ethnic minorities within the Soviet Union. Even after the collapse of the USSR, the conflict is to some extent arguably a secessionist movement by ethnic Armenians living in Nagorno-Karabakh and seeking autonomy from the government of Azerbaijan so that they can affiliate with the government of Armenia. Similarly the war in Vietnam is treated as a civil war from 1960 to 1965 but as an interstate war from 1965 to 1973. Arguably it was always an internal war, with the only change being the level of resources committed to the conflict by the intervening nation, the United States.

18. Holsti (1992: 38) notes the only exception to this is the combat between the United States and China during the Korean War. The periodicity of war among major powers, including the absence of war in Europe since the end of World War II, is discussed in Vasquez 1993. Russett (1993) alludes to it in his discussions of the "democratic peace" proposition.

19. On the "long peace" as the absence of a third world war, owing largely to the balance of terror between the United States and the Soviet Union, see Gaddis 1987.

20. The figures on annual casualties were calculated by adding the battle deaths for all COW civil wars and extra-systemic wars begun after 1945, then dividing this figure by 47, the number of years between 1945 and 1992.

21. Mao Zedong, "Strategic Problems in the Anti-Japanese Guerrilla War," *Collected Works*, vol. 2 (Beijing: Foreign Language Press, 1967).

22. The casualty figures cited here are from Sivard 1991: 22–25.

23. Scott (1977: 267) argues that "it is abundantly clear that the peasantry, not the proletariat, has constituted the decisive social base of most, if not all, successful twentieth-century revolutions." Skocpol (1979: 112–13) echoes this conclusion: "Peasant revolts have been the crucial insurrectionary ingredient in virtually all actual (i.e., successful) social revolutions to date, . . . Without peasant revolts, urban radicalism in predominantly agrarian countries has not in the end been able to accomplish social revolutionary transformations." For dissenting views, emphasizing the urban origins of Third World revolutions, see Gugler 1982 and Dix 1983.

24. Desai and Eckstein (1990: 446) characterize premodern peasant rebellions as motivated by specific local grievances resulting from peasants' perception that landlords somehow violated "the traditional obligations of privilege." These included "matters involving the rights and obligations of holding land, or . . . a demand for the abolition of the lord's monopoly over hunting and fishing rights and for access to common pastures." As such, these movements sought to restore these rights, not to transform the state or the system of land use and land tenure.

Appendix: "Correlates of War" Civil Wars, 1945–1997

War Name	War Type	Year Began	Year Ended	Duration (Days)	State Deaths	Total Deaths
Afghanistan vs. Mujahedin	revolution	1978	1992	5083	1059454	1300000
Algeria vs. Former Rebel Leaders	revolution	1962	1963	172	1500	—
Algeria vs. Islamic Rebels	revolution	1992	—	—	80000	—
Angola vs. UNITA of 1975	revolution	1975	1991	5681	345800	—
Angola vs. UNITA of 1992	revolution	1992	1994	756	100000	—
Argentina vs. Army	revolution	1955	1955	97	3000	—
Azerbaijan vs. Nagorno-Karabakh	secession	1991	1994	946	3250	20000
Bolivia vs. Leftists	revolution	1952	1952	3	1500	—
Bosnia/Herzogovina vs. Serbs	secession	1992	1995	1359	250000	—
Burma vs. Ethnic Rebels	secession	1968	1980	4679	25000	—
Burma vs. Kachin Rebels	secession	1983	1995	4359	9000	—
Burma vs. Karens	secession	1948	1951	1050	8000	—
Burundi vs. Hutu of 1972	revolution	1972	1972	26	50000	—
Burundi vs. Hutu of 1988	revolution	1988	1988	5	5000	—
Burundi vs. Hutu of 1993	revolution	1993	—	—	200000	—
Burundi vs. Tutsi Supremacists	revolution	1991	1991	39	3000	—
Cambodia vs. Khmer Rouge of 1970	revolution	1970	1975	1822	56000	185000
Cambodia vs. Khmer Rouge of 1978	revolution	1978	1991	4686	40300	200000
Cambodia vs. Khmer Rouge of 1993	revolution	1993	1997	1615	15000	—
Chad vs. Frolinat of 1966	secession	1966	1971	1689	281	3037
Chad vs. Frolinat of 1980	secession	1980	1988	3061	4700	11200
Chile vs. Pinochet-Led Rebels	revolution	1973	1973	5	100	8000
China vs. Communists of 1946	revolution	1946	1950	1499	1000000	—
China vs. Red Guard	revolution	1967	1968	596	50000	—
China vs. Taiwanese	secession	1947	1947	22	1000	—
China vs. Tibet (1950)	secession	1950	1951	454	1000	—
China vs. Tibetans	secession	1956	1959	1117	40000	100000

War Name	War Type	Year Began	Year Ended	Duration (Days)	State Deaths	Total Deaths
Colombia vs. Conservatives	revolution	1948	1949	369	1400	—
Colombia vs. Liberals of 1949	revolution	1949	1962	4856	300000	—
Colombia vs. M-19 & Drug Lords	revolution	1984	—		31000	—
Zaire/Congo vs. Denis Sassou Nguemo	revolution	1997	1997	133	4000	10000
Costa Rica vs. National Union Party	revolution	1948	1948	37	2000	—
Cuba vs. Castroites	revolution	1958	1959	202	5000	—
Dominican Republic vs. Leftists	revolution	1965	1965	130	2526	—
El Salvador vs. Salvadorean Democratic Front	revolution	1979	1992	4599	25000	69000
Ethiopia vs. Eritrean Rebels	secession	1974	1991	6357	70000	150000
Ethiopia vs. Somali Rebels	secession	1976	1977	2376	12400	39000
Ethiopia vs. Tigrean Liberation Front	secession	1978	1991	4818	15000	—
Georgia vs. Gamsakurdia & Abkaz	revolution	1991	1994	872	3000	—
Greece vs. Communists	revolution	1944	1945	1139	160135	—
Guatemala vs. Conservatives	revolution	1954	1954	23	1000	—
Guatemala vs. Indians	revolution	1966	1972	2112	58000	138000
Guatemala vs. Leftists of 1970	revolution	1970	1971	305	1000	—
Guatemala vs. Leftists of 1978	revolution	1978	1984	2225	73000	—
India vs. Hyderabad	secession	1948	1948	5	1000	2000
India vs. Sikhs & Kashmiros	secession	1985	—		30000	—
Indonesia vs. Darul Islam	revolution	1953	1953	65	1000	—
Indonesia vs. East Timor	secession	1975	1977	576	6000	16000
Indonesia vs. Leftists	revolution	1956	1960	1478	30000	—
Indonesia vs. Moluccans	secession	1950	1950	157	5000	—
Iran vs. Anti-Shah Coalition	revolution	1978	1979	485	7500	—
Iran vs. Mujaheddin	revolution	1981	1982	332	14000	—
Iraq vs. KDP Kurds	secession	1996	1996	8	1500	—
Iraq vs. Kurds & Shiites	secession	1985	1993	3287	10000	—
Iraq vs. Kurds of 1961	secession	1961	1963	798	500	3000

War Name	War Type	Year Began	Year Ended	Duration (Days)	State Deaths	Total Deaths
Iraq vs. Kurds of 1974	secession	1974	1975	382	5000	—
Iraq vs. Shammar Tribe & Pro-Western Officers	revolution	1959	1959	5	2000	—
Jordan vs. Palestinians	revolution	1970	1970	8	2100	—
Laos vs. Pathet Lao of 1960	revolution	1960	1962	639	5000	—
Laos vs. Pathet Lao of 1963	revolution	1963	1973	3591	18500	—
Lebanon vs. Leftists of 1958	revolution	1958	1958	130	1400	—
Lebanon vs. Leftists of 1975	revolution	1975	1990	5663	43800	167000
Liberia vs. Anti-Doe Rebels	revolution	1989	1990	363	10000	—
Liberia vs. National Patriotic Forces	revolution	1996	1996	138	3000	—
Liberia vs. NPFL & ULIMO	revolution	1992	1995	1039	150000	—
Morocco vs. Western Sahara	secession	1975	1983	2935	12000	16000
Mozambique vs. Renamo	revolution	1979	1992	4733	200550	1200550
Nicaragua vs. Contras	revolution	1982	1990	2955	43000	—
Nicaragua vs. Sandinistas	revolution	1978	1979	291	35000	—
Nigeria vs. Biafrans	secession	1967	1970	922	100000	1000000
Nigeria vs. Muslim Fundamentalists of 1980	secession	1980	1981	15	5000	—
Nigeria vs. Muslim Fundamentalists of 1984	secession	1984	1984	32	1000	—
Pakistan vs. Baluchi Rebels	secession	1973	1977	1651	8600	—
Pakistan vs. Bengalis	secession	1971	1971	253	500000	—
Pakistan vs. Mohajir	secession	1994	1995	423	2000	—
Paraguay vs. Leftists	revolution	1947	1947	167	1000	—
Peru vs. Shining Path	revolution	1982	1995	5051	30000	—
Philippines vs. Huks	revolution	1950	1952	670	9000	—
Philippines vs. Moros	secession	1972	1980	3000	15000	60000
Philippines vs. NPA	revolution	1972	1992	7397	40000	—
Republic of Vietnam vs. NLF	revolution	1960	1965	1864	302000	—
Rumania vs. Anti-Ceaucescu Rebels	revolution	1989	1989	2	1014	—
Russia vs. Chechens	secession	1994	1996	507	30000	90000

War Name	War Type	Year Began	Year Ended	Duration (Days)	State Deaths	Total Deaths
Rwanda vs. Patriotic Front	revolution	1994	1994	104	500000	—
Rwanda vs. Tutsi	revolution	1990	1993	1040	2000	—
Rwanda vs. Watusi	revolution	1963	1964	84	2500	—
Sierra Leone vs. RUF	revolution	1991	1996	1859	20000	—
Somalia vs. Clan Factions	revolution	1982	1997	5725	95018	—
Sri Lanka vs. Janatha Vimukthi-JVP	revolution	1971	1971	41	2000	—
Sri Lanka vs. JVP	revolution	1987	1989	853	30000	—
Sri Lanka vs. Tamils	secession	1983	—	—	9400	50000
Sudan vs. Anya Nya	secession	1963	1972	3073	250000	—
Sudan vs. SPLA-Garang Faction	secession	1983	—	—	1300000	—
Tadzhikistan vs. Popular Democratic Army	revolution	1992	1997	1884	20000	50000
Thailand vs. Communists	revolution	1970	1973	1400	1650	4000
Turkey vs. Kurds	secession	1991	—	—	28000	40000
Uganda vs. Buganda Tribe	secession	1966	1966	10	2000	—
Uganda vs. Lords Resistance Army	secession	1996	—	—	10000	—
Uganda vs. National Resistance Army	revolution	1980	1988	2756	102000	—
Yemen Arab Republic vs. Royalists	revolution	1962	1969	2485	101000	—
Yemen Arab Republic vs. Yahya Family	revolution	1948	1948	33	4000	—
Yemen People's Republic vs. Leftist Factions	revolution	1986	1986	17	12000	—
Yemen vs. South Yemen	secession	1994	1994	137	7000	—
Yugoslavia/Serbia vs. Croatians	secession	1991	1992	248	10000	—
Zaire/Congo vs. Kabila-ADFL	revolution	1996	1997	222	1000	—
Zaire/Congo vs. Katanga & Leftists	secession	1960	1965	1886	100050	—
Zaire/Congo vs. Rebels	revolution	1993	1993	8	1000	—
Zimbabwe vs. Patriotic Front	revolution	1972	1979	2557	12000	—

Source: Sarkees, Meredith Reid. 2000. "The Correlates of War Data on War: An Update to 1997." Conflict Management and Peace Science 18 (1): 123–44 (http://cow2.la.psu.edu/, last accessed September 2003).

Chapter Two

Theories of Revolution: The Evolution of the Field

Under what conditions would ordinary citizens take the extraordinary step of joining a revolutionary movement, knowing full well the grave risks to life, limb, and property that such action entails? In this chapter, I review some of the most influential contemporary works that have struggled with this question. Comparing these competing (and often complementary) arguments should provide some insight into how this field—the analysis of contemporary revolutions and civil violence—has evolved over the course of the past few decades.

The initial wave of social scientific works on revolution in the Third World focused on deprivation—in terms of economic well-being or political rights or both—as a source of grievances that motivate people to rise up in revolt. Works by James Davies (1962) and Ted Gurr (1970) inspired *deprived actor theories* of revolution, which point to inequality in income, wealth, and land ownership as sources of frustration that fuel revolutionary discontent.

Resource mobilization theory arose out of a concern with the inability of deprived-actor theories to account for the fact that conditions of deprivation and inequality are quite common among the nations of the world, whereas revolution is extremely rare. Why does revolution occur in only a small number of instances in which populations face severe deprivation? Charles Tilly (1978) points to the importance of revolutionary leadership and revolutionary organization in mobilizing discontented populations for violent collective action. In the absence of effective mobilization, deprived populations suffer in silence.

A third group of scholars, led by Theda Skocpol (1979), argue that both deprived actor models and resource mobilization theory implicitly discount the role of the state in generating the crises that sometimes degenerate into revolutionary violence. Skocpol and her colleagues "bring the state back in" to the analysis of revolution by pointing out the ways in which actions by the state are critical in determining whether discontent will arise and whether revolutionary elites will succeed in mobilizing discontented populations for revolt.

Finally, *rational actor theories* address the question that is central to this book: Regardless of the level of deprivation, the presence or absence of revolutionary leadership, or the actions of the state, why would any rational individual take up arms against the government, given the extreme risks and the uncertain payoffs that such action entails?

Reviewing the contributions of each of these schools should reveal some of the fundamental questions that have guided research on the causes, dynamics, and outcomes of contemporary revolutions. The answers that each school offers provide insights into the conditions that would make it rational for an ordinary citizen to take up arms against the government. If we know the right questions, we can proceed more effectively in formulating an understanding of why revolutions in the countryside occur in the Third World.

SOURCES OF POPULAR DISCONTENT: INEQUALITY AND DEPRIVATION

Western scholarship on the subject of Third World revolutions has followed a discernible evolutionary pattern in the years since the end of World War II. This evolution coincides in part with the changing perceptions of Western national security interests, which might be at stake in such conflicts, and in part with the ebb and flow of interest among scholars (as opposed to strategic analysts in the government) in the subject.

Soon after World War II, guerrilla insurgencies in China, Greece, the Philippines, Malaya, and Vietnam forced strategic analysts in the United States and Europe to confront the question of why peasants revolt. Because the spread of insurgencies coincided with the emergence of the U.S.-Soviet rivalry, analysts tended to treat these revolts as tactical problems in the Cold War. Guerrilla insurgency was seen as the Communist bloc's preferred strategy for expanding its influence into the Third World without risking a direct nuclear confrontation with the United States.[1] Michael Shafer (1988: 17) quotes from a U.S. National Security Council directive drafted in 1951: "Communist-controlled guerrilla warfare represents one of the most potent instrumentalities in the arsenal of communist aggression on a worldwide basis. It is therefore in the important national security interests of the United States to take all practicable steps . . . to prepare to counter such guerrilla warfare on a coordinated worldwide basis."

Goodwin and Skocpol (1989: 489–90) note appropriately that, from this perspective, revolutions occur in Third World nations when professional revolutionaries, with the backing of Moscow or Beijing, subvert indigenous regimes by employing the organizational weapon of a disciplined revolutionary party. Using the same logic, those on the other side of the political spectrum argued that the absence of revolution in many impoverished Third World nations was the result of the United States propping up corrupt indigenous regimes whose only virtue was that they endeared themselves to the capitalist West through their vociferous anticommunist rhetoric and their energetic repression of anyone suspected of sympathizing with that enemy. Both views imply that the citizens of Third World nations torn by revolutionary violence are little more than pawns in the hands of clever revolutionaries trained, armed, financed, and directed by Moscow or Beijing. Accordingly there is little if any need to consider whether domestic economic, political, or social conditions might make these people susceptible to revolutionary mobilization. Revolution results when a nation becomes infected with the virus of communist subversion. The task for the United States and its allies, then, is to counter communist subversion through the military tactics of counterinsurgency warfare.[2] The successful British counterinsurgency program in Malaysia became the model for similar efforts by the United States and indigenous regimes in other parts of the world.[3] Identifying and remedying any social, economic, or political crises that might have plagued these nations was considered a humanitarian task, unrelated to the mission of defeating the insurgency.

America's involvement in the Vietnam War and the accompanying antiwar movement and racial strife of the 1960s sparked renewed interest among social scientists in theories of civil violence.[4] To some extent, the resulting wave of behavioral research on civil violence was a reaction against the working assumption of U.S. policy toward Third World revolutions: that people could be duped into supporting a revolution when that revolution was not in their interest. Scholars posed the counterproposition: If people are willing to revolt, there must be some syndrome of social, economic, and political conditions that would make them so dissatisfied with their government that they would be willing to consider revolution as an alternative to the status quo. Those factors constitute the underlying conditions of revolution. When they are present, all that is required is some precipitating event to serve as the spark that touches off the tinderbox of popular discontent into a conflagration of revolutionary violence.[5] What, then, are the underlying social, economic, and political conditions that generate popular grievances that fuel revolution? The quest to answer this question spawned several research traditions, all based on deprived actor assumptions: Political violence is most likely to occur among populations that experience severe and sudden economic deprivation. The *inequality-instability* research program focuses on inequalities in the distribution of wealth, income, land, and power as causes of political violence. A second prominent school focuses on psychological processes of frustration and aggression that result from conditions of *relative deprivation.*

Inequality and Political Violence

One intuitively appealing explanation of the sources of revolutionary discontent is the existence of extreme inequality with respect to income (Muller 1985), land tenure (Russett 1964; Mitchell 1968; Paige 1970; Paranzino 1972; Midlarsky 1982; Midlarsky and Roberts 1985; Seligson 1996), or both (Muller and Seligson 1987). The link between inequality and political violence has a long history in the analysis of revolution. Bruce Russett (1964: 443) quotes Tocqueville: "Remove the secondary causes that have produced the great convulsions of the world and you will almost always find the principle of inequality at the bottom." Samuel Huntington (1968: 375) was quite explicit in characterizing the link between inequitable systems of land tenure and peasant-based revolution in the Third World:

> Where the conditions of landownership are equitable and provide a viable living for the peasant, revolution is unlikely. Where they are inequitable and where the peasant lives in poverty and suffering, revolution is likely, if not inevitable, unless the government takes prompt measures to remedy these conditions. . . . No group is more conservative than a landowning peasantry, and none is more revolutionary than a peasantry that owns too little land or pays too high a rental.

The sheer volume of studies based on some version of the inequality–political violence link attests to its intuitive appeal as an explanation for revolutionary violence. Nevertheless, the inequality-political violence research program has been plagued by two persistent puzzles (see Lichbach 1989, 1990). First, there has been little effort to spell out conceptually the causal links between inequality and political violence. Some degree of inequality is found in all societies, but not all societies—in fact, very few—are torn by political violence. What, then, is the mechanism by which inequality gives rise to violent conflict? Is there some threshold of inequality that must be achieved before violence is likely to occur? Or is inequality just a necessary but not sufficient precondition for political violence? If so, what other conditions must also be present for the discontent spawned by inequality to erupt into political violence? The answers to these questions would require a conceptual framework that not only spells out the causal sequence by which inequality leads to insurrection but also accounts for why insurrection does not occur in so many instances where high levels of inequality are present for prolonged periods of time. To date, no one has addressed this problem adequately.

Second, the empirical findings on the inequality-political violence link have been inconclusive, inconsistent, and at times contradictory. Lichbach surveys forty-three studies that use aggregate data (both cross-national and within countries) to test the relationship between inequality and political violence. These studies employ a variety of measures of both variables. They use a widely varying set of cases and time frames, dictated largely by availability of data. And they employ a variety of control variables. Lichbach (1989: 447–48) concludes, however, that the findings "are not robust between studies" and reveal no "laws" linking inequality to political violence. In a similar vein, Manus Midlarsky (1988: 442) concludes from his survey of existing research on the inequality–political violence nexus that "rarely is there a robust relationship discovered between the two variables. Equally rarely does the relationship plunge into the depths of the black hole of nonsignificance."

Why would the relationship between inequality and political violence be so difficult to establish empirically? Will Moore points out that we are not likely to find a robust relationship between inequality and political violence within a country over time because the distribution of land ownership, income, or wealth changes at a glacial pace, while the level of political violence can and does vary substantially on an annual, monthly, or even weekly basis (Moore, Lindström, and O'Regan 1996: 337–38). In effect, then, inequality is a constant over most time spans for which measures of political violence vary, and by definition a constant does not covary with a variable. If researchers have found statistical correlations between inequality and political violence with cross-national data, it is simply because inequality does vary from one country to another, as does the level of political violence. However, any such statistical relationship is likely to be spurious, not causal. If inequality is related to political violence in any way (which it most certainly is), the relationship is indirect, at best (Moore, Lindström, and O'Regan 1996; Lichbach 1989). Inequality may generate other conditions that are more directly related to political violence. Or inequality may contribute to the outbreak of political violence if other conditions are also present. However, inequality does not always under all circumstances give rise to political violence or to other conditions that lead to political violence. The central task for this research tradition, then, is to determine what intervening variables might account for the indirect relationship between inequality and political violence.

Relative Deprivation Theories

In 1962 James Davies (1962: 6) hypothesized that "revolutions are most likely to occur when a prolonged period of objective economic and social development is followed by a short period of sharp reversal." This development pattern, referred to as the J-curve, generates a sense of relative deprivation (RD), whereby people's expectations about what they should be achieving exceed their actual level of achievement (See figure 2.1). The prolonged period of social and economic development leads not only to increasing levels of achievement but also to rising expectations among people for achieving material well-being. A crisis such as a depression or a war brings about a sharp reversal in the level of achievement. However, according to Davies, popular expectations continue to rise, or at least they do not adjust downward with declining achievement. The widening gap between expectations and achievements produces mounting frustration. At some point, frustration generated by the gap between expectations and achievements becomes so intolerable that aggression results. If the frustration is widespread throughout society, the aggression will assume the form of collective violence. If the government is seen as being responsible for the declining levels of satisfaction, then this frustration will crystallize into what Davies terms a "revolutionary state of mind." Revolution will ensue as the aggressive effect of shared, politicized frustration.

In *Why Men Rebel*, Ted Gurr (1970), elaborates RD theory in greater detail. He points out that an intolerable gap between expectations and achievements can result from other patterns of macrosocial development besides Davies's J-curve. Gurr proposes two other patterns of relative deprivation. The first is what he terms *decremental deprivation*, where expectations remain constant but achievements decline. The second is termed *aspirational deprivation*, whereby expectations rise while achievements remain constant.

Gurr (1970) also refines Davies's original formulation by introducing the critical variable of the *coercive balance* between the government and the dissidents. Frustrated people will not take up arms against their government if the government's coercive capacity (that is, its military and police capabilities) is substantially greater than the dissidents' own coercive capacity. In short, even frustrated people are not suicidal.

Davies's and Gurr's works were provocative for a number of reasons. First, by grounding RD in frustration-aggression theory, they draw attention to the individual and what motivates him or her to participate in a revolution.[6] Second, by spelling out the dynamics of social and economic change that produce frustration, they link individual behavioral propensities (the revolutionary state of mind) to macrosocial developments (prolonged periods of systemic development followed by sharp reversals). Although RD theory is grounded in psychology, it does not depict revolutionary behavior as some sort of psychological pathology. Instead, political violence is seen as a predictable outcome of frustrations that result from the dynamics of social and economic change.

Third, RD theory explicitly rejects the notion that the revolutionary state of mind is more likely to arise among the most severely deprived, or that revolution is more likely to occur the more severely deprived the population is.

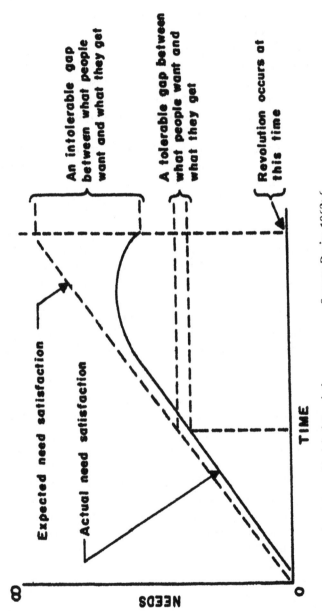

Figure 2.1. Davies' J-Curve Model of Revolution.

Source: Davies 1962: 6.

According to Davies, people experiencing the extremes of absolute deprivation are too preoccupied with the immediate rigors of mere survival to join in any organized endeavor such as a revolution. Absolute deprivation frays the fabric of social life, making cooperation among individuals difficult and highly unlikely. It is relative deprivation, not absolute deprivation, that produces the "revolutionary state of mind." People who have become accustomed to steady improvements in their standard of living but are confronted with a sharp and sudden decline in living conditions are the ones most likely to revolt. Furthermore, because they are not absolutely deprived, they have some resources to contribute to the revolutionary effort, which is not the case with those suffering from absolute deprivation.

There are, of course, a number of questions left unanswered by Davies's and Gurr's work, and efforts to test RD theory empirically have not produced convincing results.[7] At a conceptual level, RD theory has been criticized for, among other things, its reliance on frustration-aggression logic, when clearly aggression is only one of several response alternatives to frustration.[8] Others have argued that RD theory fails to specify the reference groups on which people base their expectations or the mechanisms by which individual psychological states (that is, the revolutionary state of mind) aggregate into explicitly collective action (especially violent collective action) (Wickham-Crowley 1997: 48; Park and Mason 1986).[9] Moreover, neither Davies's J-curve nor Gurr's decremental or aspirational models offer any explanation for the continued rise in expectations in the face of sudden and severe declines in individual need satisfaction. Why do people's expectations not adjust downward with declines in their achievement? This is a rather strong and counterintuitive proposition, but without it the gap between expectations and achievements never occurs, and the revolutionary state of mind never emerges.[10] However, the seminal impact of Davies's and Gurr's work cannot be discounted. It moved the field beyond the strategic and tactical analyses of the early Cold War years. Even the questions left unanswered by relative deprivation stimulated additional theory-building that advanced the field substantially.

Generally the inequality–political violence literature and the relative deprivation literature suffer from the problem of overpredicting revolution. Both theories rely on causal factors that occur far more frequently in time and space (that is, in far more nations far more often) than does widespread political violence.[11] There are numerous historical cases in which J-curve dynamics occurred but no revolution took place. One often-cited instance is the Great Depression in the United States: Why did no revolution occur in the 1930s, when clearly there was a sharp reversal in levels of achievement following the prolonged period of social and economic development that accompanied America's industrial revolution? In a similar vein, poverty and high levels of inequality in wealth, income, and land ownership are far more common than revolution. Goodwin and Skocpol (1989: 490) observe that "very many Third World countries are poor, . . . but revolutions have occurred in only a few of them, and not necessarily the poorest. Why did China and Vietnam have social revolutions, but not India or Indonesia? Why Cuba, one of the more developed Latin American countries when Castro seized power, but not Haiti or the Dominican Republic? Why Nicaragua, but not Honduras?" In his analysis of the Mexican revolution, Walter Goldfrank (1986: 105) adds that explanations of revolution based on professional revolutionaries exploiting severe deprivation "do not take us very far. Widespread oppression and inflammatory agitation occur with far greater frequency than revolutions, or even rebellion." What is special about that handful of cases of RD or severe inequality that do erupt into violence?

Neither relative deprivation theory nor inequality–political violence theory adequately addresses the question of why people who are frustrated (by a gap between expectations and achievements or by the existence of high levels of inequality) would resort to revolutionary violence rather than some other response. Even if people are frustrated with their government and willing to take up arms against it, how would they bring about the extraordinary coordination of behavior that a revolution would require? In *The Logic of Collective Action* (1965), Mancur Olson raises the problem of persuading rational individuals to participate in collective action, which inspired the rational choice research program on revolution and political violence.

RATIONAL ACTOR APPROACHES

The starting point for rational actor (RA) models of political violence is the observation that the collective action problem is largely ignored in the deprived actor research program. For the average citizen the benefits produced by a successful revolution are public goods. Public goods are distinguished from private goods by virtue of their being both nonexcludable in their supply and nonrival in their consumption. Nonexcludability refers to the fact that, once the good is supplied to one person, it is available to all, regardless of whether or not they contributed to its provision. Nonrivalness refers to the absence of crowding effects: One person's consumption of the good does not diminish the amount available for others to consume. Clean air and national defense are commonly cited examples of public goods that illustrate these two characteristics. All citizens of a nation enjoy the benefits of national defense, regardless of whether or not they pay any taxes, serve in the military, or otherwise contribute to national defense. Similarly, if the government enacts pollution control regulations, all citizens are able to enjoy the benefits of clean air, regardless of whether they pay any taxes. No one can be excluded from enjoying these goods once they are made available to anyone, and one person's enjoyment of clean air or national defense does not noticeably diminish the amount of clean air or national defense available to other citizens.

Mancur Olson argues that, given these characteristics of public goods, there is little reason for a rational self-interested individual to contribute to their production. If the goods are produced, they will be able to enjoy them, even if they do not contribute to their provision. Moreover, in large groups, each person's contribution is such a small share of the total amount needed to produce the good that the contribution or noncontribution of a single individual will not determine whether or not the good is produced. Thus rational individuals will be tempted to "free ride," which Dennis Chong (1991: 5) describes as follows: "The temptation will be to save on the cost of contributing to the public good. If others come through and produce the good, he will share in its benefits without having contributed to its cost. If the other members of the group do not produce the good, then his single contribution would not have made any difference."

The collective action dilemma, then, is that if everyone acts according to this logic, public goods will never be produced. Thus Olson (1965: 2) concludes that "rational, self-interested individuals will not act to achieve their common or group interests." The only way to induce people to participate in collective action or contribute to the provision of public goods is to offer them selective incentives: divisible benefits that can be withheld from those who do not participate in the collective action (51).

Gordon Tullock (1971) captures the relevance of Olson's argument for the question of revolution. The outcome of a successful revolution—a new regime— is a public good: Everyone will be able to enjoy the new order, regardless of whether or not they participated in the rebellion. The incentives to free-ride are especially powerful in the case of revolutionary collective action. Time and resources devoted to the cause are time and resources that could be devoted to other endeavors that promise greater private benefit. Moreover, participation in revolution is risky behavior: It involves the possibility of physical injury and death as well as fines, incarceration, and torture if one is apprehended by the government. Why assume these costs and risks if the benefits of revolution will be available to you even if you do not participate?

Tullock formalizes the logic of this dilemma in an expected utility equation that models the individual's choice between participating or not participating in a revolution. His equation can be simplified as follows:

$$E(U_i) = p_{pg} (R) + (1 - p_i) (L_i) - p_i (C_i) \qquad (2.1)$$

where $E(U_i)$ is the ith individual's expected utility from participation in revolution; R is the value that person attaches to the public goods resulting from a successful revolution; p_{pg} is that person's estimate of the probability that the revolution will succeed and produce the public goods R; L_i is the value that the individual places on the selective incentives that come from participation (such as the fruits of looting stores and houses); $(1-p_i)$ is the probability that the individual will participate, gain the selective incentives, and not get caught and punished by the government; p_i is the probability the individual will be apprehended and punished for participating in the revolution; and C_i is the value of the punishments the individual will suffer if apprehended.

This model leads Tullock to conclude that people will not participate in revolutions unless the expected private benefits of participation, $(1-p_i)(L_i)$, are greater than the expected costs of participation, $(p_i)(C_i)$; otherwise, he or she will stay home. The goals of the revolution—that is, the public goods that will result from revolutionary victory—are irrelevant to the individual's choice between participating or not. The individual will be able to enjoy those benefits whether or not he or she participates, and that participation will have no appreciable effect on the likelihood that the revolution will succeed and produce those public goods (p_{pg}).

This model has several troubling implications. First, carried to its logical conclusion, it implies that revolutions will never occur, because everyone will free-ride. The only way to avert this outcome is for someone to offer selective incentives (Li) in sufficient amounts to induce enough people to participate. Yet, we know that revolutions do occur. They do not all fall victim to the inertia of free-rider temptations.

The second implication is that the ideological goals of the revolution or the promise of a new social order are largely irrelevant to a person's choice between participating or free-riding. Instead participation is strictly a function of the selective incentives (L_i) and costs (C_i) that accrue only to participants. In effect, revolution becomes a matter not of righteous rebellion against unjust authority but "revolution for fun and profit." Participation is strictly a mercenary consideration, and whether or not the rebels succeed is strictly a function of how effective they are at manipulating mercenary incentives: Are there enough selective incentives available to lure enough mercenaries into the streets to overthrow the government?

While these conclusions do follow from the logic of Tullock's model, they also confront us with at least two anomalies. The logic of free-rider effects implies that individuals can be induced to join a revolution only by the promise of selective incentives and then only if the probability of suffering the costs of participation (death, injury, or incarceration) is relatively low. What diminishes the probability of suffering the costs of participation is the presence of a large number of other people already participating in the rebel movement. The more rebels there are, the more the state's police and security forces will be overwhelmed and, consequently, the lower will be the probability of any one rebel being among those killed, injured, or incarcerated in the uprising. This presents us with a theoretical chicken-or-egg dilemma: In order to explain the nth person's decision to join the revolt, the model presupposes that a large number of equally rational individuals have already chosen to participate. How were those individuals persuaded to do so? More specifically, how does the model account for the behavior of the early recruits to the rebellion, when the chances of being apprehended and punished by the government are much higher, and the ability of the rebel organization, still in its infancy, to offer them selective incentives is severely limited if not nonexistent (see Mason 1984: 1042–43)?

Second, if selective incentives are required to induce participation, who supplies the selective incentives, and how do they acquire the means to provide them? Few people are sufficiently wealthy to underwrite the cost of a revolution by themselves, and those who are have no reason to invest their wealth in an enterprise intended to destroy the very system from which they have so richly benefited.

The problem created by this version of the rational rebel is that it underpredicts revolution (Lichbach 1995). By the logic of Olson's free-rider dilemma, no rational individual should join a revolution unless compensated directly for it. Yet revolutions do occur, and people do participate in them for reasons other than just the selective incentives offered by the rebels. Revolutions begin with the action of individuals who are not deterred by the risks that such action incurs and who are not motivated primarily by the immediate private payoffs of revolution. And they have the skills to mobilize human and material resources for collective action and to manage those resources in such a way as to mount a viable challenge to the incumbent regime. Thus the next major school of revolutionary theory to emerge—resource mobilization theory—focuses on the critical role of political leadership and organization in solving the collection action problem.

SOCIAL MOVEMENTS, CONTENTIOUS POLITICS, AND RESOURCE MOBILIZATION

Troubled by the tendency of deprived actor models to overpredict revolutions and rational actor models to underpredict them, a number of scholars began focusing on, first, the critical role of revolutionary leadership and revolutionary organization in mobilizing dissatisfied people for the purpose of collective action and, second, the role of political opportunity structure, framing processes, and mobilizing structures in determining the timing, forms, and likely outcomes of collective action. The resource mobilization school that evolved from this research program has expanded over the years to explore the dynamics of nonviolent social movements and other forms of contentious politics.[12] Revolution is one type of social movement on a spectrum of contentious politics that includes a full panorama of nonviolent and violent collective action short of revolution.

The resource mobilization critique of deprived actor models begins with the collective action problem: Even if grievances are widespread, people still have no incentive to cooperate in collective action. For Turner and Killian (1972: 251), the level of grievance in society is largely irrelevant to the question of whether or not a revolutionary movement will arise because, "there is always enough discontent in any society to supply the grassroots movement if the movement is effectively organized and has at its disposal the power and resources of some established elite group." Rod Aya (1979: 41) adds that "fluctuations in grievances account for the outbreak of collective protest as poorly as fluctuations in the oxygen content of air explain the incidence of fires." McCarthy and Zald (1977: 1215) add that "we can go even further: grievances and discontent may be defined, created, and manipulated by issue entrepreneurs and organizations."[13] What is more critical for revolution than the level of grievance in society is the presence of revolutionary leaders who can overcome the collective action problem by mobilizing the human and material resources necessary to mount a viable challenge to the incumbent regime.

Their point of departure from rational actor models is the latter's treatment of individuals as socially isolated, atomized actors who confront the choice of whether or not to participate in collective action (and revolutionary collective action specifically) as if they had no pre-existing memberships in any social networks or organizations of any sort. Marwell and Oliver (1984: 16) counter this rational actor assumption by arguing that "collective action, in general, is not undertaken by isolated automata: rather, it is undertaken by groups of people in social interaction with one another. Thus, any analysis of a collective campaign must take account of the social organization of the population at risk."

Social movement theorists highlight the critical role of changes in the dissidents' *political opportunity structure* in determining when and if they will undertake collective action, what form that action will assume (that is, violent or nonviolent), and what the prospects of success might be for that action.[14] Aspects of the political opportunity structure that make dissident collective action more or less likely include the degree of openness of the polity (Eisinger 1973), the stability or instability of political alignments among elites and contender groups within the polity (Piven and Cloward 1977), whether or not the challenger group has allies and support groups within the polity or among other challengers (Jenkins and Perrow 1977), divisions within the governing elite (Jenkins and Perrow), the state's tolerance for protest and its willingness and ability to repress challengers, and the policy-making capacity of the government (Kitschelt 1986). Even if large segments of the population are aggrieved, and even if dissident leaders and organizations exist to mobilize them for collective action, people are not likely to join such a movement unless they perceive some change to have occurred in the stability of the dominant coalition of elites and classes and in the capacity and propensity of the state to repress dissident activity. Doug McAdam (1996: 32) contends that "changes in either the institutional features, informal political alignments, or repressive capacity of a given political system . . . significantly reduce the power disparity between a given challenging group and the state" and thereby affect the chances of dissident collective action succeeding and its participants escaping harsh sanctions. Thus, for McAdam, "revolutions owe less to the efforts of insurgents than to the work of systemic crises which render the existing regime weak and vulnerable to challenge from any quarter (24)."

Multiple Sovereignty

Charles Tilly's *From Mobilization to Revolution* (1978) stands as the most influential work on revolution from the resource mobilization school. For Tilly a revolutionary situation arises "when the government previously under the control of a single sovereign polity becomes the object of effective, competing, and mutually exclusive claims on the part of two or more distinct polities" (191). This is the condition of *multiple sovereignty.* The state no longer exercises a monopoly over the legitimate use of power within the territorial boundaries of the nation because a counter-elite has arisen to challenge the state. Challengers become revolutionary when they develop the organizational capacity to mobilize the support of a significant segment of the population to the point that, for that segment of the population, the revolutionary organization is the de facto government in their lives. Revolution, then, is the struggle between the dual sovereigns over which one will prevail as the sole legitimate authority. How does the condition of multiple sovereignty arise?

According to Tilly (1978), any polity consists of three sets of actors: a population, a government, and a set of contenders (see figure 2.2). The government is the entity that "controls the principal concentrated means of coercion within the population" (52). It is the sovereign authority that enjoys a monopoly over the legitimate use of coercion. A contender is any group that applies pooled resources in competition with other groups to influence the government in ways that advance that group's interests. An increase in a group's

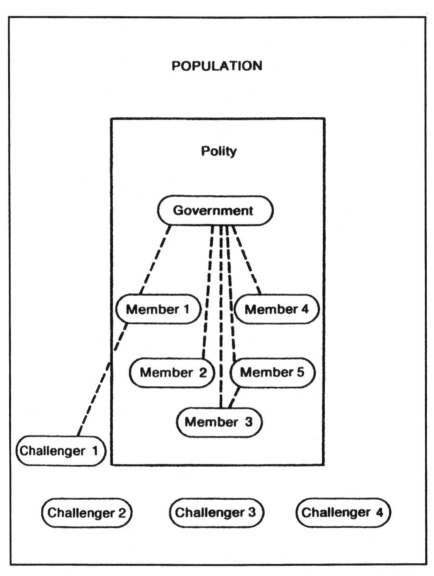

POPULATION

Polity

Government

Member 1   Member 4

Member 2   Member 5

Member 3

Challenger 1

Challenger 2   Challenger 3   Challenger 4

––– Coalition

Figure 2.2. Tilly's Model of the Polity. *Source:* Tilly 1978: 53.

power shows up as a higher rate of return (in terms of benefits received) on resources expended in its efforts to influence government action (54).

In this model, there are two types of contenders. Contenders who are members of the polity enjoy "routine, low-cost access to resources controlled by government" (Tilly 1978: 52). They are accepted by the government as legitimate players in the political process. They attempt to influence government through conventional means of political action. Challengers are contenders who are not members of the polity. They are not recognized by the government as legitimate contenders for power, and they are excluded from the conventional political contest over power and resources. To the extent that a contender can mobilize sufficient support from some segment of the population, its claims to power gain force in the competition with other contenders. The government can either admit it to the polity or resist its challenge, in which case a condition of dual sovereignty comes into being.

Contenders arise because the social transformations that occur during the course of modernization undermine existing structures of social organization and social control. Long-standing loyalties and allegiances that bound various segments of the population to some existing elite group erode, making those segments of the population available for mobilization by newly emerging elites. In agrarian societies, peasants remain loyal to the landed gentry so long as those elites provide them with access to land and emergency assistance in times of crisis, such as when floods or droughts result in crop failures. Peasant dependency on the landed elite enables the gentry to mobilize peasant support behind the gentry's efforts to influence the state to adopt policies supportive of the gentry's interests. However, when peasants are forced off the land by land pressures or by the shift to commercial agriculture, or when they leave the countryside voluntarily and move to the city to become wage laborers in an emerging industrial or commercial sector, they are no longer available for political mobilization by the landed gentry because they are no longer dependent upon them for their well-being. The landed gentry lose power in the polity, and at some point they may be excluded from the polity altogether. At the same time those peasants who are displaced from the land become available for mobilization by new elite challengers. New challengers might advocate reforms that would improve the situation of urban workers and landless peasants. If they can mobilize a significant segment of the growing urban labor force, they can challenge the government to admit them to the polity.

While these tectonic social changes may dissolve existing ties between elites and nonelites and generate grievances among disaffected nonelites, grievances alone are not sufficient to guarantee collective action. This requires organization and leaders capable of persuading the aggrieved populace to contribute to and participate in the activities of the dissident organization. Rod Aya (1984: 332–33) states this requirement quite bluntly: "Individuals are not magically mobilized for action no matter how aggrieved, hostile, or angry they feel. Their anger must first be set to collective ends by the coordinating, directing offices of organization, formal or informal. . . . There must be some kind of organization on hand to orchestrate discontent and convert it into collective action." Otherwise, "the unhappy merely brood passively on the sidelines" (Shorter and Tilly 1974: 338).

Who are the counter-elites who mobilize segments of the population for contentious political activity? Challengers can arise when changes in government policies alienate certain segments of the nation's elite, or when the dynamics of social and economic development significantly alter the ability of different elite groups to mobilize support for their claims on the government. Jack Goldstone (1991) argues that, in agrarian societies, a supply of counter-elites can emerge as a consequence of demographic pressures. During periods of rapid population growth, there is an increase in the number of children of current elites competing for what is essentially a fixed supply of elite positions, either as members of the landed gentry or as officials of the state. Their demands for official positions or for land are difficult to satisfy, because the supply of land is fixed, and the fiscal constraints impinging on the state limit its capacity to create new offices to absorb an expanding pool of elite aspirants. This leads to intensified elite rivalry and factionalism. Some of these aspiring elites become so alienated from the state that they pursue their ambitions by mobilizing popular resistance to the state's extractive demands.[15]

Mobilizing Structures

To overcome free-rider tendencies among the population they seek to mobilize, challengers rely on pre-existing *mobilizing structures,* including social networks, community organizations, and other such entities. Mobilizing structures are "those collective vehicles, both formal and informal, through which people come together and engage in collective action" (McAdam, Tarrow, and Tilly 1997: 155). Michael Taylor (1988b: 67) points to the importance of "community" in mobilizing people for revolutionary collective action, "not just because individual behavior can be more easily monitored but because a strong community has at its disposal a variety of powerful positive and negative social sanctions."

For challengers to pose a threat to the government, they must be able to persuade a significant segment of the population to withdraw their support from the government and make a commitment to the challenger's claims to sovereignty. Dissident leaders must be able to persuade the aggrieved population that their grievances are widely shared and that they can be remedied through collective action. This is referred to as the framing process.[16] Through their words and actions, dissident leaders attempt to shape reality for their potential supporters by identifying injustices and attributing them to the state or to other parties that are the target of their contentious movement. They offer their target audience positive symbols around which ordinary people join together in collective action, despite their ingrained reluctance to challenge authorities and the ever-present temptation to free-ride (McAdam, Tarrow, and Tilly 1997: 149). Existing community institutions and social networks can become effective mobilizing structures for collective action if the dissident leadership can draw on shared beliefs and worldviews that motivate and legitimize protest activity for the members of those collectivities (157).

The struggle between the state and challengers is most likely to escalate to a revolutionary situation of dual sovereignty when a coalition of challengers arises. A challenger group acting alone is more likely to resort to collective action short of revolution. The form that such action will take is, in Sidney Tarrow's words, "not born in the organizer's head but is culturally inscribed and socially communicated" (1998: 20). These "learned conventions of contention" are a part of the group's history as a group, a part that Tilly (1995a,b) termed the group's *repertoire of contention* (see also Trauggott 1995a,b). It is difficult to persuade people to participate in high-risk confrontational or violent protest at the outset of the movement. Therefore leaders of specific groups turn to the repertoire of contentious activities with which the group has experience. Because members have engaged in these forms of collective action in the past, it is easier for the group's leaders to persuade members to join in the same form of collective action again (Tarrow 1995: 99). Thus urban workers may engage in strikes, while students stage demonstrations. Landless peasants may undertake land invasions, while the urban poor may stage food riots.

None of these acts is intended to overthrow the government. Indeed, in many instances, such actions can be mobilized with a minimum of dissident leadership and organization because they involve existing mobilizing structures and forms of contention with which the participants are familiar. However, such actions are often short-lived and narrowly focused on a limited range of issues. They cannot be sustained as a credible challenge to the state without an organization that can mobilize a series of actions that sustain the pressure on the state's coercive resources. A credible challenge to the state also requires a leadership group that can translate the group's contentious behavior into demands for specific remedial actions by the state. In this manner, the contenders seek to compel the state to admit them into the polity as fully participating members.

When several challengers mobilize simultaneously and begin to cooperate as a coalition, a revolutionary situation is said to exist. In France in 1789 a coalition of peasants, bourgeoisie, and urban workers, each motivated by a different set of grievances, united to overthrow the monarchy and form the republic. Similarly in Russia in 1917 a coalition of peasants and urban workers brought about the Bolshevik victory. A revolutionary organization is the essential catalyst for the emergence of a coalition of challengers capable of overthrowing the government. The revolutionary organization coordinates the activities of the different challenger groups and thereby shapes an otherwise inchoate sequence of strikes, demonstrations, and localized peasant uprisings into an organized revolutionary challenge to the government. To do this, the revolutionary organization must persuade each challenger group to subordinate its particular agenda to the shared goal of overthrowing the government.

> The revolutionary moment arrives when previously acquiescent members of that population find themselves confronted with strictly incompatible demands from the government and from an alternative body claiming control over the government, or to *be* the government . . . and those previously acquiescent people obey the alternative body. They pay taxes, provide men to its armies, feed its functionaries, honor its symbols, give time to its service, or yield other resources despite the prohibitions of a still-existing government they formerly obeyed. Multiple sovereignty has begun. (Tilly 1978: 192)

Political Opportunity Structure

The success of a revolutionary organization is not just a function of its own organizational capacities. Often sudden and dramatic shifts in popular support occur because the population perceives the state to be weakened and ripe for challenge. While they may have been reluctant to support the movement actively up to that point (for fear of the consequences), signs of state weakness can cause them to upgrade their estimate of the revolution's chances of success and downgrade their estimate of the risks they face by participating. The result is that large numbers of latent supporters can be activated by such sudden shifts in the movement's political opportunity structure.

The circumstances most likely to bring about a critical shift in popular allegiance from the government to the challengers are (1) the sudden failure of the government to meet specific obligations that the population regards as deserved and crucial to their well-being, and (2) a rapid or unexpected increase in the government's demands on the population for the surrender of resources (Tilly 1978: 204–5). An example of the former would be when the government fails to prosecute a war effectively, leaving the population vulnerable to attack by an external enemy. In Russia in 1917 Tsar Nicholas II failed to prevent German armies from invading Russian territory. By March the provisional government of Alexander Kerensky was able to persuade enough of the population that the elected Duma, and not the tsar, was more capable of securing Russia against the Germans, and the tsar was forced to abdicate. By November the Bolsheviks were able to persuade enough peasants and workers to withdraw their support from the Kerensky government and support the Bolshevik's call for "bread, peace, and land." Thus, the Kerensky government fell to the Bolshevik challenge. A similar situation arose in China after the Japanese occupied much of northern China in 1937. The Nationalist (Guomintang) government of Chiang Kai-shek retreated to Chungking, conceding large areas of northern China to the Japanese occupation forces. In these regions the Chinese Communist guerrillas were able to build a base of popular support by offering peasants the sanctuary of rural base camps (soviets) that were relatively secure from the Japanese army. In both Russia and China, the government's failure to fulfill its obligation to protect the population from foreign invaders made it possible for challengers to mobilize a base of support sufficient to defeat the old regime in a civil war.[17]

A shift in allegiance can also occur when there is a sudden and unexpected increase in the government's demands for resources from the population. A dramatic increase in the tax burden imposed on peasants or an increase in the conscription or corvée labor demands of the state can cause people to shift their support to a challenger (Tilly 1978: 206). The burden imposed by new demands need not be so onerous as to threaten the population with subsistence crisis. Eric Wolf (1969) argues that defensive mobilization occurs when the government's new demands simply make it impossible for individuals to fulfill obligations that bind them to their community as "honorable men." Victor Magagna's analysis of peasant unrest depicts it as a reaction not to the size of elite extractions but to elite intrusions on the community's control over the allocation of that extractive burden among the community's membership: "Any change in the political links between [peasant] communities and elites that undermines the ability of community institutions to maintain jurisdiction over their members will create the potential for struggle over the extent of community autonomy. Similarly, elite projects that directly undercut community regulations concerning the use of land will likely result in acute conflict about who has the right to define the rights and duties of land tenure" (1991: 26).

The State's Response

Just as important for revolution, however, is the incapacity or unwillingness of the government to suppress the challenger coalition. This may occur because the government simply lacks sufficient coercive capacity to defeat the challengers. The Russian imperial state had depleted its coercive resources in its war with Germany, making it all the more vulnerable to the Bolshevik challenge in 1917. Incapacity of the state can also occur when the challengers manage a sudden increase in their own coercive resources by, for example, pooling the private weapons of participants or mobilizing a new contender with abundant coercive resources at its disposal. The defection of army units or the intervention of foreign troops are examples of this dynamic. Finally the government may have sufficient forces, but its leaders lack the will to use them.

The coercive capacity of a government can also erode more gradually, as a function of developmental changes in the character, organization, and daily routines of the population. As a nation undergoes the transition from agrarian to industrial society, the government may find that its system of social control and coercion, though well-adapted to an agrarian society, is inadequate for policing dissident political activity by a newly emerging urban working class. Similarly an agrarian social order built around patron-client networks may be less able to control or prevent collective action by peasants when production shifts from food crops produced by sharecroppers to commercial crops produced by landless wage laborers. Sharecroppers can be monitored by their landlord, whereas itinerant seasonal wage laborers cannot.[18]

Resource mobilization theorists address the collective action problem by highlighting the critical importance of revolutionary leadership and revolutionary organization for the inception and success of revolutionary violence. Even if grievances against the state are widespread and deeply felt, there will be no revolution unless a revolutionary leadership arises that is capable of organizing those who are aggrieved and mobilizing material resources in sufficient amounts to sustain an effective challenge to the state.

BRINGING THE STATE BACK IN

In *States and Social Revolutions* (1979) Theda Skocpol's point of departure from both the deprived actor and resource mobilization schools is that both largely ignore the proactive role of the state in generating revolutionary situations. While widespread grievances and revolutionary organization may be necessary for the revolutionary forces to take advantage of a crisis, "the fact is, no successful social revolution has ever been 'made' by mass-mobilizing, avowedly revolutionary movements" (17). The revolutionary vanguard does not create the revolutionary crisis; they simply exploit it. To explain revolutions one must look first to the generation of a revolutionary crisis within the old regime, and then identify the ways in which challengers are able to exploit that crisis for revolutionary purposes (18).

Most theories of revolution treat the state as a set of administrative, policing, and military institutions headed by an executive authority that uses state power to serve the interests of a dominant economic class. As such, the state is treated as little more than the arena in which conflicts over social and economic interests are fought. Control over the state is viewed as the stakes in the revolutionary struggle.

Skocpol contends that this perspective is flawed. The state must be viewed as relatively autonomous from the dominant economic class, with interests of its own that are distinct from those of the dominant class. It pursues those interests with a logic of its own, independent of the interests of the dominant economic class. Under normal circumstances, the state and the dominant class share an interest in keeping subordinate classes subjugated to their authority. However, the state's fundamental interest lies in maintaining social order and domestic peace and defending the nation against external threats. Under certain circumstances, pursuit of these interests can lead it to make concessions to subordinate classes if those concessions serve the state's interest in controlling the population, collecting taxes, and securing conscripts for its army (Skocpol 1979: 29–30). However, those concessions sometimes come at the expense of the dominant economic class, so that the state's pursuit of its own interests brings it into direct conflict with the dominant class. The resulting clash can generate the crisis that makes social revolution possible (25–28).

Both Skocpol and Jack Goldstone (1991) contend that whether or not this clash of interests leads to social revolution is contingent upon, first, characteristics of the state itself and, second, certain structural features of the pattern of state-society relations. Certain types of states embedded in certain patterns of social organization are more susceptible to social revolutions than others. All three of the social revolutions that Skocpol studies—France, Russia, and China—occurred in societies ruled by imperial states that governed through agrarian bureaucracies. As imperial states, they were "differentiated, centrally coordinated administrative and military hierarchies functioning under the aegis of an absolute monarchy" (Skocpol 1979: 49). As agrarian bureaucracies, they were "proto-bureaucratic" in the sense that only some offices at higher levels were functionally specialized, and only some officials and official duties were subject to explicit bureaucratic rules and formal hierarchical supervision. However, none of these states was fully bureaucratized. The traditional dominant class—the landed gentry—still permeated key portions of the state apparatus. While the monarch was the supreme authority, control over the day-to-day lives of peasants was much more decentralized. "A semiautonomous elite outside of official state office who acted as custodians of a well-articulated moral tradition" exercised varying degrees of judicial and administrative authority locally and regionally (Goldstone 1991: 5). They collected taxes and fees for the state, and they enacted and enforced regulations in the name of the state. Though formally subordinate to the monarchy, local elites exercised authority locally with a substantial degree of independence from the central state but with its formal backing. They were the local agents of the state, holding formal offices that gave them responsibility for collecting taxes, exacting corvée labor and conscripts for the army, and dispensing justice locally. They could also use their official status to serve their own interests, even at the expense of the state's.

The second feature of imperial states was that all presided over agrarian economies and social systems (Skocpol 1979: 48). Society was divided between a mass of peasant families and a small landed elite. Peasants were dependent upon the landed gentry for access to the land they needed to provide for their own subsistence needs. Market relations were extensively developed. A commercial class controlled commerce and industry, and the urban working class was dependent upon them for the wages needed to purchase the requirements for their own subsistence. However, trade and commerce remained predominantly local or regional in scope, and agriculture remained the dominant sector of the economy. Capitalist relations of production did not predominate in either the agricultural or commercial sectors.

In normal circumstances, the imperial state and landed gentry were partners in the control and exploitation of the peasantry. Local elites expected the central state to perform certain fundamental tasks of government. In return, they collected taxes for the state and enforced its directives. They expected the state to conduct successful military campaigns, maintain domestic order, regulate coinage, maintain transportation infrastructure, and provide status- or wealth-enhancing opportunities for local elites by restricting access to education, military careers, and civil service positions. Barrington Moore (1978: 20–23) adds that the population in general expected from the state (1) the defense of the nation against foreign enemies, (2) the maintenance of domestic peace and order, including protection from bandits, and (3) contributions to the material security of the population through public works and direct or indirect support of minimum subsistence guarantees. To perform these tasks, the state required revenues which were derived from land taxes on privately owned lands and rents on lands owned by the imperial state (Goldstone 1991: 5). In addition to paying taxes, the population was expected to obey the directives of the state and contribute to the national defense when necessary through military service.

In a real sense, the state and the gentry were competitors for control over the manpower of the peasantry and the surplus of the agrarian economy. The state's interest in appropriating resources was to channel them into its military or the state apparatus, or into state-controlled economic enterprises. The landed gentry's interest was to minimize state appropriations from local production. Balancing these competing interests posed a challenge. If the flow of income to the central state was insufficient, the state would be unable to fulfill its duties. If the flow of income to the central state was too great, local elites would be unable to perform their duties as agents of the imperial state. If the tax burden was shifted to the peasantry, they might be unable to produce the surplus needed to support the state and the agrarian elite. Local elites therefore generally supported state actions that sustained their authority locally but opposed state actions that threatened to concentrate power and revenues in the hands of the monarchy at expense of the agrarian elite (Goldstone 1991: 5–6). Indeed they often used their state offices to siphon off revenues for local projects that would enrich them and preserve their dominance in the local political economy.

Under normal conditions, these conflicts of interest between the state and the landed gentry would not escalate to the point of superseding their shared interest in preserving the status quo. What upset the balance and made modern social revolutions possible if not inevitable was the uneven spread of capitalist economic development (Skocpol 1979: 19). As European states industrialized, they gained power relative to other states. States that were late to industrialize perceived their international status and their national sovereignty to be threatened by the accretion of power to the more industrialized states. When this external challenge escalated to the threat of war, the state was compelled to impose extraordinary new extractive claims on the gentry, either to fight a war or to invest in a state-directed industrial revolution that would restore the nation's competitive balance with international rivals. Some late industrializing states, such as Prussia and Japan, succeeded in this endeavor.[19] Other states failed and were either defeated in war with more advanced powers (such as Russia), or they were deposed by the landed gentry's resistance to modernizing reforms and increased extractions. Thus changes in the international context strained the state's capacity to defend the nation. The state's efforts to meet these international challenges brought its interests into irreconcilable conflict with those of the dominant economic class, resulting in a revolutionary crisis of the state.

What distinguished those states that successfully adapted to modernization without social revolution from those that did not was the autonomy of the state from the agrarian elite. Skocpol (1976: 185) argues that "the adaptiveness of the earlier modernizing agrarian bureaucracies was significantly determined by the degree to which the upper and middle ranks of the state administrative bureaucracies were staffed by large landholders." In Germany, Japan, and Turkey the state bureaucracy was not staffed by large landowners. This autonomy of the state from the landed elite allowed the state to encroach upon the landed elite as necessary in order to strengthen the central state

(Trimberger 1972, 1978). In France and China the landed gentry assumed important local and regional offices in a state administrative structure that was only nominally centralized. The French monarchy even sold administrative posts to landed gentry in order to raise cash to finance wars. This allowed the landed gentry to capture control over or at least influence parts of the state's administrative machinery. From their position within that machinery, they could thwart the state's efforts to monopolize the flow of tax revenues and implement modernizing reforms.

These intra-elite conflicts were not sufficient in and of themselves to bring on social revolution. What was required in addition was the coincidence of widespread peasant revolts that "destroyed the old agrarian class relations" and thereby "weakened mainstays of the socioeconomic and political orders of the old regimes" (Skocpol 1979: 112, 113). Peasant rebellions were not unheard of in the history of these three nations or in agrarian societies generally. However, in premodern times, these revolts were sporadic, localized "momentary reactions to special grievances. Indeed, they were oriented more toward the restoration than toward the transformation of the conventional order" (Desai and Eckstein 1990: 445–45). As such, they "never achieved a successful, widespread, direct assault on the property or claims of landlords" (Skocpol 1979: 114). What was remarkable about the peasant revolts accompanying the French, Chinese, and Russian revolutions was that "they became at once widespread and directed particularly against landlords" (113). How is it that, at this historical moment in each country, peasant revolts suddenly transcended the local to coalesce into a truly nationwide uprising?

On this point Skocpol is less specific. Shared grievances are not the answer because "peasants always have grounds for rebellion against landlords, state agents, and merchants who exploit them" (1979: 115). And, indeed, despite the critical role that she attributes to national peasant revolts, she argues that, in terms of their goals, the national revolts that accompanied social revolutions "were *not* intrinsically different from previous peasant aims in rebellions or riots. Peasants participated in these revolutions without being converted to radical visions of a desired new national society, and without becoming a nationally organized class-for-themselves. Instead they struggled for concrete goals—typically involving access to more land, or freedom from claims on their surpluses" (114).

If these revolts are essential for the crisis of the state to degenerate into social revolution but, nonetheless, no different in their goals and motives from traditional peasant revolts, then how does she explain the unprecedented coincidence of peasant revolts on a nationwide scale?

On this matter Skocpol is less exacting than she is in her analysis of the role of the state in revolution. She argues that, where agricultural production is organized around large estates worked by serfs or landless laborers, spontaneous peasant uprisings are rare, because peasants are impoverished and subject to close supervision by landlords or their agents. Where peasants work their own land, either as smallholders or renters, peasant revolts are much more common, because the ties of peasant community unite families in opposition to landlords (1979: 116).

Skocpol's work does succeed in "bringing the state back in" to the analysis of revolution. The state is more than just a neutral arena in which contending groups play out their struggles for power. The state is more than just the stakes in those struggles. The state plays an active role in generating the crises that aspiring revolutionaries exploit. And these crises emerge because the state is compelled by changing circumstances in the international environment to pursue policies that bring its interests into direct conflict with those of the dominant economic class in whose name the state is supposedly governing.

Skocpol compelled a generation of scholars to consider not just the proactive role of the state in the dynamics of revolution but the structural features of social systems that render them susceptible to revolutionary challenge. However, in taking on this task, she arguably pays less attention to the dynamics of grassroots mobilization that is essential if the crisis of the state is to become a full-blown revolution and not just a palace coup or some other form of intra-elite conflict that fails to penetrate to the foundations of society. Similarly Tilly and most resource mobilization theorists argue that the level of grievances in society is far less relevant to the emergence of social movements than the existence of effective revolutionary leadership and organization. One could argue that, by focusing on the role of revolutionary leadership and organization, these theorists may have gone too far in discounting the processes by which peasants and other nonelites become alienated from the regime and susceptible to the mobilization appeals of revolutionary elites. Skilled leaders may be able to mobilize some forms of collective action regardless of the level of grievance in society. However, to say that they could organize a strike or a public demonstration or a petition drive with ease is not to say that they could mobilize an armed rebellion regardless of the level of grievances among the population. Revolution involves far greater risks than any other forms of collective action. While leadership skills and organization are critical to the success of any such movement, one cannot ignore the processes by which peasants become so marginalized that they become willing to assume the extraordinary risks inherent in supporting a revolutionary insurgency.

CONCLUSION

The works of Davies, Gurr, Tullock, Lichbach, Tilly, Skocpol, Goldstone, and others highlight the questions that must be addressed if we are to explain the causes and dynamics of contemporary Third World revolutions. Most of the cases these scholars examine are what some have termed "classic" revolutions of the early modern era. The revolutions in France, Russia, and China occurred within nations that were members of the major power system, and (with the arguable exception of China) they occurred prior to the end of World War II. The revolutions that are the concern of this book occurred after World War II in the peripheral regions of Asia, Africa, and Latin America. Are there differences in these two classes of revolutions? Certainly there are. Skocpol, for one, observes that, whereas the French, Chinese, and Russian revolutions occurred in large, autocratic, partially bureaucratized agrarian monarchies, modern social revolutions (such as Cuba and Vietnam) have taken place in "small, formerly colonial countries situated in highly vulnerable and dependent positions within the world capitalist economy and international states system" (Skocpol 1979: 288). Do these differences render the theories discussed in this chapter irrelevant to the explanation of contemporary Third World revolutions? Not at all. Theda Skocpol (1994) points to at least three aspects of commonality between classic revolutions and contemporary revolutions.

First, in all of the classic revolutions, peasant rebellion played a critical role in weakening the economic control of the dominant economic classes and the coercive monopoly of the state. The same is true of contemporary revolutions in the Third World. I noted in chapter 1 that most contemporary revolutions are "revolutions in the countryside," in the sense that they usually originate in rural areas and draw upon the peasantry as their support base. They differ from traditional peasant revolts in that from their start they are explicitly revolutionary in their goals, their organization, and their national scope. Revolutions in the countryside seek not to restore the stability of the old order but to destroy it and replace it with a new order.

This brings us to a second common theme in the classic works on classic revolutions. All of them point to coincidence of social revolution with the fundamental social, economic, and political transformations that occurred in these societies as a direct (or indirect) result of industrialization. Social revolutions occur in societies in transition from one historical epoch to another. Thus, when peasant revolts occur, of necessity they play a role different from their traditional restorative purpose. Restoration of the old order is not an option, because the traditional order has already been irrevocably disintegrated by the nation's incorporation into the emerging global economic order dominated by the industrializing powers of Europe. Similarly peasant revolts in the Third World cannot restore the old order there because that order has been destroyed by colonialism and the subsequent incorporation of the nation into the international division of labor as producers of raw materials for export to the industrial north. Thus the choice between revolution and restorative rebellion is not available to revolutionary elites or their peasant supporters in the Third World.

This brings us to a final point of commonality between contemporary revolutions and the classic revolutions of the early modern era: International forces played a central role in generating the crises that gave birth to revolutions, and those same forces influenced the course of the revolutions once they were under way. The next chapter concerns the incorporation of the Third World into the global economy and the ways in which the resulting disruption of traditional patterns of social organization rendered these nations susceptible to revolutions in the countryside.

NOTES

1. Among the works that reflect this view of Third World insurgencies are Tanham 1961, Osanka 1962, Deitchman 1964, McCuen 1965, Valeriano and Bohannan 1962, and Thompson 1966.

2. The theme of external subversion as a primary cause of revolution in the Third World has persisted among segments of the policy-making establishment. Ronald Reagan's National Bipartisan Commission on Central America (1984: 17), charged with analyzing the causes of revolutions in that region, stated that "if wretched conditions were themselves enough to create such insurgencies, we would see them in many more countries in the world." While that statement is true enough, the report then goes on to pinpoint intervention by Cuba, the Soviet Union, and their surrogates as the primary factor determining whether revolutionary violence will erupt from conditions of poverty and powerlessness. The not-so-subtle implication is that, in the absence of Soviet-Cuban intervention, there would be no revolutions in Central America, or in any other Third World nation, regardless of how impoverished its people or how repressive its government.

3. An excellent discussion of how the successful counterinsurgency operation in Malaysia influenced U.S. strategy and tactics in Vietnam—and why the analogy was misguided—is found in Khong (1992: 89–96). See also the works of Sir Robert Thompson (1966), the architect of the British program in Malaysia, and Shafer 1988: ch. 5 on the evolution of U.S. counterinsurgency doctrine.

4. A number of useful reviews of this literature are also available. Goldstone's (1986) anthology provides a useful and carefully chosen sample of important works. Rule 1988 is especially valuable for the comprehensiveness of its coverage and rigor of its analysis.

5. Eckstein (1965) saw this distinction between underlying causes and precipitating events as essential in making revolutions amenable to systematic analysis. Colburn (1994: 40–46) discusses this distinction and its applicability to contemporary Third World revolutions. See also Smelser 1963. For critiques of this perspective, see Aya 1979, DeNardo 1985.

6. The classic models of frustration-aggression that Gurr and Davies refer to are found in Dollard et al. 1939.

7. Feierabend and Feierabend (1966, 1972) found mixed support for a relationship between "systemic frustration" and political instability. Miller, Bolce, and Halligan (1977) found little empirical support for the J-curve in their analysis of urban racial violence in the United States during the late 1960s (see Crosby 1979 for a critique of their analysis). Grofman and Muller (1973) found little empirical support for Davies's J-curve and instead found some empirical evidence supporting a V-curve, whereby political violence is more likely to occur after a period of prolonged decline in achievement is followed by a sharp increase in achievement. Moreover, most of these studies are plagued with methodological problems. Most rely on aggregate data to test what is quite explicitly an individual-level psychological theory. And most rely on cross-national data to test a theory that is explicitly cast in terms of changes over time within a society. As such, many of these studies suffer from the same problems of spuriousness discussed earlier with regard to the inequality-political violence link. See Rule 1988: 207–21 for an especially thorough critique of empirical studies on relative deprivation theory. Other reviews of relative deprivation theory include Korpi 1974, Gurney and Tierney 1982, and Brush 1996.

8. Korpi (1974) argues that not all forms of relative deprivation are likely to lead to conflict. He develops a political process model, owing more to Tilly than to Davies, to demonstrate that only Gurr's progressive relative deprivation is likely to increase the likelihood of conflict significantly.

9. Panning (1983) develops a formal model of the relationship between inequality and relative deprivation, with social comparison (that is, people's tendency to compare themselves to others, as opposed to their own situation at some earlier point in time) as critical to whether inequality generates RD and RD results in conflict.

10. Park and Mason (1986) address the question of the dynamics of popular expectations by locating relative deprivation theory in a stage-based model of political development. Crosby (1979) also addresses this issue by distinguishing between expectations as "just deserts" versus expectations as one's subjective estimate of the likely future.

11. Roderick Aya (1979) and James DeNardo (1985), among others, express similar reservations about what they term the "spark and tinder" (DeNardo) or "volcanic" (Aya) logic of deprived actor theories of revolution, including works by Eckstein (1965), Davies (1962), Gurr (1970), Smelser (1963). DeNardo argues, "The implicit assumption is that a revolutionary explosion will occur with high probability, if not certainty, when the underlying conditions are ripe, and the paramount issue is to know what conditions constitute ripeness" (1985: 9).

12. Excellent review articles that trace the evolution of this field and map its intellectual terrain include McAdam, Tarrow, and Tilly 1996, 1997. Collections of articles from this school include McAdam, McCarthy, and Zald 1996, and McAdam and Snow 1997.

13. McCarthy and Zald are referring to peaceful nonviolent social movements in the advanced postindustrial societies of Western Europe and North America, not revolutions in the Third World. They see the West as having achieved, for the first time in

history, a level of wealth and prosperity that allowed society to sustain an emerging class of more or less professional movement activists and entrepreneurs.

14. The concept of political opportunity structure was raised by Lipsky (1968) and made explicit by Eisinger (1973), Tilly (1978), McAdam (1982), and Tarrow (1994). See also Tarrow 1988, 1996b for reviews of the development and use of this concept.

15. On elite competition and revolution, see Goldstone 1991.

16. On the framing process, see Snow and Benford 1992, Snow et al. 1986.

17. The Russian and Chinese revolutions are two of the cases treated by Skocpol (1979). For a different but by no means incompatible perspective on these two revolutions, Wolf (1969) analyzes them from the perspective of peasants. Both works owe some intellectual allegiance to Barrington Moore's (1966) classic treatment.

18. The question of what conditions make peasants more or less inclined to engage in collective action is a central issue of this book, one that is more appropriately addressed in later chapters. For now, I note that Wolf (1969), Paige (1975), Migdal (1974), Scott (1976), Popkin (1979), Skocpol (1979, 1982), and Goodwin and Skocpol (1989) weigh in on this issue.

19. On elite-directed "revolutions from above," see Trimberger 1972, 1978. See also Moore's (1966) chapter on Japan and his discussion of Prussia, as well as Skocpol's (1979) discussion of state autonomy from the dominant economic class as a condition making revolution less likely in late industrializing societies.

Chapter Three

Dependent Development and the Crisis of Rural Stability

This book concerns peasant-based revolutions in the Third World. The Third World encompasses over 150 nation states in Asia, Africa, and Latin America. As a group this collection of nations is far more varied and diverse than the advanced industrial societies of Europe, North America, and Japan. The abundance of religions, languages, cultural traditions, and political, economic, and social systems found in the Third World makes Europe and North America appear relatively homogeneous by comparison.

If the Third World is so diverse, how is it that these nations came to be the near-exclusive locus of revolutionary violence between 1945 and 1989? What common developmental experiences led such a heterogeneous collection of nations to become so uniformly susceptible to revolutions in the countryside? The short answer is that their shared experience as colonies or neocolonial dependencies of European nations and the United States imposed an element of uniformity onto the developmental paths of this otherwise widely disparate collection of social systems. Beginning in the nineteenth century, European colonial powers harnessed the economies of Asia, Africa, and Latin America for the purpose of producing raw materials to fuel Europe's emerging industrial sector. As the industrial revolution reached maturity, Europe and North America turned to the same regions for a variety of luxury crops to feed the appetites of the North Atlantic region's growing middle class. The exploitation of Asia, Africa, and Latin America as suppliers of raw materials, as markets for finished goods, and as sites for investment opportunities became a central element in the economic and military strategy that North Atlantic states pursued to enhance their own competitive positions in the emerging world system (Walton 1984: 145).

Even after gaining independence, many former colonies remained caught up in a pattern of dependent development, exporting raw commodities to the north and importing capital, technology, and manufactured goods from the north. As recently as 1959–1961 agricultural commodities still constituted 75 percent of all nonpetroleum exports from the nations of Latin America, Asia (excluding Japan), and Africa; over 90 percent of these exports went to the industrialized market economies of Europe, North America, and Japan (Paige 1975: 1). Over time the unfavorable terms of trade that accrue to raw materials exporters served to retard and distort the diversification of Third World economies and polarize the distribution of wealth and income within those societies.[1]

The impact of colonialism and neocolonialism was by no means confined to the economic arena. Eric Wolf (1969: 276–77) depicts what he terms "North Atlantic capitalism" as a cultural system that transformed the patterns of social organization in peripheral regions by imposing its central ideological principle: "that land, labor, and wealth are commodities that are produced not for use but for sale."

> To the Mexican Indian, to the Russian and Vietnamese peasant, land was an attribute of his community. . . . Even the Chinese peasant, long used to buying and selling land, regards land as more of a family heirloom than a commodity. Possession of land guaranteed family continuity, selling it offended "the ethical sense" . . . If land was to become a commodity in a capitalist market, it had first to be stripped of these social obligations . . . either by force which deprived the original inhabitants of their resources in land . . . or . . . by furthering the rise of "the strong and sober" entrepreneurs within the peasant communities, who could abandon their ties to neighbors and kin and use their surpluses in culturally novel ways to further their own standing in the market. (277–78)

Initially European colonial penetration of Asia and Africa was geared toward shifting agriculture to the production of export crops. This required the concentration of land ownership in the hands of those who could and would convert land use from subsistence crops to export crops. The shift in land use resulted in the displacement of peasant smallholders and tenants from the land, relegating them to the status of landless seasonal wage laborers. Displaced from the land, peasant cultivators faced the erosion of the traditional survival strategies by which they and their families had gained some security against the risk of subsistence crisis.

New forms of agricultural production created new sources of conflict within these societies. The old sources of contention between traditional landed patrons and peasant clients were transformed into new forms of conflicts between agro-export entrepreneurs and their now-landless wage laborers. Colonial rule largely prevented those conflicts from erupting into overt violence. The British suppressed an insurgency in Malaysia, Zulu resistance in South Africa, the Mau Mau uprising in Kenya, and periodic disturbances in the Indian subcontinent. The French were less successful after World War II at containing indigenous revolts in their North African and Southeast Asian colonies. However, they did successfully contain indigenous resistance in their colonies prior to the war.

With the dismantling of colonial empires after World War II, the newly installed states of the former colonies were confronted with new forms of popular contention from peasants and urban nonelites. Rural populations in an otherwise diverse collection of social systems—from Nicaragua, El Salvador, Guatemala, and Peru to Vietnam, Cambodia, and Laos, to Zimbabwe, Angola, and Mozambique—became uniformly susceptible to the appeals of a new type of dissident political leader. Whereas premodern revolts had been led by alienated elements of the indigenous elite seeking to restore the old order, the new social movements were led by Western-educated activists who sought not to restore the old order but to create a new one (White 1974: 78; Colburn 1994: ch. 2). However, the very same developmental trends—domestic and international—that generated popular grievances in the first place also served to weaken the capacity of Third World states to respond to popular challenges with remedial policies (Goldstone 1997: 108–09).

This chapter describes the patterns of rural social organization and production that prevailed prior to the Third World's integration into the global economy. The common feature of most premodern agrarian societies was the pervasiveness of patron-client networks. Clientelist mechanisms bound peasants to powerful landed patrons through debt and other obligations. In return, landed patrons provided peasant clients with security against the risk of subsistence crisis. The stability of patron-client networks was undermined by the Third World's integration into the global economy, either as colonies or as neocolonial dependencies producing commodities for export to the industrial north. As a result, the legitimacy of regimes that sustained the agro-export economy eroded, and peasants became susceptible to the appeals of dissident political leaders intent on reforming or destroying those regimes.

PATRON-CLIENT NETWORKS OF SOCIAL CONTROL

Prior to the industrial revolution, a hierarchical pattern of social organization evolved in premodern peasant communities that has been characterized as a system of patron-client politics.[2] Patron-client politics were based on a pervasive network of "vertical exchange relationships between peasants and agrarian elites in which the legitimacy of the elites, both collectively and individually, [was] directly related to both the balance of goods and services transferred—the terms of trade—between them" and the distribution of the risks of agriculture that were inherent in those exchanges (Scott and Kerkvliet 1977: 441). The relationship between landed patron and peasant client was multifaceted, diffuse, face-to-face, and based on personalistic ties, not written contracts. From the peasant's point of view, the legitimacy of the clientelist exchange is based on the subsistence ethic: What peasants wanted was some insurance against the risk of subsistence crisis that would put their very lives in jeopardy. In return, they were often willing to accept highly inequitable terms of trade that virtually guaranteed their perpetual poverty and dependence on the patron. In return for providing subsistence insurance, the patron could extract most of the peasant's surplus up to the limit of a household's minimum subsistence requirements.

Terms of Trade

Terms of trade refers to the flow of goods and services between patron and client. In exchange for use of a plot of land, peasant cultivators were expected to provide the landed patron with some combination of crop shares, free labor, and a variety of other services as the patron demanded. These could include tending the patron's livestock and providing household services such as cooking, cleaning, gardening, and gathering wood for fuel. Peasant clients were also expected to show deference to the patron through ritualized patterns of behavior, such as removing their hat and lowering their eyes in the presence of the patron. They were also expected to support the patron politically by deferring to his instructions on matters such as whom to vote for in elections. In return, the patron provided his clients with access to land and some combination of goods and services that amounted to a subsistence floor (Scott 1976). These services included such things as emergency grain; loans of seed, tools, and draft animals; rent delays; cash loans; and other material benefits that allowed a peasant household to avert an imminent crisis of subsistence. In addition, patrons typically assumed responsibility for subsidizing local festivals and organizing the community for any public works projects that were necessary to sustain local commerce and agriculture. They dispensed justice locally and provided their clients with protection, not just from bandits and other predators but from the state and other outside agents who might assert a claim to a share of the peasant's time, labor, or crops. As such, local patrons served as a buffer between the peasant and the state.[3]

Benedict Kerkvliet's interviews with peasants who participated in the Huk Rebellion in the Philippines depict the diffuse, personalistic character of the relationship between patron and client. Tenants on large rice plantations in the Philippines first had to clear the land for the landlord and prepare it for rice growing, a process that often took two years. Tenant and landlord shared production expenses, and at harvest the peasant turned over as much as 55 percent of his crop to the landlord. The peasants also did odd jobs for the landlord, built irrigation canals on the plantation (under the landlord's direction), and were generally at his beck and call. In return they received the right to farm a plot of land and to keep 45 percent of its yield in rice. They were free to grow food on their household plot, to cut wood for fuel on the plantation's uncleared land, and to catch fish in the irrigation streams and canals on the plantation. They could also turn to the landlord for help in emergencies, such as when a member of the family fell ill. The landlord provided tenants with loans for production and for emergencies and often overlooked unpaid loans when he knew the tenant was experiencing hard times. None of these agreements was written down; they were simply based on custom (Kerkvliet 1977: 6–7).

Distribution of the Risks of Agriculture

For peasants living perilously close to the margins of subsistence, how the risks of agriculture were distributed between patron and client was often more critical than the terms of trade that prevailed in the exchange. The risks of agriculture are those events in markets, weather, and the natural environment over which the peasant has no control but which could drastically affect the size and market value of his crop. Weather-related disasters such as floods, droughts, and storms could devastate a peasant's crop, as could insect infestations or plant diseases. Likewise, radical fluctuations in the purchase price of production inputs or the sale price of crops could jeopardize the farmer's margin of security against subsistence crisis and financial insolvency. Emergency grain, rent delays, and other benefits a patron provided could make the difference between survival and disaster for a peasant household.

A peasant's willingness to accept the inequity of clientelist exchanges may seem puzzling when viewed from the perspective of conventional notions of the utility-maximizing rational actor. However, for James Scott, the rationality of peasants' behavior under conditions of insecure subsistence is evident:

> Living close to the subsistence margin and subject to the vagaries of weather and the claims of outsiders, the peasant household has little scope for the profit maximization calculus of traditional neoclassical economics. Typically, the peasant cultivator seeks to avoid failure that will ruin him rather than attempting a big, but risky, killing. In decision-making parlance his behavior is risk aversive; he minimizes the subjective probability of the maximum loss. (1976: 4)

The conservatism of peasant subsistence farmers is rational given the thin margin between maximum production and starvation, a margin that was reduced by the extractions of the landed patrons (Paige 1975: 26–27). However, those extractions were tolerated only so long as they came with the guarantee of a subsistence floor that protected the peasant against the risks of agriculture. Jean Oi (1989: 14) notes that violations of the subsistence ethic were what prompted peasants to action: "The amount of the harvest left [to the peasant] is likely to be more important than the amount taken [from the peasant] . . . in prompting peasants who live on the edge of subsistence to political action."

The asymmetry in the distribution of power between patron and client was a function of the patron's control over access to land. In an economy where most of the population lived perilously close to the margins of subsistence and few if any occupational alternatives to agriculture existed, demand for land was highly inelastic (Scott and Kerkvliet, 1977: 442). In other words, demand for land did not decline with increases in its effective price.[4] Therefore peasant farmers submitted to almost any terms a landowner dictated if, in return, they gained access to enough land to provide for their families' subsistence needs. Under these circumstances each client was far more dependent upon the benefits provided by the patron than the patron was upon the goods and services that any one client could provide him. The loss of their patron's beneficence could be disastrous for a peasant household because it would cast them into the pool of landless laborers, devoid of any subsistence guarantees and exposed to the risks of agriculture and the uncertainties of the markets for land, labor, and food. By contrast, the defection of one client from a patron's domain had little if any effect on that patron's well-being because the defector could easily be replaced from the same pool of landless laborers.

PATTERNS OF LAND TENURE AND
PEASANT SUBSISTENCE SECURITY

The terms of trade and distribution of risks that prevailed between patrons and clients in agrarian societies varied according to whether peasants existed as smallholders, tenants, resident workers on a large estate, or landless wage laborers. Eric Wolf (1969), Jeffrey Paige (1975), James Scott (1976), and Samuel Popkin (1979) have argued that the differences in the exchange relationships between lord and peasant correlate with variations in their propensity for revolt. By contrast Joel Migdal (1974: 229–30) argues that peasants whose traditional subsistence strategies were most rapidly and thoroughly disrupted by the penetration of global market forces were the ones most likely to respond to dissident political movements. Whether their political activity assumed a revolutionary form was a function not of economic conditions or depth of grievances but of "the degree to which revolutionary leadership appears, with an organizational framework capable of absorbing peasants and then expanding power through recruitment" (231–32). Theda Skocpol (1982: 364) concurs in arguing that structural dislocations can make any class of peasants available for mobilization by revolutionary organizations: "There is no reason why organized revolutionary movements, once on the scene, cannot appeal to many different kinds of agrarian cultivators." Certainly different classes of peasants were affected differently by the shift to export agriculture. Whether this correlates with differences in their propensity to participate in revolutionary activity is an issue to which I shall return later.

The differences that did distinguish these classes of peasants can be understood as differences in the terms of trade and distribution of risks facing each class, and these differences were a function of land use and land tenure patterns. Land tenure and land use varied widely, from commercial plantations to hacienda systems to corporate villages of smallholders and tenants. In most settings, though, a small elite controlled access to land, and a large peasant majority worked the land as smallholders, tenants, landless laborers, or resident workers on large estates.

Corporate Villages

Corporate villages consisted of a collection of peasant households that, as a community, exercised de facto control over production on the lands surrounding the village. Corporate villages of tenants and smallholders were found where the dominant crops were labor intensive, the crop cycle was one year or less, labor was cheap, and there were no appreciable economies of scale to be gained from large field production (see Stinchcombe 1961: 169). In some cases, the land was owned by an absentee landlord and farmed by village members in family-size tenancies. This pattern was especially common in rice growing regions because the production characteristics of rice required frequent and close cooperation among village members for the construction and maintenance of the water systems that were necessary for rice production (Popkin 1979: 96–97). Corporate villages were also found in parts of Latin America in regions where land was not suited to export crop production by large plantations. There, villages owned land communally (the *ejidos*) and members farmed the land in family-size plots.

In both cases, village authorities, chosen from among the member households, made decisions concerning the allocation of plots among households, access to village commons such as pasture, and the distribution of tax burdens among households. Village authorities also organized the members for any cooperative endeavors that were essential to maintaining production and commerce in the village. Samuel Popkin (1979: 36) describes the essence of village governance as follows: "Where there were communal pastures, the village decided how many animals each family could pasture; where the fields belonging to each family were intermingled and unfenced, the village determined the times for planting, harvesting, and grazing; where there was irrigated agriculture, the village decided when the fields would be flooded and apportioned the work of maintaining common irrigation works." The village headman and council also served as intermediaries between the landlord and the residents and between the state and the residents. They adjudicated disputes between members and allocated the community's tax, corvée labor, and military conscript obligations among the member households (88–95).

Although residents of corporate villages had more control over the day-to-day management of production than did peasants on commercial estates or haciendas, they were still dependent on powerful patrons for credit, seed, tools, draft animals, and (in the case of tenants) access to land. Even villages of smallholders, though not directly dependent upon patrons for land, nevertheless were compelled to turn to them for benefits that were their only margin of safety against financial insolvency. James Scott (1976: 80) points to debt as the shackle that bound the smallholder into clientelist dependency: "The smallholder's need for cash for production costs, taxes, and consumption led to indebtedness and often to the loss of land. Local largeholders became the creditors of a smallholding clientele who mortgaged their land by what was called *vente à réméré* (conditional sale). When the smallholder failed to make the required payments, his land passed into the hands of the creditor and he became a tenant." Smallholder villages were only one bad crop year away from being converted into tenants, as creditors foreclosed on their land for failure to pay their production credit debts.

The status of tenants was even more precarious. How precarious was in part a function of whether tenancy was based on sharecropping or a fixed rent. The terms of trade and distribution of risks differed somewhat between these two forms. Under sharecropping the landlord assumed a greater share of the risks of agriculture than in a fixed-rate tenancy. If the sharecropper experienced a bad year, the landlord's income declined as well. In good years, however, the landlord could extract most if not all the tenant's surplus as payment for subsistence security that the landowner provided during bad years (Scott 1976: 79). This limited the peasant's incentives to improve his land or make other investments because the benefits of increased output would be shared with the landlord or even expropriated in total by him as payment for subsistence guarantees.

Under fixed-rate tenancy, the tenant paid the landlord a fixed rent in cash or in kind, regardless of the size of his yield. Peasant cultivators had more incentive to increase their productivity because they kept any surplus above the fixed rent. However, the peasant also assumed a greater share of the risks of agriculture than in a sharecropping arrangement. The rent owed to the landlord was the same, regardless of the peasant's output in a given year, and the rent payment had to be made even if the peasant's production fell below the requirements for rent plus subsistence needs. This left the household dependent upon the landlord for subsidies or rent delays in years when production fell below this minimum.[5]

In corporate villages of tenants, there were inherent conflicts between cultivators and land owners. As long as production technology remained rudimentary and capital scarce, the landlord and the tenant were in a zero-sum competition over the fruits of the land and the distribution of the risks of agriculture: How much of the crop would the landlord extract and how much insurance (and in what forms) would he provide? The tenant viewed the absentee landlord as an unnecessary claimant on his production. The landlords were not residents of the village. They exercised almost no control over the production process, and they were largely out of touch with their tenants, pursuing lifestyles that were decidedly different from their tenants. As such the peasant could produce his crop as well if not better without the landlord as with him. The landowning class appeared "alien, superfluous, grasping and exploitive" (Stinchcombe 1961: 170–71), and peasant cultivators were, in effect, waiting for the opportunity to lay claim to their land as smallholders.

Hacienda Systems

In hacienda systems, which were common in Latin America, land was held in large estates with production divided into two segments. The estate's domain lands were devoted to large field production of food crops for national markets, with surrounding marginal lands given over to subsistence cultivation by resident laborers. Hacienda agriculture prevailed where capital was scarce, labor was plentiful, and the market was limited.[6] Because the hacienda produced for a national market (and not usually for export), the estate owner's access to capital was limited to that which could be accumulated from the national market. Given the high levels of poverty typical of societies organized around hacienda agriculture, there simply was not much investment capital generated from the domestic economy. Therefore the hacienda relied on labor as its primary variable production input (Stinchcombe 1961: 167–69). Indeed, Paige (1975: 12) argues that, with capital scarce, labor plentiful, and production technology primitive, *hacendados* (estate owners) made almost profligate use of labor on the estate.

Hacienda agriculture is distinguished from commercial plantations by its reliance on a resident labor force compensated with subsistence plots and other clientelist guarantees rather than contract laborers compensated with cash wages. For the *hacendado* maintaining a resident workforce was preferable to hiring wage laborers because the cost of cash wages exceeded the cost of providing resident workers with housing and subsistence plots. Where the estate's domain lands were planted in especially labor-intensive crops (such as sugar, cotton, or tobacco) or in crops with a narrow window of opportunity for planting and harvesting (such as coffee, tea, or rubber), a shortage of labor at harvest or planting could be disastrous for *hacendados*. Therefore they placed a premium on ensuring an adequate supply of labor. Labor was relatively cheap, especially in cash terms, and hacienda owners endeavored to keep it so by monopolizing the local supply of land and limiting the availability of occupational alternatives to agriculture. Thus hacienda owners had a voracious appetite for land—including marginal lands that were of no value in producing cash crops—and they were ardent opponents of industrial development. By limiting the availability of land and jobs, the *hacendado* was able to bind the local peasantry to him through ties of clientelist dependency (Wolf and Mintz 1957). Resident workers were provided with housing and a small plot of land where they could grow food crops for their own consumption. In return they were expected to provide the landlord with labor on the domain lands and other services as he demanded. This could include domestic services, cooking, gathering fuel, and tending the *hacendado's* livestock.

The combination of housing and a subsistence plot, along with other benefits provided by the landlord as needed, amounted to a subsistence floor for peasant laborers. For the *hacendado* they served as a substitute for cash wages, and they bound peasants to the estate, guaranteeing an adequate labor force at critical planting and harvesting times. The peasants' marginal existence and lack of opportunities outside the estate left them with no alternative but to comply with the labor demands of the *hacendado*. Indeed, considering the alternatives, a permanent position on an estate offered peasants the most secure subsistence guarantees available in the local economy. However, their situation was tenuous. Their wages were usually well below market rates, if they received any cash wages at all. They had no legal claim to the plot they cultivated, and they were subject to eviction at the whim of the estate owner. This could occur when, for instance, the market price of the cash crops that could be produced on their subsistence plots came to exceed the value that the landlord placed on the peasant's services. In this circumstance the landlord was free to evict the peasant, replace him with temporary wage laborers as needed, and plant his subsistence plot in cash crops. It could also occur when the supply of landless laborers increased to the point that the landlord found it profitable to replace resident workers (to whom he was obligated to supply subsistence security) with temporary wage laborers (to whom he provided no clientelist guarantees).

Plantation Systems

Plantation agriculture is distinguished from the hacienda by virtue of its concentration on export crop production, its greater reliance on wage labor rather than on debt peonage, and its requirement of a substantial long-term capital investment in the crop, land improvements, or machinery for production and processing (Stinchcombe 1961: 173). Wolf and Mintz (1957: 380) characterize plantation agriculture as "an estate, operated by dominant owners (usually organized into a corporation) and a dependent labour force, organized to supply a large-scale market by means of abundant capital, in which the factors of production are employed primarily to further capital accumulation without reference to the status needs of the owner." Plantation agriculture was often built around crops that required several years for maturation (such as rubber, coffee, and other tree crops) or crops that required substantial processing before shipping (such as sugar). For Paige (1975) the distinguishing feature of a plantation is that the landowners derive their income primarily from returns on capital rather than from land directly, while peasants in a plantation system derive their income from wages, not crop shares.

In a plantation system, crops were planted in large fields, with planting and harvesting being highly labor-intensive endeavors. Production was managed by a corporate organization that, in principle, was subject to the discipline of market forces. Often this translated into minimizing the size of the resident labor force and relying on seasonal workers as needed at critical points in the crop cycle. Since production was for cash-based markets, seasonal laborers worked for cash wages, not crop shares. Only a minimal staff of resident workers were allowed to maintain subsistence plots on lands too marginal to plant in cash crops. Because plantations did not maintain a large resident labor force, they generally did not maintain large amounts of marginal or unused lands; that would represent idle capital (Wolf and Mintz 1957: 399–401).

Plantation laborers existed outside the boundaries of the clientelist network. Their income was strictly a function of the supply and demand for seasonal labor. Relations between seasonal workers and management were impersonal and rationalized in the sense that the plantation owner seldom provided workers with any benefits beyond wages, and certainly nothing that even approached the level of a subsistence floor. Likewise the workers felt no sense of obligation, loyalty, or deference to the plantation owner.

Landlessness and Clientelist Stability

Regardless of whether plantations, haciendas, corporate villages, or some mixed arrangement prevailed in a society, the size of the landless population played a crucial indirect role in determining the terms of trade and distribution of risks that prevailed between landed elites and other classes of peasant. In an agrarian society the landless served as a ready pool of competitors for the positions held by tenant farmers, resident workers on estates, seasonal laborers, and (to a lesser and more indirect extent) for the land farmed by smallholders as well. The larger the size of the landless population, the weaker was the bargaining position of each of these other classes of peasant clients. The more landless laborers there were, the more easily a landlord could replace a recalcitrant tenant with a landless peasant who was willing to accept a smaller crop share, a higher fixed rent, and fewer services. Barrington Moore argues that absentee landlords in China relied on the presence of a steady surplus of landless peasants to extract ever larger crop shares from their tenants (Moore 1966: 168). In his study of the Huk Rebellion in the Philippines, Benedict Kerkvliet (1977: 17–19) notes that the population of the Philippines doubled between 1903 and 1939, creating severe land pressures that landlords exploited to their own advantage: "If for some reason a landowner forced a tenant to leave, the tenant had far less hope than before of finding another landowner. The other side of the coin was that landowners could demand more from tenants and threaten to replace anyone who refused their terms. And as they became more concerned about making profits, their terms became stiffer and more strictly enforced" (18).

Likewise resident workers on an estate could be compelled to provide the estate owner with more labor for lower wages and fewer services if there was a large pool of landless peasants ready to take their positions and accept the terms the landlord dictated. Even smallholders were affected negatively by a large landless population. A large landless population could squeeze the smallholder out of the seasonal work on neighboring estates that was one of his hedges against financial insolvency. His creditors would be more tempted for foreclose on his land because a large landless population drives up the rent the creditor could earn from that land if he took ownership of it. Finally the relative size of the landless population was a barometer of the stability and legitimacy of patron-client networks: Growth in the size of the landless population (relative to other peasant classes) was an indicator of eroding patron-client bonds and a portent of peasant unrest to come.

WHICH PEASANTS REBEL?

A number of scholars have argued that variations in the patterns of land use and land tenure not only determine the terms of trade and distribution of risks that prevail between lord and peasant; they also correlate with differences in the propensity of different classes of peasants to support revolutionary movements or to engage in other forms of contentious activity, such as land invasions.

One school of thought contends that regions dominated by corporate villages were the most prone to revolution. Two features of corporate villages are usually cited to support this argument. First, because residents of corporate villages controlled their own land, they often came to view landlords as dispensable exploiters whose elimination would increase the peasant's own share of the fruits of the land (Stinchcombe 1961: 171). In the eyes of the village residents, any clientelist protections that absentee landlords might offer them could be replaced by cooperative arrangements among the villagers themselves. If not, the loss of those protections would be more than offset by the increase in peasant income that would result from elimination of landlord extractions. Second, the residents of corporate villages also had greater capacity to mobilize for collective action. Because the landlord was not a resident of the village, his capacity to monitor and preempt peasant organization was weak. The residents themselves already had in place a variety of formal institutions and informal social networks that had evolved over time to mobilize the members for the community projects and cooperative endeavors necessary to sustain agricultural production and community life. These mobilizing structures could be readily adapted to more explicitly political contention, such as land invasions, rent strikes, or even clandestine support of guerrilla insurgents.

By contrast, manor or hacienda systems are viewed by these same scholars as infertile grounds for the growth of peasant radicalism and revolution. Landlords in manorial or hacienda systems enjoyed a greater capacity to monitor peasants through their daily supervision of the resident laborers' work on the domain lands. The paternalistic protections they provided resident workers not only bound them to the estate but also made them more reluctant to jeopardize subsistence guarantees by engaging in any sort of dissident activity. Moreover, resident workers were subject to manipulation by the *hacendado*. He could play them off against each other in the competition for better housing and subsistence plots or supervisory positions on the hacienda staff. The political quiescence of hacienda peons was further reinforced by the existence of a pool of landless laborers ready and willing to take the place of a resident worker who violated the norms of deference and subservience between lord and peasant.[7]

Paige (1975: 42–43) contended that when residents of haciendas did revolt, their goals were typically confined to local and immediate concerns of seizing land and other assets from the hacienda owner, not the revolutionary destruction of the prevailing system of land tenure and political power. Such revolts were likely to occur only when the power of the landed elite was weakened by such things as the state's defeat in a war. However, once peasants seized land, the movement quickly subsided, because hacienda peons lacked the political organization to sustain or expand the movement to national revolutionary dimensions.

There is less consensus on the revolutionary potential of independent small-holders and landless laborers. Arthur Stinchcombe (1961: 172–73) views small-holders as unlikely candidates for revolutionary collective action because they were isolated from each other physically and socially, and they competed with each other for land and credit. As a group, smallholders tended to be "poor in politically talented leaders, relatively unable to put together a coherent, disciplined class movement controlled from below" (173). "Political movements of smallholders tend to be directed primarily at maintenance of the price of agricultural commodities rather than at unemployment compensation or other 'social security' measures" (172). Paige (1975) echoes this view by asserting that smallholders were more likely to engage in "reform commodity movements" aimed at getting better prices for their crops. They were unlikely to risk their status as landowners by joining an armed challenge against the government.

By contrast, Eric Wolf (1969: 291–93) argues that "middle peasants" with secure access to land of their own which they farm with family labor were the most likely source of revolutionary support. As independent producers, they were less subject to manipulation by landlords, and they had the most to lose from the disruptions generated by the penetration of market forces. Scott (1976: 36–37, 208–09) suggests that where smallholders remained dependent on local patrons for seasonal employment and other services as their only hedge against financial insolvency, they were susceptible to revolutionary appeals because they were vulnerable to the unpredictability of markets and the manipulation of patrons.

Similarly there is a lack of consensus on the revolutionary potential of landless laborers. One perspective is that landless laborers are difficult to organize and less likely to protest than are tenants or smallholders (Popkin 1979: 250). Scott (1976: 213) contends that the shift of peasants from landed categories (tenants, smallholders, and resident workers) to the landless migratory laborer category "works against economic and political cooperation at the village level. . . . The withdrawal of a substantial fraction of the adult males from the village is likely to deprive it of much of its lower class leadership." Eric Wolf argues that the landless lacked "tactical power" in that, among other things, they were dependent on the landlord for most if not all their income. He concludes that "poor peasants and landless laborers, therefore, are unlikely to pursue the course of rebellion, unless they are able to rely on some external power to challenge the power which constrains them" (Wolf 1969: 290).

For Jeffery Paige (1975: 48–51), the revolutionary potential of wage laborers depends more on the type of land owner. He views landless laborers as a rural proletariat more than able to organize for collective action against landowners. Whether their activism escalated into revolutionary conflict depended on the interests and behavior of the landowners themselves. On commercial plantations producing for export, wage laborers were capable of organizing, but the result was more likely to approximate a labor movement. The workers demanded (and received) concessions on wages and working conditions, and the landowners could afford to make some concessions, thus defusing the revolutionary potential of worker activism. Where the primary crop allowed year-round harvesting, the plantation owners had more to lose from a work stoppage than from the concessions they might make to keep the harvest going and their processing plants working. Owners could afford to make concessions because their income was derived from returns on capital, not from land per se. Any losses in income could be offset by increases in productivity and by replacing workers with capital.

Paige diverges from most students of peasant revolts by concluding that the most politically volatile classes were tenants and workers on migratory labor estates. Sharecroppers on large manorial estates that produced labor-intensive crops for export were, in Paige's view, the most potentially revolutionary class of cultivators. Such estates differed from haciendas in that there was no division between domain lands and subsistence plots cultivated by resident workers. Instead the estate was simply divided into a number of family-size tenancies, with the landlord demanding that the peasant plant most of his land in export crops, though some portion of the tenant's land might be given over to subsistence cultivation. With such crops, there was usually nothing to be gained from processing the crop on-site or growing them in large field plantings. Therefore the estate owner had little incentive to make large investments in processing equipment; his income was still almost exclusively from the land, not from capital (1975: 60). This put the landed elite and peasant cultivators in a zero-sum competition over the fruits of the land. The landlord's goal was to maximize the amount of land devoted to export crops and minimize the amount tenants devoted to subsistence cultivation, while the tenants' incentives were exactly the opposite. The tenant knew that nearly all of his export crop output would be expropriated by the landlord, and even the peasant's compensation for his agreed-upon share of that crop would be determined by the landlord, not by market forces. Therefore his incentive was to devote as much of his land as possible to subsistence crops that sustained his family.

Paige concludes that sharecroppers on such estates shared several characteristics with wage laborers on commercial plantations, but it was the differences between estate owners and plantation owners that made this mix especially volatile. Sharecroppers, like plantation laborers, had weak ties to the land: They could be evicted on a whim, and any improvements they made in their land would likely benefit the estate owner, not the sharecropper. Because they lived on an estate with other sharecroppers, they were capable of producing the sort of social networks and cooperative relations with their fellow estate residents that could evolve into peasant solidarity organizations. Unlike hacienda peons, however, they were relatively independent producers who relied very little on the estate owner for the day-to-day necessities of production. As such, they were relatively free from the close scrutiny and supervision of the estate owner (1975: 60–61). In these circumstances, peasant sharecroppers could engage in agrarian revolt when they perceived that the power of the landlord or the power of the state that sustained the landed elite was weakened.

Finally some scholars argue that the debate on which classes of peasants are more or less revolutionary is irrelevant. Theda Skocpol (1982: 364) contends that "There is no reason why organized revolutionary movements, once on the scene, cannot appeal to many different kinds of agrarian cultivators, including traditional ones." What can be said is that different patterns of land use and land tenure created different structures of political opportunity for different classes of peasants, and the different patterns of social organization that evolved around different land tenure patterns also generated differences in the form and capacity of existing mobilizing structures to organize peasants for collective action. Relatively autonomous villages of smallholders and tenants were less subject to the daily scrutiny of the state and landed elites. Village institutions as well as social networks based on ties of kinship, neighborhood, and production practices made it easier for peasants in this environment to organize for collective action. By contrast, resident workers on haciendas were subject to the scrutiny of the *hacendado,* and they were far more dependent upon him for their subsistence security than were peasants in corporate villages. Hence resident workers often lacked the capacity to mobilize for collective action against their landlord, and they often lacked the will to do so as long as engaging in such action jeopardized the subsistence security that came with their permanent position on the estate. Nonetheless, as Paige and others argue, when external events weakened the landlord's hold over them or the capacity of the state to defend the landed elite by repressing peasant activism, resident workers could be mobilized for actions such as land seizures and attacks on the landlord.

Furthermore, dramatic changes in the patterns of land use and land tenure, changes brought about by the shift to agro-export production, undermined whatever pattern of clientelist social organization prevailed in the countryside. In this manner the shift to agro-export agriculture could leave peasants of any class economically marginalized, vulnerable to subsistence crisis, and therefore susceptible to the appeals of dissident leaders seeking to mobilize grassroots support for an organized challenge to the incumbent regime. Disrupting existing patterns of clientelist social organization is precisely what happened as a result of the Third World's integration into the global economy. The diverse patterns of rural social organization found across Asia, Africa, and Latin America were subjected to a common developmental trauma that set the people of these nations on a path of dependent development that, in some cases, contributed to the emergence of revolutionary movements in the countryside.

THE CREATION OF THE PERIPHERY

The industrial revolution that swept Europe in the eighteenth and nineteenth centuries transformed the economies of that region and, in so doing, altered profoundly the course of European social and political development. This same industrial revolution also had direct and lasting effects on the economies and social systems of Africa, Asia, and Latin America. It transformed those regions into a thoroughly integrated economic periphery of the industrial north. They became crucial but dependent units, whose role in the emerging global economic system was to produce raw material inputs for the industrial economies of Europe, North America, and later Japan.

Their new role in the global economic system necessitated a transformation of the way production was organized within those societies. Specifically the agricultural sector, long the dominant sector of the economy, was transformed from the production of subsistence crops for local consumption to the production of cash crops for export. Eric Wolf observes, "During the latter part of the nineteenth century, . . . whole regions became specialized in the production of some raw material, food crop, or stimulant . . . [which] had consequences at the level of household, kin group, community, region, and class" (1982: 310). This shift in production transformed existing patterns of social organization, effectively eroding traditional patron-client networks. As a result, ever-increasing proportions of these regions' rural populations were left largely devoid of any means of subsistence security and therefore vulnerable to fluctuations in the markets for land, labor, and food. However, as Wolf (314) points out, the people of those regions did not choose to produce these commodities by some Ricardian or Smithian law of comparative advantage. Rather, this choice was forced on them by the European powers, with devastating consequences for the traditional social order and for the survival strategies of individual households in the countryside of Asia, Africa, and Latin America. As Joel Migdal so aptly puts it, "despite the nineteenth-century liberal credo of free trade and the invisible hand, the hand that helped achieve these goals was actually quite visible," especially to peasant farmers in the Third World (Migdal 1988: 56).

Beginning in the late fifteenth century, expanding global trade routes began to link Europe with Asia, Africa, and Latin America.[8] For the most part, however, contact with European traders was limited in volume, confined to a few ports or inland enclaves, and conducted through middlemen from the indigenous population (Migdal 1988: 52–53; see also Wolf 1982). The volume of trade was certainly not sufficient to dictate the social organization of production in these societies. Existing patterns of production and exchange, built around patron-client networks, remained largely intact and geared primarily to local needs. If a particular export crop did require modifications in land tenure and land use, local strongmen would engineer the changes, either directly through coercion or indirectly by persuading landed patrons in the interior to compel peasant clients to shift production to the new crops (Migdal 1988: 53). As such, the European trade tended to reinforce local elites' grip on social control within their own society, and "the market [was] held at arm's length" (Redfield 1960: 29).

The industrial revolution changed all that. In a matter of a few decades, the rapid growth of European industrial production generated a dramatic increase in the demand for a small set of agricultural commodities. Some (such as cotton, rubber, sisal, and palm oil) were in demand as inputs for new industries. Others (such as coffee, cocoa, sugar, and tea) were in demand because rising incomes in the north led to growth in consumer spending on goods that previously would have been considered luxuries beyond the means of all but the elite. As the real wages of industrial workers grew, more of these goods came within the buying power of middle- and working-class consumers in Europe and North America.

Europe's imperative to supply its industries with raw materials and its population with food touched off a new era of colonial expansion aimed primarily at Africa and Asia (Wolf 1982: 313). In the latter half of the nineteenth century, European armies conquered the inland kingdoms of Africa, the British subjugated the Indian subcontinent, and the French colonized much of Southeast Asia. In Latin America, where most of the region had secured independence from Spain or Portugal by 1825, European traders found it more cost-effective simply to persuade the small landed elite in those countries to shift production to the requisite export crops. This was easy enough to accomplish, because there was enough money to be made to enrich the local elites and still allow Europeans to profit handsomely from the trade.

Whether through direct colonial domination or neocolonial co-optation of local elites, harnessing production in these regions to the demands of European markets involved dramatic changes in land use and land tenure. Colonial authorities or their local surrogates altered land tenure laws in order to facilitate the consolidation of landholdings into large tracts for export crop production. The result was the rapid consolidation of land ownership into haciendas, estates, and ranches in many parts of the Third World. Both the number of family farms and their average land allotment shrank, while the number of landless and land-poor peasants increased. In Mexico by 1910, there were 300 haciendas containing at least 25,000 acres each. Eleven of them had more than 250,000 acres each. Altogether, estate owners in Mexico had acquired more than 2.25 million acres of communal property *(ejidos)*. Less than 1 percent of families owned 85 percent of all farmland, while 90 percent of villages had almost no communal land (Migdal 1988: 63; see also Vilas 1995: 51). In Zimbabwe (Rhodesia) at the end of the colonial period, the commercial sector of the agricultural economy consisted of some 6,000 farms owned by white settlers and averaging 2,500 hectares in size. These farms accounted for only 0.1 percent of all farms but covered 15.3 million hectares, or 39 percent of all farmland. By contrast the peasant sector included 750,000 households on 16.3 million hectares, consisting of smallholdings of 2 to 4 hectares, plus some land devoted to communal pasture (Bratton 1990: 268).

THE EROSION OF CLIENTELIST STABILITY

As the value of the export crops that a landowner could raise on a given plot of land came to exceed the returns he could extract from peasant clients growing subsistence crops, landed patrons resorted to a number of devices to displace subsistence cultivators from the land and convert that land to export crop production. The mechanisms varied depending on whether the peasants existed as smallholders, tenants, or resident workers on existing estates. Because tenants had no legal claim to the land they farmed, they could simply be evicted and their land converted to export crop production. As the size of the landless population grew, the wage rate for agricultural labor declined, presenting estate owners with an incentive to replace resident workers with temporary wage laborers to whom they owed no clientelist services above and beyond cash wages. Discharging estate workers had the further advantage of freeing up for export crop production lands that previously had been devoted to subsistence cultivation by resident workers. If the lands were not suitable for export crops, they could be rented out at rates that were pushed up by the same growth in the landless population.

Smallholders could be pressured through more indirect means to sell off their land to neighboring estate owners. Many smallholders relied on seasonal wage labor on neighboring estates as a hedge against financial insolvency. With the supply of landless laborers growing, these opportunities became increasingly scarce, and the wage rate declined accordingly. Neighboring estate owners could also manipulate smallholders' access to credit and other clientelist services in such a way as to push them into financial insolvency and compel them to sell off their land. Not surprisingly, the neighboring estate owner was the only one with sufficient capital to buy up the smallholdings and convert them to export crop production.

The major structural consequence of this transformation of land tenure and land use patterns was a shift in the distribution of the rural population among the various land tenure categories. Tenants, resident workers, and smallholders were displaced from the land and cast into the growing population of landless seasonal laborers. As such, an ever-growing share of the rural population was forced into a marginal existence outside the boundaries of traditional patron-client networks which, however exploitive and inequitable, had provided them with some measure of security against the risk of subsistence crisis. Deprived of traditional survival strategies, landless peasants were at the mercy of fluctuating markets for land, labor, and food.

The very same changes in land use and land tenure that pushed peasants into the landless category also contributed to deteriorating conditions in these markets. Assuming that the amount of arable land is fixed, any increase in the number of landless peasants inevitably drives agricultural wages down. The supply of wage laborers increased, while at best the demand for labor remained relatively stable because it was a function of the supply of arable land. In many regions the demand for labor actually declined, because the production characteristics of many export crops required less labor per acre of land than did traditional subsistence crops. Cotton production became increasingly mechanized after World War II, reducing the demand for labor on cotton estates and making it more profitable for landowners to substitute large-field plantings for the patchwork of sharecroppers dividing their land between cotton and subsistence crops. The expansion of cattle ranching was even more devastating to peasant agriculture. Ranching was the most land-intensive type of agriculture to be introduced to these regions. Compared to most row crops, ranching displaced far more subsistence cultivators from the land, while creating far fewer wage labor positions to absorb them. Conservative estimates indicate that cotton produced six times more employment per acre than cattle ranching. Sugar provided seven times as many jobs, and coffee created thirteen times as much employment as cattle ranching (Williams 1986: 117). Therefore shifting land to cattle production displaced peasant cultivators without creating any occupational alternatives for families displaced from the land. With demand for agricultural labor declining as a result of the same shift in land use that had increased the supply of landless laborers, wages and household incomes declined as well. Brewer (1983: 400) notes that in El Salvador, among those employed in agriculture during the 1970s, agricultural wages were sufficient to provide only about 50 percent of the income needed for subsistence.

A further effect of these shifts in land use was a reduction in the supply and an increase in the price of basic food commodities and other subsistence goods. The same process that pushed peasants off the land and denied them the wherewithal to grow their own food also reduced the supply of food available in local markets, as food crop production was displaced by export crops (see, for instance, Durham 1979: 30–36; Brockett 1988: 76–85; Vilas 1995: 44–46). As demand for cotton grew after World War II, expanded production in the Pacific coastal plain of Central America displaced peasant subsistence cultivation. Between 1948 and 1950–1951 corn acreage (an indicator of the extent of subsistence cultivation) declined by more than 8,000 acres in El Salvador's eight most important cotton-growing *municipios*. By 1951, 20 percent of that nation's crop land was planted in cotton and 50 percent in corn; by 1971 cotton consumed more than 50 percent of crop lands, while corn consumed only about 20 percent (Williams 1986: 55). The result was that local supplies of food declined. Between 1948 and 1978 food production per capita declined by 17 percent across Central America (Vilas 1995: 45). At the same time, those displaced from the land turned to the market to buy the food that previously they had produced for themselves. Thus market demand for food crops increased at the same time that local supplies were diminishing. This resulted in high rates of inflation in the markets for these basic commodities at the same time that wages were declining. In El Salvador, for instance, between 12 and 30 percent of the population did not earn enough income to meet the government's estimate of the minimum needed for bare subsistence, and about 60 percent of the rural population did not earn enough to provide an adequate diet (Montgomery 1995: 23). In El Salvador, Guatemala, and Honduras during the 1970s an estimated half or more of the population consumed less than 90 percent of the recommended daily caloric intake; in Guatemala the poorest half of the population was estimated to consume only about 61 percent of the recommended number of calories (Brockett 1988: 84).

Some nations addressed this problem by importing large amounts of grain. Cheap food imports were intended to keep prices down for the urban poor and for landless peasants, in hopes of dampening any unrest among those segments of the population. However, importing grain by itself did nothing to put cash in the hands of those households that were in most urgent need of it. Carlos Vilas (1995: 45) notes that "the majority of Central American peasants who stopped producing corn . . . did not switch over to eating imported corn; they simply began to eat less." For peasants who still had land, cheap food imports depressed the price they could get in local markets for their surplus crops. In effect they had to compete with grain producers all over the world. The result was a decline in their income, making them even more vulnerable to eviction from their land (Graham 1984: 175). Furthermore food import policies consumed valuable foreign exchange that otherwise would have been available for job-creating investments in industrial expansion. Industrialization could have relieved some of the pressures in local markets for land and labor by expanding occupational alternatives to agriculture. To the extent that foreign exchange had to be used to pay for food imports, there was less available to purchase equipment or service loans for the expansion of the industrial economy.

The deteriorating plight of peasant households was further exacerbated by the rapid growth in population that accompanied the Third World's entry into the global political economy. The dynamics of the demographic transition occurring in the Third World are well documented and extensively analyzed (see, for instance, Saunders 1986). The major effect of this process was that annual population growth rates in the Third World often ranged from 2.5 to 3.5 percent, which meant that the population was doubling every twenty to thirty years. Moreover most of this growth occurred within the peasant and urban poor segments of the population, where income-earning opportunities were already scarce (Goldstone 1997: 103–04).

Population growth generated further upward pressure on the rental price of land and downward pressure on the size of a limited and shrinking supply of tenant plots. Lands that were not suitable for export crops could be subdivided into ever smaller plots and still earn higher per acre rents for the land owner. Population growth created further downward pressure on agricultural wages and thereby increased the incentives for commercial estates to replace resident workers with seasonal employees. Finally population growth intensified inflationary pressures in the market for food by pushing up demand while supply remained stagnant or, in many cases, declined as a consequence of the displacement of food crops by export crops.[9]

EVERYDAY FORMS OF PEASANT RESISTANCE

The integration of the Third World into the global economy undermined indigenous patterns of social organization that, by one means or another, had afforded peasant cultivators some measure of security against the risks of subsistence crisis. Displaced from the land, peasant cultivators were confronted with deteriorating conditions in the markets for land, labor, and food.

However, contrary to the logic of deprived actor models, marginalized peasants are not likely to engage in spontaneous acts of rebellion. They are more likely to seek relief from their economic distress through what Scott (1985), Colburn (1989), and others have termed "everyday forms of peasant resistance."

In the Third World it is rare for peasants to risk an outright confrontation with the authorities over taxes, cropping patterns, development policies, or onerous new laws; instead they are likely to nibble away at such policies by noncompliance, foot dragging, deception. In place of land invasion, they prefer piecemeal squatting; in place of open mutiny, they prefer desertion; in place of attacks on public or private grain stores, they prefer pilfering. When such stratagems are abandoned in favor of more quixotic action, it is usually a sign of great desperation. (Scott 1985: xvi)

For several reasons, peasants preferred everyday resistance to any form of collective action. Everyday forms of resistance required little or no planning or coordination with others. They required no contributions of scarce resources to an organization capable of planning and organizing dissident collective action. Everyday forms of resistance also avoided direct confrontation with authorities (Scott 1986: 6). This is an important consideration, given the overwhelming advantage in coercive capacity that landlords, in alliance with the state, enjoyed over peasants. Everyday forms of resistance could usually be undertaken covertly, so that the chances of detection and punishment by the authorities were rather low. In short, they are low-cost, low-risk strategies. Forrest Colburn (1989: x) adds that, when these tactics succeeded, they produced direct private benefits that enhanced the individual's welfare: "Whether it be a poached rabbit that provides a hearty stew or desertion from an ill-fated army that saves a life, commonplace resistance assists those who all too often live close to the margin of survival." Unlike the public goods of collective action, one did not have to share these benefits with others who may or may not have participated in the anonymous "little acts" of resistance. In short, free-riding was not an option when it came to everyday forms of peasant resistance, and the success of everyday resistance was not contingent upon the absence of free-riding by others.

Thus the almost reflexive response of displaced peasants was to pursue one of several more conventional escape valves by which peasants have traditionally sought relief from their immediate economic distress. One option was migration to another region where there were unused lands, better terms of trade from landlords, or occupational alternatives to agriculture. However, the very trends that led to their declining economic situation in the first place also served to foreclose many of these traditional escape valves. With the value of land increasing, land use became saturated. There simply was not much if any unused land available for cultivation. Population pressures exacerbated this problem by driving up the agricultural density (that is, the person-to-land ratio). The tendency for export crop production to become concentrated in one or two major crops meant that the terms of employment available from landlords in different parts of the country became rather uniform. Therefore migration in search of better terms of trade and a more favorable distribution of risks was foreclosed by the homogenization of landlord-tenant relations brought about by a mono-crop economy.

The same forces of dependent development that touched off the erosion of traditional patterns of social organization also served to restrict the growth of occupational alternatives to agriculture. The profits that accrued from export crops were seldom invested in local industries that could relieve pressures in the markets for land, labor, and food by providing industrial jobs. Landed elites usually preferred to devote their earnings either to consumption or to more lucrative and safer investments in the industrial north. Furthermore landed elites often feared that industrial growth would hurt export agriculture by driving up agricultural wages at the expense of profits.

Even if they were to invest in local industry, it is doubtful that the resulting rate of job creation would have been sufficient to absorb the growth in the labor force that resulted from the high rates of population growth typical of Third World societies. Rapid population growth retarded economic development by driving up the dependency ratio—the ratio of children and elderly (who are too old or too young to work) to the size of the working age population—so that more of the nation's economic surplus had to be devoted to consumption by the dependent population instead of investment in economic growth. Thus rarely was industrial growth sufficient to absorb the growth in the urban labor force brought on by demographic transition and rural-to-urban migration that accompanied dependent development. Murray Gendell (1986: 64–65) estimates that an annual growth in GDP of 8 percent would have been required to absorb the growth in the labor force of Latin America that was projected to occur between 1975 and 2000.

The most likely response to land pressures in the countryside was for displaced peasants to migrate to urban areas, not because they were drawn by the prospects of economic opportunity but because they were compelled to do so by "push" factors—that is, land pressures in the countryside—not "pull" factors, such as expanding industrial employment (Walton 1984: 150). Gendell (1986: 60–63) has shown, for instance, that the great rural-to-urban migration in Latin America in the last half of the twentieth century simply shifted the problem of unemployment and underemployment from the countryside to the city. Moreover this migration did not even relieve land pressures in the countryside to any appreciable degree. Between 1950 and 1960, a net rural-to-urban migration of eleven million people occurred in the seven nations of Argentina, Brazil, Chile, Colombia, Ecuador, Peru, and Guatemala. Yet during the same time there was a natural increase of nineteen million in the rural populations of these countries (Barraclough and Domike, 1970: 68). Thus the urban population was swollen by push factors in the countryside, but booming population growth meant that land pressures were not alleviated by this migration; indeed land pressures became more severe as a result of population growth.

Because urban migration was almost totally the result of rural push factors, it resulted in the literal creation of urban poverty and a proletariat divided between the new service sector and the informal, subsistence economy (Walton 1984: 147). Recent migrants from the countryside were crowded into slums and squatter settlements, surviving in underemployment through personal services, petty commerce, hustling, and sundry vices, including theft and prostitution. An informal economy was created that subsidized the upper classes and capital-intensive industries through cheap labor and services. At the same time, a small "labor aristocracy" grew in the modernized and often foreign-owned industrial and commercial enterprises. Thus migration to urban areas did little to relieve the economic marginality that pushed landless peasants to the city in the first place. High rates of unemployment and underemployment persisted because of continuing land pressures, unabated population growth, and the absence of sufficient job growth in the industrial sector.[10] One-third of Central America's urban workers were employed in the informal sector as of 1982, and the proportion rose to 40 percent by 1988–1989 (Vilas 1995: 157). Hernando de Soto (1989: 12) estimates that, as a result of rural-to-urban migration in Peru and the inability of the formal economy to absorb this migrant population, 48 percent of Peru's economically active population and 61 percent of all work hours were devoted to informal-sector activities, contributing almost 40 percent of the nation's gross domestic product.

What, then, was the fate of displaced peasants, condemned to the insecurities of seasonal wage labor in the countryside and unemployment or underemployment in the city? The Third World's integration into the global political economy disrupted peasant subsistence strategies, and this certainly engendered in them the sorts of grievances that deprived-actor theories of revolution point to as necessary preconditions for violent revolution. Certainly being pushed off one's land with little or no prospects for alternative means of employment would make one dissatisfied with the current regime, especially when that regime actively manipulated land tenure and land use laws to the detriment of peasant cultivators as a class. The resulting exposure to the risks of subsistence crisis could eventually make one desperate enough to consider participating in revolutionary violence, should it erupt. After all, a peasant's very survival could be jeopardized by changes in land use and land tenure, regardless of whether or not he or she participates in any dissident activity. The additional risks to life and limb that accompany involvement in an armed uprising may be only marginally greater than the risks associated with doing nothing. Therefore, by the logic of deprived-actor models of revolution, participation in an armed rebellion could become a reasonable behavioral choice for marginalized peasants.

However, peasants do not typically, frequently, or inevitably rise up in spontaneous revolt, even when dramatic changes in land tenure, land use, income, employment, and authority structures leave them economically deprived. The conditions that deprived-actor theories posit as causes of revolution occur far more frequently in time and space than do revolutions. Roderick Aya (1979: 42) notes, "There are many situations on record where 'severe and persisting grievances' abound and are clearly perceived as such, but where victimized people lack the political wherewithal to galvanize anger into action, or else face such comprehensive repression that any but the most cautious petition for redress is well-nigh suicidal." James Scott (1976: 4) adds, "If anger born of exploitation were sufficient to spark a rebellion, most of the Third World (and not only the Third World) would be in flames." James DeNardo (1985: 17) adds:

> If we considered a complete census of *all* the historical instances of economic catastrophes; rapid economic growth; turns past the apex of J curves; class, ethnic, or colonial oppression; relative or absolute deprivations; population explosions; political unresponsiveness; or ruthless repression . . . we would find that only the tiniest fraction of the events that are said to make revolutions inevitable actually predated an uprising or an insurrection, however pitiful or short-lived. (italics in original)

In short, there is nothing inevitable about a revolution erupting as a consequence of the social dislocations that accompany an agrarian society's integration into the global economic system. And there is nothing inevitable about an individual's participation in a revolutionary movement when he or she is victimized by those dislocations. How then do revolutions in the countryside come about in that tiny sample of all cases in which the underlying conditions are ripe? Exposed to the exigencies of the markets for land, labor, and subsistence goods, displaced peasants became susceptible to mobilization appeals by a variety of counter-elites who offered ways to restore some measure of subsistence security. The next chapter addresses the questions of who these counter-elites are and what strategies they employ to induce marginalized peasants and urban residents to participate in grassroots collective action aimed at remedying the structural sources of their economic distress.

NOTES

1. The "terms of trade" argument was first made by Argentine economist Raoul Prebisch (1950, 1959, 1964). In simple terms, the price of manufactured goods, capital,

and technology imports tends to rise over time relative to the price of raw material exports. As a consequence, raw material exporters face declining net barter terms of trade: A given amount of raw material exports allows them to purchase a smaller and smaller amount of manufactured goods imports. Productivity gains are lost to these declining terms of trade, and economic growth and diversification stagnate. The dependency school that evolved out of this argument is most notably represented in the works of Cardoso and Faletto (1979), Dos Santos (1983), and Furtado (1964), among others.

2. On patron-client politics, see also Powell 1970, LeMarchand 1972, Scott 1972, 1976, and excellent anthologies by Eisenstadt and Lemarchand (1981) and Schmidt et al. (1977).

3. For instance, tax burdens were usually distributed among households by the patron, rather than directly levied on households by the state in the form of a head tax or hut tax. Indeed the head or hut tax was one device colonial powers used to break the power of local patrons in order to extend the authority of the colonial administration down to the village level and thereby undermine the competing authority of the local elites (see Scott 1976: 99–102, 107–110). As long as the patron controlled the distribution of tax burdens locally, he could reduce the burden on those households that were least able to pay and constrain the ambitions of more prosperous households by imposing a greater share of the burden on them. By manipulating these exchanges, the patron could command the support and loyalty of his clients: Their loyalty was to their patron as an agent of the state, not to the state per se.

4. George Foster (1965) describes land as a "limited good" in peasant society: It is highly valued as something essential to survival, but its supply is limited, and there is no way to increase the supply.

5. The different developmental implications of these two systems of tenancy can be profound. Barrington Moore (1966) notes the contrast between imperial China's system of sharecropping and Tokugawa Japan's system of fixed-rate tenancy. He argues that the differences in the incentives and rewards available to peasants in the two systems help to explain why Japan was able to modernize under the Meiji Restoration, whereas the Chinese imperial system collapsed in the face of a peasant-led revolution.

6. Wolf and Mintz (1957: 380) characterize the hacienda as "an estate, operated by a dominant land-owner and a dependent labour force, organized to supply a small-scale market by means of scarce capital, in which the factors of production are employed not only for capital accumulation but also to support the status aspirations of the owner." Arthur Stinchcombe (1961: 168) adds that "neither the value of land nor the value of labor is great and . . . calculation of productive efficiency by the managers of agricultural enterprises is not well developed."

7. Popkin (1979: 256) adds that the same condition holds for tenants as well: "Tenant movements are likely to be more successful in areas where there is no class of permanent laborers for the landlords to use against the tenants."

8. For some of these regions, the impact of early European expansion was disastrous. Witness the decimation of indigenous populations in Central America and the Caribbean in the wake of Spanish colonization. On this, see Wolf 1982.

9. Moreover, the effects of population pressures are not linear, as Jack Goldstone (1997: 104) illustrates. Consider a situation in which 20 percent of the population is

employed in the industrial sector, 60 percent in agriculture or petty commerce, and 20 percent is unemployed or underemployed. If that nation experiences a 20 percent increase in population, even a 50 percent growth in the industrial sector would absorb only half the extra population, resulting in a 50 percent increase in the size of the unemployed or underemployed population. If population grows by 50 percent, even a doubling of the industrial sector will still result in a 150 percent increase in the size of the unemployed or underemployed population.

10. Booth (1991: 41) notes that underemployment, defined as an inability to find full-time work or taking wage labor because of insufficient land for family subsistence, is believed to be from one to five times the official unemployment rate in Central America.

Chapter Four

Mobilizing Peasant Social Movements

Under what circumstances would a rational peasant, even one confronted with the grave risk of a subsistence crisis, choose to get involved in a revolutionary movement? Why would he or she abandon everyday forms of resistance (which require little or no cooperation with others) and join forces with other like-minded peasants in a political movement intent upon compelling the incumbent regime to undertake reforms or face the possibility of being overthrown in a revolution?

The central issue of this chapter is why rational individuals join social movements, especially revolutionary movements. What Mark Lichbach (1995) terms the rebel's dilemma and Gordon Tullock (1971) describes as the paradox of revolution is a special case of the collective action problem delineated by Mancur Olson (1965): A rational person cannot be expected to participate in any form of collective action, violent or nonviolent, because the benefits of collective action are public goods that will be available to that person whether or not he or she participates. If a reform-minded social movement succeeds in persuading the regime to undertake reforms, everyone will benefit from those reforms, regardless of whether or not they participated in the movement. Likewise, if a revolution succeeds in overthrowing the regime and establishing a new order, everyone will be able to enjoy that new order, even those who did not contribute to the revolutionary victory. By not participating, the actor avoids the costs and the risks of participation—which are substantial in the case of a revolutionary movement—but still receives the benefits. Therefore the rational course of action is to free-ride. The rebel's dilemma arises from the fact that, if everyone followed this logic, no one would participate in revolutions, and therefore no revolutions would ever occur. Yet revolutions do occur, even if they are rare. And sometimes they do succeed in overthrowing the incumbent regime.

Mark Lichbach (1995) has catalogued over forty different solutions to the collective action problem.[1] Some of these involve the use of selective incentives: private benefits that can be withheld from those who do not participate in the collective action.[2] It is safe to say that every revolutionary organization uses selective incentives as part of its mobilization strategy. On the other hand, it is also safe to say that no revolutionary movement has ever succeeded in building a base of popular support sufficient to challenge the regime (much less overthrow it) by relying exclusively or even predominantly on selective incentives. Social movements—and revolutionary movements especially—require something more.

A second set of solutions focuses on preexisting social networks and community institutions as mechanisms to overcome the collective action problem.[3] Marwell, Oliver, and Prahl (1988: 502) observe that, among students of collective action, "it is widely agreed that participants in social movement organizations are usually recruited through preexisting social ties and that mobilization is more likely when the members of the beneficiary population are linked by social ties than when they are not."[4] While Olson may be correct in assuming that "unconnected self-interested individuals will not spontaneously make small contributions which make no detectable difference in the provision of an expensive collective good," most people do not lead solitary, atomized lives governed only by pure self-interest and unaffected by any consideration of the behavior of others (Oliver 1993: 274). Yet, only if we assume such an existence does the collective action problem arise.

"What [Olson's] view misses is the degree to which individuals are already embedded and ontologically invested in various kinds of social structures and practices" (McAdam, Tarrow, and Tilly 1996: 26). They are members of families, neighborhoods, villages, or other communities. Their lives are embedded in already existing networks of social relations that exist in part for the purpose of coordinating the behavior of individuals in activities that produce mutual benefit. Social networks and community institutions have at their disposal a variety of social incentives to induce members to participate in collective action. Community members are aware of and familiar with these incentives, who allocates them, and by what criteria. Therefore they can and do anticipate how others in the community will react to a call for action, and they can estimate quite accurately the consequences they will suffer if they do not respond to the appeal in the same manner as their comrades. Thus rational actors, as members of communities, can be induced to contribute to public goods and to participate in collective action, even in the absence of selective incentives.

However, a national social movement, whether reformist or revolutionary, is not likely to emerge spontaneously from community-based social networks.

A social movement requires leadership and organization to sustain collective action over time and to coordinate activities among communities. This is especially true for revolutionary movements. Thus another set of solutions—from the resource mobilization school—emphasizes the importance of social movement organizations as agents that induce latent supporters of a cause to contribute to or participate in its activities.[5] Resource mobilization theories suggest that, for opposition social movements to arise in Third World nations experiencing the dislocations described in chapter 3, dissident leaders must first establish social movement organizations for the purpose of soliciting support from aggrieved peasants and coordinating collective action among peasant communities. They do so by framing the issues confronting peasants in such a way as to convince peasants, first, that their troubles are shared by others beyond the boundaries of their own immediate community. Second, dissident leaders must convince peasants that the conditions that gave rise to their grievances are unjust and by no means inevitable. Third, they must politicize the movement by persuading peasants that the state is either responsible for their grievances or has the capacity to remedy them. Finally, dissident leaders must persuade peasants that only if each member of each community contributes to the success of the movement will they be able to succeed in bringing pressure to bear on the state to compel it to undertake reforms.

Under normal circumstances these mechanisms—selective incentives, preexisting social networks, and social movement organizations—can be used to mobilize rational actors for participation in conventional forms of cooperation (such as local public works projects) and nonviolent forms of contentious action (such as rent strikes or demonstrations). Revolutionary violence, however, is not normally a part of most communities' repertoires of contention. Revolution involves substantial risk to life and property for participants, far in excess of the risks they might anticipate from participating in nonviolent forms of contentious action. Nonetheless, once people are mobilized for familiar, nonviolent forms of collective action, it is possible for a revolutionary organization to "capture" this social movement as a support base for a revolutionary movement.

After spelling out the rebel's dilemma and its implications, I describe the mechanisms that evolved in Third World societies for the purpose of mobilizing people for nonviolent collective action. Once a nonviolent social movement has been established, the escalation to revolutionary violence is largely a function of the state's response to nonviolent collective action (a subject discussed in chapter 5). If the state responds with repressive violence, participants in nonviolent social movements may conclude that they have no choice but to shift tactics to revolutionary violence.

THE REBEL'S DILEMMA

The rebel's dilemma depicts the collective action problem in revolution as a prisoner's dilemma game.[6] In this model a rational individual—let us call her Carla—is faced with the choice of participating or not participating in a revolution. Let us assume that Carla sympathizes with the goals of the rebels. She believes that the current regime is oppressive and unresponsive to popular demands, and that wealth and opportunities are unfairly monopolized by a small number of privileged elites. Through their alliance with the military, those elites are able to keep wages low and profits high, capturing for themselves and their collaborators in the military the fruits of the labor of peasants and workers. Peasants and workers are relegated to grinding poverty, their very subsistence threatened by landlessness, frequent unemployment and underemployment, low wages, and the human corollaries of poverty: disease, malnutrition, and misery. Carla believes that this system will not change without a violent challenge. In short, her moral commitment is to the goals of the revolution. But does she participate in it?

The choice facing her can be represented by the decision matrix in table 4.1. The payoffs to Carla from each of her possible choices are contingent upon

Table 4.1

		Everyone Else's Choices	
		Join the Rebels	**Don't Join the Rebels**
Carla's Choices	**Join the Rebels**	*Benefits:* Rebel Victory	*Benefits:* None (no rebellion occurs)
		Costs: Time, Resources spent in Rebellion, Risk of sanctions by government	*Costs:* Time, Resources spent in Rebellion, Risk of sanctions by government
	Don't Join the Rebels	*Benefits:* Rebel Victory	*Benefits:* None (no rebellion occurs)
		Costs: None	*Costs:* None

what "everyone else" does, and she cannot know with certainty what "everyone else" will do. The dilemma for Carla is that, no matter what everyone else does, the best choice for her (in terms of her own self-interest) is to not participate in the rebellion.

Consider first the case where "everyone else" stays home (so there is no movement to challenge the existing regime). Carla's choice here is obvious: She too stays home. It would be dangerously foolish for her to take up the sword of rebellion by herself. Without the support of others, her one-person protest would be easily crushed by the regime, with Carla being jailed, killed, or "disappeared." Participating under these circumstances would be the height of folly.

When "everyone else" does participate in the rebellion, Carla's choice is less obvious, but the logic is still compelling: She still stays home. If enough others join in so that a rebellion breaks out and the rebels win, then the difference to Carla between participating and not participating is simply a function of the costs of participation. The benefits to Carla—the public goods of revolutionary victory—are the same whether she participates or not. But if she joins the rebels, she expends a certain amount of her own time and resources in rebellious activity, and she puts her own life in jeopardy in the process. Yet the outcome of the rebellion is not altered by her participation, because she is only one of the many thousands whose participation is required for the rebels to win. She gets the same benefits if she stays home, but she also avoids the costs and the risks of participation. In short, there is no advantage to her from participating. No matter what "everyone else" does, the rational course of action for Carla is to stay at home.

The logic of the rebel's dilemma argues against revolution ever occurring because individual self-interest argues against a rational person ever participating. First, the benefits of revolution are uncertain and unknown. They are uncertain in the sense that the probability of rebellious collective action even occurring is extremely low, and the chances of it succeeding are even lower.[7] To quote James Scott (1985: 29):

> Peasant rebellions, let alone peasant "revolutions," are few and far between. Not only are the circumstances that favor large-scale peasant uprisings comparatively rare, but when they do appear the revolts that develop are nearly always crushed unceremoniously. To be sure, even a failed revolt may achieve something. . . . Such gains, however, are uncertain, while the carnage, the repression, and the demoralization of defeat are all too certain and real.

The benefits of revolution are unknown in the sense that no one can be sure whether the postrevolutionary order will be a substantial improvement over the status quo. Many is the revolutionary movement that failed to deliver on its promised utopian social order, instead imposing, on the very social groups it claimed to represent, a new system of control that was no less harsh and objectionable than the old order.[8] Quoting Scott again: "All too frequently the peasantry finds itself in the ironic position of having helped to power a ruling group whose plans for industrialization, taxation, and collectivization are very much at odds with the goals for which peasants imagined they were fighting." (1985: 29)

Second, whether or not the revolt succeeds is independent of any one person's participation or nonparticipation in it. The effort required to overthrow an entrenched political regime is so monumental that thousands must contribute if the revolution is to succeed. Any one person's contribution to this effort amounts to only a minuscule portion of the total effort required for victory. Therefore Carla's contribution will not be missed if she stays home; the revolution will succeed or fail regardless of whether or not she participates.

Third, participation is costly. The time, energy, and material resources that one contributes to the rebellion could be devoted to other endeavors that have a much greater chance of producing direct benefits for the individual. Food and money donated to the rebels is food and money not available for one's own consumption. Time spent serving in a guerrilla unit is time not spent cultivating one's fields, earning wages, or engaging in other activities that will produce direct benefits for oneself and one's family.[9]

Finally, participation in rebellion is extremely risky, because governments fight back with a vengeance. Governments kill known or suspected rebels and their sympathizers, their supporters, their families, and even their neighbors. Knowing this adds to the temptation to stay out of the crossfire between rebels and regime, at least until victory is all but assured and one can jump on the rebel bandwagon with little risk to life, limb, or property.

Thus the logic of collective action would lead us to conclude that rebellious collective action should be extremely rare.[10] Even in situations where large numbers of people are in such distress that they would welcome a successful revolution, a revolutionary organization will not readily, naturally, or automatically emerge. Even if a revolutionary organization does arise, most of those who would benefit from its success will not join the movement. Even those who do support the rebels will provide support only intermittently and only with low-cost, low-risk forms of support (Lichbach 1995: 16–17). Thus Lichbach (12) concludes that even among those who prefer a rebel victory to the current regime, at least 95 percent of them, 95 percent of the time, in 95 percent of the settings do not rebel. Their behavior is consistent with what Olson would predict. It is also consistent with the observation that the social and economic conditions scholars have depicted as causes of revolution occur far more frequently in time and space than do violent revolutions aimed at remedying those conditions.

Yet empirically we know that revolutions do occur and that ordinary people do participate in them, even if they constitute only a tiny minority. Rebellions are made by small minorities.[11] It is that 5 percent or so of the population that is of interest to us: How is it that they overcome the rebel's dilemma?

Solutions to the rebel's dilemma involve dispensing selective incentives, harnessing preexisting social networks and community institutions, and building an effective social movement organization that frames the issues so they appeal to peasants, dispenses selective incentives that induce their participation in movement activities, and coordinates activities nationwide so that collective action is sustained and widespread rather than intermittent, isolated, and localized. These are the roles that all social movement organizations—whether revolutionary or reformist—perform. What distinguishes revolutionary movements from reformist movements is, of course, that the former seek to overthrow the incumbent regime, not reform it, and they use insurgent violence, not nonviolent protest, as their dominant tactical repertoire.

Revolutionary movements do not spring up fully mature out of nothing. Nor does the transition from political tranquility to revolutionary instability occur in a single leap. Rather it occurs as a process of escalation, from relatively minor and localized acts of contention to more organized but still nonviolent dissident social movements and finally to organized revolutionary violence. Revolutionary leaders do not begin their political careers as revolutionaries. They do not make a sudden leap from political noninvolvement to revolutionary activism. Instead most of them begin their careers much more modestly, as student activists, union leaders, party politicians, civil servants, or leaders of other legal opposition organizations.[12] Their involvement in revolution does not occur as a choice from a menu that includes various other forms of less radical and less violent forms of opposition politics. They come to revolutionary activism in response to the state's repression of the nonviolent opposition movements in which they begin their political careers. Revolutionary organizations are not usually created from scratch. Their ancestry can usually be traced to legal political parties, peasant associations, student organizations, labor unions, or some other legal opposition organization.[13] Indeed most revolutionary organizations are assembled from the remnants of legal organizations after they have been shattered by the repressive arm of the state.

Finally, rank-and-file participants in revolutions are not people who were previously unaffiliated with any dissident organization and who suddenly choose to abandon total noninvolvement in favor of total commitment to revolutionary collective action. Revolutions are made by people who are active members of already existing communities, social networks, and nonviolent social movements.

Revolutions occur when existing dissident organizations decide to adopt revolutionary violence as a strategy rather than continue with nonviolent tactics that have produced no results and have left them exposed to the government's repressive tactics.[14] In effect, they have already solved the collective action problem, but for the purpose of nonviolent collective action. Thus most revolutions take place by separating the collective action problem from the rebel's dilemma, in the sense that they establish the means to mobilize supporters for nonviolent collective action, and later, in response to government repression, they use that capacity to build support for the more extreme goal of revolutionary change.

We turn now to the strategies nonviolent social movements use to solve the collective action problem and build a base of support for their movement. Whether that movement retains its reformist goals or reconstitutes itself as a revolutionary movement is largely a function of how the state responds to nonviolent collective action, a subject discussed in the next chapter.

SELECTIVE INCENTIVES

The only solution that Mancur Olson allows for the collective action dilemma in large groups is the provision of selective incentives:

> Group action can be obtained only through an incentive that operates, not indiscriminately, like the collective good, upon the group as a whole, but rather *selectively* toward the individuals in the group. The incentive must be "selective" so that those who do not join the organization working for the group's interest, or in other ways contribute to the attainment of the group's interest, can be treated differently. (1965: 51; emphasis in original)

Unlike the public goods of collective action, selective incentives are both excludable and subject to crowding effects: They are available only to those who participate in the collective action, and one person's consumption of these benefits does diminish the amount available for others to consume.

All social movements—whether revolutionary or reformist—make use of selective incentives to enlist supporters. Public television stations offer patrons coffee mugs, calendars, video cassettes, and umbrellas in return for contributions to public broadcasting, which the patrons could watch even if they did not contribute. Reformist social movements offer participants similar sorts of tangible benefits as well as a variety of "soft incentives," including the "entertainment value" of participating in protest activities (Tullock 1971), and a sense of self-esteem from participating in a cause one values (see Opp 1986: 88–89). Revolutionary social movements also make use of selective incentives to build a base of support among the civilian population and to induce some of their numbers to participate actively in the movement as combatants. Goodwin and Skocpol (1989: 494) describe the use of selective incentives by revolutionary movements:

> In addition to collective goods, revolutionary organization may also offer selective incentives to encourage participation in various sorts of activities, particularly dangerous ones like actual guerrilla warfare. Such incentives for actual or potential cadres and fighters and their families may include extra tax or rent reductions or an additional increment of land beyond that allocated to supporters in general. In any event, it is the ongoing provision of such collective and selective goods, not ideological conversion in the abstract, that has played the principal role in solidifying social support for guerilla armies.

The point to emphasize here is not what appears to be obvious: that people will provide acts of support in return for private benefits. The important point is what Goodwin and Skocpol assert is *not* the basis of peasants' conversion to a revolutionary movement: It is *not* the ideological appeal of the rebels but their ability to provide tangible material payoffs to their supporters that wins peasants over initially. Conversion to the goals of the revolution comes later.[15]

While the selective incentive solution can account for a peasant's initial acts of support for a social movement, it falls far short of providing a complete explanation of how dissident social movements—revolutionary or reformist—emerge and develop. Pamela Oliver (1993: 273) points out the logical flaw inherent in the selective incentive solution: Someone has to pay for the selective incentives, but Olson's logic implies that no rational person should be willing to devote his or her private wealth to the dispensation of selective incentives when the public goods that will result from the ensuing collective action will be available to that person even if he or she does not underwrite the cost of selective incentives. In practical terms the selective incentive solution assumes the existence of an organization with the capacity to pay for and dispense selective incentives. It cannot explain why anyone would form such an organization in the first place, since there are no selective incentives available to induce them to take on that task. In short, while selective incentives may account for the participation of the *n*th rebel or demonstrator, this solution cannot explain the behavior of the first rebel (Mason 1984; Van Belle 1996).[16]

A second limitation of the selective incentive solution is that a social movement (violent or nonviolent) built exclusively through selective incentives would, in all likelihood, be prohibitively expensive (Van Belle 1996: 109; Lichbach 1994b: 390). The cost of providing selective incentives grows with increases in group size, even if it does grow at a decreasing rate.[17] If every rank-and-file participant in the movement had to be provided with private benefits sufficient to overcome his or her estimated costs of participation, the movement would go bankrupt long before it had a chance to succeed (see Chong 1991: 32–33). This is especially problematic for revolutionary social movements, given the extreme risk that supporters assume by participating in them. People may be willing to contribute to public television in return for a coffee mug or an umbrella, but doing so does not involve substantial risk to life and property, whereas participating in a revolutionary movement does. Thus the cost of the selective incentives required to offset the risks of participation in a revolutionary movement is likely to be prohibitive. Moreover, opposition social movements (and revolutionary movements in particular) are subject to outbidding by the regime: The state has far more resources at its disposal to compete with dissidents in the provision of selective incentives in return for political support (see Lichbach 1994b: 391).

A third issue is that a dissident social movement built exclusively on selective incentives is not likely to be very cohesive or resilient over the course of its struggle with the government. This is another logical conundrum for selective incentives solution: Selective incentives should be equally appealing to someone who does not support the goals of the movement. If the value of these goods exceeds the costs of participation, then it is rational for an individual—whether a supporter or opponent of the cause—to "pay the entry fee" (Chong 1991: 33). James DeNardo (1985: 56) points out that discounting public goods as a motivation and relying exclusively on selective incentives "implies that socialists will gladly participate in fascist demonstrations, and vice versa, if the organizers simply provide enough coffee and doughnuts to the marchers."

If supporters can be counted upon only as long as side payments are forthcoming, then the movement is likely to collapse during those periods in the ebb and flow of political contention when the movement's strength (and therefore its ability to dispense selective incentives) declines relative to that of the regime. If the movement suffers a setback, the costs of that defeat are likely to be magnified by the desertion of supporters who, based on the defeat, perceive the movement to have lost its capacity to provide them with selective incentives. In short, to the extent that a social movement relies on what amounts to mercenaries, the movement is likely to fail because its support base will dissolve at the first sign that the leaders might not be able to deliver on their promise of selective incentives.

Selective incentives provide only part of the solution to the rebel's dilemma. Selective incentives can account for the recruitment of the marginal supporter to an already existing social movement but cannot account for the creation of the dissident organization that dispenses selective incentives. Selective incentives cannot explain the participation of those who join a dissident social movement early, when the risks of participation are at their greatest and selective incentives are nonexistent. More important, they cannot explain why people would join an explicitly *revolutionary* social movement. Even if selective incentives are available, the risks to life, limb, and property that accompany revolutionary activism are so extreme that no amount of private incentives would be sufficient to offset this risk. Even for nonviolent social movements, the poverty, powerlessness, and inertia characteristic of peasant life in the Third World suggest that the obstacles to mobilization are onerous. How then do we account for the emergence of contentious social movements and the participation of peasants in them?

SOCIAL MOVEMENT ORGANIZATIONS

According to resource mobilization theory, the solution to the collective action problem is found in the emergence of effective movement leaders who are capable of mobilizing the human and material resources necessary to mount a viable challenge to the incumbent regime (McCarthy and Zald 1977; see also Frohlich, Oppenheimer, and Young 1971). From this perspective, the reason that widespread and deeply felt grievances are far more common in the Third World than are active social movements is that effective social movement entrepreneurs and social movement organizations are so rare. Those few cases where organized opposition does arise are distinguished not by the severity of popular grievances but by the presence of effective opposition leaders and movement organizations. Without dissident leadership and organization, popular grievances may occasionally erupt in local uprisings, but those events will be short-lived, localized, and quickly defeated by the regime.

Social movement activists solve the collective action problem by persuading potential supporters who would otherwise free-ride that (1) their contribution is needed, however small it may be; (2) if they do contribute, there will be other rewards (selective incentives) that are available only to those who contribute; (3) if they contribute, others will as well; and (4) their contributions will not be in vain because the leaders have the skills and the organizational capacity to aggregate the contributions of many people to produce the public benefits of reform or revolution. To do this, opposition leaders must frame the issues so as to convince the aggrieved population that the status quo is not inevitable, that many others share their dissatisfaction, and that others will be willing to join a movement for change if they are assured that enough like-minded individuals will participate as well (Kuran 1995: 285).

The framing process involves several dimensions. First, dissident leaders seek to expose the regime's vulnerability. They may engage in contentious acts themselves in order to demonstrate that dissent is possible and that the regime's capacity to suppress it is far from absolute. By publicizing the hidden discontent simmering among the population—and getting away with it—dissident activists encourage the belief among people that a vast majority of their fellow citizens share their preference for change, whether it be change in policies through reform or a change in regime through revolution. Second, dissident leaders seek to mold people's preferences by identifying the wrongs in the existing order and persuading the population of the virtues of the alternative order they seek to create (Kuran 1995: 286). They politicize grievances by depicting them as the result of state action or inaction. They try to persuade the aggrieved population that only the state can remedy the conditions that are the source of their grievances, and the state will not act unless forced to do so by a determined population willing to challenge the state collectively. Third, dissident leaders make joining the public opposition more attractive by making it appear less risky. Through the events they organize, leaders generate a support network for those who declare themselves opponents of the regime and proponents of reform. In so doing they not only reduce the risks of dissent, they enhance the reputational benefits of dissent. Once people are convinced that others in their community are supporting the dissident movement, they feel more comfortable doing so as well. They perceive the risks of participation as being lower because so many others are supporting the movement. Moreover, they feel social pressure to participate: No one wants to be known as a government collaborator in a community of opposition supporters.[18]

While these arguments suggest how dissident leaders overcome collective action problems, the question remains: Why would they undertake this activity rather than some other, less risky path? Berejikian (1992: 650–51) points out that there is no reason to assume that villagewide contempt would be sufficient to induce a peasant to assume the extraordinary risks of engaging in open revolt. Besides, reputational effects still require an explanation of how the rest of the community came to participate in collective action themselves. McCarthy and Zald (1977) see the affluence of the West as giving rise to a new class of professional social movement entrepreneurs. Clearly this is not the case in the Third World. The profound poverty in which most peasants live leaves them with few resources of time or money to contribute to social movements. Moreover, the social movement entrepreneurs that McCarthy and Zald see in such ample supply in advanced industrial democracies are much scarcer in rural communities of the Third World. Besides the lack of educational opportunities that would allow people to develop the skills needed to be an effective movement entrepreneur, such skills are not in great demand in a subsistence economy.

Finally, movement entrepreneurship is discouraged by the state and other authorities. Activists in the Third World face severe legal, economic, and social barriers to their efforts. Governments often restrict the kinds of activities they are allowed to use. Mass demonstrations, for instance, are often severely restricted, if not outlawed. Many regimes use a corporatist strategy of pre-emptively organizing peasants and workers. They establish unions and peasant associations under state auspices and use the existence of these state-sanctioned entities as a pretext to deny legal status to competing organizations that seek to mobilize peasants, workers, and the urban poor outside the auspices of the state. In contrast to their Western counterparts, social movement entrepreneurs in the Third World must appeal to a population whose poverty severely constrains their ability to support a social movement of any sort. They simply do not have the disposable income to devote to something so speculative and risky. Moreover, they are much more vulnerable to intimidation and threats by employers, landlords, and other nongovernmental authorities who hold sway over some aspect of their lives. Sharecroppers risk eviction for participating in a reformist social movement. Wage laborers can be fired from their jobs for participating in dissident activities. Where then do Third World revolutionary leaders come from, and why do they devote their time and energies to such a high-risk endeavor?

One motivation, mentioned earlier, is *leadership benefits*.[19] For a revolutionary movement, leadership benefits include political office in the postrevolutionary regime. Leaders of reformist social movements can use the movement as their electoral base in a bid for public office. Leadership benefits are private goods in the sense that they are excludable, rival, and available only to the leaders of the movement. Political office comes with the benefits of power, wealth, and other perquisites. A social movement activist or revolutionary leader who assumes office in the new government can use the power of that office to shape policy in ways that benefit himself and his personal client group. Former activists typically live far more comfortably than they did prior to assuming office, and far more comfortably than their followers do after the revolution. As an extreme example, Van Belle (1996) cites the case of Zairean president Mobutu Sese Seko, who is estimated to have amassed a personal fortune of several billion dollars despite the fact that, during his rule, personal income in Zaire declined by 3.9 percent, and the nation experienced the second worst growth record in the world. Zaire went from being self-sufficient in agriculture to importing 30 percent of its food. After twenty-three years as the leader of the Southwest Africa People's Organization (SWAPO) guerrillas, Sam Nujoma was elected the first president of the newly independent nation of Namibia. The *New York Times*[20] reported that forty-three former guerrillas who were elected to parliament and held ministerial or deputy minister posts in the cabinet received a salary of $55,000 a year, plus allowances for housing, furniture, electricity, telephones, and drivers. They also received a free television satellite dish, cellular phones, and $1,500 in "pocket money" over and above hotel and meals when they traveled abroad. While these amounts are certainly not excessive compared to what top government officials in other nations are paid, they do represent leadership benefits to those who joined the Namibian independence movement early and served in the leadership of SWAPO.

Access to leadership benefits helps us understand why people join a social movement early, before the movement has the capacity to dispense selective incentives. Leadership benefits are not only excludable; they are also limited in supply. Social movements can attract early recruits by offering them opportunities for upward mobility if they are willing to join the movement before bandwagon effects set in and the pool of leadership benefits is exhausted (Migdal 1974: 242).

Attracting supporters early is especially crucial for revolutionary social movements because the risks to early joiners are so severe, and the prospects for rebel victory are remote. As long as the rebel numbers are small, the probability of any one rebel being detected, apprehended, and punished by the government is still prohibitively high for most sympathizers. Under these circumstances it is necessary for the rebels to offer something more than the conventional ration of selective incentives. Upward mobility is important as a selective incentive at this stage because it is a benefit that will continue to pay off for the recipients throughout the course of their lives, should the revolution succeed and they survive.

What types of individuals are likely to pursue leadership positions in the dissident movement's organization? Skocpol (1979: 165) notes that the leadership of the French, Russian, and Chinese revolutions all "precipitated out of the ranks of relatively highly educated groups oriented to state activities or employments . . . especially from among those who were somewhat marginal to the established dominant classes and government elites of the Old Regimes." Van Belle (1996: 115) suggests that it should be those who possess "a diverse and distinctive set of skills, experiences, and dispositions that would preclude the most impoverished" from assuming this role. Kuran (1989: 42) contends that revolutionary leaders are "individuals with an exceptional ability to detect and help expose the incumbent regime's vulnerabilities." This aspect of a revolutionary entrepreneur's role suggests to Samuel Popkin that the skills they need above all else are "communications skills to provide peasants with the signals and incentives necessary to collective action and organization building. . . . Village-level entrepreneurs [in Vietnam] were persons with extensive experience in the few roles in an agricultural society in which communication skills were developed: teachers, drivers, river boat pilots, itinerant actors, NCOs from the French Army" (1988: 17).

This implies that those most suited to this role are those who have had at least some formal education and some experience in formal organizations.

This would include frustrated elite aspirants, former elites, or children of middle-class families who have sufficient education but little or no opportunities for elite positions in the current social order. They are individuals who have the abilities to compete for leadership goods in the current social system but who have been excluded from that competition for reasons other than merit. Skocpol notes that:

> The leaders of the French Revolution were "marginal" because they tended to come from lesser, provincial urban centers and/or from the lower levels of the former royal administration. . . . Most of those in top and intermediate level positions of leadership [in the Russian and Chinese revolutions] came either from dominant-class backgrounds or from families on the margins of the privileged classes. . . . Moreover, both revolutionary leaderships included very high proportions of people who had received formal secondary and (domestic or foreign) university educations. (1979: 166)

While leadership benefits may explain why certain people will assume the risks required to initiate and maintain a revolutionary organization, this concept still does not explain why they would invest their time and energy in such a high-risk endeavor with such a low prospect of success. Kuran (1995: 286) cautions that "one must not exaggerate the role of such motives as fame, political power, and pecuniary gain," because most revolutionaries are smart enough to realize that the chances of their succeeding are rather slim. The same argument applies to reformist social movements as well. Besides, with their skills, most dissident leaders could have done quite well if they had collaborated with the regime early in their careers, when the prospects of revolutionary victory were extremely remote. Why would they not commit themselves instead to an endeavor that had a far greater chance of succeeding and posed far fewer and less ominous risks to their lives and property?

As alluded to earlier, most revolutionary leaders do not begin their political careers as revolutionaries. Nor do the political organizations they head begin as revolutionary movements. Instead most revolutionaries begin as activists pursuing reform through legal means, and they do so by leading legal opposition organizations engaged in peaceful forms of collective action aimed at pressuring the state into undertaking reforms. It is only after the state responds with violent repression that the leaders of nonviolent social movements turn to revolutionary violence. Some of them succeed. Many do not: The state successfully crushes their movements. One factor that distinguishes those who make the transition to effective revolutionaries from those who do not is their ability to build a base of grassroots support.

GRASSROOTS ORGANIZATIONS
AND COMMUNITY INSTITUTIONS

Contemporary Third World revolutionary movements were not built from scratch, nor were supporters recruited one-by-one by offering selective incentives. Instead, dissident leaders took advantage of already existing social networks, community institutions, and other mobilizing structures to recruit supporters in groups. Olson's rational actor is also a member of a family, a neighborhood, a village, and other types of communities. As such, his or her social life is governed by the rules and routines of social networks that have evolved in part for the purpose of coordinating the behavior of members to produce mutual benefit. These social networks of "interdependence and coordination can change individual decisions even without private incentives, and . . . many collective goods can, in fact, be provided by a small number of individuals making large contributions through an appropriate technology" (Oliver 1993: 274). In the case of local collective action, the "appropriate technology" consists of those pre-existing social networks. In the case of a national social movement, it consists of the social movement organization. In short, rational actors, as members of social networks and participants in social institutions, can be induced to contribute to the provision of public goods, even in the absence of selective incentives.

In terms of rational choice, these existing social institutions—be they the governing councils of corporate villages, churches, schools, extended family and clan ties, neighborhoods, or others—have, in effect, solved the free-rider problem. They have developed the mechanisms necessary to mobilize members of the community in cooperative endeavors that produce collective goods for the entire community. Accordingly they can be adapted for other, less conventional purposes as well, including contentious political action. Dissident leaders can harness them as mobilizing structures to build a support base for a national social movement.[21] Sidney Tarrow (1994: 22) observes that "the mobilization of preexisting social networks lowers the social transaction costs of mounting demonstrations, and holds participants together even after the enthusiasm of the peak of confrontation is over. In human terms, this is what makes possible the transformation of episodic collective action into social movements." This strategy is especially useful in impoverished rural areas of Third World nations, where community members lack the resources and the will to participate in national social movement organizations led by activists who are not members of their community.

Members of existing social networks bring to a social movement experience in various kinds of collective action. These "repertoires of contention" consist of "limited numbers of historically established performances linking claimants to the objects of their claims" (McAdam, Tarrow, and Tilly 1996: 23).[22] They represent a set of collective behaviors with which the members of the community have had some experience. Based on this experience, community members already know how to organize themselves for these forms of collective activity, and they have reason to expect that these contentious acts will produce collective benefits. Individual members have some assurance that, if they make their contribution, others will do so as well. Thus "workers know how to strike because generations of workers struck before them; Parisians build barricades because barricades are inscribed in the history of Parisian contention; peasants seize the land carrying the symbols that their fathers and grandfathers used in the past" (Tarrow 1998: 21). Students in China drew on the experience of demonstrations in 1976, 1978, and 1986 to mobilize their members for the Tiananmen Square movement of 1989.[23] Based on previous experience, they knew how to organize street demonstrations, and participants had some assurance that others would participate as well. They also believed that they could demonstrate with little risk of violent repression by the state. Unfortunately they miscalculated the state's willingness to use repressive violence.

Traditionally in agrarian societies the targets of most of grassroots contentious actions have been local authorities, such as landlords or local government officials. And these actions have been focused on local issues, such as the terms of trade and distribution of risks between landlords and peasants, or the availability of public services and public works (such as schools, roads, bridges, or water systems) from the government. For pre-existing social institutions to be activated in support of a sustained national social movement that addresses national issues requires the intervention of social movement leaders and organizations from outside the community.

Dissident leaders can harness existing social networks for movement activities that go beyond those networks' existing repertoires of contention. In so doing they harness those social networks as mobilizing structures for a sustained national social movement. This is achieved through framing processes, by which dissident leaders identify injustices that afflict the community and attribute them to the state or some other entity that is the intended target of the movement. Movement leaders "underscore and embellish the seriousness and injustice of social conditions or redefine as unjust and immoral what was previously seen as unfortunate but perhaps tolerable" (Snow and Benford 1992: 137). On the one hand, this strategy facilitates the mobilization process for the social movement leaders, because they can mobilize entire communities at a time. On the other hand, this kind of appeal makes it easier for members of the community to adapt their repertoires of contention to the new broader movement, because its goals are presented to them as compatible with the goals for which they are accustomed to cooperating. As McAdam, Tarrow, and Tilly (1997: 157) put it, "well-established organizations or associational networks . . . become effective mobilizing structures because they can draw on shared beliefs and worldviews that motivate and legitimate protest activity." It is the task of dissident leaders to construct a political reality for the potential participants that makes use of symbols and identities with which they are already familiar. In so doing, the leaders redefine local groups' collective identity so that members feel a commitment to participate in or otherwise contribute to the national movement's success. However, as Tarrow (1998: 110) notes, "movement entrepreneurs cannot simply adapt frames of meaning from traditional cultural symbols: if they did, they would be nothing more than reflections of their societies' values and would be inhibited from challenging them." Leaders must use traditional symbols to attract nonelites to a new set of values and beliefs about the state that will make them more willing to challenge the state.[24]

PEASANT-BASED SOCIAL MOVEMENTS

In Third World social movements, there are at least two paths by which pre-existing social networks can be mobilized in support of social movements that extend beyond local concerns (and local action) to pose a challenge to the state itself. First, where the traditional institutions of agrarian communities remain intact, those institutions can be co-opted by national social movements for contentious collective action. The corporate village, for instance, is essentially a set of local institutions that exist for the purpose of organizing villagers for public works projects and other cooperative ventures, eliciting contributions from members for those projects, and identifying and sanctioning free-riders who try to avoid contributing to the projects. Under certain circumstances, a national social movement can "capture" those village institutions and harness their mobilizing capacity in the service of its national agenda. In Vietnam the Vietminh were highly successful at this strategy, relying on already existing village institutions to mobilize members in support of the Vietminh's revolt against the French and, later, against the United States and the government of South Vietnam.[25]

Revolutionary organizations or reformist social movements can also come into being where traditional village institutions have eroded but new agents or political entrepreneurs have succeeded in establishing new grassroots organizations. Displaced peasants and urban poor participate in grassroots organizations because they provide their members with both selective incentives and public benefits, in return for their participation in and contributions to the new organization's program of nonviolent collective action. In many Latin American nations, Catholic priests and lay catechists, inspired by the doctrines of "liberation theology," have mobilized the poor for collective action in Christian base communities (CEBs, or *communidades eclesiales de base*). CEBs organize cooperation among poor villagers for projects such as building schools and clinics, establishing food cooperatives, and child care cooperatives. The collective action mobilized by CEBs addresses specific needs of poor households. CEBs not only empower the poor to address their own immediate needs; they have also established mechanisms of cooperation that opposition political parties and other social movements can harness to elicit the support of the entire community for their national agenda of reform.

Village Institutions

In regions where agricultural production is still organized around corporate villages, village residents can and do routinely cooperate in the production of collective goods. Village-based institutions of social control have evolved over time to serve as mechanisms for coordinating the production activities of member households and enforcing cooperation among residents for community projects that are essential to the welfare of the entire village. Members cooperate in the construction of roads, bridges, walls, and other public works projects that are essential for local commerce. They also cooperate in the timing of planting, harvesting, and other stages in the crop cycle, such as flooding of fields in rice production or pasturing livestock in fields after harvest (see Magagna 1991). Village institutions are valued by residents because they provide highly valued services, including some forms of subsistence insurance. They also dispense justice locally by distributing land among households, regulating the use of village commons, and resolving disputes according to agreed-upon community norms and rules. Thus members more or less willingly endow the village council or headman with the authority to compel members to participate in essential community projects.

Villagers are able to overcome collective action problems in part because village institutions allow the careful monitoring and sanctioning of free-riding. The typical village is small enough that most members know most of the other members on a face-to-face basis. Mancur Olson (1965: 33–36) acknowledges that free-riding poses less of a problem in small groups, because free-riders can be detected and sanctioned more easily than in large groups. A household that does not contribute its fair share to the community welfare can be sanctioned by the community in a number of ways, including limiting that family's use of common grazing land, allocating them smaller or inferior plots of land, or, in the extreme, expelling them from the community.

A second reason that village members are more likely to contribute to public goods is that, in smaller groups, each person's contribution may be essential to the group's success in producing the public goods. If one person withholds his or her support, that might be sufficient to preclude the production of the public goods. Therefore people are less inclined to believe they can free-ride and still enjoy the benefits of collective action. Effective leaders often try to convince constituents that the goals they seek are all-or-nothing goods: Either everyone contributes, or the public goods will not be produced (Chong 1991: 14–15). Popkin notes that Vietminh leaders often convinced villagers to contribute to their movement by breaking up the goals of the movement into a series of smaller steps, all of which were essential to achieving the ultimate goal of revolutionary victory. "If a large goal can be broken into many small independent pieces, all of which are necessary to the larger goal, the free-rider problem can be overcome, for if each person has a monopoly on a necessary factor for the final goal, all contributions are essential" (1988: 15).

Contributions to collective endeavors is also enforced by reputational effects. Villagers have to interact with other members of the community on a continuing basis, and any failure to do their fair share of the community work will become known. As Michael Taylor observes, "An individual joins or contributes or participates [in collective action] because he is asked tacitly or overtly pressured by friends, colleagues, co-workers, or co-members of the association's local branch. He cannot say no to them; he is afraid of losing their approval, respect or cooperation" (1988b: 84). Their reputation in the community will suffer, and this will have negative consequences for their own well-being and social mobility in the village.[26]

Popkin (1988: 20–21) argues that, for these reasons, villagers can be mobilized locally, not necessarily for revolutionary violence but for far less risky nonviolent collective action aimed at providing direct material benefits to participants. Leaders of dissident social movements can take advantage of existing village institutions to mobilize villagers for dissident collective action aimed at pressuring the state to undertake reforms that will benefit the entire community. The same mechanisms that coordinate the timing of planting, harvesting, and flooding the fields of rice farmers can be used to organize those same families for a rent strike, a land invasion, or some other form of collective dissent.

For social movements to enlist the support of entire villages, they must first win each community's support by mobilizing them for local projects that produce immediate and tangible benefits. In effect the social movement can present itself as an alternative to the existing elite, rivaling landlords and government officials for the loyalty of the village by offering them more collective benefits at a lower cost. As Popkin (1979: 246–47) observes, "traditional arrangements can be improved on and landlords outbid by persons willing to provide the same services at lower cost (and higher dignity)." In so doing, the social movement enhances its own ability to mobilize that village in support of the movement's agenda "by helping them to break their dependence on, and control by large landowners and/or village officials" (Popkin 1988: 10). Popkin (1979) notes that members of the Cao Dai movement in Vietnam were able to enlist support among villagers by intervening on their behalf with French colonial officials. As much as 60 percent of the movement's original members were employees of the French colonial administration. As such, they had knowledge of how the French bureaucracy worked, while peasants' ignorance of French bureaucratic procedures made them easy victims of landlords, local officials, and other better-connected traditional authorities. Cao Dai members presented themselves to peasants as intermediaries who could help them navigate their way through the French administration and thus avoid being so easily exploited. By offering peasants protection from predatory local authorities, Cao Dai could win their support and loyalty.

Mobilizing entire communities in support of a nonviolent social movement is far easier than mobilizing them directly into revolutionary collective action. First, the kinds of local projects that a reformist movement would undertake involve far less risk for the community than does revolutionary collective action. Contributing one's share of the labor and materials required to construct a levee that protects the village from floods or an irrigation channel that brings water to everyone's fields does not inevitably put a person at risk of violent reprisals by the state.

Second, the benefits of such projects are tangible and immediately available, even if some portion of them are nonexcludable public benefits that even nonparticipants will enjoy. Everyone in the village will benefit from such endeavors in tangible terms, such as greater crop yields or less frequent crop losses from flooding. The benefits from revolutionary action are unknown, uncertain, and in the distant future.

Third, in a small group such as a village or a local peasant association, it is much easier to enforce sanctions against free-riding. Because the members of the village know each other, they can readily determine who among them failed to participate in the project, and they can impose sanctions on those free-riders. Knowing this, most members of the village are far more likely to reject the free-rider option and instead participate in the collective action (Popkin 1988: 21). To free-ride is to risk losing access to these assets. Thus the capacity of village institutions to detect and punish free-riding gives those institutions the capacity to mobilize village members for collective action.

Grassroots Organizations

Chapter 3 describes the developmental trends that resulted in the displacement of large numbers of peasants from the land and their marginalization in the agro-export economy. Many traditional village institutions that might have been useful for mobilizing peasants behind reformist social movements eroded with this transition to export agriculture. This was especially true in Latin America. The horizontal ties of community that bound peasants together in corporate villages in Southeast Asia were largely absent in Latin American hacienda systems. In their place was a system of vertical dependency that bound peasant cultivators to powerful *hacendados,* severely limiting their autonomy and hence their ability to organize for collective action of any sort.[27] Elsewhere the bonds of community that held together peasant villages on communal lands were destroyed when communal lands (*ejidos*) were expropriated for conversion into plantation production of export crops. Peasants were displaced from the land and relegated to the pool of landless seasonal laborers, cut off from any social networks that could be used to mobilize them in support of a reformist social movement. How, then, were populations in such circumstances mobilized for revolutionary violence?

Movement activists can establish new grassroots institutions that provide displaced peasants with the services and material benefits they used to get from landed patrons or village institutions. In effect, activists can fill the institutional void in peasants' lives that resulted from the disruption of traditional patterns of social organization, including patron-client networks. And they can do so at what amounts to a lower cost to the peasant than landed patrons typically extracted in return for subsistence guarantees. Joel Migdal (1974: 239) argues that "revolutionaries must no longer wait for the collapse of the state through an instantaneous mobilization of large numbers into violent action. Rather, by painstakingly building institutions, which are merely sets of routinized behavior patterns that cluster around certain specific functions, they can increasingly gain control over the political environment." The same argument holds for reformist social movements. Indeed more commonly it is not committed revolutionaries who painstakingly build up these grassroots institutions. Rather it is other types of activists whose initial goal is not the violent overthrow of the regime but the reconstruction of a viable community that will serve the immediate needs of its residents. In Central and South America, it was Catholic priests and lay catechists who built Christian base communities, not for the purpose of revolution but to enable the members of their parishes to cooperate in activities that would provide them with some relief from their poverty.

Grassroots organizations can be effective in overcoming collective action problems in a number of ways. First, they facilitate collective action simply by bringing together people who otherwise live in the social isolation of rural poverty. This is especially important to displaced peasants. Even when they have access to land, they usually live in isolation from fellow cultivators (at least under most cropping and land tenure patterns).[28] Landowners who rent land to sharecroppers or hire large numbers of agricultural laborers usually take steps to minimize the extent to which peasants under their control can communicate with each other. Grassroots organizations can overcome this isolation.

Second, grassroots organizations are usually small and composed exclusively of people from humble backgrounds. As such they serve as a nurturing environment for movement leaders and activists. Individuals who would have been crowded out of leadership positions in large, bureaucratic reformist parties, unions, or peasant associations can assume active leadership roles in local grassroots organizations. In the process, some of them develop the communication skills that allow them to move into leadership roles in larger organizations, including national social movements. As such, the new leaders nurtured in grassroots organizations come to serve as links between local organizations and national social movements. The national movement can recruit leaders of local organizations and count on them to mobilize their local constituents in support of the national movement.

Third, people will participate in grassroots organizations because they are rewarded with selective incentives: One has to participate in and contribute to many of the organization's projects in order to receive its benefits. For instance, one can use the services of a child care cooperative only by contributing some of one's own time to the cooperative. One can enjoy the benefits of a food cooperative only by contributing to the cooperative's ability to make bulk purchases. Thus the initial payoffs from participation are immediate and tangible.

Fourth, as with village institutions, grassroots organizations are usually small groups in which all members know each other. Olson (1965: 33–36) explicitly argues that the smaller the group is, the easier it is to identify free-riders and sanction them, even if the sanctions amount to nothing more than ostracism or shaming. In addition the smaller the group is, the more essential any one person's contribution is to the success of the organization. The members of grassroots organizations are likely to believe that their own contribution, however small, is essential to the success of the collective action. They are also more likely to believe that, if they contribute their share, they can count on others to contribute as well. In short, free-riding by any one member is less appealing because it might preclude the production of any public benefits.

UP FROM THE GRASSROOTS

Mobilizing people in villages and other grassroots organizations overcomes a major structural obstacle to explicitly political collective action. As more people experience success at grassroots collective action, it is a much smaller step for them to apply their organizational resources, leadership skills, and collective action repertoire to a more explicitly political program of pressuring the state to undertake reforms that will alleviate the structural causes of their poverty and economic insecurity. All that is required is an organization that can appeal to local grassroots organizations, frame issues so as to persuade members to support a national movement, and coordinate the activities of local units.

The leap to national political activism requires that local grassroots organizations begin cooperating with each other in a coordinated program of political action that reaches beyond the local level. Often the catalyst (and the immediate beneficiary) for such efforts is an existing opposition political party that is intent upon building a base of popular support sufficient for it to challenge the incumbent officeholders at the polls. If elections are relatively open and fair, then this is simply a matter of mobilizing voters. "Capturing" grassroots organizations is an efficient way to do this, because the members are already mobilized for some forms of collective action. All that the party has to do is persuade the leadership of grassroots organizations to get their constituents to vote for that party. If (as is more often the case) electoral rules constrain the opposition's ability to compete fairly, or if election results are manipulated by the incumbent elite to preclude victory by opposition parties, then the opposition party may also solicit grassroots support for unconventional tactics such as street demonstrations. Demonstrations may be used to articulate a reform agenda and to compel the state to allow fair competition at the polls. Whether through elections or demonstrations, grassroots organizations provide opposition parties with a ready pool of supporters who are already organized for and experienced in collective action.

Opposition parties in Third World nations traditionally have faced an uphill struggle in appealing to peasants as individuals to support their electoral challenge to powerful and entrenched incumbents. Even promises of economic reforms that would benefit marginalized peasants are rarely sufficient to bring them out to the polls because, in the absence of grassroots mobilization, peasants all too easily succumb to free-rider tendencies and refrain from voting at all. For some it is a matter of not being able to escape the psychological shackles of patron-client networks in which their lives are embedded. They vote the way their patron instructs them. Otherwise they risk losing the subsistence security that their patron provides them. Where election results are subject to manipulation and fraud by the incumbent elite, voting for reformist parties is at best an act of futility. People know that the reformers will not be allowed to take office, no matter what the true results of the vote count may be. For others, refraining from voting is a matter of fear: Voting for the opposition in an election that is far from free, open, and fair. It can be a risky act of defiance. One cannot be sure that ballot secrecy will be honored in a corrupt election system. Those who vote for the opposition might be identified and targeted for reprisals ranging from eviction from their land or dismissal from their job to "disappearance."

Examples abound of electoral fraud and manipulation in nations experiencing rural instability. In the 1972 national elections in El Salvador, the reformist National Opposition Union (UNO, consisting of the Christian Democratic Party, the social democratic National Revolutionary Movement, and the Communist National Democratic Union) appeared to have defeated the conservative incumbent National Conciliation Party (PCN) for the presidency and at least a plurality if not a majority of the seats in the legislature. However, as the counting of the votes was getting under way, the Salvadoran military suspended public announcements of the tallies and seized the ballots. They sent in a team to nullify ballots marked for UNO, mark blank ballots for PCN, and substitute PCN ballots for UNO ballots as necessary to produce a PCN victory without altering the total vote count (Stanley 1996: 89). The 1972 election signaled to the opposition that they would not be allowed to win power by legal means. Soon thereafter, opposition violence began to escalate.

Opposition parties lack the resource base and the organizational infrastructure to overcome the political inertia of marginalized peasants or the powerful influence of local patrons who would oppose any reforms that might threaten their control over peasant clients. However, once displaced peasants are mobilized by grassroots organizations, opposition parties can increase their own support base substantially by "capturing" these grassroots organizations. Instead of appealing to peasants as individual voters, the party can win blocs of votes by persuading the leaders of grassroots organizations to endorse their challenge and deliver the votes of their already mobilized constituents. This is precisely why UNO was able to challenge the incumbent oligarchy in El Salvador in 1972. By then large numbers of peasants and urban poor had been mobilized by CEBs. UNO succeeded in persuading the leaders of grassroots organizations to deliver their members' votes for UNO. The fact that it took blatant fraud to deny UNO the election victory is indicative of UNO's success at capturing grassroots organizations as a support base for their electoral challenge.

The question then becomes how will the state respond to this expansion in support for opposition parties. By capturing grassroots organizations, opposition parties significantly enhance their ability to challenge incumbents' policies and even their claims to state office. In the face of this challenge, the state has two broad options. It can undertake reforms designed to remedy the conditions that gave rise to popular grievances in the first place. This is the accommodative strategy. Alternatively the state can repress organized opposition by targeting their leaders, members, and supporters with violent reprisals. What determines which strategy a state will choose and what are the likely outcomes of each choice? This question is the subject of chapter 5.

NOTES

1. Lichbach (1995: 21) categorizes these solutions according to two dimensions: whether the actors involved do or do not discuss their situation with each other (resulting in either planned or unplanned action), and whether the entities involved in collective action are individuals or already existing groups (resulting in spontaneous or contingent solutions). Combining these two dimensions results in a four-fold categorization of solutions: (1) market-based solutions (no prior deliberation and action by individuals acting on their own), (2) contract solutions (actors do deliberate but as individuals acting on their own), (3) community solutions (no prior deliberation but action by individuals as members of pre-existing groups), and (4) hierarchy solutions (prior deliberation by individuals as members of pre-existing groups). Lichbach 1992 presents an earlier effort to catalog the solutions to the collective action problem that are found in the literature, noting the remarkable lack of consensus that has emerged from these efforts. See also Lichbach 1997 and McAdam, Tarrow, and Tilly 1997 for a debate on the rational actor versus political process or social movement approaches to collective action problems.

2. See Moore 1995: 426–34 and DeNardo 1985: 52–57 for a discussion of the various selective incentive solutions that have been offered for the rebel's dilemma. Other works that address the rebel's dilemma are Tullock 1971 and Leites and Wolf 1970, among others.

3. In the first edition of *Power in Movement,* Sidney Tarrow (1994: 221n. 14) quotes another economist, Albert Hirschman, on one irony surrounding the publication of Olson's *The Logic of Collective Action:* "Olson proclaimed the impossibility of collective action for large groups . . . at the precise moment when the Western world was about to be all but engulfed by an unprecedented wave of public movements, marches, protests, strikes and ideologies" (Hirschman 1982: 78). Indeed the Watts riot in Los Angeles occurred in the same year that *The Logic of Collective Action* was published.

4. Among the works that emphasize the influence of pre-existing social networks and social ties on participation in collective action are Hardin 1982; Oberschall 1973, 1993; Tilly 1978; Chong 1991; Taylor 1988a; McAdam 1982; and Tarrow 1998.

5. McCarthy and Zald 1973, 1977 represent the seminal works on the importance of social movement organizations. See also McCarthy 1996 for a review of works on

social movement organizations, placing them in the broader context of other types of mobilizing structures.

6. The example that follows is derived from Lichbach 1995: 4–5. Earlier treatments of the collective action as a prisoner's dilemma game are found in Hardin 1971, 1982; Sandler 1992: ch. 2; and Chong 1991: 4–7.

7. Confirming this, Mason, Weingarten, and Fett (1999) note that, of the fifty-seven civil wars and separatist conflicts listed in the Correlates of War that began and ended between 1945 and 1992, the rebels won only 28 percent of the time, whereas the government defeated the rebels in almost half of the cases.

8. Christine Pelzer White (1974: 77) describes the recurrence of this pattern in Vietnamese history:

> Land-poor peasants repeatedly revolted against the Vietnamese landed elite or rose up to expel Chinese or Mongol invaders and overthrow their landholding Vietnamese collaborators. If successful, the victorious leader would proclaim himself king and return most of the land of the supporters of the defeated regime to the peasantry as communal land, a traditional institution of peasant land tenure. However, the new king would also award large tracts of private land to his major lieutenants and members of his family, thereby forming a new landed elite and laying the basis of a new cycle of land concentration. Later, as the dynasty weakened, this elite would expand its holdings, causing a rebellion of the increasingly impoverished peasantry.

9. See Oliver and Marwell 1992 for a comparison of the value of money versus time as contributions to collective action.

10. Mark Lichbach summarizes the case:

> The benefits derived from changing unpopular policies or regimes redound to all members of the dissident group, including those who have not participated in the group's activities. The costs of participation, however, are paid only by those who participate. Some costs (e.g., wages foregone at an income-producing job) could be minimal. Other costs (e.g., jail, injury, or even death) are maximal. The level of costs depends on an unknown: the regime's response strategy. But if the individual receives the benefits regardless of whether or not he or she participates, why participate and pay *any* costs? (Lichbach 1995: 16; emphasis in original)

11. As Lichbach (1995: 18) notes, "the study of collective dissent involves the study of minorities and not the majority, exceptions and not the rule."

12. Joshua Nkomo, one of the leaders of the Zimbabwean revolution, began his career as a trade unionist and president of the National Democratic Party (NDP) before he became a leader of the Zimbabwe African People's Union (ZAPU), one of the two major guerrilla organizations in the Rhodesian civil war. Robert Mugabe, the leader of the other guerrilla organization, the Zimbabwean African National Union (ZANU), was also an active member of NDP and ZAPU before he split with Nkomo and formed his own guerrilla organization (Scarritt 1991: 246–47). Guillermo Ungo, who served as president of the Democratic Revolutionary Front (FDR) in El Salvador, had been a candidate for vice president in 1972, running with José Napoleon Duarte on the UNO ticket (National Opposition Union, a coalition of the Christian Democratic Party, the

National Revolutionary Movement, and the National Democratic Union). Indeed it is generally believed that the UNO won the 1972 election, but the Salvadoran military subverted the vote counting and denied Duarte and Ungo their offices, forcing them into exile (see Montgomery 1995: 62–64).

13. As noted earlier, the two guerrilla organizations in Zimbabwe began as political parties. The Faribundo Martí Liberation Front (FMLN), the coalition of guerrilla groups in El Salvador, was made up of at least five different guerrilla organizations that at one time had been legal opposition parties (Montgomery 1995: 103–05). Even the Shining Path movement in Peru began as a faction of the Peruvian Communist Party.

14. Goldstone (1994: 149–55) discusses the case where an already existing group, one that engages in collective action for the benefit of its members, chooses to shift strategies to revolutionary violence. He contrasts this with the case of a group that forms for the purpose of engaging in revolutionary collective action.

15. In commenting on peasant involvement in the Russian, French, and Chinese revolutions, Theda Skocpol (1979: 114) asserts that "peasants participated in these revolutions without being converted to radical visions of a desired new national society, and without becoming a nationally organized class-for-themselves. Instead they struggled for concrete goals—typically involving access to more land, or freedom from claims on their surpluses."

16. One solution to this dilemma is "leadership goods": things such as high office in the postrevolutionary regime. These are a special set of selective incentives that will be available only to the leaders of the rebel movement, if they survive. I discuss this subject in the next section of this chapter. For a more complete treatment of the subject, see Van Belle (1996).

17. As the group gets larger, the risks to the next recruit become smaller. The larger the rebel force, the less likely any one of them is to be a victim of violence. Therefore the cost (in terms of selective incentives) of recruiting the nth rebel should be less than the cost of recruiting each previous convert, all else being equal.

18. Dennis Chong (1991: 51–61) highlights the importance of reputational effects in overcoming free-rider temptations among civil rights activists in the 1960s. Michael Taylor (1988b: 84) stresses the importance of reputation in mobilizing villagers to participate in collective action.

19. Leadership benefits are a special case of what Frohlich, Oppenheimer, and Young (1971) refer to as a "revolutionary surplus" which motivates dissident entrepreneurs to take on the task of establishing a social movement organization. If political entrepreneurs are willing and able to invest in the organizational infrastructure necessary for the initiation of contentious collective action, then they may be able to extract a revolutionary surplus from their supporters, and this becomes their payoff. A revolutionary surplus exists when the contributions that leaders elicit from the supporters exceed the amount needed to provide the public goods and selective incentives they promise to their supporters. In effect, it amounts to a "profit" that the leaders can keep for themselves.

20. Donald G. McNeil, "Free Namibia Stumps the Naysayers." *New York Times,* 16 November 1997, p. 14.

21. Mobilizing structures are defined as "those collective vehicles, both formal and

informal, through which people come together and engage in collective action" (McAdam, Tarrow, and Tilly 1997: 155).

22. Tilly addresses the concept of repertoires of contention and how they change over time in Tilly 1995a,b. See also Traugott 1995a in his excellent anthology on the subject.

23. On the student movement in China, see especially Zhao 1998, Walder 1998, and Mason 1994.

24. See Snow et al. 1986 on different types of framing processes and the ways in which movement leaders bring into alignment their own values with the values of those they seek to mobilize for contentious collective action.

25. Popkin (1988, 1979) discusses the mechanisms used not only by the Vietminh but also the Cao Dai and Hoa Hao sects as well as the Catholic Church in mobilizing peasants. See also Migdal 1974.

26. Of course, as Berejikian (1992: 651) points out, the reputational cost argument—that people will participate in collective action rather than suffer the ostracism of community members—fails to explain how the others in the village came to prefer collective action over free-riding. Who pressured the first convert?

27. See Paige 1975: 40–45, Stinchcombe 1961, and Wolf and Mintz 1957 on the disadvantages hacienda peasants face in trying to organize for collective action.

28. On the isolation of smallholders and the resulting difficulty in organizing them for collective action, see Paige 1975: 45–48.

Chapter Five

The Response of the State: Reform or Repression?

Faced with a growing (but as yet peaceful) opposition social movement, the state can choose between two alternative strategies to defuse the challenge. It can initiate reforms aimed at relieving the immediate economic distress of displaced peasants and urban poor and ameliorating the structural sources of the poverty that gave rise to popular grievances in the first place. Alternatively the state may choose to repress opposition organizations and intimidate their supporters into withdrawing their support from the movement.

In most cases, states pursue some mix of reform and repression. Governments in many Third World nations have tried to recapture popular support by undertaking bold initiatives such as land reform, public works programs that provide jobs for the unemployed, or food import programs that increase the supply and reduce the price of subsistence goods. Reform programs such as these are intended to restore some measure of economic security to the urban and rural poor, who constitute the support base for most reformist social movements. In this manner, reformers in the state hope to pre-empt popular support for opposition movements generally and for revolutionary insurgencies specifically. In Peru, when peasant uprisings and land invasions in the early 1960s coalesced into an organized insurgency, the army was sent in to quell the rebellion. In 1968 some of the same officers who had fought in the counterinsurgency campaign staged a coup, and the junta they subsequently installed immediately embarked upon a sweeping land reform program designed to pre-empt revolution by relieving peasant economic distress.[1] Similarly in El Salvador in 1979 a military coup brought to power a junta that initiated a major land reform program for the purpose of pre-empting popular support for a growing revolutionary insurgency.[2] In the Philippines during the 1950s, President Ramon Magsaysay combined a land reform program with the promise of amnesty to Huk guerrillas in an effort to lure them away from the leadership of the Huk rebellion (Kerkvliet 1977: 238–42). In these and other cases, land reform was initiated not for economic reasons but for the political purpose of restoring popular support for the incumbent regime by giving people a stake in the survival of the current state.

The alternative to the reformist response is for the state to undertake violent repression of any organized opposition. Dissident leaders in any number of Third World nations have been imprisoned, tortured, exiled, or "disappeared" by the state in an effort to suppress nonviolent social movements. In El Salvador 8,000 civilian noncombatants were victims of death squad violence in 1980 alone, and the number rose to over 13,000 in 1981 (Simon and Stephens 1982). Over the course of Guatemala's protracted civil war, over 35,000 civilians were killed by the state or its paramilitary surrogates (Ball, Kobrak, and Spirer 1999: 8). Repression may deter people from acting on their grievances. They might come to fear that they too will become targets of state repression. Or they might withdraw their support for a reformist social movement out of concern that the movement's prospects for success will be severely disrupted by the state's program of repression. Under these circumstances, any further contributions to the opposition movement would be an exercise in futility. However, the grievances that gave rise to their support for the movement in the first place remain unresolved by repression.

This leads us to the central question of this chapter: If repression does nothing to restore popular support for the state—and in some circumstances can even increase support for the opposition—why would a state, itself composed of supposedly rational individuals, pursue a policy of escalating repression? As I suggested in the previous chapter, it is the state's response to nonviolent opposition challenges—movements that seek reform, not revolution; movements that employ nonviolent tactics, not revolutionary violence—that determines whether those social movements will adopt the goals and strategy of revolution. Thus the logically prior question might be whether certain types of regimes are more or less likely to respond to opposition movements with repression rather than reform and, if so, why? What aspects of the institutional structure, intra-elite politics, and accompanying patterns of state-society relations make some states more likely to respond to opposition challenges with repressive violence?.

A number of scholars have speculated on whether certain types of regimes are more likely to generate revolutionary opposition and, within this category, whether certain subtypes are more likely to be overthrown by revolutionary movements. Thus, Goodwin and Skocpol (1989) argue that "closed authoritarian" regimes are more likely to generate organized revolutionary challenges and that, among closed authoritarian regimes, those of the neopatrimonial or "sultanistic" variety are more likely to be overthrown by such movements (see also

Goodwin 1997). Whatever state characteristics might be associated with revolutionary movements, those Third World states that have faced revolutionary challenges share what Barry Buzan (1983), Joel Migdal (1988), Mohammed Ayoob (1992, 1995), and Brian Job (1992) have termed the "weak state syndrome." This condition makes revolution more likely in two ways. First, when weak states are confronted with an opposition social movement, even a nonviolent one, their institutional weakness makes them more likely to experience the sorts of intra-elite conflicts and institutional failures that alter the political opportunity structure facing dissident elites in such a way as to embolden them. When an opposition challenge instigates factional conflicts within the state, dissidents may take the resulting failure of the state to respond quickly and decisively as an opportunity for them to escalate their challenge to revolutionary proportions, in hopes of toppling the regime. Second, the weak state syndrome imposes constraints on the state's capacity to respond with effective reforms that would accommodate the demands of the opposition and thereby restore some measure of popular legitimacy to the state. The very conditions of dependent development that characterize these nations' development (discussed in chapter 3) often leave the state without the institutional machinery, economic resources, or political will to address opposition challenges through more accommodative programs of reform. Hence the almost reflexive response of the state to any reformist social movement is to increase the level of repressive violence directed against opposition leaders and their actual, suspected, or potential supporters. Escalating repression is perpetrated not necessarily because it has a high probability of success but because the weakness of the state precludes its resort to less violent alternatives.

THE STATE AND SOCIAL REVOLUTIONS

To understand why certain types of states are more susceptible to revolutionary challenge than others, we must first spell out a classification scheme for Third World states. Juan Linz (1975; see also Linz and Stepan 1996: ch. 3, 4) has developed a systematic categorization of nondemocratic regimes. Included among the categories are totalitarian, post-totalitarian, corporatist, bureaucratic authoritarian, and neopatrimonial or sultanistic regimes.[3] Are there characteristics of these regime types that make one or another type more or less susceptible to revolutionary challenges?

Goodwin (1997: 16–21) delineates five state practices or characteristics that make certain types of regimes especially susceptible to revolutionary challenges. First, state sponsorship or protection of unpopular economic and social arrangements serves to make the state itself the source of blame for grievances in the countryside. Inequitable land tenure arrangements and oppressive labor conditions are hardly rare in Third World nations. However, when those arrangements are seen as enjoying the sponsorship or protection of the state, then the state—not the landed elite or the factory owner—becomes the focus of popular grievances. When strikes and demonstrations are routinely crushed by the state, when the state imposes restrictions on the rights of peasants and workers to organize and to engage in dissident activities targeted on what they perceive to be unjustly exploitative economic elites, then the state itself becomes a target of popular opposition. Land invasions or strikes that might have targeted landlords or factory owners are seen as futile so long as the state announces itself as the guarantor of those elites. Thus "the economic grievances of groups excluded from the political system tend to be quickly politicized." The state itself becomes "a highly visible focus of opposition and a common enemy for groups and classes that may be nursing different sorts of economic and political grievances" (Goodwin and Skocpol 1989: 496).

Second, excluding newly mobilized groups from state power or state resources may leave them with few alternatives beyond a direct challenge to the state's authority. Exclusionary regimes are intolerant of grassroots mobilization of any sort. They respond with repression to any hint of a challenge to their power, policies, or prerogatives. "They readily turn to vicious repression when faced with demand for even the most moderate political or economic adjustments" (Goodwin and Skocpol 1989: 496). Even moderate reformers are confronted with the choice of abandoning their cause or resorting to revolutionary violence. In this manner, exclusionary regimes tend to radicalize moderate or reformist politicians. Reformists who eschew violence run the risk of becoming marginalized, because their natural constituency comes to see them as hopelessly ineffectual. By default, then, the appeals of revolutionary dissidents begin to attract more popular support (Goodwin 1997: 18).

Third, indiscriminate but not overwhelming state violence against mobilized groups and opposition political figures tends to radicalize grassroots supporters of dissident leaders. Just as leaders are radicalized by repression targeted against them, so their grassroots supporters are radicalized when repression extends beyond dissident elites to include the anonymous rank-and-file supporters of opposition social movements (Mason and Krane 1989). The indiscriminate use of repression leads to "the diffusion of the idea that the state needs to be violently 'smashed' and radically reorganized" (Goodwin 1997: 19).

Fourth, the "weak policing practices and infrastructural power" of exclusionary regimes means that radicalized groups are able to establish security zones within the territory of the state from which they can sustain an armed challenge to the state (Goodwin 1997: 19). Eric Wolf (1969: 290) highlights the importance of "tactical leverage" in building a revolutionary movement. If the policing powers of the state are geographically uneven, rebels can establish their own base of operations in remote regions that are relatively secure from state repression. From that base, they can attempt to outbid the state for the support of the population by offering them benefits that the exclusionary state is either unwilling or unable to offer. Secure base areas also allow rebels to offer peasants protection from the repressive arm of the state. Among authoritarian regime types, neopatrimonial states tend to be especially ineffective at policing their territory, because the military itself is staffed with personnel who are evaluated not on the basis of their performance but on the basis of their loyalty to the dictator. Corruption and venality are endemic to neopatrimonial military establishments, and divisions within the officer corps not only exist but are often encouraged by the dictator in order to prevent a unified military from staging a coup (Chehabi and Linz 1998b). Corruption and inefficiency are tolerated so long as the military demonstrates its loyalty to the dictator. But the result is a "deprofessionalization" of the military that limits its capacity to extend its authority throughout the territory and effectively preserve the stability of the state.

Fifth, the corrupt and arbitrary rule of sultanistic or neopatrimonial regimes tends to alienate, weaken, or divide elite groups and external supporters who normally would share the state's interest in repressing opposition challenges. For this reason, exclusionary regimes often cannot easily defeat revolutionary movements once they come into existence because the coalition of economic elites and military leaders who support the regime under normal circumstances is likely to disintegrate in times of crisis. A turning point for the Somoza regime in Nicaragua was when Anastasio Somoza assumed control of the national reconstruction committee established in the wake of the devastating earthquake of 1972. From this position he profiteered shamelessly at the expense of not only the victims of the quake but his middle-class allies as well. The resulting defection of a significant portion of the middle class eventually hastened the collapse of his regime (Booth 1985: 88). Thus patrimonial regimes are especially susceptible to sudden collapse due to defections by the military or the middle class at critical junctures in a struggle with an organized opposition. Their susceptibility to divisions within the elite also serves to alter the political opportunity structure available to revolutionary leaders. Signs of division within the ruling coalition are readily apparent, and their appearance emboldens the opposition to escalate its level of violence. Such divisions can encourage latent supporters of the rebels to jump on the opposition bandwagon because the associated risks are diminished by the appearance of defections among the coalition of elites that controls the state.

REGIME TYPES AND REVOLUTION

If these characteristics make a state more or less susceptible to revolutionary challenge, can we say that certain types of regimes—from among those categories delineated by Linz—are more likely to generate revolutionary challenges? And among those states, are certain types more likely to be overthrown by revolution, whereas others are more likely to weather the revolutionary storm? First, the emerging consensus is that democracies are relatively immune from revolution. As Goodwin and Skocpol (1989: 495) observe, "the ballot box . . . has proven to be the coffin of revolutionary movements." This argument has found empirical support in tests of the domestic version of the "democratic peace" proposition: Just as democracies rarely if ever go to war with other democracies, so they are relatively immune to civil war as well. The democratic peace proposition holds that democratic norms and institutions allow nonviolent forms of protest, facilitate the peaceful resolution of conflict through bargaining, and constrain leaders from resorting to force for fear of the electoral repercussions. Thus the grievances that might fuel revolution in a nondemocracy can be addressed through nonviolent means in a democratic state because the leaders are subject to the discipline of the ballot box.

Totalitarian and Post-Totalitarian Regimes

Among the nondemocratic types of Third World states, totalitarian and post-totalitarian states are viewed as the least susceptible to revolutionary challenge. Totalitarian states (such as Cuba, Vietnam, or the Stalin-era Soviet Union) are guided by an all-encompassing, unified, and thoroughly articulated utopian ideology. That ideology is used to justify the state's monopolistic control over the economy and the complete elimination of all autonomous social organizations. The entire society and the economy are completely etatized. The state strictly enforces its hegemony through its monopoly of coercive resources, which it uses to monitor and pre-emptively eliminate dissidents before they can build an opposition social movement. Such regimes are rarely faced with revolutionary challenges because they do not tolerate any form of autonomous social organization that could evolve into an opposition movement. Thus the Stalin-era Soviet Union, Mao-era China, and Castro's Cuba effectively pre-empted revolutionary challenges from ever emerging.

Post-totalitarian states (such as the Brezhnev-era Soviet Union) evolve from totalitarian origins and still manifest the institutional characteristics of the totalitarian state. However, economic growth and development necessitate the state's increasing reliance on a technocratic elite, with the result being a waning of the intensity and pervasiveness of ideological commitment on the part of state officialdom and on the part of an increasingly diverse society. Still, the state's overwhelming coercive capacity and its intolerance of autonomous social organizations make such states relatively immune to revolutionary challenges. Brezhnev suppressed those who engaged in overt dissent and allowed no dissident organizations. While mass demonstrations did occur in China in 1976, 1978, 1986, and 1989, Deng Xiaoping never allowed them to coalesce into any permanent dissident organization. When in 1989 dissidents exceeded the boundaries of what had been tolerated in earlier demonstrations, he crushed the movement and jailed or exiled its surviving leaders.

Corporatist Regimes

For very different reasons, Goodwin and Skocpol argue that "'inclusionary' authoritarian regimes—including fascist and state-socialist regimes, as well as the single-party corporatist regimes found in some nations of Africa and Asia—have so far been immune from revolutionary transformations" (1989: 495). Corporatist states manage to avoid revolution by engaging in the preemptive mobilization of workers and peasants through state-sponsored labor unions and peasant associations. The stability of the corporatist state is preserved by a system of bargaining between the state and the representatives of those groups. The state confers benefit flows upon recognized groups that guarantee their members a measure of economic security. In return, those groups are expected to accede to the state's monopoly on policy making and leadership selection. In effect, corporatism amounts to an office-based form of patron-client network whereby the state provides subsistence guarantees in return for popular support (see Malloy 1977). As an example, Mexico managed to avoid serious revolutionary challenges during the 1970s and 1980s, when most of the rest of Central America was experiencing protracted revolutionary insurgencies. Certainly Mexico's immunity from revolutionary challenge is not a function of its military being more harshly and thoroughly repressive than its Central American counterparts. On the contrary, the Mexican military is usually depicted as the rare case of a Latin American military that is subordinate to civilian rule (see, for instance, Ronfeldt 1986). Instead the PRI (Partido Revolucionario Institucional, the dominant party in Mexican politics since 1929) preserved the domestic peace—that is, avoided both military coups and revolution in the countryside—through a corporatist system of benefit flows to key popular sectors, including urban workers, peasants, civil servants, intellectuals, and the business community.[5]

What types of regimes, then, are most susceptible to revolutionary challenge? Huntington (1968: 275) argues that "the great revolutions of history have taken place either in highly centralized traditional monarchies (such as France, Russia, and imperial China) or in narrowly based military dictatorships (Mexico, Bolivia, Cuba)." When states fail to incorporate newly mobilized groups into the political system, they often face revolutionary challenges from those groups. It is the unwillingness or inability of the state to develop institutions capable of channeling the demands of newly mobilized groups into nonviolent forms of participation that leaves the state vulnerable to revolution. Goodwin and Skocpol are more specific, noting that "exclusionary" authoritarian regimes, especially of the neopatrimonial and sultanistic variety, are especially susceptible to the emergence of broad revolutionary coalitions (Goodwin and Skocpol 1989: 496–500). Wickham-Crowley (1992: 158–60) concurs to an extent in depicting "patrimonial praetorian" regimes, or "mafiacracies," as the most vulnerable to revolutionary challenge. Examples of these regimes include those of the Somoza dynasty in Nicaragua, Mobutu Sese Seku in Zaire, Idi Amin in Uganda, the Shah of Iran, Manuel Noriega in Panama, Jean-Claude Duvalier in Haiti, Rafael Trujillo in the Dominican Republic, Fulgencio Batista in Cuba, and Ferdinand Marcos in the Philippines.[6]

Neopatrimonial and Sultanistic Regimes

Sultanistic or neopatrimonial regimes are characterized by a personalist dictatorship, in which the chief executive maintains authority through a network of loyalists tied to him through patronage. His exercise of authority is unrestrained by either the rule of law or ideological principles.[7] The distinction between the private interests of the ruler and the public interests of the state or nation are purposely blurred. The institutions of the state are staffed by people chosen on the basis not of their competence or qualifications but of their loyalty to the dictator. And their loyalty is based not on any unique personal mission or charismatic qualities that attract them to the leader but on a mixture of fear and greed, lubricated by a steady flow of patronage benefits and vivid memories of the fate of those who incur the wrath of the leader (Chehabi and Linz 1998b: 7; see also Bratton and Van de Walle 1994: 458). The ruler tolerates no autonomous mobilization of groups in society, nor does he grant institutional autonomy to agencies of the government (such as the military) or to sectors of the nation's economic elite (Goodwin 1997: 498). Even routine bureaucratic administration in government and market transactions in the private economy are subject to arbitrary intervention and subversion by the leader, with no requirement for him to justify his actions to those affected.

As such, sultanistic regimes are more likely to generate opposition among the military and the economic elite, "from landlords, businessmen, clerics, and professionals, who resent [the dictator's] monopolization of key sectors of the economy, [his] heavy-handed control of the flow of ideas and information in schools and the press, [his] subservience to foreign powers, and the general climate of corruption" (Chehabi and Linz 1998c: 41).

These conditions make sultanistic or neopatrimonial regimes especially susceptible to sudden defections by the military and broad coalitions of the middle class. Many times opposition movements are led by former loyalists to the dictator who have fallen out of his favor (Bratton and Van de Walle, 1992, 1994, 1997). They can often find allies among alienated sectors of the middle class, who have the resources to support an opposition movement and have no reason to oppose a revolutionary movement that, if nothing else, would free them from the arbitrary interventions of the dictator. Moreover, dictators eventually die, and the tenuous personal loyalty that preserved the regime does not readily pass on to their heirs. Often the coterie of loyalists who did the dictator's bidding, administered the state, and preserved him in power begins plotting and maneuvering among themselves in the struggle over succession. The death of the dictator and any signs of conflict over succession signal the weakening of the state, which can encourage dissidents to seize the opportunity to mount a challenge to the regime.

However, there is nothing inevitable about revolution in neopatrimonial regimes, nor is their collapse in the face of an armed revolutionary challenge inevitable. Richard Snyder (1992) points out that, while regimes in Nicaragua, Iran, and Cuba were overthrown by revolutionary movements, the Philippines experienced a transition to civilian rule, while Haiti and Paraguay experienced transitions to military rule. For Snyder the key variables determining the fate of such regimes are the institutional autonomy of the military, the strength and autonomy of domestic economic elites, and the organizational strength of revolutionaries. Where the military retains a substantial degree of autonomy from the dictator, that body can pre-empt revolution by removing the dictator in a coup and either assuming control themselves (as in Paraguay) or passing power to a new civilian government (as in the Philippines). When the dictator's corruption and authoritarian monopoly of power serve to exclude the middle class and other economic elites from political power and patronage, they can be expected to join a multiclass coalition in opposition to the dictator. If, at the same time, the military is so thoroughly co-opted by the dictator that it is incapable of autonomous action against his excesses, the middle-class coalition may turn to the revolutionaries as their only allies in an effort to remove the dictator. This was the fate of the Somoza regime in Nicaragua (Snyder 1992: 383, 386–87; see also Booth 1985).

On the other hand, neopatrimonial regimes do not inevitably generate revolutionary movements with the organizational capacity to mobilize popular
support behind their cause. The very repressiveness of the regime can prevent
the emergence of an effective opposition movement. Alternatively the dictator's patronage machine can be used to co-opt moderate opposition leaders,
so that they do not become so alienated that they opt for revolutionary action
as the only alternative. The Mobutu regime in Zaire was able to remain in
power for so long in part because Mobutu either co-opted opposition leaders
or played them off against each other along regional or ethnic lines so that no
unified opposition movement was able to develop until the 1990s. If a revolutionary opposition does arise, it may be incapable of defeating the regime's
military in the battlefield, especially if the military enjoys enough institutional
autonomy that its leaders can insulate the armed forces from the debilitating
effects of corruption and the dictator's use of patronage to staff the military
leadership. Indeed, if the military enjoys sufficient autonomy and has maintained a certain degree of professionalism, then when faced with a revolutionary challenge it may form a coalition with disaffected segments of the
middle class to remove the dictator and suppress the revolutionary movement. Snyder (1992: 383) suggests that this dynamic characterized the "people
power" victory over the Marcos regime in the Philippines, a victory that pre-
empted revolutionary victory by the revolutionary New People's Army.
    In summary Snyder notes that,

> neopatrimonial regimes which effectively co-opt elites through institutionalized
> patronage networks may inhibit the growth of both radical and moderate oppo-
> sition.... On the other hand, neopatrimonial regimes which exclude elites from
> patronage ... tend to encourage the growth of opposition.... Revolution is the
> likely outcome ... where a coherent revolutionary movement challenges the dic-
> tator and where the armed forces lack the autonomy to act against him. Military
> dictatorship is the probable outcome in cases ... where no coherent revolution-
> ary or moderate oppositions emerge ... and where the armed forces have the au-
> tonomy to turn against the dictator.... Civilian rule is the likely outcome in cases
> ... where a powerful moderate civilian opposition and a revolt by key segments
> of the military can dislodge the dictator and enable the civilian opposition to
> take control without opening the way for a seizure of power by revolutionaries.
> (384)

Thus the characteristics of the state and the patterns of state-society relations do affect the likelihood that the state will be confronted with a revolutionary challenge. Those same factors affect whether the state will or will not
prevail over its revolutionary challenger. In general, revolutions are more likely
among those states that suffer from the weak state syndrome, whereby some

sector of society does not accept the legitimacy of the state and the state lacks the institutional capacity and political will to respond to grassroots challenges with reforms that would restore the state's legitimacy in the eyes of alienated sectors of society. The weak state does not have the institutional capacity to prevent dissident social mobilization. When faced with such a challenge, it is compelled by its institutional weakness to respond with repressive violence.

THE STATE FORMATION PROCESS

How, then, do we account for the pervasiveness of weak states in the Third World? Why have more states not evolved with the institutional capacity to build a base of popular legitimacy and respond to dissident challenges with reformist measures that preserve the state's legitimacy and preclude the need for revolutionary violence? The weak state syndrome is a direct result of the way in which the state formation process transpired in the Third World. It differed radically from the process by which the strong states of Europe and North America evolved over the course of the early modern era. It was indelibly influenced by the Third World's colonial legacy.

Both Skocpol and Goldstone point to the importance of unprecedented challenges to the state emanating from the international environment as catalysts for the internal conflicts that eventually escalated into revolution. In the case of France and Russia, it was the challenge posed by competition among industrializing states on the European continent. In the case of China, it was the threat of European imperialism, which brought on the collapse of the imperial system, and the Japanese invasion, which undermined the legitimacy of the Nationalist (Kuomintang) regime.

Challenges emanating from the international arena have also rendered Third World states susceptible to revolutionary unrest. These challenges, however, are of a different order from those described by Goldstone and Skocpol. For the Third World, the legacy of their colonial experience and their dependent position in the global economic system (discussed in chapter 3) contributed to the institutional weakness of the state and the underdevelopment (or distorted development) of the economy. These conditions not only fueled opposition challenges but constrained the ability of the state to respond to those challenges with reform rather than repression.

The state formation process in the Third World was fundamentally different from the process by which the modern nation state came into existence in Europe. European state formation was a prolonged and bloody enterprise, lasting several centuries, marked by territorial wars between emerging expansionist states and internal conflicts aimed at subduing local authorities who resisted the central state's efforts toward internal hegemony. The outcome of this process was the modern European nation state system, populated by a relatively small number of strong states with secure borders and a monopoly of power and force within those borders. By contrast, the territories of Asia, Africa, and Latin America were colonial appendages to European powers, and state formation in the Third World was a direct outgrowth of the dismantling of those colonial empires.

> The original purposes of colonialism . . . never included state-making. . . . Imperialism was driven by a variety of purposes: trade, slavery, exploitation of resources, "civilizing" the barbarians, religious conversion to Christianity, ending the Arab slave trade, . . . securing strategic territories, and emulation: if the British were expanding in Africa, the Germans had to do the same. . . . The colonial leaders, encompassing the military, government officials, colonial societies, political parties, and the churches, never assumed that some day the subjugated peoples should or could create a state form of political organization. (Holsti 1996: 61–62)

Mohammed Ayoob (1995: 30) describes state formation in early modern Europe as occurring in three phases:

> (1) the establishment of a centralized "absolutist" state at the expense of feudal order that had begun to lose much of its economic and political utility; (2) the merging of the subject population of the centralized monarchy into a people with a common history, legal system, language, and religion; . . . (3) the gradual extension of representative institutions (dictated by the need to co-opt into the power structure new and powerful social forces that emerged as a result of the industrial revolution).

The first two stages were accomplished largely by force. The first phase, beginning around the middle of the seventeenth century, was marked by frequent and prolonged wars among European powers over territory and national survival. Indeed territorial issues, including the very survival of the involved states as sovereign territorial entities, were the dominant causes of well over half the wars that occurred in Europe between 1648 and 1989.[8]

The outcome of the first stage was a drastic reduction in the number of sovereign entities on the European continent and, among those that survived the process, the creation of a strong central state with the institutional capacity to provide for the nation's international security and domestic stability as well as its economic development. The modern nation state and the nation state system emerged from these wars as a consequence of the territorial absorption of smaller protostates by emerging strong states. Charles Tilly (1990: 45–46) notes that, in the year 1500, a minimum of 80 and a maximum of 500 autonomous political entities dotted the European landscape. This collection included a hodgepodge of tributary empires, free cities, ecclesiastical proto-states, dukedoms, hereditary kingdoms, and even Arab tribal organizations in parts of Spain. Over the next four centuries, wars of territorial conquest and a few deliberate federations reduced the number to somewhere between 20 and 100 states, depending on how one counts the papal states, the members of the German Federation, the autonomous segments of Switzerland, and a few other entities. By the end of World War I, the roster included only about 25 states. Kal Holsti (1996: 42) adds that the range of state types had also been reduced to include only two forms: the modern territorial nation state and the dynastic multinational empire. Within two decades all the latter had collapsed, leaving the modern nation state as the sole type of sovereign political entity making up the core of the major power system.

Strong centralized states developed because European states were faced with the imperative of fighting wars or being absorbed by ambitious neighbors. A monarch's ability to wage war depended on his ability to raise enough conscripts and enough revenues to sustain the war effort. This required a state apparatus that could overcome any efforts by local elites, feudal or otherwise, to resist the state's extractive claims. Local and regional elites had to be subordinated to the will of the monarch. Crucial to this task was the central state's exclusive command over the use of force. Concentrating military force in the hands of the central state thus became a crucial step in the creation of the modern nation state (Tilly 1985: 172–75; 1990).

The outcome of the second phase was the creation of a "nation," in the sense of a people with a shared sense of national identity. Once rulers had established a centralized state at the expense of the feudal order, they used the machinery of the strong state to effect the coercive assimilation of the people within its boundaries into a nation marked by a common language, culture, religion, and history. Ayoob (1995: 73) notes that this was not an enterprise conducted by liberals or advocates of the welfare state. Forging a nation involved the application of force by the state, from the forced assimilation of populations absorbed as a result of territorial conquest to the mobilization of the masses for war in the name of national preservation and national honor. Linguistic minorities were compelled to adopt the national language. Religious minorities were compelled to adopt the state-sanctioned religion. Dissidents of all varieties were repressed or expelled. Coercion was supplemented with persuasion as well. Political leaders manipulated national symbols and promulgated new doctrines of nationalism to enlist grassroots support and loyalty to the new state (Holsti 1996: 50).

Only after establishing a coherent sense of nationhood was the state compelled to extend representative institutions and participatory rights to ever larger segments of the subject population. This it did only gradually and only in response to pressures generated by newly emerging social groups who could demonstrate to state elites that their support was essential to the continued growth and prosperity of the nation. As Stein Rokkan (1975: 598; quoted in Ayoob 1995: 30) notes, "Western nation-states were given a chance to solve some of the worst problems of state-building before they had to face the ordeals of mass politics."

The European states that survived this Darwinian process were the ones that overcame these challenges. However, they had centuries to complete the process. By contrast, state formation in much of the Third World was telescoped into decades or even years. While pursuing the task of state-building, European regimes did not have to contend with the intrusion of a highly developed, highly integrated global economic and political community dominated by strong states with the military capacity to project force far beyond their borders and the economic capacity to influence the developmental trajectory of Third World economies. The Third World did.

STATE FORMATION PROCESS IN THE THIRD WORLD

The state formation process in the Third World—in the nations susceptible to revolutions in the countryside—began from a radically different starting point (decolonization), followed a radically different developmental trajectory, and was constrained by international and domestic forces that were not present when Europe was undergoing its state formation process. Instead, the reality facing Third World leaders is that the intrusive pressures of the contemporary international system compelled them to telescope the state formation process into the shortest time possible. Otherwise they risked having their nation marginalized in the global economy, subordinated in the global political community, and decimated in the global strategic environment.

Whereas the state formation process in Europe was predominantly a matter of the internal consolidation of power in response to external threats, state formation in the Third World was fundamentally conditioned by external actors—namely the European colonial powers—pursuing their interests, not the internal politics of the nation itself. In addition, the nascent postcolonial state was conditioned by internal challenges to the legitimacy of the state, not external challenges to the sovereignty of the nation. Internal challenges could take the form of ethnic, regional, or religious minorities seeking secession, power-sharing, or greater autonomy within the newly independent nation, or they could take the form of class-based revolutionary challenges by peasant cultivators and landless laborers seeking some restoration of subsistence security.

State formation in the Third World was distorted and retarded by the colonial experience in at least four ways. First, colonialism left them with a set of boundaries that in many cases (especially in Africa) were artificial. National boundaries often had little correspondence to the natural geographic groupings of peoples. Second, colonialism left them with economies that were inextricably tied to the global economy as producers of raw commodities, a status that denied the state and the nation the resources necessary to foster the level of economic growth and development that, over the long term, could have allowed the postcolonial state to build a base of popular support. Third, colonialism left them with a set of political institutions that were ill-suited to the arduous tasks of state formation and nation building. Finally, the colonial experience left them as new members of an international community that bestowed sovereignty on the state—whatever state there might be—at the expense of the self-determination of its people. In effect, the international community guaranteed the territorial integrity of the postcolonial nation state, even when that territorial configuration confronted the state with separatist or irredentist challenges that the new state was incapable of resolving by either peaceful or violent means.

Boundaries

Most Third World nation states owe their territorial boundaries to colonialism, not to any process grounded in internal development or external expansion, as was the case with European nation states. In Africa especially, European powers drew colonial boundaries guided primarily by the goal of avoiding conflicts among themselves over territory.[9] Colonial boundaries were drawn with no concern for the geographical distribution of indigenous peoples. As a consequence the populations that were subsumed within the territorial boundaries of each African colony had no pre-existing identity as a recognized community prior to the colonial era.

The newly independent nation states of the Third World came into existence simply by the colonial powers granting independence to their colonies. In so doing, the colonial powers bequeathed to the newly created postcolonial state a set of territorial boundaries that in many cases enclosed a number of distinct and sometimes hostile ethnic, religious, and communal groups. In other cases the formal borders of the newly independent nation state divided previously homogeneous ethnic communities between two or more states. Immediately upon gaining independence the new states found themselves confronted with secessionist or irredentist challenges or both (Ayoob 1995: 34–35). Ethiopia, for instance, was faced with secessionist movements in Eritrea and Tigre and became embroiled in an irredentist war with Somalia over the Ogaden region. As Robert Jackson (1987: 525) puts it, "The political map of Africa is devoid by and large of indigenous determination in its origins. All but a very few traditional political systems were subordinated or submerged by the colonialists. Decolonization rarely resulted in their elevation."

The legacy of colonial boundaries was that the new states presided over no single unified "nation," in the sense of a people with a shared culture, language, history, or any sense of shared identity.[10] Instead the new nations consisted of a mosaic of "nations" (Buzan 1991: 98), divided by considerations of region, language, ethnicity, religion, and social and economic institutions.

"For many colonies, this was not a case of a reasonably homogeneous historic, ethnic, language, and/or religious group claiming an upgrade of status from a 'people' into a state, as happened in Europe in 1919. It was, rather, the literal creation of a nation out of dozens, and sometimes more, of 'peoples' not unified sentimentally with anything resembling the early twentieth century European nationalism" (Holsti 1996: 70). If there was to be a sense of nationalism uniting the citizens under a common national identity, it would have to be created.

The nation building process—creating a shared national identity from the mosaic of subnational identities within the boundaries of the state—was accomplished in Europe by forced assimilation carried out by a strong state over the course of several generations. The resulting European ideal of modern nationalism was adopted by indigenous leaders of anticolonial movements as a justification for their independence movements. Once independence was achieved, those same leaders (now the newly empowered heads of state) continued to use the principle of nationalism to justify their efforts to consolidate and centralize power within the new state and to extend the authority of the central state throughout the territorial domain of the nation. Nationalist leaders did not challenge the existence of the postcolonial state or the boundaries it inherited from the colonial power. What was at issue for them was simply who would control the state (Smith 1983: 50; cited in Holsti 1996: 70). Nationalist leaders believed that they, like their European counterparts before them, could forge nations simply by gaining mastery over the machinery of the new state and applying it in the task of creating a new national identity. However, another component of the colonial legacy was that the postcolonial state lacked the institutional capacity and the economic resources necessary to carry out this project. Moreover, given the intrusive pressures of the Cold War international system, the new leaders did not have the luxury of time to complete the multigenerational task of forging a new sense of national identity.

State Capacity

The tendency of colonial powers to employ indirect rule and divide-and-rule strategies to control the population in their colonies reinforced powerful centrifugal tendencies within those societies (Migdal 1988). These pressures made it even more difficult for the postcolonial regime to consolidate power in a strong and effective central state. Through coercion and co-optation, colonial powers employed existing networks of local authorities (including patron-client networks, tribal organizations, village institutions) to transform local production so it served colonial power's economic interests. Rather than colonize their African and Asian holdings with a large contingent of British citizens, the British government preferred to leave in place indigenous local elites and simply co-opt or coerce them into serving as agents of British rule. Through this means, the British colonial state established a network of in-digenous intermediaries "who combined the useful authority derived from some customary title to office with the literate skills and exposure to basic ad-ministrative training that would make them serviceable auxiliaries of the would-be Weberian state" (Young 1994: 150). This strategy was especially suc-cessful in Uganda and northern Nigeria, where the British found strong struc-tures of social control already in place and willing collaborators among those in command of those structures (Young 1988: 42–43).

For the system of indirect rule to serve the interests of the colonial power, the control that local authorities exercised over the population and over pro-duction within their domain had to be strengthened. In reinforcing the au-thority of local strongmen at the expense of the central state, however, the colonial powers reversed the conventional (European) process of state build-ing, whereby local authorities would have been supplanted by or subordinated to the central state (Ayoob 1995: 35–36). The crucial first step in European state formation had been the subjugation of traditional authorities such as lo-cal strongmen. By empowering their counterparts in colonial territories, the colonial powers reinforced the local population's dependence on these strong-men for their survival. As a consequence, their primary loyalties were to the strongmen, not to the central state. Thus indirect rule set in motion and rein-forced centrifugal tendencies that would impede the postcolonial state's ef-forts to build a strong central authority and a sense of national identity. It re-inforced subnational identities that revolutionary movements could play upon in their efforts to mobilize support for revolution (Migdal 1988).

Upon granting independence to their colonies, imperial powers typically took no special steps to endow the newly formed state with the resources or institutional capacity necessary to subdue the networks of local authorities who had served as the de facto collection agents, enforcers, and production supervisors for the colonial administration. Nor was the postcolonial state en-dowed with the capacity for such conventional development tasks as infra-structure development and public works construction. Typically the one asset with which the postcolonial state was well endowed was coercive capacity. Ei-ther the colonial powers bequeathed to their indigenous successors a standing army and police force staffed and trained to subdue the indigenous population, or the new state itself was constituted from a national liberation movement whose success was based upon force of arms. Under colonial rule the coercive machinery had been used not to subdue local strongmen but to support them in their maintenance of order at the local level. In this sense, the basis for a protection racket between local authorities and the military was already in place: As long as the military preserved the dominance of local authorities over the local economy, those strongmen cared little about how the military and its civilian allies in the capital used the central state to enrich themselves.

Economic Underdevelopment

The burdens of the colonial legacy also delayed, retarded, or distorted the transformation of postcolonial economies from agro-export systems to diversified, industrialized, modern economies. Chapter 3 argued that colonial rule and the demands generated by Europe's industrial revolution disrupted stable and relatively self-sufficient agricultural economies by converting them from the production of food crops for local consumption to cash crops for export. Besides disrupting the lives of peasant cultivators, this transformation also retarded the growth and development of the nation's economy and thereby denied the postcolonial state the resource base needed to fulfill the tasks of statebuilding and nation-building. Had the new state been able to offer citizens the benefits of economic growth and development, it could have given them a positive reason to support and identify with the new state. Lacking that capacity, the postcolonial state had only its coercive capacity to induce compliance with its nation-building agenda.

The shift to export crops during the colonial era drained the colonial economy of any economic surplus it was capable of generating. The profits generated by export crops accrued not to indigenous traders and entrepreneurs—who might have invested some or all of that surplus back into the local economy—but to European trading companies that exported the surplus back to the colonial power's economy. The result was "a massive net transfer of surplus from the Third World to the metropolitan heartland" (Ayoob 1995: 35).

Colonialism and postcolonial patterns of dependent development also decimated the class of native traders and financiers who had dominated the monetized sector of the precolonial economy. Indigenous traders, who could have served as the entrepreneurial class that Rostow (1990) and others have depicted as the essential driving force behind economic modernization, were squeezed out of the market by European trading companies. As the postcolonial state confronted the challenges of nation and state building, it did so presiding over an economy that, to varying degrees, had been bled dry by colonial powers, deprived of the entrepreneurs needed to lead the nation's economic modernization, and bound into dependent status in the global economy. Consequently the postcolonial economy was incapable of generating the revenues needed by the state to pursue more accommodative strategies of nation building, strategies that would have built support, loyalty, and national identity on the basis of the positive rewards of citizenship in the new nation. Lacking this alternative, the state was left with coercion and repression as the default option in pursuing its developmental imperatives.

The International Context

Besides the internal predicaments of state building and nation building that were part of their colonial heritage, postcolonial states faced an external predicament as well. With independence they entered a highly developed international system structured by rules, norms, and institutions that they had no role in shaping. Instead the very powers that had subjugated them as colonies and bound them into patterns of postcolonial dependency dominated the institutions of the international community and shaped the rules governing interactions between nations. Among the most sacred of these norms was the principle of national sovereignty and its geopolitical corollary: the inviolability of national borders. Despite the fact that the formal borders of postcolonial states encapsulated ethnic groups that resisted assimilation and continue to pose a threat of armed secession, irredentism, or revolution, the community of nation states continued to recognize and guarantee the inviolability of the new states' borders.

At least it did so until 1991. Kal Holsti (1992: 15) notes that not a single Third World nation disappeared from the map between 1945 and 1991, despite the fact that many of them amounted to geopolitical fictions.[11] Instead over a hundred new nation states were added to the nation state system during that time. In contrast, territorial absorption of one state by another and the division of empires into constituent nation states were integral aspects of the European state formation process. However, former colonies, once granted independence, acquired the right to exist as sovereign states even when many did not possess "much in the way of empirical statehood, disclosed by a capacity for effective and civil government" (Jackson 1987: 529). Third World states that, in an earlier era, would not have been considered viable and would have been absorbed or otherwise reconfigured by the international community as part of a strong state were nevertheless preserved in a condition of juridical statehood (Jackson 1987; Jackson and Rosberg 1982).

Preserving these states only served to compound the challenge of nation building and state formation by precluding one solution to it: secession.

Because the state formation process in the Third World differed so thoroughly from what had unfolded over several centuries in Europe, the result was also fundamentally different. Kal Holsti (1996: 79) summarizes the argument: "the universalization of the territorial state format does not mean that all states share the same characteristics. . . . Artificial states—the creations of colonial organizations and international organizations—are in many ways fundamentally different from states that grew slowly through an organic process involving wars, administrative centralization, the provision of welfare entitlements, and the development of national identities and sentiments."

Whereas Europe entered the twentieth century as a system of relatively strong states, the Third World struggled through the last half of that century with a large number of weak states.

THE WEAK STATE SYNDROME

Mohamed Ayoob (1995: 28–29) argues that the sources of the internal insecurity that confronts most contemporary Third World states are the same as those that European state makers had to overcome: (1) the lack of unconditional legitimacy for state boundaries, state institutions, and regimes, (2) inadequate social cohesion marked by the lack of a sense of nationhood or shared identity among the population, and (3) the absence of societal consensus on fundamental issues of how social life, the economy, and the political system should be organized. However, contemporary weak states lack the institutional capacity, the political will, and the economic resources to confront these challenges in the same manner—or with anything approaching the same prospects for success—as their counterparts in eighteenth- and nineteenth-century Europe, North America, and Japan.

The predicament that weak states face is that the threats to the state's security are internal, not external, in origin. Social organizations other than the state (such as ethnic groups, clans, and communal groups) compete with the state for the loyalty of part of the population. For instance, peasants identify themselves as members of a village first, not as citizens of the state that governs them. Members of ethnic minority groups identify themselves with that group first, not with the nation state that subsumes them within its borders. Loyalties are subnational, not national, in their focus. As a consequence the legitimacy of the national state is fragile at best.

The only asset with which the state is more heavily endowed than the leaders of these subnational groups is its coercive capacity. As Barry Buzan (1983) argues, "Weak states either do not have or have failed to create a domestic political and social consensus of sufficient strength to eliminate the large-scale use of force as a major and continuing element in the domestic political life of the nation." Instead of representing the entire nation, the state is seen by one or more significant social group as representing the interests of a particular ethnic group (as is the case with many multiethnic states), a particular social sector (such as the agrarian elite in Latin America), or an economic or military elite (as was the case in Nicaragua under Somoza or the Philippines under Marcos). As such, the state lacks popular legitimacy in the eyes of those who are not members of its favored group. The alienated segments of society may withhold their support from the state, either tacitly by neglecting to comply with state laws and regulations and evading taxes or actively by organizing opposition movements to challenge the incumbent regime.

Because the state feels threatened by alienated social groups, it responds by increasing its coercive capacity. Its spending priorities are skewed heavily toward developing its security forces so it can defend itself against anticipated challenges to its authority. In so doing, the state drains resources from investment in other programs that might enhance economic growth and prosperity and thereby improve the well-being of its citizens. Military spending comes at the expense of the economic well-being of those very segments of the population whose loyalty to the state is most fragile. They remain impoverished, and the state's legitimacy is even further undermined in their eyes. Realizing this, the state feels compelled to invest further in its repressive capacity. This syndrome, which Brian Job (1992) calls the "insecurity dilemma," constrains the willingness and the ability of the weak state to respond to opposition challenges with economic reform, as opposed to violent repression.

The consequences of this cycle of insecurity between the state and various subnational groups are, first, less effective security for all sectors of the population. Those groups that are the target of repression will certainly feel less secure; those that have not yet been targeted will learn what fate awaits those who dare to challenge the state and its policies. Second, the insecurity dilemma diminishes or retards the capacity of the central state to provide services to its constituents, services that would enhance their well-being and thereby give them a positive reason to support and identify with the state. Resources that could have been invested in programs that would produce benefits for citizens are instead diverted to the military and the internal security forces. Third, the insecurity dilemma increases the state's vulnerability to influence by outside actors. The state may feel compelled to turn to external benefactors to supply it with the coercive resources it needs to secure itself against internal challenges. Even if its benefactors are not foreign powers but instead are certain segments of the dominant economic class (for instance, the landed elite, the agro-export elite, or, as dependency theories argue, multinational corporations), the state is weakened by its dependence on them for the resources necessary to defend itself against domestic challengers. In order to remain worthy of their support, the state becomes more constrained in its capacity to initiate reform programs that might be detrimental to the interests of its benefactors, even if those programs might enhance popular support for the regime.

If the state lacks the capacity to forge a strong nation state, then what does it do? While the weak state syndrome implies that Third World states will find it difficult to consummate the state formation process along the same lines that their European counterparts did, they usually do have the capacity to resist opposition challenges. The incumbents can preserve themselves in power. However, if that is all they can do, if they lack the capacity to bring about economic and social development, then for what other purposes can and will they employ the institutional machinery of the weak state? One obvious answer is the preservation of their own control over the state and the enrichment of themselves and their allies.

FROM WEAK STATE TO PROTECTION RACKET STATE

The repressive violence perpetrated by many Third World states has often been wildly disproportionate to any threat posed by opposition movements. Certainly it has been far in excess of the level of violence required to repress the opposition challenge (Stanley 1996: 18–20; Pion-Berlin 1989: 4–5). Thus we cannot view state repression as a strictly reactive and proportionate response to opposition challenges.

The extent of repression in many Third World nations is difficult to explain as the choice of a single rational actor. If we conceive of the state as a unitary actor, we would have to conclude that the states that perpetrate such excessive repression are irrational or arational at best. Any single actor who responded with such excess would have to be judged pathological. However, to account for repression as the policy choice of a pathological state is unsatisfying and unconvincing. It is true that on occasion an individual who arguably is pathological has captured power in a state and has engaged in such brutal repression that it could only be the result of his pathology. Idi Amin is an example of such a ruler. While he was in power in Uganda from 1971 to 1979, between 250,000 and 350,000 Ugandans were killed by state security forces (Brogan 1990: 108). However, to attribute more than a handful of cases to pathological leaders would leave us with the question of how so many states could have fallen under the sway of psychopaths.

Stanley and Tilly have suggested that such repression can be viewed as the outcome of bargaining among factions within the state in what they have likened to a protection racket. Stanley depicts the state, especially the weak state in the Third World, as a coalition of actors or factions, with each faction rationally pursuing its own set of institutional and personal interests. Policies—including the choice between repression and reform, and the choice of what level of repression to impose—can then be understood as the outcome of bargaining among these factions. Even the excessive levels of repression that we have witnessed in a number of states can be attributed to one or more factions within the regime using violence in the pursuit of its primary goal: the control of state power, with all its ensuing benefits. Even if it appears irrational in terms of national goals such as securing domestic peace, the violence can be seen as a coldly rational strategy on the part of one faction to enhance its control over the state.

The social systems in which protection racket states emerge are grounded economically in export agriculture. In many of them, export agriculture was established not through the invisible hand of the market but through the very visible and bloody hands of what Barrington Moore (1966: 434–35) terms "labor-repressive agriculture." In this system a small landed elite enlists the support of the military to enforce, through violence against the peasants, the consolidation of land ownership into large agro-export estates. The military's collaboration is required to expel peasants from the land and to suppress any peasant resistance to this sort of land reform in reverse. Once the agro-export economy is installed, a key to its continued prosperity is maintaining an ample supply of low-cost labor. The swelling ranks of the landless laborers obviously fulfills that need. However, their increasing immiserization makes them susceptible to mobilization appeals by opposition movements intent upon instituting redistributive reforms. Land reform, redistributive tax policies, minimum wage laws, and even industrial development programs would threaten the economic dominance of the agro-export elite. Agrarian reform would deprive them of all or part of their land, which is the basis of their wealth and their power over the peasant masses. Redistributive tax policies would diminish their control over income flows in the economy. Minimum wage laws and industrial development programs would raise the cost of labor and thereby reduce their profits from exports while undermining their control over the lives of landless laborers who have no occupational alternative to agriculture. Thus, once the system of labor-repressive export agriculture is in place, the civilian elites who control that sector of the economy still need the services of the military to suppress labor activism in the countryside and protect them against reformist movements that might threaten their economic hegemony.[12] Hence the military's role in the protection racket is, first, to enforce the consolidation of land holdings and, second, to maintain the labor-repressive regime that keeps the cost of labor low and the supply of labor ample enough to preserve the profitability of export agriculture.

How does the landed elite induce the military to act in their interest? In return for repressing labor activism and preserving the economic dominance of the agrarian elite, the military is allowed to exercise control over the machinery of the state. Under these circumstances, the military can convert the state into what amounts to a protection racket: "The military earn[s] the concession to govern the country (and pillage the state) in exchange for its willingness to use violence against class enemies of the country's relatively small but powerful economic elite" (Stanley 1996: 6–7). Through its control over the machinery of the state, the military can preserve its priority claim on the state's budget, protect its institutional dominance and privileges, and enrich its officer corps. The landed elite should be willing to acquiesce in this "pillage of the state" up to the point that the cost to them of repression—the rent they must allow the military to extract from the agro-export economy—equals the cost of acceding to the wage demands of labor.

What explains the often wildly excessive levels of violence it perpetrates is the military's need to demonstrate to the agrarian elite that the threats to their continued economic hegemony are grave and can be suppressed only by diligent military action. Stanley describes this process as follows:

> Conspicuous acts of violence against supposed enemies of the state can enable a repressive regime or coercive state agencies to develop and maintain a civilian constituency. By committing acts of repression, the coercive apparatus sends signals to social elites that threats from below still need a firm hand. This may help convince groups within the upper and middle classes who might otherwise become restive that they still need the services of a highly autonomous, authoritarian regime, thereby forestalling pressures for political liberalization. (1996: 37)

Tilly (1985: 171) suggests that the military in protection racket states often exaggerates the threats that exist and even creates threats (or at least the appearance of threats) when none exist simply to legitimize their claim to control over the state and their demands for more resources. Tilly is describing the military in early modern European states. He argues that states even instigated fights with neighboring states in order to justify greater extractions from society. Stanley argues quite convincingly that the militaries of contemporary Third World states use the same tactic against alleged internal "enemies" in order to justify their continued hegemony within the state. In return for protecting the economic hegemony of the agrarian elite, the military is allowed to engage in rent-seeking behavior, claiming resources far in excess of what is required to sustain its capacity to suppress opposition challenges. Thus the level of repression that it perpetrates on society often far exceeds the level required to suppress the opposition, because higher levels of violence can be depicted as a response to more severe threats to the status quo, threats that require additional resources for the military and continued acquiescence to their control over the state.

The protection racket state is most likely to occur in precisely the type of system that is susceptible to revolutions in the countryside. The agro-export elite dominates the economy to the point that it controls not only agriculture but banking, finance, and whatever manufacturing might exist. If no independent urban middle class emerges, then intra-elite bargaining can be confined to two sets of actors: the military and the agro-export elite. Once a protection racket bargain is struck between these two factions, it can be preserved so long as the military can repress grassroots challenges and the agrarian elite can preempt the emergence of an urban middle class capable of challenging its dominance over the economy.

WEAK STATES AND THE CHOICE BETWEEN REPRESSION AND REFORM

When opposition challenges arise, any state must decide what mix of reform and repression is appropriate for its response. Given the institutional weakness of many Third World states and the character of intra-elite politics that prevail within them, we would expect them to choose repression over reform, even though repression in and of itself does nothing to resolve the grievances that gave rise to opposition challenges in the first place. Moreover, as Lichbach (1987) and Mason and Krane (1989) have argued, repression can, under certain circumstances, increase rather than deter support for opposition movements, including revolutionary movements. Nonetheless, reform strategies are likely to be eschewed by weak states for a number of reasons.

First, the kinds of reforms that would be required to accommodate opposition demands in agro-export economies—land reform, for example—would amount to a breach of the protection racket agreement between the military and the agrarian elite. Given this, it should not be surprising that, first, land reform is rare in such states and, second, when it does occur, it is usually only after the protection racket has been broken through a coup or a revolution. Thus Peru's land reform of 1968 was initiated by a military junta after a coup. Likewise the Salvadoran land reform program of the early 1980s followed a coup in which a group of younger progressive officers overthrew the antireform government of General Carlos Romero.

Second, most agro-export economies are characterized by extraordinarily high population-to-land ratios. Land reform by itself cannot relieve the economic distress of large portions of the economically marginalized population. There simply is not enough land available to give the landless population sufficient acreage to make them economically self-sufficient. Therefore reform must involve more than just the redistribution of land. It must address the problems of unemployment and underemployment through policies that expand the availability of occupational alternatives to agriculture. Typically this means industrial development.

A state that lacks the capacity to defuse opposition challenges through structural reforms is left with repression as its only alternative for dealing with this challenge. The very conditions of dependent development that gave rise to opposition movements in the first place constrain the capacity of the state to respond to those challenges with anything other than repression. Reform programs require resources. The state has to be able to raise sufficient revenues to finance any programs designed to relieve poverty and provide new economic opportunities for marginalized nonelites. The state must also be able to address the structural sources of poverty: It must have the institutional capacity (and the political will) to redistribute wealth more equitably, so that the returns on the nation's economic assets benefit a larger share of the nation's population. To redistribute wealth and income requires substantial state autonomy from the dominant economic classes. However, in most weak states, especially those whose economy is grounded in labor-repressive agriculture, the autonomy of the state as well as its capacity to generate sufficient revenues and to redistribute wealth is severely constrained by the very conditions that gave rise to poverty and organized opposition movements in the first place.

First, the highly skewed distribution of land, wealth, and income that is typical of peripheral societies results in high rates of unemployment and underemployment. This severely restricts the tax base from which the state can extract the revenues necessary to finance reform programs. The vast majority of the population is so impoverished that they have little income beyond subsistence for the government to tax. In short, the state lacks a tax base that is sufficiently broad and deep to generate the revenues needed to finance economic development and reform initiatives.

Second, those who do have taxable income or assets are politically capable of resisting state efforts to raise tax rates or to redistribute wealth and income at their expense. Given the low level of industrialization in most peripheral economies, the major form of taxable wealth and income is export agriculture. Farmland by itself is a rather unstable revenue base upon which to build a more equitable and prosperous society. The revenue flows a state can generate from land taxes are limited at best and fluctuate with the value of the land, which is itself a function of the "boom and bust" cycles typical of world markets for the crops grown on the land. Whatever industry the nation's economy might have is often foreign-owned or owned by the same agro-export elite who control the agricultural economy. As such, industrial assets and the income they produce are often insulated from taxation as part of the protection racket agreement. Foreign firms are often able to extract special tax exemptions from Third World governments as incentives to invest in the country in the first place. Any efforts by the state to shift the tax burden onto multinational corporations or the indigenous economic elite (both agro-export and industrial) will meet resistance. Industrial elites can threaten to liquidate their assets and emigrate, touching off a wave of capital flight that would cripple the economy further.

Foreign economic benefactors, including private banks, foreign governments, and international agencies such as the International Monetary Fund (IMF), also pressure the state to minimize the tax burden on industrial firms. The IMF, for instance, can use the terms of the loan packages it provides to pressure Third World states into moderating or abandoning redistributive policies, including tax increases on foreign capital. Indeed IMF conditionality usually specifies that the state reduce taxes on capital while simultaneously reducing if not eliminating subsidies on fuel, food, housing, and other basic necessities that provide the poor with some relief from the exigencies of the markets for land, labor, and subsistence goods. Because such austerity measures typically result in sharp increases in unemployment and prices as well as declines in wages, they often stimulate increased opposition activity, as the poor protest the additional hardships imposed on them by these policies. The state sees repression as the necessary response to this escalation in opposition activity, because to accede to opposition demands would be to violate the conditionality of external assistance, thereby jeopardizing its continued provision.

The most direct and immediate constraint on the willingness and ability of weak states to undertake reform rather than repression is the intra-elite politics typical of the protection racket state. Those who control the land have both the capacity and the will to resist any state efforts to redistribute wealth and income. They can effectively prevent reformers from within the state from imposing substantial new land taxes on them for the purpose of financing economic reform and development programs. They will be especially inclined to use their clout if the purpose of those reforms is to redistribute income, land, and wealth more equitably but at their expense. The military's own control over the state is predicated upon its protecting and preserving this landed elite's monopoly over land ownership. To initiate land reform is, therefore, to attack the exchange that is at the heart of the coalition that controls the protection racket state. If the military were to initiate land reform, it would lose the landed elite's support for the military's continued control over the state. Therefore the military in protection racket states can be expected to preempt any efforts to initiate significant land reform or other redistributive reforms. Should civilian reformers somehow gain nominal control over the legislature or the executive and try to initiate redistributive reforms that threaten the income, wealth, and prerogatives of the agrarian elite, those elites can call on the military to launch a coup and install in power a junta that will pre-empt reforms. In Guatemala, for instance, when the popularly elected President Jacobo Arbenz initiated a land reform program in 1954, he was overthrown in a military coup organized and financed by the U.S. Central Intelligence Agency. Arbenz's reform would have expropriated unused farmland, most of which was owned by the United Fruit Company, an American firm. (See Schlesinger and Kinzer 1983; Brockett 1988: 100–04; Handy 1994.)

In summary, weak states in peripheral societies typically lack the redistributable resources, the institutional machinery, and the political will to pursue more accommodative responses to opposition challenges. Conversely the one response for which weak states do have the requisite institutional capacity is repression. The coercive machinery of the weak state is usually the most longstanding, well-funded, and well-developed set of policy instruments at the disposal of government elites. The military in weak states thus feels compelled to respond with repression in part by default: Coercion is the only response for which they have the institutional capacity and the political support from both indigenous economic elites and their foreign benefactors.

In bureaucratic authoritarian states, the willingness of the military to exercise its capacity by intervening in civilian politics and repressing political opposition movements is reinforced by what George Lopez (1986) has termed the "national security ideology," in which the military leadership believes that political tranquility is a prerequisite to economic development and that political turmoil scares off investment and thereby retards development.[13] The military sees itself as the one institution capable of preserving social stability and quelling turmoil, not just in times of strife but at all times. In effect, the military believes it should exercise a veto over the civilian regime in the name of political stability. This national security ideology and the policies that flow from it are reinforced by the generous military assistance that metropolitan powers such as the United States are usually willing to offer compliant Third World regimes. Foreign patrons willingly subsidize the military establishment in friendly Third World nations in order to preserve in power a regime that is not antagonistic to the foreign patron's own economic and strategic interests. Moreover, Ted Gurr (1986) points out that regimes that have been successful in the past at suppressing opposition through violent repression are likely to resort to such tactics in the future, regardless of the character of the opposition organizations, the nature of their demands, or the composition of their base of popular support. Hence the almost reflexive response of weak states to opposition challenges is to increase the level of officially sanctioned violence directed against the opposition leaders and their actual, suspected, or potential supporters.

This raises the question that is the subject of the next chapter: If weak states are expected to respond to opposition challenges with repression rather than reform, does this strategy work, in the sense of suppressing opposition activity and preserving the stability of the current distribution of economic and political power? Or does repression lead to an increase in opposition activity and a shift in the form that it assumes, from nonviolent to violent? This question has been at the center of the scholarly debate on the opposition-repression nexus. Sophisticated theoretical arguments and empirical tests have been advanced in support of positive, negative, and curvilinear relationships between repression and opposition. The next chapter explores the logic underlying these competing hypotheses and presents the argument that the effects of repression vary, depending upon whether it is targeted on opposition leaders, rank-and-file supporters of opposition organizations, or members of the general public whose affiliation with and support of opposition organizations is not fully known by the agents of repression.

NOTES

1. On the political motivations for the Peruvian coup and the junta's land reform program, see Caballero 1981b; Handelman 1975, 1981; Kay 1983; Lastarria-Cornhiel 1989; McClintock 1998. On the peasant unrest that motivated the coup, see Paige 1975: 131–39; Hobsbawm 1974.

2. On the coup in El Salvador and the subsequent attempts at land reform, see Montgomery 1982, 1995; Baloyra 1982; McClintock 1998; Shulz 1984; Simon and Stephens 1982; Stanley 1996.

3. Citations on regime types in the Third World are too numerous to document fully. A few useful sources include Malloy 1977 on corporatism, Collier 1979 and O'Donnell 1973 on bureaucratic authoritarianism, Bratton and Van De Walle 1994 and Theobold 1982 on neopatrimonial regimes. Chehabi and Linz 1998a is an excellent recent collection on sultanistic regimes.

4. On the democratic peace, see Russett 1993. Krain and Myers 1997 presents empirical evidence in support of the domestic version of the democratic peace. See also Rummel 1995, Hegre et al. 1999.

5. In 1929 the Partido Nacional Revolucionario (PNR) was created. In 1946 its name was changed to Partido Revolucionario Institucional.

6. See Chehabi and Linz 1998b: 8. Chehabi and Linz 1998a contains chapters on Trujillo, Batista, Somoza, Duvalier, Marcos, and the Shah.

7. The term *sultanism* was coined by Max Weber to characterize an extreme form of patrimonial authority. Juan Linz (1975) revived its use in his classification of non-democratic regimes. For a discussion of the contemporary revival of the concept and the cases in which it has been applied, see Chehabi and Linz 1998b,c, Theobold 1982, Bratton and Van De Walle 1994, among others.

8. As Anthony Giddens (1987: 112) puts it, "It was war, and preparations for war, that provided the most potent energizing stimulus for the concentration of administrative resources and fiscal reorganization that characterized the rise of absolutism."

9. On the impact of colonialism in Africa, see Young 1994.

10. The Minorities at Risk data set includes seventy-four black African minority groups as compared to forty-three in Asia, which has a much larger total population. Ethnic minorities constitute 42 percent of the total population of Africa, compared to a global average of 17 percent. In three African states, all the population consists of ethnic minorities that are "at risk" according to MAR criteria; in eight other African nations, over half the population consists of "at-risk" minorities, and in another four, over 40 percent are minorities at risk (Scarritt 1993: 254–55; Scarritt and MacMillan 1995: 328). Approximately 45 percent of the ethnic minorities in Africa have engaged in armed rebellion, and almost all of these incidents have occurred after independence (Scarritt 1993: 260; Scarritt and MacMillan 1995: 331).

11. The lone exception is the creation of Bangladesh through the partitioning of Pakistan.

12. Rueschmeyer, Stephens, and Stephens (1992: 163–65) argue further that plantation agriculture that is concentrated in labor-intensive crops tends to rely more on repression because the landowners' dependence on labor leaves them vulnerable to demands for higher wages.

13. On the bureaucratic authoritarian state, see O'Donnell 1973, 1979, 1988.

Chapter Six

State Repression and the Escalation of Revolutionary Violence

When confronted with a reformist social movement, the state can respond by accommodating the movement's demands through policy reforms, or it can repress the movement by arresting, "disappearing," or killing its leaders and intimidating nonelite members into withholding further support from the movement. In a nation with a large and growing population of impoverished, marginalized peasants, the most likely response of the weak state is to repress the opposition challenge. As I argued in chapter 5, the type of state that tends to evolve in such environments often lacks the institutional capacity, redistributable resources, or political will to undertake significant reforms. Hence it resorts to repression almost by default.

However, repression will not necessarily bring an end to opposition challenges. Indeed the state's resort to repression confronts participants in nonviolent social movements with a choice of their own: Do they withdraw from the political arena, or do they shift tactics from dissent to violent revolution? The leap to revolutionary collective action is more conceivable for those already engaged in nonviolent activism because it represents a tactical shift in the form of collective action; their participation in nonviolent reformist social movements means that they have already overcome collective action problems. The existence of an organized social movement means that the organizational machinery is already in place to build and sustain a revolutionary social movement. All that is required is that the movement's leaders shift strategy to apply that machinery in a program of revolutionary violence. While this is certainly no easy task, in fact this is how most revolutionary organizations come into being. If an opposition social movement does make the transition to revolutionary violence, will those peasants who supported its reformist agenda and participated in its nonviolent program of collective action follow the movement's leaders to the hills to become guerrilla fighters?

This chapter is concerned with how aggrieved peasants respond to varying mixes of repression and accommodation on the part of the state. The state and its revolutionary opposition compete with each other for the support of peasants and other nonelites by offering them variable mixes of rewards and punishments. Each seeks to elicit behaviors that are supportive of its own claims to power and authority, and each seeks to deter behaviors that are supportive of its rival's claims to power and authority. Rather than be caught in the crossfire between government and opposition, most peasants would prefer to remain uninvolved, devoting their energies instead to the everyday tasks of securing subsistence. However, as the competition between state and opposition escalates, the option of remaining uninvolved may eventually be foreclosed. Caught in the crossfire between regime and rebels, peasants must choose between supporting the government, supporting the rebels, or supporting neither. This chapter presents a model of the decision calculus by which peasants make that choice. Within this framework, I explore the impact of competing insurgent and counterinsurgent strategies on the distribution of popular support between the rebels and the regime.

REFORM, REPRESSION, AND THE RATIONAL PEASANT

How does the state respond to an opposition social movement energized by the mobilization of grassroots collective action? The state can attempt through reforms to accommodate the demands of economically marginalized peasants and urban nonelites, or it can attempt through repression to intimidate peasants into withholding their support from the opposition. The particular mix of repression and reform that the state adopts will depend upon the resources at its disposal, the difference in the expected payoffs (in terms of political stability) from investing marginal resources in repression versus reform, and the state's autonomy from the dominant economic elite whose wealth, income, and political power will be diminished by any redistributive reforms (Lichbach 1984).

Reform

Accommodative strategies such as land reform or employment programs are designed to restore popular support for the state by providing peasants with new flows of material benefits that relieve their immediate economic distress and restore for them some measure of economic security. In return, the beneficiaries are expected to refrain from participating in dissident activities and withdraw their support, material and otherwise, from dissident organizations. Accommodative reforms are intended to pre-empt support for revolution by giving peasants a stake in the endurance of the current regime and thereby restoring its claims to popular legitimacy.

In an agrarian economy with large numbers of landless or land-poor peasants living perilously close to the margins of subsistence, land reform has often been advocated as a remedy for rural unrest. While land reform programs face opposition from powerful domestic constituencies—that is, the traditional landed elite—regimes faced with the prospect of rural insurgency are often encouraged and sometimes pressured by external benefactors to undertake land reform in return for the economic and military assistance they need to shore up the regime against an insurgent challenge. The United States backed land reform programs by the governments of South Vietnam, the Philippines, and El Salvador as ways to restore stability to regimes faced with mounting unrest in the countryside. Other nations, including Peru and Bolivia, initiated land reform on their own, as a way to pre-empt revolution in the countryside.[1]

Although land reform is often portrayed as a remedy for rural unrest in the Third World, its record of success at inoculating peasants against the appeals of guerrilla insurgents has yet to be established. Indeed one is hard pressed to cite any instance in which agrarian reform implemented amid an ongoing civil war has effectively dissipated that conflict. Of the two cases that Prosterman and Riedinger (1987) analyze in which reform was undertaken by a regime during an ongoing civil war, one (South Vietnam) must be deemed a failure because the incumbent regime was eventually overthrown, and the other (El Salvador) did not witness any dissipation of revolutionary violence for more than a decade after land reform was initiated. Despite the loss of thousands of lives in counterinsurgent combat and the expenditure of billions of dollars in U.S. aid to support land reform in Vietnam and El Salvador, neither regime was able to win the hearts and minds of peasants to the point that they could defeat their insurgent challengers.

By Prosterman and Reidinger's (1987: 12) own reckoning, the most significant land reform programs have been undertaken by newly established regimes that had recently seized power in a revolution or a coup (for example, Cuba, Russia, China, Ethiopia, Nicaragua, Mexico, and Bolivia), or that had recently been installed by a foreign power occupying the nation after a major war (for example, Japan, South Korea, and Poland). The common sequence of events appears to be the overthrow of an existing regime, followed by a radical redistribution of land by a new regime, followed by a period of relative peace in the countryside. Perhaps, then, the alleged remedial effects of land reform are based on little more than the logic of negative cases: If the *anciens régimes* in

Cuba, Russia, China, Ethiopia, and Nicaragua had undertaken agrarian reform, perhaps they never would have been overthrown. But then again, perhaps they would have. Even agrarian reforms implemented amid conditions of peace have not always immunized regimes against later insurgent challenges, as postreform conflicts in Nicaragua, Peru, and Ethiopia indicate.

The belief in the stabilizing effects of agrarian reform emerged as a corollary to the widely accepted link between highly inequitable land tenure systems and political unrest in the countryside. In chapter 2, I quoted Samuel Huntington on the inequality-instability link and the remedial effects that land reform should have on it. His words bear repeating here:

> A government can . . . significantly affect the conditions in the countryside so as to reduce the propensity of peasants to revolt. While reforms may be the catalyst of revolution in the cities, they may be a substitute for revolution in the countryside. . . . Where the conditions of land-ownership are equitable and provide a viable living for the peasant, revolution is unlikely. Where they are inequitable and where the peasant lives in poverty and suffering, revolution is likely, if not inevitable. . . . No social group is more conservative than a landowning peasantry, and none is more revolutionary than a peasantry that owns too little land or pays too high a rental. (1968: 375)

Roy Prosterman, the architect of "land to the tiller" programs in both South Vietnam and El Salvador, summarizes the empirical evidence for the suspected correlation between landlessness and revolution in the countryside: "In this century landless populations have constituted one-quarter or more of the total population in twenty-two countries. Of these, so far fifteen have experienced revolution or protracted civil conflict" (Prosterman and Riedinger 1987: 25).

The arguments of Huntington, Prosterman, and others of similar persuasion still find an audience among top policy makers, as evidenced by the following passage from a 1982 speech by Thomas Enders, then U.S. Assistant Secretary of State for Inter-American Affairs, in which he addresses the importance of the U.S.-sponsored land reform program in war-torn El Salvador: "For the United States, it is vital to carry the agrarian reform through [in El Salvador]. Peasants who have become landowners will be a strong bulwark against the guerrillas" (quoted in White 1984: 17). It was Enders who brought in Roy Prosterman to advise the Salvadoran government and the U.S. Agency for International Development (USAID) on the Salvadoran land reform program.

By the logic of Huntington and Prosterman, land reform is supposed to pre-empt peasant support for revolution by restoring their economic security and giving them a stake in the endurance of the incumbent regime. To borrow the famous metaphor coined by Mao Zedong, the "sea" of peasant supporters in which the guerrilla "fish" must sustain itself is effectively drained by land reform, and the revolutionary threat should decay with the restoration of the incumbent regime's legitimacy in the eyes of a peasantry newly endowed as landowners.

Land reform is intended to shift peasant preferences in favor of the regime, something that the more repressive responses to political opposition usually fail to do. By increasing the income of peasants, land reform strategies raise the effective price that revolutionary organizations must pay to elicit supportive behaviors from peasants. As peasant incomes rise, the opposition should face decreasing marginal returns on the benefits they offer as selective incentives for participation in opposition activities.[2]

Of course, the effectiveness of land reform in restoring peasant loyalty and pre-empting their support for a rural insurgency is in part a function of the design and implementation of the program. How many households receive land reform benefits? Are those segments of the peasantry that are most susceptible to opposition appeals benefited by the land reform program? Do they receive benefits in amounts sufficient to restore to them some measure of economic security? As the examples of El Salvador and Peru illustrate (see chapters 8 and 9), land reform programs that do not provide enough benefits to enough peasants and do not provide benefits to the most volatile segments of the peasantry often do not have the desired effect that Huntington predicts (see Mason 1998).

Repression[3]

Besides reform, the other broad response of a state faced with an opposition social movement is to repress the challengers. Repressive violence by the government can be applied reactively or proactively. Indeed governments seldom wait for opposition movements to resort to violent tactics of their own before initiating a program of repressive violence. It is usually the government's proactive resort to violent repression that accounts for an opposition movement's shift from reform to revolution.

More often than not, the scope of state repression far exceeds the scope of the challenge confronting the state. Rudolph Rummel (1994) estimates the death toll from state-sanctioned killing of civilians to be almost 170 million in the twentieth century, a figure that is more than four times the total number of battle deaths for all the century's interstate and civil wars up to 1987. Examples of the extremes to which states will go in order to suppress opposition movements are far too numerous to list. Stanley (1996: 18–19) notes that the military government of Guatemala killed about 10,000 civilians during the

1960s in an effort to suppress a band of 500 guerrillas. In the early 1970s another 15,000 civilians were "disappeared" by the Guatemalan state. Altogether over 35,000 civilians were killed or disappeared by the by the army, the police, or death squads (Ball, Kobrak, and Spirer 1999: 8). Pion-Berlin points out that the Argentine state began its "dirty war" against the civilian population after it had largely annihilated the incipient guerrilla movement. In 1974, 137 guerrillas were killed by the armed forces of the state, while 109 army and police officers were killed by the rebels. By 1977 the guerrillas had suffered over 2,000 dead, and they had ceased all military operations. However, it was at this point—precisely when the rebels had been effectively suppressed—that the government escalated its use of repression against civilians. The infamous "dirty war" that followed claimed the lives of over 20,000 Argentine civilians after the guerrilla movement had been eliminated (Pion-Berlin 1989: 4–5).

THE SPIRAL OF REPRESSION AND REVOLUTION

What effects does repressive violence have on peasant behavior? The state hopes that it will deter them from supporting opposition organizations. In some cases, such as Argentina, that seems to be what happened. In other cases, however, repression seems to have increased popular support for the revolution. How do we account for these contradictory patterns? The impact of repression on the distribution of popular support between the government and the opposition depends in part on whether the government targets its violence against leaders of nonviolent opposition organizations, the rank-and-file supporters of those organizations, or groups of citizens with little or no demonstrable affiliation with the opposition.

Opposition Leaders

The most restrictive strategy for repressive violence is to target the leaders of nonviolent social movements. These include the leaders of political parties, labor unions, peasant associations, and other grassroots organizations that have had success at mobilizing peasants for nonviolent collective action. Usually targeting the leaders of such groups is the earliest and most common form of repressive violence to occur, and it appears long before the political struggle between the state and the opposition has escalated to the point of intractable civil war. The purpose of such repression is to "decapitate" the opposition. If the leaders are eliminated, the capacity of their organizations to reward their supporters will decline, and this should reduce supporters' willingness to continue participating in opposition activities or contributing to the organizations.

This form of repression can include legal and quasi-legal measures, such as restricting the kinds of activities organizations are allowed to undertake. It can also include imprisoning or exiling movement leaders. In the extreme, the government may resort to "disappearance," assassination, or other forms of death squad violence. Such violence is intended to induce compliance through fear. It is sanctioned by the state, either explicitly through policy pronouncements or implicitly through the lack of effort on the part of the state to curtail such acts. The extent to which the state sanctions such violence is reflected in the composition of the death squads themselves and the patterns of violence they perpetrate. Death squads may consist of secret police, special counterinsurgency units, or regular units of the armed forces. They may also include paramilitary units structured along military lines but organizationally autonomous from the state's security forces, at least formally. These include regional and local militias, mercenaries, private armies, and vigilante units that act in the service of local elites who share the state's desire to preserve the economic and political status quo (see Mason and Krane 1989). Often the state will deny responsibility for death squad violence because to admit responsibility would be to signal the population that the state will no longer tolerate nonviolent political opposition. However, the state's lack of effort to curtail death squad activity is a clear indication of its tacit acceptance of such violence.

Targeting the leadership of opposition organizations can reduce peasants' willingness to support opposition activity, at least for the short term. However, decapitation achieves this effect not so much by inducing the fear among peasants that they too might become victims. After all, so long as the victims are restricted to a small number of high-profile leaders, their anonymous peasant supporters will not necessarily conclude that they are likely targets of death squads. However, those same supporters are likely to withdraw their support out of a sense of futility. Decapitating opposition organizations reduces supporters' estimate of the payoffs—both public goods and selective incentives—that they can expect in return for their support. With the movement leadership imprisoned, exiled, or dead, peasants are not likely to receive any payoffs in return for their acts of support, regardless of how strongly they may sympathize with the stated goals of the movement. More important, their estimate of the chances that the movement will achieve its reformist goals declines with the elimination of opposition leaders and the demise of the organizations they lead.

I argued in chapter 4 that people can be induced to contribute to the provision of public goods even in the absence of selective incentives. What makes them willing to do so is the presence of leaders who have the organizational resources and leadership skills to ensure that the contributions of many individuals—each of which is by itself insignificant in determining whether the collective action succeeds—will in fact be aggregated in such a way as to produce the public goods. Workers are more likely to strike for higher wages and better working conditions if there is a union leadership that can enforce prohibitions against free-riding, translate striker solidarity into negotiable demands, and bargain with employers for the satisfaction of those demands. Peasants are more likely to engage in work stoppages or land invasions if they know there is a peasant association that can enforce prohibitions against defections and translate their actions into negotiable demands for higher wages, lower rent, land reform, or other concessions. When the leaders of such movements are eliminated by death squads, their peasant supporters begin to doubt whether the movement can still deliver selective incentives or achieve its reformist goals. Targeting opposition leaders is an example of what Leites and Wolf (1970: 79–81) refer to as "degrading the production function" of the opposition organization. Supporters withdraw their support in order to save the costs of such support and avoid the risks of detection and punishment by the state for supporting the opposition.

Of course, repression of this sort does nothing to enhance popular support for the state. After all, eliminating opposition leaders does not resolve the grievances that motivated peasants to support the movement in the first place. Indeed it is likely to shift popular preferences against the state and reduce the level of active support the state can elicit from its constituents. By repressing the opposition leadership, the state closes off a source of benefits flowing to peasants. This generates resentment against the state. Therefore latent support for the opposition will probably increase, even if active support for opposition activities does wane.[4]

Finally, decapitating opposition organizations is not likely to end opposition activity. Mark Lichbach has demonstrated that repression of nonviolent opposition results in an increase in the level of violent opposition activity. The degree to which violent activity increases depends on the relative effectiveness of violent versus nonviolent tactics for the opposition. If nonviolent tactics have been effective in the past (that is, they have produced benefits for the opposition), then repressing them should result in an increase in the level of violent activity that "will more than offset the decrease in the group's nonviolent activities, and hence the opposition group's total conflict activities will increase" (1987: 285). In other words "if government increases its repression of the opposition group's tactic that is more effective at obtaining a desired government policy for the group, then the group's total conflict activities [violent and nonviolent] will increase" (1987: 286). How does this come about? How does repression of nonviolent action result in an increase in opposition violence?

If the top leaders of reformist social movements fall victim to repressive violence, then their remaining lieutenants are likely to reconstitute themselves as a covert or insurgent organization and shift tactics from nonviolent to violent opposition.[5] For them to continue the same strategy of nonviolent opposition in the face of mounting state repression would be to leave themselves vulnerable to the same kind of repression that befell the leaders. Unlike their anonymous peasant supporters, however, the surviving leaders and activists cannot simply withdraw from the political arena. They have to assume that they too might be on the government's target list. Therefore the only choice for them is to go underground in search of security from state-sanctioned repression. With nonviolent tactics now being violently repressed, they have little choice but to shift tactics from nonviolent to violent opposition. Because they begin without an extensive support base for insurgent violence, they are likely to commence their campaign of violence with terrorist strikes, such as car bombings and other acts that are difficult to defend against. Terrorist strikes mark the first step in the transition from nonviolent opposition aimed at reforming the status quo to insurgent violence aimed at overthrowing the regime.

Rank-and-File Supporters

If opposition activity does not dissipate substantially (as the government hopes) but instead shifts to more violent forms, then the state is likely to expand its targeting of repressive violence to include known or suspected supporters of opposition social movements. This can include the rank and file members of the very unions, peasant associations, student organizations, and political parties whose leaders were eliminated by death squads. It can also include occasional and intermittent participants in discrete opposition activities, such as strikes and demonstrations, as well as those who occasionally provide material and other forms of support to opposition organizations. The state's goal in expanding its targeting is to deter people from participating in nonviolent activities or supporting the nascent violence of the opposition movement.

This targeting strategy is likely to have two different effects on two different segments of the peasant population. First, those who have not previously been involved in opposition activities may be deterred from doing so in the future, even if they sympathize with the movement's goals. To support the movement now is to risk becoming a victim of the state's expanded program of repression. So long as the state confines its targeting to known participants in opposition movements, it may temporarily pre-empt any growth in the number of people willing to join such movements or actively support their programs. Nonsupporters will continue to withhold support, because they fear reprisals. However, expanding repression in this manner does nothing to enhance support for the state among this segment of the population. Latent support for the opposition is likely to grow, in the sense that the number of people who would prefer the opposition to the current regime but are unwilling to act on this preference (because of fear) is likely to increase. The popular legitimacy of the regime erodes further, as the targeting of repression expands. Whatever support the state can elicit from citizens will become more strictly coercively induced. Compliance out of fear is not the same as obedience out of loyalty. To the extent that people engage in behaviors that are supportive of the state, they do so not because they prefer the state to the opposition but because they fear reprisals if they do not perform the acts of citizenship that the state demands of them. Support that is coercively induced can easily be reversed. All the opposition has to do is disrupt the effectiveness of the state's coercive capacity, and support based on fear will dissipate.

Expanding the targeting of repressive violence has quite a different effect on peasants who have actively supported the opposition movement in the past: They are not likely to withdraw their support from the opposition. To the contrary, they are likely to shift to higher levels of support and more violent forms of support, especially since nonviolent forms of dissident activity are now being repressed. They must presume that they too are on the state's target list. Therefore simply withdrawing from the political arena now will not necessarily exempt them from repressive violence. Instead they too will have a powerful incentive to go underground and join the surviving leaders of now-targeted opposition organizations. Revolutionary victory becomes even more urgent for them, because that is the only way they can be assured of security against that state's repressive violence. With the ranks of the underground opposition swelling with peasant supporters fleeing expanded state repression, the reconstituted opposition gains the capacity to escalate its own program of violence from sporadic terrorist strikes to guerrilla insurgency.

Benedict Kerkvliet's study of the Huk Rebellion in the Philippines reveals precisely this sort of dynamic at work. The Hukbalahap were peasant guerrillas who had fought against the Japanese in World War II. When their landlords returned from exile after the war, the Huk veterans were treated not as heroes of the resistance but as potential troublemakers who needed to be watched carefully. Huk veterans played a key role in mobilizing village support for opposition candidates in the 1946 elections, and they hoped that by electing progressive politicians to office they would get reforms of the land tenure system that would improve the lot of peasant sharecroppers. Instead they became targets of political violence by the landed elite. Kerkvliet (1977: 143) reports the following from his interviews with former Huk rebels:

> Many who in April [the time of the 1946 elections] had expected things to improve were rebelling by the next September. Why? Typical reasons were, "We were forced to because of what the landlords and constabulary were doing," "civilian guards and the PC [the national police] had me on their wanted list,"

"government soldiers tried to arrest me because I was in the PKM [the National Peasants Union]," "the landlords' armed guards killed my brother."

The Politically Uninvolved

When enough rank-and-file supporters have fled to the now-violent opposition, the movement becomes capable of expanding its tactical repertoire beyond isolated terrorist strikes to include a full range of guerrilla operations. Rebel tactics can include assaults on government troops and military bases, as well as attacks on the economic infrastructure that sustains the state's ability to wage war and to reward its own supporters. At this point the goal of insurgent violence is not to persuade the state to undertake reforms but to overthrow the state by means of revolutionary violence; the struggle between state and opposition has escalated to civil war.

Faced with a guerrilla insurgency, the state often responds by escalating its own repressive violence to target those who are merely suspected of being rebel supporters. The rationale for this strategy is the notion that, to defeat a guerrilla insurgency, the army must first deny the guerrillas the civilian support base that is essential for the rebels to sustain their own operations. Recalling Mao's famous metaphor, this counterinsurgent strategy is referred to as "draining the sea."

However, "draining the sea" confronts the military with the nearly impossible task of distinguishing the guerrilla irregular and his or her covert supporters from the otherwise neutral peasant. On the one hand, the military fears that if its units in the field are too careful in trying to distinguish neutrals from guerrilla supporters, they will be unable to disrupt the rebels' support base sufficiently to defeat the rebels. On the other hand, if they are indiscriminate in their attacks on civilians, they run the risk of driving otherwise neutral peasants into the arms of the rebels.

This effect can be termed the counterinsurgency dilemma. The overriding desire of the soldier in the field is to survive the mission. All too often this leads counterinsurgent units to engage in overkill. The standards of evidence they use to distinguish the guerrilla supporter from the uninvolved civilian are rarely sensitive to the need to avoid punishing neutrals. Instead their treatment of civilians is dictated by their own desire to survive the mission, which all too often comes to mean eliminating any civilians whom they suspect might pose a threat to the soldiers' own lives. All peasants are suspects, and any stores of supplies are viewed as potential caches for the rebels. As Leites and Wolf (1970: 91) put it, without sufficient training or adequate intelligence to allow them to target rebel supporters and only rebel supporters, counterinsurgency units "may not feel too guilty about fulfilling their professional duty of spending ammunition."

The counterinsurgency dilemma is that, instead of diminishing support for the rebels, targeting the insurgents' civilian support base can actually drive otherwise neutral peasants into the arms of the rebels. As government troops become more indiscriminate in their use of violence, the probability of an uninvolved peasant becoming a victim of state-sanctioned violence is no longer strictly contingent upon his or her own covert or overt support for the rebels. Refraining from supporting the rebels no longer exempts one from counterinsurgent violence. When government troops execute those who are merely suspected of supporting the rebels, when they raze entire villages because some of the residents are suspected of being rebel supporters, or when they use air strikes and other tactics that rely on superior firepower but do not discriminate between insurgents and innocents, otherwise neutral peasants may find it to be in their interest to emigrate or join the rebels in search of protection, not against the risks of agriculture that normally underlie peasant risk aversion, but against the risk of violent death at the hands of the state's own counterinsurgent forces.

Under these circumstances, all that the rebels need to do in order to win the support of peasants caught in the crossfire between rebels and regime is to offer them sanctuary from counterinsurgent violence. If the rebels can establish secure base areas in remote regions of the countryside, peasants threatened by the repressive arm of the state can be persuaded to emigrate to those regions, especially if they are landless and otherwise devoid of clientelist ties that would limit their mobility. Thus the indiscriminate application of repressive violence renders the otherwise uninvolved peasant susceptible to rebel appeals that promise sanctuary from repressive violence. In this manner, indiscriminate repressive violence ceases to deter and, indeed, stimulates a shift in peasant support from the state to the insurgents.

THE CALCULUS OF FEAR

Once the conflict between government and opposition has escalated to civil war, the question of whether the government or the rebels will prevail depends in no small part on the distribution of popular support between government and rebels.[6] Government and rebels compete for the support and loyalty of peasants and other nonelites by manipulating benefits and sanctions. They offer public benefits and selective incentives, and they threaten punishments in return for specific acts of support. They also seek to go beyond just eliciting discrete acts of support. They seek to win the loyalty of peasants. Loyalty involves a preference for victory by one side over the other and a willingness to support that side, even in the absence of immediate payoffs.

The calculus by which peasants choose between supporting the government, supporting the rebels, or supporting neither can be conceived of as a function of the difference in the net payoffs (expected benefits minus expected punishments) they expect to receive from supporting the state, the rebels, or neither.[7] One's expected payoff from supporting the state (or the rebels) will be in part a function of the benefits one receives from the state (or the rebels), minus the costs of engaging in the required acts of support. In this sense, the choice between supporting the state, the rebels, or neither is similar in logic to conventional forms of consumer behavior or voter behavior.[8] People purchase goods from Store A or Store B, depending on which one offers the best deal for the dollar. In a similar fashion, people choose between competing parties in an election by determining which one will give them the most (in terms of public goods and selective incentives) in return for their vote and other acts of electoral support. Obviously the crucial difference that distinguishes behavioral choice in a revolution from both consumer choice and voter choice is the risk of punishment at the hands of one side (state or rebels) if one is discovered to be providing support to the other side. In a civil war, people know that the state will punish them (perhaps with death) for supporting the rebels. They also know that the rebels will punish them for supporting the state. Citizens do not have to consider similar risks in deciding which party to vote for in an election or which store to visit to buy groceries. Political parties do not threaten the lives of people who vote for their rivals, nor do stores threaten the lives of customers who patronize their competitors. States and revolutionaries locked in civil war do. This condition profoundly alters the decision calculus by which people choose between supporting the state, supporting the rebels, or supporting neither. It introduces the "calculus of fear" into their behavior.

For an individual caught in the crossfire of civil war, the major uncertainty in their choice between the rebels and the state is the likelihood that his or her support for one party will be detected and punished by the other. From experience, most people know with some degree of certainty what benefit flows they can expect from the state or the rebels in return for certain acts of support. Likewise most people have some idea of what penalties the state or the rebels might impose on them if they are caught supporting the rival. They also know what kind of regime they will live under if the government defeats the rebels, and they have at least the rebels' ideological vision of what the postrevolutionary regime will be like, should the rebels prevail. What is difficult to estimate (because it changes with the ebb and flow of the war) is the likelihood of being caught either by the state or the rebels.

In large part, the probability of detection is a function of how many others also choose to engage in similar acts of support. The more there are, the lower the chances are that any one person will be detected and punished. The fewer there are, the greater the chances are that any one person will be detected and punished. Just how many others are actively supporting one side or the other can be estimated only with considerable uncertainty.

On what basis, then, does an individual determine what the chances are of supporting the rebels and getting away with it? They know that the state has invested a certain amount of resources in its coercive machinery, and that this investment gives the state the capacity to detect and punish a certain level of rebel support. They also know that the number of people providing support for the rebels exceeds the number of people the state can monitor. In other words, enforcement by the state is not perfect or leakproof.[9] Thus, for a given level of state coercive capacity, each citizen's chances of being detected and punished for supporting the rebels is a function of the ratio between the state's coercive capacity and the number of others who are already supporting the rebels. The larger the size of the rebel support base, the more the state's coercive capacity will be crowded or overwhelmed, and therefore the more likely it is that our sample citizen will be able to support the rebels and get away with it (see Frohlich and Oppenheimer 1973: 75–76).

The problem for our citizen, then, is that he or she cannot know with any certainty how many others are providing support for the rebels. However, he or she does have some sense that, at some level of rebel support, the risks of being caught and punished are low enough that it is worthwhile to take that risk and support the rebels. If the payoffs from supporting the rebels are great enough, then the threshold at which it becomes rational to support them is lower. In other words, the greater the payoffs from supporting the rebels, the greater the risk of detection a person is willing to accept in order to get those payoffs. Conversely, the lower the risk of detection, the lower the payoffs have to be in order to make it rational for a person to engage in acts of support. Thus rebels can increase their support base by either offering supporters more rewards in return for their acts of support or by engaging in actions that reduce the state's enforcement capabilities.

This logic implies that rebels will find more fertile recruiting ground among two segments of the peasant population. First, those who are worse off economically should be more susceptible to rebel appeals, because any package of benefits the rebels offer will be more valued (that is, have greater marginal utility) to them than to peasants who are better off economically. Moreover, the worse off one is economically, the less one puts at risk by supporting the rebels. The second segment of the population that should be receptive to rebel appeals consists of young, ambitious peasants who see involvement in the rebel organization as an opportunity for upward social mobility. The prospect of leadership benefits, such as government office in the postrevolutionary state (should the rebels win), is often sufficient to attract early participants from this group, even when the risks of participation are still substantial. (The age effect is discussed in more detail later.)

To counter the rebels' efforts, the state can pursue varying mixes of coercion and persuasion to enhance its support among the population. The state can increase the severity of the penalties it imposes on rebel supporters. Increasing the severity of penalties is intended to deter support for the rebels by making it more costly should one be detected. The state can also increase its policing efforts (that is, increase its capacity to monitor and detect civilian support for the rebels). Increasing the state's policing capacity is intended to deter support for the rebels by increasing citizens' estimate of the probability that, if they support the rebels, they will be caught and punished. Alternatively, the state can increase the level of benefits (both public goods and selective incentives) that it provides to its supporters. For instance, land reform and jobs programs represent benefits programs that are intended to reduce the level of rebel support by giving people a positive reason to support the state. Redistributive reforms also raise the price the rebels must pay (in the form of selective incentives and public goods) in order to induce supportive behaviors from those same citizens. This reform strategy not only elicits supportive behaviors from citizens, it shifts their preferences in favor of the state as well.

What this logic suggests is that the effect that different insurgent and counterinsurgent strategies have on the distribution of popular support between regime and rebels may be less a function of popular preferences with respect to the outcome of the conflict. Instead, the ebb and flow of popular support is more likely to be a function of the relative success of the state versus the rebels at manipulating people's short-term estimates of fear and gain. It also suggests that the behavior of peasants caught in the crossfire between rebels and regime may be determined more by the calculus of fear than by the pursuit of benefits, more by short-term estimates of fear and advantage than by the depth of one's commitment to revolutionary ideals. This is something that successful guerrilla leaders have long understood, even if social scientists have not. Quoting a Vietcong commander, Leites and Wolf (1970: 149) note that the Vietcong applied this logic in their tactical calculus: "We knew the people wanted nothing but peace for themselves . . . we had no illusion that they were for us . . . we knew that when we left they'd serve the GVN [government of Vietnam]. . . the people would submit to whoever was wearing a gun." Similarly DeNardo (1985: 26) notes that "most of Mao's followers [during the Chinese Communist revolution] only became revolutionary *after* they joined the movement" (emphasis in original). What drove them into the arms of the Chinese Communist guerrillas was the promise of protection against the often indiscriminate violence of Japanese forces occupying northern China where Chinese Communist Party (CCP) guerrillas operated. It is only after the rebel army won their initial support out of fear that they could begin winning their loyalty by offering rewards.

At the same time, peasant preferences between the contenders cannot be totally discounted. Although one's immediate behavioral choices may be predicated on short-term estimates of personal risk and reward, people realize that their supportive behaviors, along with those of others, contribute to the ability of one side or the other to win the conflict eventually. As such, their preferences for one side or the other may be reflected in the "price" they demand for their acts of support. While the prospect of contributing to the victory of their preferred side may not be sufficient in itself to induce someone to engage in risky acts of support, it can lower the amount of benefits they expect in return for those acts. Likewise, one's preference can affect the amount of risk one is willing to assume in order to provide acts of support. It can also raise the price one charges the rival (that is, the less preferred) contender for acts of support and reduce the amount of risk one is willing to assume in order to engage in those acts.

In summary, the state and the rebels compete for the hearts and minds of peasants and other nonelites by pursuing strategies that involve (1) increasing their capacity to detect and punish acts of support for their rival, (2) increasing the severity of the penalties they impose on the rival's supporters, and/or (3) increasing the supply of benefits (both public goods and selective incentives) they provide to their own supporters. The state's goal in manipulating these variables is to reduce each citizen's estimate of the number of others supporting the rebels. To the extent that the state succeeds, peasants' estimate of the chances that they can support the rebels and get away with it will decline. Conversely the goal of the rebels is to devise a strategy that will increase each citizen's estimate of their chances of supporting the rebels and getting away with it. Both the rebels and the state can manipulate the same variables in this struggle. They can also attack each other's ability both to provide benefits to constituents and to detect and punish the rival's supporters. This calculus of fear can be used to assess the impact on peasant support of varying mixes of benefits and coercion which are the substance of insurgent and counterinsurgent strategies.

INSURGENCY AND THE RATIONAL PEASANT

There is an asymmetry between the level of popular support required by the state to defeat the rebels, on the one hand, and the level of support required by the rebels to undermine the stability of the state, on the other (Leites and Wolf 1970). For the state to defeat the insurgents, it must turn the population against the rebels to the point that they actively cooperate in locating and destroying the rebel organization. By contrast, for the rebels to prevail, all they require from the population at the outset is passive tolerance of their existence. Passive tolerance allows the insurgent organization to survive and build its strength. For the state to prevail, it must deny the rebels even passive tolerance on the part of peasant populations.

What kinds of acts of support do governments and rebels try to elicit from peasants and other nonelites? Leites and Wolf (1970) depict the forms of rebel support as a set of discrete behavioral syndromes that can be arrayed along a continuum from the most to the least supportive. Each level of support involves different levels of risk for the peasants and requires different levels of commitment to the rebel cause. At the least supportive end of the scale is a pattern of active and overt support of the government and equally active and overt betrayal of the rebels. At the other end of the scale is overt participation in the rebel organization and its operations. In between are patterns of support ranging from passive tolerance of the rebel's presence to active but covert support of their operations.[10] What mixes of rebel benefits and sanctions might induce each level of nonelite support? What counterinsurgent strategies is the government likely to respond with in order to deter or prevent people from providing this form of support?

Betrayal

Betrayal involves peasants providing the state with intelligence on rebel organizations and operations. This information allows the government to target its violence precisely against the rebels and their known supporters while minimizing "collateral damage" that might drive otherwise neutral citizens into the arms of the rebels. Betrayal can be especially devastating to a rebel movement in the early stages of its existence, when the rebel forces are heavily outnumbered and outgunned by the government army. The imbalance in force strength early in a civil war means the state can crush a nascent rebellion if only a few peasants provide government troops with accurate intelligence on rebel locations, movements, and activities.

The early defeat of a rebel insurgency is quite common. Mason, Weingarten, and Fett (1999) find that, in the fifty-seven civil wars in their data set, rebels were defeated in the first year of the war in fifteen of those cases, which represents over half the rebel defeats. Ché Guevara's failure to rally Bolivian peasants to his call for revolution illustrates the point that the first task of the rebels is to deter betrayal until they can build the capacity to enlist active forms of support from peasants and other nonelites. Timothy Wickham-Crowley (1992:

117) points out that farmland was relatively abundant in Bolivia at the time of Guevara's campaign. As a consequence, most peasants reacted with indifference to Guevara's appeal to take up arms against landlords, the Bolivian state, and their North American benefactors. It took only a few informants among the mass of otherwise indifferent peasants to provide the Bolivian army with enough information on Guevara's movements to enable them to track him down and annihilate his small band before they could build a base of support among the peasantry. Wickham-Crowley suggests that betrayal may be more difficult to deter when land is relatively abundant and peasants have little incentive to assume the risks inherent in providing even covert support to guerrilla insurgents.

Though the chances of being caught by the rebels may be small, peasants know that the punishment for betrayal can be harsh. For the rebels to counteract government intelligence gathering, they must increase their own capacity to detect and punish betrayal. They cannot simply buy off informants by promising to match or exceed the payoffs the government offers for information. As long as the rebels lack the capacity to detect and punish betrayal, informants could simply accept the rebels' payoffs and continue to inform on them anyway. For this reason, rebel tactics for dealing with betrayal usually focus on precisely targeted but extremely violent reprisals. Wickham-Crowley (1990: 217) notes that rebels are usually more effective than the government at identifying informants, largely because the rebels tend to establish a permanent (if clandestine) presence in a region, while the government relies on periodic sweeps by military units that then return to their barracks, isolated from the civilian population. For this reason, the rebels are usually better able to sort out the "traitors" from the mass of anonymous peasants. They tend to be more precise though no less brutal than the government in punishing betrayal. Threatening informants with death may deter them more effectively than increasing the probability with which they expect to be caught and punished by the rebels. Adding to its own intelligence gathering capacity (that is, its capacity to identify government informants) is extremely costly for the rebels. Incremental increases in detection capacity may be less cost-effective at deterring betrayal early in the conflict than simply threatening known betrayers with harsher penalties, including death. No amount of government benefit can offset the risk of assassination. Besides, government forces seldom provide much in the way of direct payoffs for the information that peasants provide them, and certainly not enough to offset even the slim possibility of death at the hands of the rebels. Unless government forces can also protect informants from rebel reprisals, the calculus of fear dictates that one would plead ignorance when government troops ask for information.

Passive Tolerance

The minimum level of support that the rebels hope for, especially in the early stages of the rebellion, is that peasants simply avoid involvement on either side of the conflict, refrain from taking any action against them (especially betrayal), and in their passivity allow the rebels to operate in their vicinity. Leites and Wolf (1970: 10) observe that, "the only 'act' that [the rebel] needs desperately from a large proportion of the populace is *nondenunciation* (that is, eschewing the act of informing against R[ebels]) and noncombat against it." Joel Migdal (1974: 249) observes, "in the early stages of revolution, revolutionaries stake their lives on the hope that peasants will not expose them to authorities."

As a form of tacit support, passive tolerance requires no commitment of time and resources on the part of peasants. It also poses little risk for them. As long as the government forces do not punish villagers for pleading ignorance to questions concerning rebel activity in their area, peasants have little to fear from tacitly supporting the rebels by simply avoiding any involvement in the conflict. By doing nothing, residents allow the rebels to exist.

Passive tolerance is critical in the early stages of a rebellion because the rebels are outnumbered and outgunned by the state. Their numbers are small, their organization is fragile, and their capacity both to challenge the state and to provide benefits for their supporters is very limited at this stage. A rebellion could easily be annihilated in its infancy if the population did not tolerate the rebels' existence by declining to inform on them.

Although the odds are stacked against the rebels early in the civil war, they have a decided advantage over the government in their struggle to elicit tacit support from rural populations. Winning passive tolerance is not especially costly for the rebels. They do not have to provide substantial flows of benefits to peasants, since tacit support has few if any opportunity costs for the peasants. Rebels can cultivate this level of support largely by playing on the grievances peasants have against the state and by taking advantage of peasants' lack of commitment to the state (Migdal 1974: 248; Leites and Wolf 1970: 10). As noted in chapter 3, the sort of socioeconomic setting in which rural rebellions occur is hardly conducive to widespread commitments of loyalty to the state. At its best, the state is a matter of indifference to peasants. At its worst, the state is an intrusive force that exacts payments from them, provides them little in the form of public goods or services, and uses intimidation as a normal part of its interaction with them. In this environment, it does not require much persuasion for the rebels to induce people to do nothing to help the state defeat them.

Ideological appeals that promise a better tomorrow are less relevant at this early stage. Rebels often recruit from villages in the region where they operate, and ties of family and community can help to persuade residents to refrain from informing on the rebels (Race 1972: 72–73). Simply treating peasants with respect, paying them a fair price for food and other purchases, and helping out with community projects such as harvesting, planting, and repairing roads, bridges, and water systems are often sufficient to induce tolerance on the part of peasants. Jeffrey Race interviewed a hamlet chief from the South Vietnamese province of Long An, who described how the Vietcong won the loyalty of a villager:

> [The peasant] would be building a house. The Vietcong would come by and help him put it up. . . . The next time they came by and asked for a meal, he would invite them in. But when they took a meal it was not like our soldiers' way: burst in, demand food, sit around while it was being fixed, eat, and finally grab a couple of chickens and run off. Instead, the VC would go into the kitchen, clean the rice, and while they were waiting for it to cook, they would sweep the house, wash the dishes, and set the table. When the meal was over, they would clean up, and then thank everyone politely. So the owner of the house would think, "the soldiers come in here as if they owned the place, but this other fellow is very polite and helps me out." Naturally, he let the Vietcong eat at his house all the time. This is how the Vietcong gained people's support. (73)

Mao Zedong pioneered this "people's war" strategy of winning the support of peasants by providing them with services, treating them with dignity and respect, and using these everyday forms of interaction as opportunities to persuade them—by word and deed—that the revolutionaries would create a more abundant and just social order when they prevailed.[11] When they entered a region, CCP cadres began by addressing specific mundane problems in the lives of villagers, such as the shortages and high prices of salt, rice, and other basic necessities, or the need for a bridge in a particular community. Resolving these problems induced the sort of tacit support that allowed the CCP to extend its authority in the region.

Covert but Active Support

Passive tolerance increases the range of territory over which insurgents can operate, with the range being circumscribed more by constraints of rebel logistics and organization than by the extent of peasant support for their cause. However, for the rebels to sustain their operations, at some point they need some peasants to go beyond mere passive tolerance and provide them with active forms of support. For most peasants most of the time, their acts of support will be covert. These include providing sanctuary, food, shelter, and other logistical aid for rebel operations, as well as intelligence on the movement of government forces. Civilians who provide this kind of help do so covertly, in that they conceal their acts in order to avoid punishment by the state. They are part-time supporters who continue to carry on their daily routines as citizens of the regime, even as they engage in occasional acts of covert support for the revolutionaries. Nevertheless, compared to passive tolerance, covert but active support represents a quantum leap in commitment to the rebel cause. By providing such support, peasants do risk detection and retribution by the government. They expose themselves to the risk of denunciation by neighbors, friends, or relatives.

To induce this level of commitment, rebels often begin by cultivating exchange relationships with peasants on an individual basis. Individual peasants or small groups provide discrete acts of support to the rebels in return for private rewards or selective incentives. In return the rebels provide the supporter with payments in cash or in kind. However, at this point, the peasant does not want to become known to the government or to his neighbors as a supporter of the rebels. Therefore the rebels must also be able to offer some protection against retaliation by the government's forces and denunciation by other peasants. This can involve simply concealing the exchange from other peasants. Or it can involve some demonstration of their effectiveness at identifying and eliminating local landlords, government officials, and informants (Leites and Wolf 1970: 10–11). Once tacit support allowed CCP guerrillas to operate more freely in a region, Mao would elicit more active forms of peasant support by compelling local landlords to accept rent reductions and even modest land reform programs.

As the level of rebel activity escalates further and the capacity of the rebel organization to provide benefits increases, peasants will seek collective gains for their village, ethnic group, or other solidarity unit in return for group support for the rebels. Where some aspects of traditional village social organization remain viable, the revolutionaries can "capture" the support of whole villages by offering residents a better exchange rate than the state on the variety of transactions that make up the fabric of the village's links to the outside world (Migdal 1974: 249–50). Where traditional patron-client mechanisms of subsistence security have eroded, rebels can capture the support of entire villages by restoring the effectiveness of village institutions and becoming, in effect, the new patrons. With landlords and agents of the state eliminated or intimidated into inaction, rebels begin establishing an institutional presence in the form of peasant cooperatives, clinics, and schools for villagers and their children. This stage marks a critical threshold of peasant participation in rebel institutions. Once villagers have a stake in the survival of these grassroots institutions, they have a stake in the survival of the rebel organization. The CCP used this strategy in China, and the Vietcong emulated it in South Vietnam. If the rebels do this, they gain access to market and non-market exchange flows in the community from which they can extract a revolutionary surplus to support their own organization. This revolutionary surplus—usually extracted in the form of "war taxes"—can also be used to provide the selective incentives needed to induce other sympathizers to become active supporters.

By making use of traditional village institutions, the rebels also relieve themselves of the need to establish and maintain their own enforcement machinery in the village. As long as the village as a unit is receiving collective benefits from the rebels, the village as a community has an incentive to use its own policing capacity to enforce prohibitions against both free-riding and denunciation of the rebels to the government. As long as the rebels can protect the village from reprisals by the state and prevent the state, landlords, or other authorities from collecting rents and taxes, it can elicit support from villagers, as long as its war taxes are less than the rent and taxes the villagers were paying to the other authorities.

The decision calculus discussed earlier suggests that peasants are more likely to engage in covert support as their chances of detection and punishment by the government decrease and the payoff for these acts, especially in the form of rebel-provided selective incentives, increase. Of these two variables, the more salient one should be the risks of reprisals by the government. Anything the rebels can do to decrease the chances of covert supporters being identified and punished by the government should increase the willingness of peasants to provide them with covert support. Offering a higher price for such support might increase a peasant's present income, but the penalties the government can impose in reprisal—penalties such as confiscation of a peasant's land and other property, imprisonment, torture, or even death—will have a far more substantial and lasting effect on the individual's well being, to say the least. Therefore rebel tactics aimed at inducing active but covert forms of support often center more on reducing the government's capacity to detect and punish covert support. It is also cheaper for the rebel organization to accommodate peasants' fear of reprisal by taking steps to conceal transactions and eliminate local agents of the state than it is for the rebels to pay a higher price for support while doing nothing to minimize the risk of reprisal. Just as the most cost-effective way for them to deter betrayal may be to increase the severity of the punishments imposed on informants, so the cheapest way to induce covert support should be to reduce the probability of those acts being detected and punished by the government.

To counter rebel success at inducing covert support, states often employ "input denial" strategies, such as interdicting supplies, making pre-emptive purchases of subsistence goods in local markets, and denying the rebels the human resources they need through such measures as relocating populations away from rebel-controlled zones and conscripting young males into the army (Leites and Wolf 1970). One example of this was the "strategic hamlet" program implemented in South Vietnam in 1962. Stanley Karnow (1983: 255) describes this program as a plan "to corral peasants into armed stockades, thereby depriving the Vietcong of their support." The program turned out to be a failure, as Karnow notes:

> In reality, the program often converted peasants into Vietcong sympathizers. Peasants in many places resented working without pay to dig moats, implant bamboo stakes, and erect fences against an enemy that did not threaten them but directed its sights against government officials. . . . Even peasants who agreed to join local self-defense groups were disenchanted when the government failed to furnish them with weapons, and many were antagonized by corrupt officials who embezzled money earmarked for seed, fertilizer, and irrigation as well as medical care, education, and other social benefits. (257)

Many input denial strategies impose hardships on peasants and thereby induce resentment against the state. The affected population suffers a loss of income which undermines their loyalty to the regime and shifts their preferences in favor of the rebels.

Active and Overt Support

Some of those who provide active but covert support to the rebels will eventually shift to overt forms of support. Active and overt support involves direct participation in at least some of the rebels' operations some of the time. Those who make this level of commitment are full-time participants in the revolutionary organization. They have abandoned all pretense of being neutral or pro-regime and instead have committed themselves publicly to the support of the rebels.

More risk-acceptant peasants join first. Their addition to the rebel force reduces the risks of penalties for subsequent recruits and enhances the rebels' prospects of victory, eventually inducing more risk-averse sympathizers to join as well (Lichbach 1995: 114–16). These risk-takers and innovators are usually the younger and more ambitious peasants in a village. Young peasants who have some education, training, or special skills but who feel that they will never be able to fully exploit their talents under the current social order are attracted to the rebels by the promise of upward mobility in the form of leadership benefits. The prospect of a new social order free of the traditional ascriptive barriers that currently constrain their mobility appeals to them, perhaps enough to make it worthwhile for them to assume the risks inherent in being an early recruit to the rebel cause. They are more likely to act on this opportunity if they already have a history of activism, are integrated into networks of other activists, have some personal tie or regular contact with someone who is already a participant in the movement, and are relatively free of personal constraints that would make participation potentially costly (McAdam 1986: 71; McAdam and Paulsen 1993: 644).

For a number of reasons, young adults with such ambitions are more likely to become activists and militants than are older adults with the same abilities and ambitions.[12] First, young adults are less likely to have established a family. Therefore they do not have those responsibilities to constrain them in making the choice between participating or not participating in a revolutionary organization. Those with a family must consider how the risks they take on by joining the movement will affect not only their own personal well-being but the well-being of their spouse and children as well. Those with no family responsibilities are free from those constraints. Second, young adults are less likely to have their own farms, businesses, houses, or other assets that would be put at risk if they joined the movement. In short, they have less to lose. Third, because they are young, whatever punishments they risk will be discounted to present value over a longer remaining life span and, therefore, will have a lower present value. Finally, the value of any benefits they gain from participation will be compounded over a longer remaining life span than is the case for older peasants.

To support the rebels overtly is extremely risky, and peasants will not assume such risks unless they have some assurance that their support will not be suicidal. This assurance can come about in several ways. First, active and overt support becomes more likely as the rebels gain all but unchallenged control over entire villages and regions and establish themselves as the sole functioning authority in that region. Eric Wolf (1969: 293) refers to this as "tactical power." Location in outlying areas that are beyond the reach of the coercive power of the state and landlords allows rebels much greater tactical flexibility in building institutions and providing services that will induce peasants to abandon the state and support them. To the extent that they are beyond the reach of the state and landlords, rebels can establish their own local monopoly over the organized use of force and thereby become the de facto government in that region of the country. Such control implies that they can protect supporters from government reprisals, in which case peasants need not conceal their support. Unchallenged rebel control in an area also implies that they can detect and punish acts that are supportive of the government. When rebel control in a region is so nearly complete, the price that they have to pay for peasant support, in the form of benefits, is reduced because of their substantial ability to detect and punish nonsupport and betrayal. In this situation, peasants have the choice of supporting the rebels or leaving the region for some other area that is not under rebel jurisdiction.

Finally, active and overt support becomes more likely as the state's application of repressive violence becomes more widespread and more indiscriminate. When one is in danger of becoming a victim of counterinsurgent violence regardless of whether one has or has not provided support for the rebels, there is little additional risk associated with supporting the rebels. All that the rebels have to do in return is offer protection.

One strategy that governments have used to undermine active and overt support for a protracted insurgency is to offer amnesty to guerrillas if they will put down their arms and withdraw their support from the rebel leadership. Most negotiated settlements to civil wars include as a necessary component some sort of amnesty for both sides. Benedict Kerkvliet (1977: 238–42) argues that support for the Huk rebellion in the Philippines declined after 1951 precisely because Ramon Magsaysay, first as secretary of defense (1950–1953) and then as president (1954–1957), reformed the military's counterinsurgency strategy to reduce drastically the level of sanctions that peasants faced. In addition, he provided subsidies to peasants in the form of rural development projects (credit, health clinics, irrigation canals, and wells). He even offered homestead lands to Huk soldiers who would surrender under a grant of amnesty. The effects of this two-pronged strategy were that large numbers of Huk soldiers surrendered, and much of the movement's civilian base withdrew their support from the rebels and began to support the government. By the end of 1954, the rebellion had faded away.

CONCLUSION

A central issue in research on state-sanctioned terror is whether, and under what conditions, repressive violence deters or induces a shift in popular support away from the state and toward the opposition. This chapter describes the ways in which variations in the targeting of state-sanctioned repressive violence affect the ebb and flow of popular support in societies torn by civil violence and repression. Carefully targeted repressive violence may reduce the level of active support for an opposition movement in the short term, but it does nothing to restore peasant loyalty to the state. The social, economic, and political conditions that gave rise to peasant grievances in the first place remain unchanged. And those grievances remain unresolved. Support for the opposition may decline, because peasants see it as futile. Surviving opposition leaders are likely to shift to violent tactics of their own, since nonviolent tactics have been repressed. If the state responds to the emergence of opposition violence by escalating its own repressive violence and expanding its targeting, it may eventually induce an increase in active support for the rebel opposition.

This analysis of the effects of repression on peasant support contains some implications for policy makers as well. United States policy toward Third World insurgencies has consistently treated them as military problems whose resolution was simply a matter of implementing the appropriate counterinsurgency tactics and backing those tactics with sufficient firepower. Policy debates over "low-intensity conflict" have tended to focus more on questions of how military force structure, training, equipment, and tactics could be configured to optimize the prospects of battlefield success against a guerrilla army (see Klare and Kornbluh 1988). Little attention has been devoted to how these counterinsurgency tactics affect the political support and loyalties of peasants. This analysis suggests that, ultimately, nonmilitary initiatives such as negotiated cease-fires and amnesty programs designed to integrate an insurgent opposition back into the mainstream of politics may be a less costly way to bring a protracted insurgency to a peaceful conclusion. In the absence of any credible assurances against violent reprisals, rebels have nothing to lose by continuing a program of violent opposition.

The analysis also suggests that structural reform in the local economy is essential to the long-term stability of any regime in these nations. Where nonmilitary options such as land reform have been tried, the assumptions underlying their design and implementation often have been equally simplistic. The idea behind such U.S.-backed land reform programs in Vietnam and El Salvador was that "land to the tiller" programs would "win the hearts and minds" of rural populations by giving them a stake in the status quo (Prosterman 1981). However, such programs ignore the marginal economic existence of the newly created peasant smallholder. By themselves, such programs do not reduce the beneficiaries' vulnerability to either the economic risks of agriculture or the political risks of repressive violence. Any land reform program that does nothing to reduce the economic marginality of beneficiaries or to create occupational alternatives to agriculture for nonbeneficiaries has little hope of remedying the underlying sources of instability. Moreover, economic reforms that do nothing to reduce the threat of repressive violence are unlikely to succeed. Unchecked repression by foes of reform within the regime can undermine the success of land reform by intimidating potential beneficiaries into abandoning their right to claim title to land.

NOTES

1. On the Salvadoran reform, see Strasma 1989; Brockett 1988; Mason 1986a. On the Philippine land reform, see Riedinger 1995. On the Peruvian land reform, see Ma-

son and Schwartzfager 1989; McClintock 1998. Thiesenhusen (1995) discusses the politics and economics of land reform in a number of Latin American cases, and Prosterman, Temple, and Hanstad (1990) compile studies of land reform in a number of cases in Africa, Asia, and Latin America. See also Mason 1998.

2. On the other hand, Leites and Wolf point out that while programs of economic reform may elicit increased support for the government, there will not necessarily be an equivalent reduction in the level of support for the opposition. Programs that increase peasant income may end up subsidizing some activities that are supportive of the opposition. Peasants can and often do use some of their increased income to support opposition organizations, the very ones that the state is trying to defeat by initiating land reform in the first place (1970: 19–20).

3. Much of the following discussion is derived from Mason and Krane 1989 and Mason 1989, 1996.

4. Latent supporters are people who prefer the rebels to the incumbent regime but are unwilling to act on their preference out of fear of retribution by the state.

5. As noted above, most revolutionary leaders begin their political careers in legal political parties, labor unions, and other organizations. It is only after those organizations become the target of repression that they shift from nonviolent to revolutionary activism. Fidel Castro, for instance, was trained as a lawyer and was a founding member of the Orthodoxo reform party in Cuba. It was only after General Fulgencio Batista seized power in a military coup in 1952, thereby pre-empting elections in which Castro intended to run for office, that Castro turned to armed insurrection (DeFronzo 1996: 178–80). Nelson Mandela was the leader of the opposition African National Congress when the government of South Africa outlawed the party in 1960 and imprisoned Mandela. Joshua Nkomo, leader of the Zimbabwe African People's Union, began his political career as a trade union organizer in Rhodesia. Both he and Robert Mugabe, leader of the rival Zimbabwe African National Union (ZANU), led their parties to revolutionary violence after the government of Rhodesia banned them and imprisoned or exiled most of the leaders of ZANU and ZAPU (Scarritt 1991: 246–47). Repressing those who organize nonviolent forms of collective action (demonstrations, strikes, and electoral campaigns) simply compels the new opposition leaders to adopt violent tactics of their own.

6. Of course, some revolutions are defeated by a sudden blow to the revolutionary leadership. This was the case in Ché Guevara's abortive insurgency in Bolivia. A more recent example would be the near collapse of the Shining Path movement following the capture of the movement's leader and founder, Abimael Guzmán. Even though Shining Path units continue to operate in some parts of Peru, the movement poses no threat to the survival of the Peruvian regime.

In other cases, governments are defeated because they collapse due to sudden defections by the military or a collapse in the military's willingness to fight. This was the case with the Mobutu regime in Zaire, the government of South Vietnam in 1975, and the Rwandan regime in 1994. However, in these cases, defection occurs when segments of the military conclude that defeat is imminent or the current regime is so discredited that it can never regain its legitimacy.

7. The following is derived from Mason 1996, 1989. The model is derived from Frohlich and Oppenheimer's (1973, 1974) model of the rational tax evader.

8. For works that model the revolutionary behavior of peasants in this manner, see Grossman 1991; see also Gupta 1990: ch. 4; Sandler 1992: 182–88.

9. It would simply be too costly for the state to maintain a police force large enough to monitor every potential rebel supporter. All that the state has to do is maintain a force large enough to make peoples' estimate of the chances of detection large enough to deter them from engaging in support for the rebels. See Frohlich and Oppenheimer 1973, 1974; Mason 1989, 1996.

10. On the forms of nonelite support for insurgent opposition and the escalating sequence in which they emerge, see Leites and Wolfe 1970 and Migdal 1974: 4–51, among others. Many of these behaviors—whether supportive of the government or of the rebels—are not easily translated into monetary terms. Nevertheless, they are costly to the individual in the sense that they represent time, energy, and material resources devoted to the advancement of a political cause and therefore not devoted to the individual's own income-producing or consumption activities. In other words, engaging in support behaviors represents opportunity costs. In this sense, the supportive behaviors that an individual provides to the government or the rebels may be conceived of as the equivalent of taxes (in the form of direct payments in cash or in kind) or in the form of opportunity costs that he or she pays to the government or the rebels. They can also be seen as investments: The individual makes the contribution now in hopes that it will bring greater return in the future. See Marwell and Oliver 1993: 16–18. On contributions of time versus money (or other tangible resources) see Oliver and Marwell 1992.

11. Migdal (1974: 245–46) quotes Mao from his essay "Mind the Living Conditions of the Masses and Attend to the Methods of Work": "All problems facing the masses in the actual life should claim our attention. If we have these problems at heart and solve them to the satisfaction of the masses, we shall really become the organizers of the life of the masses."

12. On youth participation in radical political movements, see Goldstone 1991: 136–39.

Chapter Seven

Win, Lose, or Draw: How Civil Wars End

On July 17, 1979, Anastasio Somoza Debayle fled Nicaragua as the rebel forces of the Sandinista National Liberation Front (Frente Sandinista de Liberación Nacional, or the FSLN) marched into the capital of Managua to take power. The FSLN triumph ended eighteen years of guerrilla insurgency that had culminated in eighteen months of nationwide civil war. It also ended a forty-three-year dictatorship by the Somoza family (see Booth 1985). The Sandinista victory represented the first successful revolution in the Western Hemisphere since the Cuban revolution of 1958–1959. Soon the Sandinista regime was itself faced with an armed challenge by the U.S.-backed Contra rebels. The decade-long Contra war ended in 1990, when Violetta Chamorro won the presidential election over the Sandinista incumbent Daniel Ortega.

On September 12, 1992, armed agents of the Peruvian government burst into a safe house in Lima and captured Abimael Guzmán, leader and founding father of the Shining Path (Sendero Luminoso) revolutionary movement. Within weeks police had arrested another 1,000 suspected Senderistas, including twelve of the nineteen central committee members. The threat of a Shining Path victory, which had been looming ominously when the year began, had waned by the end of 1992. While Shining Path guerrillas still operate in some regions of Peru, the movement no longer poses a revolutionary threat to the government of Peru (see McClintock 1998; Palmer 1992).

On January 16, 1992, Alfredo Cristiani, president of El Salvador, signed a peace accord with the leaders of the FMLN revolutionary movement (the Frente Faribundo Martí de Liberación Nacional, or the Faribundo Marti National Liberation Front), marking the end of a civil war that had lasted over a decade and resulted in the death of some 70,000 Salvadorans. The agreement marked the first negotiated end to a civil war in the Western Hemisphere since the Colombian National Front pact of 1958 ended one of that nation's protracted civil wars, a period referred to simply as *la violencia*. The Salvadoran pact mandated reforms of the electoral and judicial systems, demobilization and reintegration into society of FMLN guerrillas, reductions in the size and jurisdiction of the armed forces, a purge of its officer corps, and the creation of a new civilian police force to replace the old police, the national guard, and the treasury police, all of which were irrevocably tainted by their involvement in death squad activity (Montgomery 1995). The FMLN entered the new political regime as a party running candidates for office. To date, the hostilities have not resumed.

These three cases illustrate the possible outcomes of civil war. In Nicaragua the rebels won. The Sandinistas overthrew the incumbent regime and established a new political, economic, and social order. In Peru the government of Alberto Fujimori defeated the Shining Path guerrillas, at least in the sense that Shining Path no longer represents an imminent threat to the survival of the incumbent regime, a threat they did pose in 1992. (This case is discussed in detail in chapter 9.) And in El Salvador the government of President Alfredo Cristiani and the FMLN guerrillas reached a negotiated settlement that ended the war and allowed the reintegration of the revolutionaries into Salvadoran political society. (The revolution in El Salvador is discussed in detail in chapter 8.) How do we account for these different outcomes?

Students of revolutionary violence have devoted considerable attention to the question of what causes revolution in the countryside. However, until recently very little effort has been devoted to studying the processes by which civil wars come to an end, whether by a negotiated settlement between the incumbent regime and its revolutionary challenger or by a military victory by one side or the other. The inattention to how civil wars end can be attributed to a number of common perceptions about the nature of revolution in the countryside and the international context in which such wars occur.

First, most students of civil wars have consistently discounted the prospects for peaceful settlements to civil wars, largely because until recently few civil wars ever did end in a stable negotiated settlement. Paul Pillar (1983: 25) finds that less than one-third of the civil wars in his data set ended in negotiated settlement. Stephan Stedman (1991: 5–9) finds that twenty of sixty-five civil conflicts in his data set ended through negotiation, but only eleven of the sixty-five ended in a settlement that did not involve partition of the nation, the withdrawal of a colonial power, or the mere ratification of one side's battlefield dominance.

Second, arranging a settlement in a civil war is fundamentally more difficult than mediating interstate conflicts. Roy Licklider (1993a: 4) explains why this is the case: "Ending international war is hard enough, but at least there the opponents will presumably eventually retreat to their own territories. . . . But in civil wars the members of the two sides must live side by side and work together in a common government to make the country work. . . . How do groups of people who have been killing one another with considerable enthusiasm and success come together to form a common government?"

An often-quoted passage from Fred Iklé's book reiterates this dilemma: "In conflicts that are predominantly civil wars . . . outcomes intermediary between victory and defeat are difficult to construct. If partition is not a feasible outcome because the belligerents are not geographically separable, one side has to get all, or nearly so, since there cannot be two governments ruling over one country, and since the passions aroused and the political cleavages opened render a sharing of power unworkable" (1971: 95).

Yet, since the end of the Cold War, a number of civil wars have been concluded through negotiated settlement. UN-mediated peace accords brought an end to civil wars in El Salvador, Nicaragua, Guatemala, Angola, Mozambique, Bosnia, and Cambodia, to name but a few. The recent proliferation of peace agreements in civil wars led scholars such as Roy Licklider (1992, 1993a, 1995) to examine the conditions that make civil wars amenable to peaceful resolution and the conditions that make those settlements hold.[1] Patrick Regan (1996, 2000) has analyzed the effects of outside intervention on the outcome of civil wars. Barbara Walter (1997) explores the critical role of third-party intervention in bringing about peaceful settlements to civil wars. Mason and Fett (1996) explore the characteristics of a civil war that make it more or less likely to end in a negotiated settlement as opposed to a military victory by either the rebels or the government. Mason, Weingarten, and Fett (1999) extend that analysis to consider the factors that influence whether civil wars end in a government victory, a rebel victory, or a negotiated settlement. Others have contributed detailed case studies of the conditions that affect the successful resolution of specific civil wars (see Licklider 1993b; Damrosch 1993; Zartman 1995).

This chapter explores the question of how civil wars end. Once a revolutionary social movement has mounted an armed challenge to the regime, what factors determine whether the government wins, the rebels win, or the two parties negotiate a peace agreement? The analysis begins with a discussion of the decision calculus by which rebels and governments choose between quitting or continuing to fight, in anticipation of eventual victory. This decision calculus suggests a set of conflict characteristics that influence each actor's choice between quitting or continuing to fight. From this, I draw some inferences concerning what conditions might influence whether a civil war will end in a victory by the government, a victory by the rebels, or a negotiated settlement.

WIN, LOSE, OR DRAW

Once the war is underway, the possible outcomes are (1) victory for the government, (2) victory for the rebels, or (3) a negotiated settlement. What factors influence which outcome will result in any given civil war? One place to start is with a simple model of the decision calculus facing the government (G) and the rebel leadership (R), as they struggle to bring the war to a conclusion that is favorable to their interests.[2] The goal of the rebels may be to overthrow the existing government and replace it with a new configuration of government institutions staffed by new personnel (a revolution), or the rebels may seek independence from an existing government by partitioning the nation and creating a new sovereign nation state out of some portion of the existing one (a separatist or secessionist war). The goal of the government is, quite obviously, to defeat the rebels and retain control over the machinery of the state and the territory of the nation.

During the course of the war, G and R are each confronted periodically with the choice between continuing to fight or quitting. For the war to end, it must be the case that either G or R or both decided to quit fighting. Accordingly there are four possible outcomes resulting from their joint decisions: G wins, R wins, G and R conclude a negotiated settlement, or the war continues. Following Stam (1996: 34–37), the four possible outcomes can be represented as an iterated two-person game, depicted in figure 7.1. If R continues fighting and G quits, R wins, and the government is overthrown. If G continues fighting and R quits, G wins, and the revolt is defeated. If both G and R choose to quit at the same time, the civil war ends in a negotiated settlement. If neither decides to quit, the civil war continues until some future point when one or both of them do quit.

Each actor's decision can be depicted as a function of that actor's expected benefits from victory, the rate at which it is absorbing costs of war and inflicting costs on its rival, and the duration of the war (Mason and Fett 1996; Mason, Weingarten, and Fett 1999; see also Stam 1996: 40; Bennett and Stam 1998: 347). Each side will continue to fight unless the expected costs of fighting exceed the expected benefits of victory. If only one side decides that the costs of continuing

		GOVERNMENT	
		Fight	**Quit**
REBELS	**Fight**	Civil War Continues	Rebels Win
	Quit	Government Wins	Negotiated Settlement

Figure 7.1. Civil War Outcomes as a Function of Rebel and Government Choices.
Source: **Derived from Stam 1996: 35.**

to fight exceed the benefits of victory, that side quits, and its rival wins. If both sides conclude that continued fighting will be more costly than the benefits of eventual victory, then both will quit fighting and enter into a negotiated settlement. At any given time, continued fighting is the dominant strategy for both sides, because to quit fighting without guarantees that one's rival will do likewise is to expose oneself to defeat through capitulation (Stam 1996: 353).

Given this logic, it is clear why negotiated settlements are so rare in civil wars and why, when they do occur, they are often unstable: Cease-fires often break down and fighting resumes.[3] For a settlement to be feasible, both R and G must simultaneously conclude that quitting is preferred to continued fighting. Either party can unilaterally preclude a settlement by continuing to fight, and either party can unilaterally repeal a settlement by resuming the fight. If one or both parties prefer continued fighting, it must be the case that they expect to win at some later point, or they expect to achieve more favorable settlement terms in the future. In either case, as long as one or both parties expect their net benefits from victory (or a future settlement) to exceed the benefits they can get from a settlement now (or from defeat), they have a strong incentive to continue fighting.

How do the parties decide whether to continue fighting or quit? We can represent each actor's decision calculus as a simple utility function, much like the individual's choice between participating or not participating in the revolution. For each party, there are three possible outcomes of the civil war: win, lose, or draw. We can assume that a win is their most preferred outcome and a loss is their least preferred outcome, with a draw (settlement) preferred to a loss but not to victory. Given this, we first model the choice between quitting and continuing to fight.[4] Both the government and the rebels presume that if the conflict continues, it will eventually terminate either in victory by one of them or in some later negotiated settlement. In the meantime, each party will continue to absorb the costs of continued conflict (C_C) from the present time (t_0) until that time in the future (t_V) when it estimates that it will achieve victory. Thus each party's subjective expected utility from continuing to fight can be expressed as follows (equation 7.1):

where EU_C is the expected utility of continuing the conflict, P_V is that party's estimate of the probability that it will eventually achieve victory, U_V is the util-

$$EU_C = P_V(U_V) + (1 - P_V)(U_D) - \sum_{t_i=0}^{t_V} C_{t_i} \qquad (7.1)$$

ity that party expects to receive from victory, $(1 - P_V)$ is its estimate of the probability that it will suffer defeat, U_D is the negative utility that party expects to suffer from defeat, and C_{ti} is the rate at which that party absorbs costs of continued conflict. The cost variable is expressed as a rate in the sense that it is that party's estimate of the average amount of human and material losses it suffers per day, week, month, or other increment of time (t_i). Because C_{ti} is a rate, it must be summed from the present until that point in the future, t_v, when the party in question estimates that it will be able to achieve victory.[5]

Equation 7.1 suggests several factors that enter the decision making of both the government and the rebels. Two factors affect a party's estimate of the expected costs of continued conflict. One is the rate at which it is absorbing costs. The higher that rate is, the more quickly the mounting costs of continuing to fight will approach the expected benefits of victory. The other factor is the actor's estimate of the amount of time it will take for them to achieve victory. The longer it will take for that party to win, the greater will be the total accrued costs of conflict. Thus any factor that either extends a party's estimate of the amount of time required to achieve victory or increases the rate at which it is absorbing the costs of war will decrease that party's willingness to continuing fighting in pursuit of victory, all else being equal. Generally a party will continue to fight as long as the payoff it expects to receive from victory exceeds its estimate of the costs it will have to absorb in order to achieve victory. The first factor each party must consider, then, is the probability of achieving victory. If a party believes it has a good chance of winning, it has little reason to quit now. Conversely a party that estimates its chances of victory to be remote might prefer to negotiate a settlement now rather than continue fighting. Any concessions it could secure in the settlement would leave that actor better off than the fate that awaits them with the defeat that appears inevitable if not imminent. However, if their rival has a similar read on the tide of battle, that rival has little reason to make any concessions now, since victory appears imminent. Under these circumstances, the losing party has to consider whether it would be better off simply quitting and accepting defeat or continuing to fight in hopes of turning the tide of battle and eventually winning or persuading its rival to negotiate a settlement agreement. A negotiated settlement becomes likely, then, only when both parties estimate the expected payoffs from victory to be less than the accrued costs of achieving that victory. This captures the logic of William Zartman's concept of "mutually hurting stalemate," a condition whereby "the countervailing power of each side, though insufficient to make the other side lose, prevents it from winning" (Zartman, 1993: 24).

A less obvious implication of equation 7.1 is that both parties must also discount their estimate of the payoffs from victory by the costs they will have to absorb in order to achieve victory. Even if one party estimates that it has a very good chance of eventually winning, it may still be willing to accept a settlement now if, in its estimate, the accumulated costs of winning

$$\sum_{t_i=t_s}^{t_v} C_{t_i} \tag{7.1a}$$

would be so great that victory would be pyrrhic. If victory can be achieved only by protracted or intense fighting, there may be a set of settlement terms that would leave that party better off than they would be after a prolonged and costly battle to victory.[6]

Equation 7.1 depicts an actor's choice between continuing to fight in anticipation of eventual victory or quitting now and accepting defeat. The other possible outcome (besides winning or losing) is to make an agreement with the other party for both sides to quit fighting (declare a cease-fire) and negotiate a settlement to the war. The expected utility from a negotiated settlement can be represented as follows (equation 7.2):

$$EU_S = U_S + \sum_{t_i=0}^{t_V} C_{t_i} - \sum_{t_i=0}^{t_S} C_{t_i} \qquad (7.2)$$

where EU_S is the expected payoff from a negotiated settlement, and U_S is the payoff that the actor will receive from the settlement. We can assume that the settlement payoff (U_S) is less than the payoff expected from victory (U_V). However, each actor must consider that, by negotiating a settlement now, both parties avoid the additional costs of conflict

$$\sum_{t_i=t_S}^{t_V} C_{t_i} \qquad (7.1a)$$

Instead, each actor absorbs only those additional costs of conflict that will accrue between the present (t_0) and that point in the near future when the settlement goes into effect (t_S).

Combining equations 7.1 and 7.2, it becomes apparent that the variables affecting an actor's choice between quitting or continuing to fight are (1) the probability of victory, (2) the costs of continued conflict, (3) the additional time needed to achieve victory, (4) the costs of defeat, and (5) the terms of settlement. From this, some propositions can be derived concerning the characteristics of a civil war that affect whether the outcome will be a rebel victory, a government victory, or a negotiated settlement.

DETERMINANTS OF CIVIL WAR OUTCOMES

The decision calculus described above suggests a set of factors that should influence whether a civil war ends in a government win, a rebel win, or a negotiated settlement. Any factor that reduces a party's estimate of its probability of victory, increases the rate at which it absorbs the costs of conflict, or extends its estimate of the time required to achieve victory should make that party more willing to quit rather than continue fighting. If one side decides to quit, the other wins. If both sides decide that continued conflict is futile, then a negotiated settlement becomes feasible. Within this logic, certain characteristics of the conflict, the government and rebel organizations, and the international environment should influence the outcome of the civil war by affecting one or both parties' probability of victory, the rate at which they are absorbing the costs of conflict, or the length of time required for one or the other party to achieve victory.

Roy Licklider (1993a: 14–17) has delineated five sets of factors that are relevant to explaining how civil wars end. These are (1) the stakes over which the conflict arose, (2) the internal politics of each side in the conflict, (3) the military balance in the field, (4) the role of third parties, and (5) the nature of the polity that emerges from the settlement.

Indivisible Stakes

The decision calculus discussed earlier implies that any factor that increases the benefits of a settlement (U_S) or decreases the benefits of a victory (U_V) makes a settlement more appealing. Conversely any factor that increases the benefits of victory should increase an actor's willingness to continue fighting.

The major reason that civil wars are more difficult to resolve than interstate conflicts is the indivisibility of the stakes in a civil war. Paul Pillar (1983: 24) describes the stakes dilemma as follows:

> The likelihood that the two sides in any dispute can negotiate a settlement depends greatly on whether compromise agreements are available. If the stakes are chiefly indivisible, so that neither side can get most of what it wants without depriving the other of most of what it wants, negotiations are less apt to be successful. Stakes are usually less divisible in civil wars than in other types of war; the issue is whether one side or the other shall control the country. . . . Each side in a civil war is a traitor in the eyes of the other and can never expect the enemy to let it live in peace. The struggle for power becomes a struggle for survival as the options narrow to the single one of a fight to the finish. As a result, few civil wars end through negotiation unless they become highly internationalized.

Stakes of a civil war are difficult to quantify. What we can do is distinguish among types of civil wars that presumably involve different stakes: revolutions versus secessionist wars and ethnic conflicts versus ideological conflicts. These conflict types differ from each other in terms of the goals of the rebels and, therefore, the benefits of victory and settlement.

Revolution versus Secession

First, we can distinguish between civil wars that are revolutions and those that are secessionist revolts. In a revolutionary civil war, the rebels seek to overthrow the government and take its place as the government of a sovereign nation state. In a secessionist revolt, the rebels seek not to overthrow the government but to gain independence from it; their goal is to create two sovereign nations out of one.

A number of scholars have argued that a revolutionary conflict (whether ethnically based or not) should be more difficult to conclude through a negotiated settlement than a secessionist war because the stakes—that is, control over the institutions of the state—are more nearly indivisible. Unlike a secessionist revolt, the two parties in a revolution cannot retreat to separate territories and maintain their own independent capacity to defend themselves against a resumption of hostilities. A settlement to a revolutionary war requires the dismantling or merging of two separate armies with two separate command structures, each of which has been dedicated to the defeat of the other. It requires two competing elite groups to cease their efforts to annihilate each other and share power in the routine tasks of running a single government. By contrast, a secessionist revolt can be resolved through an agreement that grants to the rebels greater regional autonomy within the current regime, formalized through federal or consociational arrangements. Whatever the specific terms of the agreement, it is at least possible in a secessionist revolt to craft an arrangement in which both the government and the rebels continue to exist as relatively distinct organizational entities, with each enjoying some guarantees against retribution by the other and some autonomous authority over a segment of the territory and population of the original nation state.

Similar logic suggests that rebels are more likely to win a secessionist war than a revolution, and the government is more likely to win a revolution than a secessionist war. A government faced with a secessionist revolt does have the option of conceding defeat and still continuing to exist as the government of a sovereign nation, though one that is diminished in territory, resources, and population. The government of Pakistan continued to exist after conceding defeat in the secessionist war in Bangladesh in 1971. Ethiopia continued to exist as a sovereign nation after the secession of Eritrea in 1991. Concession is not an option in a revolution. Victory by the rebels in a revolution means the destruction of the existing government and, in all likelihood, the death or exile of its leaders. Thus the costs of defeat for a government are greater in a revolution than in a secessionist war. For this reason, victories by the rebels should be more frequent in secessionist conflicts than in revolutions.

Ethnic versus Ideological Conflicts

Those civil wars in which the belligerents are divided by issues of ethnic identity should be more difficult to resolve by a negotiated settlement than civil wars that are ideologically based.[7] Issues of ethnic identity are more nearly indivisible and therefore more nearly nonnegotiable than are ideological issues, such as the distribution of land, income, or wealth, civil and political rights, or the proper institutional configuration of the state. In an ethnically fragmented society, a negotiated settlement cannot resolve the deeply held and culturally grounded beliefs that are the source of ethnic conflict. Ethnic conflicts are subject to settlement by formulae that guarantee or at least enhance the autonomy and security of the contending ethnic groups. Included among these are federal or consociational arrangements as well as outright partition—the division of one nation state into two. Federalism grants limited regional autonomy to geographically concentrated identity groups and guarantees them some level of representation in the national government. Consociational arrangements likewise grant ethnic groups autonomy over the selection of their own leaders and the management of public affairs internal to the group. Each group is guaranteed some power-sharing stake in the national government as well (Lijphart 1969). Power sharing arrangements require at a minimum: "(1) joint exercise of governmental power; (2) proportional distribution of government funds and jobs; (3) autonomy on ethnic issues (which, if groups are concentrated territorially, may be achieved by regional federation); and (4) a minority veto on issues of vital importance to each group" (Kaufmann 1996: 155).

However, federal and consociational formula often do not hold up over time, because the circumstances that made the original formula acceptable to all parties changes over time. When Lebanon gained independence in 1943, the National Pact defined a consociational power sharing arrangement between the nation's Shiite, Sunni, and Maronite Christian communities. The presidency (the most powerful office) would always be held by a member of the Christian community, while the prime minister would be a Sunni Muslim, and the president of the Chamber of Deputies (the presiding officer of the legislature) would be a Shiite Muslim. Seats in the legislature would be divided between Christians and Muslims on the basis of a six-to-five ratio. Over time, the Shiite population grew more rapidly than the other two, yet Shiites remained the least wealthy of the three communities, and they were confined to the least powerful positions in the national government. The Lebanese formula was irrevocably undermined by the influx of Palestinian refugees from Jordan and the West Bank following the 1973 Yom Kippur War, and civil war ensued (Deeb 1980). Thus differential rates of population growth and economic development in time undermined the legitimacy of the original power sharing formula, especially in the eyes of the ethnic group that was most disadvantaged in the original formula.

We would expect the chances of a victory by the rebels to be lower in ethnically based civil wars than in ideological civil wars, in part because ethnic identity facilitates the government's task of identifying, monitoring, and sanctioning actual or potential supporters of the rebels. Conversely the government's chances of winning should be lower in ideological civil wars than in ethnic civil wars, because it is more difficult for the government to identify, monitor, and punish actual or potential supporters of the rebels when those supporters cannot be identified by ethnic markers. This leaves government armed forces susceptible to the counterinsurgency dilemma (described in chapter 6), whereby troops, seeking to minimize their own risks in the field, sanction neutrals and thereby create an incentive for uninvolved peasants to turn to the rebels in search of protection against indiscriminate repression by the government (see Mason and Krane 1989; Mason 1989, 1996).

The Nature of the New Order

Whether a revolution ends in a government victory, a rebel victory, or a negotiated settlement, the postrevolutionary order will be fundamentally different from the old regime in any of several ways. The fate of those who participated in the revolution on both sides, as leaders, foot soldiers, and civilian supporters, will be dramatically affected by the outcome. If the government wins, what will be the fate of defeated rebels, their leaders, and their civilian supporters? If the government is defeated, what will be the institutional configuration of the new regime, and what will be the fate of deposed government leaders and their military forces? Government and rebel leaders must consider these aspects of possible outcome scenarios as they choose between continuing to fight and quitting.

Elites on both sides have to be more concerned than nonelite participants with what their fate will be after the war is over. Obviously, if the leaders on either side come to believe they will lose, they must assume that they will be executed by the victors unless they can flee to exile in another country. And if leaders anticipate victory, they must assume that they will be better off than before the conflict. But how do leaders estimate their personal fate in a settlement outcome? Can the leaders on either or both sides be confident that their personal security will be guaranteed in the new order if one of the conditions of that new order is that they lay down their arms? What settlement terms are required to assure both sides that their rival will not violate the conditions of the settlement, take up arms, and annihilate them? Devising stable power sharing arrangements that assure both sides of an acceptable degree of security is the most intractable aspect of settling a civil war and the one feature that makes negotiated settlements so much more difficult in civil wars than in interstate wars.

Harrison Wagner (1993: 260–61) points out another formidable obstacle to the stability of a civil war settlement. The willingness of both sides to consider a negotiated settlement implies that "neither combatant has been able to disarm its adversaries." Therefore any settlement will require that all the adversaries retain some semblance of their organizational identities after the war, even if they are disarmed. In effect the settlement leaves the nation one step— that is, rearming—away from what Charles Tilly (1978) terms a condition of "dual sovereignty," which is a defining characteristic of a revolutionary situation. The collapse of two peace settlements in Angola illustrates the fragile nature of negotiated settlements to civil wars, especially when the settlement does not disarm the rival armies or integrate them into a single force.

Military Balance in the Field and the Costs of Conflict

One critical determinant of whether a civil war will end in a victory for the rebels, the government, or neither is the balance of military capability between the two contenders.[8] The balance of military forces affects the outcome of the conflict in three ways. The relative size and capability of their respective armies affects the probability of each side attaining victory. The intensity of the conflict—the rate at which both sides are consuming human and material resources in the prosecution of the war—affects the length of time they can sustain military operations and the total costs of achieving victory. Finally, the duration of the conflict affects the total costs of victory (as opposed to a settlement) and therefore the expected net payoff from victory for each side.

Relative Size and Capability of Military Forces

On this dimension, civil wars differ profoundly from interstate wars, in that presumably all rebel movements begin with the disadvantage of having to build their forces from scratch. They start out with a force level of near zero, and they must build their troop strength in the shadow of an already existing army controlled by the very state that the rebels seek to overthrow. Rebel recruiting is inhibited by the extreme risks facing recruits, especially in the early stages of the rebellion. Nonelites are not likely to support a rebel movement that has little prospect for victory, even if they prefer the rebels to the incumbent regime. To do so would be suicidal. Thus the greatest danger to a revolutionary movement is in the early days of the conflict, when it is seriously outgunned by the government and vulnerable to early annihilation. Mason, Weingarten, and Fett (1999) find that the government won 58 percent of the civil wars that lasted one year or less and 64 percent of those that lasted five years or less. Indeed it appears that if governments are to win, it almost always occurs early: twenty-five of the twenty-eight government victories occurred in the first five years of the conflict.

Given the government's advantage over the rebels in the early stages of a civil war, the initial goal of the rebels must be simply to survive this phase of the conflict until they can demonstrate their capacity to win (or at least avoid annihilation). If the rebels can survive their initial disadvantage, the government's advantage in the battlefield begins to erode, simply as a matter of its failure to defeat the rebellion. As the rebels demonstrate their ability to sustain effective combat operations against the government, more and more latent supporters will begin to discount their initial estimates of the risks associated with supporting the rebels. At some point they will commit to the rebels as active, overt supporters (full-time guerrillas). Moreover, if the government fails to defeat the rebels early, it is likely to escalate its level of repression which, as I argued in chapter 6, can lead to a counterinsurgency dilemma. Additional supporters may be driven to the rebels' side by the fear that indiscriminate state repression puts them at risk of death or injury, regardless of their support or nonsupport of the rebels.

Conflict Intensity

Each side in a civil war can be conceived of as an organization that mobilizes human and material resources for the purpose of waging battle (see Leites and Wolf 1970). Fighting consumes those resources, and both the government and the rebels hope to achieve victory before depleting their resource base. Unlike an interstate war, however, both the government and the rebels draw on the same population base and the same economy for the resources needed to sustain their respective operations (barring subsidies in the form of third-party intervention, which I discuss later). This implies that the higher the rate at which the civil war is consuming the pool of human and material resources available to both sides, the more likely the two sides are to seek a negotiated settlement. With both sides drawing on the same finite pool of resources, the ability of both parties to continue waging war declines as those resources are depleted. Their estimates of their own probability of ever achieving victory should decline as well, all else being equal. For these reasons, increases in the intensity of armed conflict should be associated with increases in the likelihood of both parties deciding to quit and seek a negotiated settlement.[9]

Duration

The decision calculus implies that any variable that extends the time horizon of a party's anticipated victory will make that party more inclined to quit rather than continue fighting. Mason and Fett (1996) found strong empirical support for this proposition. Likewise Stam (1996: 71) argued that, for inter-state wars, "the longer a war drags on, the more decision makers update their beliefs about their ability to absorb costs and inflict punishment. . . . We should then expect to see the probability of both sides quitting rising over time—in turn leading to a rising probability of draws" (see also Bennett and Stam 1996). This tendency should be even stronger in civil wars since, as noted above, both the government and the rebels draw on the same finite pool of resources to sustain their operations, and these resources are depleted over time.

Participants in a civil war constantly adjust their estimates of the likely outcome of the conflict as they obtain new information on the progress of the war. Duration is one indicator of the course of the war. As a civil war drags on, each party is likely to increase its estimate of the amount of additional time required to achieve victory. As the prospects for victory begin to appear more distant in the future, one's estimate of the total costs that will have to be absorbed to achieve victory mount accordingly. Since the payoffs from victory are more or less fixed, the net benefits of victory (that is, the benefits from winning minus the accumulated costs required to achieve victory) begin to decrease with time, making an actor more willing to accept a settlement in the present that allows that actor to avoid the additional costs required to achieve victory.

In addition, people discount future benefits in any decision they make. Accordingly the longer the estimated amount of time required to achieve victory, the lower will be an actor's estimate of the present value of the payoffs of victory. In this case, not only must one discount the payoffs over a longer time span, but they must be discounted further by the fact that the future payoffs from victory are by no means certain. Finally, as a civil war drags on without either side being able to subdue its rival, each side is likely to lower its estimate of ever defeating the rival. These effects of conflict duration capture the logic underlying Zartman's "mutually hurting stalemate." Mason and Fett (1996) find that the strongest predictor of a negotiated settlement to a civil war is its duration: The longer the war lasts, the more likely it is to end in a negotiated settlement.

One corollary of this proposition is that civil wars of short duration are more likely to end in a government victory or a rebel victory than in a negotiated settlement. Bennett and Stam (1998: 364) find support for this in interstate wars as well: Wars that conclude quickly do so with victory by one side or the other. Mason and Fett (1996: 360) find similar support for this proposition with respect to civil wars: Civil wars of short duration are substantially less likely to end in a settlement than in victory for one side or the other.

Victory by the government should be more likely than victory by the rebels in short wars. All rebel movements begin with an overwhelming disadvantage in military capability. To have any chance of victory, the rebels must avoid annihilation in the early stages of the conflict by the vastly superior forces of the government. Not all rebel movements succeed in this endeavor.

For several reasons, victories by the rebels should be more likely in protracted civil wars rather than short wars. First, the rebels start off with a decided military disadvantage, which is why the government is expected to prevail in short wars. Second, if the rebels survive the dangerous initial period of the civil war, their ability to mobilize supporters should increase with time, all else being equal. The longer the war lasts, the more viable the rebel organization will appear to latent supporters. As it becomes more apparent to the population that the rebels will not be suppressed quickly, potential supporters who had withheld support out of fear become more willing to join or otherwise support the rebels. Their fears diminish as the rebels demonstrate their survivability. Moreover, as the size of the rebels' military force grows, recruitment of additional supporters becomes marginally easier. Assuming the government's military capacity remains constant, increases in the size of the rebels' forces decrease the likelihood of any one rebel becoming a casualty, which makes it easier for the rebels to persuade the next supporter to join the movement (Mason 1996, 1989). Finally, as the civil war proceeds and the rebels gains strength, bandwagon effects can occur if it begins to appear that the rebels have a chance of winning (Lichbach 1995, 115–16).

What is surprising is that Mason, Weingarten, and Fett (1999) also find that rebels win in short wars as well: Nine of the sixteen rebel victories occurred in the first year of the conflict, and twelve of the sixteen rebel victories occurred in the first five years. In most of these cases, the governments in question were some form of neopatrimonial dictatorship, such as the Mobutu regime in Zaire or the Somoza dynasty in Nicaragua. Such regimes lack a base of popular legitimacy. Often their militaries are ineffective fighting forces because, as discussed in chapter 5, promotion through the ranks in such regimes tends to be based on personal ties to the dictator, not competence. Thus patrimonial regimes often lose early, not so much as a result of rebel strength but because of their own lack of popular legitimacy or effective military capabilities. When faced with an armed challenge, the regime can implode, especially if military units defect rather than fight. Thus the Mobutu regime quickly collapsed when rebel forces, aided by the Tutsi rebels in neighboring Rwanda, mounted an offensive. Similarly the Somoza regime in Nicaragua collapsed after only eighteen months of full-scale civil war.

Finally, Mason, Weingarten, and Fett (1999) find that, while rebels rarely lose protracted civil wars, neither do they often win them. Instead the most likely outcome is a negotiated settlement: Eleven of the eighteen cases that lasted more than five years ended in a settlement rather than a victory for one side or the other. The rebels' ability to survive their early vulnerability does allow them to avoid defeat, but it does not necessarily guarantee them victory. Instead the steady rebel gains in relative strength that tend to occur as civil wars drag out usually result in what William Zartman (1993: 24; 1989: ch. 6) has termed a "mutually hurting stalemate," in which "the countervailing power of each side, though insufficient to make the other side lose, prevents it from winning."[10] According to Zartman, a mutually hurting stalemate is most likely to result in a negotiated settlement.

The Role of Third Parties

The role of third parties can work to enhance the likelihood of a negotiated settlement, enhance the prospects of one side or the other winning, or prolong the conflict by preventing one side from falling to defeat on the battlefield. Jane Holl (1993: 286) notes two bases for third-party intervention in civil wars. First, when the war threatens to widen to other nations in unacceptable ways, those nations may decide to intervene in order to prevent the diffusion of conflict. Part of India's reason for intervening in the civil war in Sri Lanka in 1987 was to prevent the spread of Tamil militancy to its own Tamil Nadu province.[11] Second, when a third party has some former involvement with one of the belligerents—for instance, the former colonial power of a nation torn by civil war—that party may feel a moral imperative to intervene in the civil war. France took a leadership role in efforts to suppress or mediate conflicts in its own and Belgium's former colonies, including Congo/Zaire, Rwanda, Chad, and Algeria. Similarly, during the Cold War, the United States and the Soviet Union both developed commitments to Third World regimes, and when incumbent governments in those nations were threatened by civil war, their superpower sponsor often intervened to prevent their overthrow. Cuban troops were airlifted into Angola to prevent the Soviet-backed government there from being overthrown by U.S.-backed UNITA guerrillas (see Rothchild and Hartzell 1995).

Generally third-party involvement takes one of two forms. Third parties may intervene militarily on one side or the other in order to prevent a battle-field defeat for that party or to enhance that party's chances of achieving final victory. This form of intervention is referred to as biased intervention. Biased intervention may be direct, with the third party providing troops and equipment, or it may be indirect, with the third party simply subsidizing the war effort of its favored party. Rarely does biased intervention take the form of direct military action. Exceptions would be the U.S. intervention in Vietnam, the Soviet intervention in Afghanistan, and the Soviet airlift of Cuban troops to Angola. More frequently, major power intervention occurs indirectly in the form of material support to the government or the rebels. This can include military equipment, supplies, training, advisors, or simply financial support.

Biased intervention is intended to enhance the recipient's chances of winning the civil war by subsidizing its capacity to conduct and sustain military operations. Thus the United States provided material support to the Afghan *mujahideen*, the Nicaraguan Contras, and the UNITA rebels in Angola. The Soviets provided assistance (through Cuba) to FMLN guerrillas in El Salvador and the Sandinista rebels in Nicaragua.

Because biased intervention increases one actor's willingness and ability to continue fighting, that actor should become less willing to accept a negotiated settlement than it would have been in the absence of the intervention subsidy. For a settlement to work, all parties involved in the conflict must agree to lay down their arms and accept the terms of the settlement. Where biased intervention is direct and extensive, the intervening party may have the capacity to veto a settlement unilaterally by refusing to quit fighting (thereby compelling the government and the rebels to continue fighting as well). Under these circumstances, a negotiated settlement becomes less likely, simply because it requires the compliance of more parties. Cuba's reluctance to withdraw its troops from Angola prolonged the civil war there by impeding negotiations toward a peaceful settlement.

The other form that third-party intervention can take is mediation. Virtually every negotiated settlement involves some form of third-party intervention as a neutral mediator (Walter 1997). Governments and rebels that have long been at war with each other are not likely to sit down at the bargaining table unless some neutral third party initiates the process, agrees to serve as a mediator, and is able to convince both sides that they (the mediators) are committed to forging a peace settlement that is acceptable to both parties. In many recent cases, the United Nations has assumed this role. UN supervision of negotiations and enforcement of the settlement terms occurred in El Salvador, Cambodia, Angola, and Nicaragua. Ultimately third-party mediation involves some package of incentives that is intended to make the payoff from a settlement preferable to continued conflict for both the rebels and the government. In effect this form of intervention amounts to a third-party subsidy of the settlement outcome, making it more attractive than continued conflict for both warring parties.

Third-party mediation efforts can take any number of forms. At a minimum it involves providing the neutral forum and mediation services needed to facilitate the negotiations. It can also involve policing a truce to ensure that neither side takes advantage of the cessation in hostilities to improve its battlefield position. Peacekeeping of this sort—policing a truce—is more difficult in a civil war than in an interstate war. Peacekeeping usually involves maintaining a buffer zone to separate the combatants (see Karns and Mingst 1998). In a civil war, especially one involving guerrilla insurgency, the government and the rebels are not so easily separable, because there are usually no clearly delineated battle lines, and the two armies do not necessarily occupy two distinct and separable territorial domains. Thus it is difficult for the mediator to create a buffer zone when the armed forces and the civilian support base of the two combatants live among each other.

The most extreme form of neutral third-party mediation is "peacemaking"—when a third party intervenes militarily with the intention of suppressing the fighting capability of both the government and the rebels and compelling them to cease hostilities. This occurred in Bosnia and Somalia, successfully in the former but not in the latter (Karns and Mingst 1998).

Internal Politics of Each Side

The final source of difficulty in bringing civil wars to a conclusion concerns the internal politics of the contending parties involved in the conflict. Governments and revolutionary organizations are, to varying degrees, coalitions of groups and leaders. Chapter 5 discussed the ways in which bargaining between the military, civilian elites in the government, and the dominant economic elite in a regime can affect the state's choice between repression or reform as a response to an opposition challenge (see Stanley 1996; Skocpol 1979). In a similar fashion, revolutionary movements usually consist of coalitions of political organizations, each of which has its own constituency (such as peasants, workers, or students) and each of which may have its own set of distinct goals that motivate its participation in the revolution. In some cases (for instance, El Salvador) each partner in the coalition also had its own military organization before entering the coalition.[12] Both the government and the rebels approach the question of conceding defeat, seeking a negotiated settlement, or continuing to fight not as unitary actors but as coalitions whose top leadership must consider how their coalition partners will react to the choices they make.

Government leaders often find themselves cross-pressured by civilian economic elites, on the one hand, and their military establishment, on the other. Civilian economic elites, especially the commercial and industrial sectors, often are more willing to make concessions to the rebels if doing so can bring an end to the armed conflict. Continuing the war threatens them with destruction of their assets. It also encourages capital flight and certainly discourages new investment. It depletes the income of consumers as well. Thus commercial and industrial elites are likely to be more willing to agree to a settlement to the war as long as the settlement allows them to stay in business. From their perspective, war is bad for business.[13]

On the other hand, the military leadership is often far more reluctant to support a settlement for fear that they may be subjected to retribution by a postsettlement government that includes elements of the rebel leadership. As noted in chapter 6, most of the casualties in civil wars are not combatants but unarmed civilians, and the overwhelming majority of civilian casualties are attributable to actions by the government's armed forces. If the terms of the settlement do not guarantee the military immunity from prosecution for violence against unarmed civilians, military leaders can be expected to oppose the settlement. Unlike civilian economic elites, the military has the capacity to act decisively to veto a settlement. They can stage a coup to remove from power those civilian politicians who negotiated the settlement. Or they can violate the cease-fire and plunge the nation back into civil war. For these reasons, many negotiated settlements to civil wars include amnesty provisions for government and rebel soldiers. Without such guarantees, combatants can effectively veto the settlement by refusing to lay down their arms and abide by the cease-fire. The peace settlement in El Salvador provided amnesty for the Salvadoran military, while the agreements that ended the Contra war in Nicaragua also provided amnesty for the Contras.

A second issue in a negotiated settlement that is critical to the military's interests is how the settlement resolves the question of merging two armies that have been killing each other with considerable vigor during the course of the war. A settlement agreement that leaves both the rebel army and the government's military intact as separate entities is almost certain to fail. Yet merging two armies into one is perhaps the most difficult obstacle to overcome in settlement negotiations. Members of both armies are unlikely to participate in this exercise, unless there are guarantees in place that protect them from retribution at the hands of their former rivals. How positions in the new army's officer corps are apportioned between the leaders of the two contending armies is often a source of tension which can motivate soldiers on one side or the other to take actions that pre-empt the consummation of the peace settlement. Thus, no matter how much the civilian leaders on both sides may prefer a settlement to continued conflict, their military wings can veto any settlement whose terms do not provide the combatants with sufficient guarantees of personal safety.

After a decade of civil war in Rwanda, leaders of the Tutsi RPF (Rwanda Patriotic Front) rebel forces and the government of President Juvenal Habyarimana of the MRND Party (Mouvement Révolutionnaire National pour le Développement, or the National Revolutionary Movement for Development) began negotiations aimed at reaching a peace settlement that would reintegrate the Tutsi rebels into Rwandan society. A critical element of the peace accord was the merging of the two military forces: Military command positions would be divided equally between MRND and RPF, with the MRND gaining only a 60–40 advantage in total troop numbers (Clapham 1998: 202–03). Not surprisingly, the Arusha accords were not popular among Habyarimana's own party or the Rwandan military (LeMarchand 1994: 597). While returning from a round of negotiations in Dar es Salaam on April 6, 1994, Habyarimana's airplane was shot down, more than likely by disgruntled members of the Rwandan military. The extremists in the MRND assumed the role of spoilers in the peace process. They killed their own leader when he made concessions that they considered unacceptable. They then blamed his death on the Tutsi and used this charge to mobilize Hutu civilians for renewed attacks on Tutsi civilians and Hutu supporters of the Arusha accords. Thus began the slaughter that reached genocidal proportions in the spring of 1994. Gérard Prunier (1995: 239–48) estimates the final death toll at between 800,000 and 850,000, with another 300,000 fleeing the country as refugees.

Similar coalition politics appear in rebel organizations as well. Revolutionary movements often consist of coalitions of organizationally distinct and relatively autonomous guerrilla armies. The rebel coalition can include relative moderates as well as hard-liners among their numbers. Often there is little to unite them other than their desire to overthrow the incumbent regime (DeNardo 1985: 254–57; Maranto 1988: 140). The different leaders of these armies are likely to manifest different degrees of willingness to risk their forces in battle and to accept a settlement short of victory.

Robert Maranto (1988) analyzes the politics within rebel coalitions as a collective action problem. While the ultimate victory over the government may be a collective good that is nonrival and nonexcludable, the final distribution of power within the new regime (including government offices, the composition of the postrevolutionary military, and the redistribution of wealth and income flows) is very much a matter of zero-sum bargaining over divisible, excludable goods: Whatever offices one rebel group claims are not available for other coalition members.

These concerns over how the spoils of victory should be distributed affect the willingness of rebel factions to commit their forces to battle at various stages of the revolution. Likewise competition within the rebel coalition over the spoils of victory affects each faction's willingness to enter into negotiations with the government over a possible settlement. Maranto argues that smaller members of the rebel coalition are more likely than large members to free-ride, allowing their larger coalition partners to assume a greater share of the burden of battle while they hold their own forces in reserve, in hopes of claiming a larger share of the spoils of victory. Free-riding is also more likely early in the conflict, when the risks are greater and the prospects for victory more uncertain (Maranto 1988). As the rebels approach victory, free-riding becomes less prevalent, as groups maneuver to stake their claims to a greater share of the spoils of victory. At the same time, the larger members of the coalition, especially those that have been shouldering a disproportionate share of the burden of fighting early in the conflict, may be less inclined to share the fruits of victory with their smaller coalition partners. Accordingly, they may be tempted to betray those coalition partners whose continued contribution is not deemed essential to the achievement of victory. As victory becomes imminent, larger members of the rebel coalition may seek to minimize the size of the winning coalitions. Maranto (1988: 141) suggests that the North Vietnamese Army may have done this to the Vietcong during the Tet Offensive of 1968: "Hanoi ordered the offensive which decimated the fully mobilized NLF, while the less committed North Vietnamese military forces suffered far fewer casualties. Some American military analysts see this as a partly purposeful effort by the Hanoi politburo to eliminate their Southern Communist competitors for power. . . . Some surviving NLF cadres seem to agree with this interpretation, and lament the Northern domination of united Vietnam."

If the rebels and the government decide to cease firing and explore the possibility of a negotiated settlement, the same coalition politics come into play. The diverse factions that make up a revolutionary coalition may be united in their desire to overthrow the incumbent regime, but they may differ substantially on what new order they seek to create, should they win. Rebel goals can range from merely seeking changes in certain policies of the current government to replacing certain personnel in that regime. In the extreme, their goal may be the destruction of the incumbent regime and its replacement with a completely new set of institutions staffed by a completely different set of people. Differences in goals—especially in the scope of revolutionary change they are willing to accept and the groups in whose interests they claim to be fighting—mean that groups in the rebel coalition will have differing propensities to accept negotiated settlements short of complete victory (see Stedman, 1991: 10–11).

Clashes over whether or not to engage in negotiations and, if so, what minimum terms are acceptable, can be debilitating for a government or a rebel coalition. They can pose considerable personal risks for any leader who might consider committing his or her organization (government or rebel) to negotiations. For a settlement to come about, the moderate elements in both the government and the rebel coalition (that is, those willing to negotiate) must not only come to agreement on a new order. Each must be able to control its coalition partners, in the sense of being able to keep them from disrupting the negotiation process. Hard-liners in the government and radicals in the rebel coalition can disrupt peace negotiations by unilaterally violating the ceasefire, in hopes of driving the rival coalition away from the bargaining table. It will be more difficult for moderates in the government to maintain popular support for their negotiating position (and for the very idea of a peace agreement) if the radicals in the revolutionary coalition stage an offensive while the negotiations are underway. Indeed moderates in the government risk being overthrown in a hard-liner coup if radical elements of the rebel coalition stage an offensive while negotiations are underway. The same holds for the moderates in the rebel coalition: An escalation in repression or counterinsurgency violence by government hard-liners will make it difficult for rebel leaders to convince their followers and coalition partners that negotiations are worth pursuing at all. They risk being discredited and even deposed by the radicals in the rebel coalition. Thus, for negotiations to proceed, the moderates on both sides have to be strong enough to prevent their coalition partners from subverting the negotiation process by escalating violence.

CONCLUSION

Although the understanding of the causes and dynamics of civil war has grown substantially with the proliferation of research on this topic, it is only recently that scholars have turned their attention to the conditions that determine whether governments confronted with a revolutionary challenge will win, lose, or draw. This chapter presents a model of the decision calculus by which participants in a civil war would choose between continuing to fight in anticipation of eventual victory or quit either in defeat or under the terms of a negotiated settlement. The model suggests that any factors that (1) lower each actor's estimate of the chances of victory, (2) increase the rate at which both are absorbing costs, or (3) increase the estimated time required to achieve victory make a negotiated settlement relatively more attractive. Conversely, factors that (1) increase one actor's probability of victory, (2) decrease one actor's estimate of the costs of victory, or (3) decrease the time required for an actor to achieve victory enhance that actor's likelihood of winning.

Empirical studies suggest that the government's chances of subduing a rebellion decline over time, but not necessarily to the advantage of the rebels. As conflicts become protracted, the most likely outcome is not a victory by either side but instead a negotiated settlement. These findings suggest that, as wars become more protracted, interested third parties should find both sides in a civil war more willing to submit to mediation efforts. Continued fighting beyond some point ceases to be a quest for victory and instead amounts to negotiation of settlement terms through violence. Less destructive alternatives are available.

NOTES

1. The peace in El Salvador and in Nicaragua has lasted long enough that neither nation appears likely to degenerate into a resumption of civil war. Indeed both nations appear to have made successful transitions to democracy. The Angolan peace has broken down at least twice since the initial agreement was signed in 1991. Cambodia has been troubled by instability at the center, but so far conditions have not deteriorated to the point that civil war has resumed.

2. This model is presented in Mason and Fett (1996) and Mason, Weingarten, and Fett (1999). Much of the discussion of the model that follows is derived from those two works.

3. Licklider (1995) discusses the factors that contribute to the stability versus the breakdown of civil war settlements.

4. The expected utility model is derived from Wittman's (1979) model of how interstate wars end.

5. Tsebelis (1989) has criticized the application of expected utility models to situations in which game theoretic models are more appropriate. Mason, Weingarten, and Fett (1999) conclude that an expected utility approach is best suited to the situation depicted here, where the concern is with which attributes of a conflict affect its outcome, not how a choice made by one player during one iteration of a civil war game affects the choice of the other player.

6. In other words, even if $P_V > (1 - P_V)$ for a party, it may still prefer a negotiated settlement now, if the accrued costs of continuing to fight on to victory exceed $P_V (U_V) - U_S$.

7. Patrick Regan (2000: 77) argues that interventions are more likely to succeed in bringing a civil conflict to a conclusion when the conflict in question is ethnically based rather than ideological. However, he is concerned simply with whether the conflict was brought to a conclusion, regardless of whether by government victory, rebel victory, or negotiated settlement. And he is concerned only with those cases in which third-party interventions occurred.

8. Citations on the importance of the military balance in determining the outcome of interstate conflicts are too numerous to list here. Licklider (1995, 1993a) lists it as one of the five major determinants of negotiated settlements to civil wars. Gurr (1970) lists the balance of coercive capabilities between government and dissidents as a major determinant of whether or not deprivation would result in revolution. Zartman's (1993) "mutually hurting stalemate" constitutes another version of this concept.

9. Mason, Weingarten, and Fett (1999) find high battle death rates to be associated with either a rebel victory or a negotiated settlement.

10. By contrast, Zartman argues, a mutually hurting stalemate can be quite stable and sustainable by both sides in a civil war (1993: 26). Unlike an interstate war, neither side in a civil war has the option of withdrawing from the fight and returning to the ordinary tasks of governing. A settlement regime will require that former enemies not only coexist but cooperate under a single set of government institutions. Faced with that outcome, a weakened insurgency can simply withdraw into the hills and avoid further action until it rebuilds its strength. Similarly the government can simply

withdraw to the capital, concede portions of the countryside to the rebels (temporarily), and build its strength in order to reassert its authority in the countryside at some later date. Unlike a negotiated settlement to an interstate war, the settlement of a civil war inevitably means both the government and the rebel organization will, in some sense, cease to exist in their current configurations. While that outcome may be preferable to total defeat, it is, in the eyes of both the government and the rebels, closer to defeat than to victory. Therefore both sides are often willing to live with a hurting stalemate that, in the case of an interstate war, would induce both sides to settle.

11. On India's intervention, see Austin 1995; Pfaffenberger 1988; Rupesinghe 1988.

12. The Salvadoran FMLN consisted of a coalition of five guerrilla organizations. The FPL (Fuerzas Populares de Liberación, or Popular Forces for Liberation), the ERP (Ejército Revolucionario del Pueblo, or the Revolutionary Army of the Poor), FARN (Fuerzas Armadas de Resistencia Nacional, or the Armed Forces of National Resistance), the PRTC (Partido Revolucionario de los Trabajadores, or the Workers' Revolutionary Party) and the PCS (Partido Comunista de El Salvador, or the Salvadoran Communist Party). Cynthia McClintock (1998: 48) points out that each group maintained its own leaders, its own organizational structure, its own internal governance. There was no single leader of the FMLN. Hugh Byrne (1996) argues that the lack of coordination between the groups hindered their ability to wage an effective armed struggle against the Salvadoran state. See also Stanley 1996. The FMLN and the Salvadoran civil war are discussed in more detail in chapter 8.

13. William Stanley (1996) argues that such transformation occurred among the governing elite of El Salvador over the course of the 1980s. Land reform eroded the power of the traditional agro-export elite, and a new generation of commercial elites, based in finance, export processing, and commerce, eclipsed them as the dominant force in the governing ARENA (Alianza Republicana Nacional, or National Republican Alliance) party. The commercial elite had little interest in continuing a war that threatened the infrastructure and investments that were essential to their own prosperity. Tom Gibb (1992: 20–21) characterizes the Cristiani government as "highly capable business people and technocrats" whose "main interest is not in controlling [state] power or government for itself but in creating the best conditions for their own businesses to flourish."

Chapter Eight

Reform, Repression, and Revolution in El Salvador

In the autumn of 1978, several small guerrilla armies in El Salvador were staging armed assaults at least once a week, including attacks on the U.S. Embassy, a Bayer Pharmaceutical plant, an electric generation facility, as well as police stations and government offices throughout the nation (Dunkerley 1985: 117). The emergence of a coordinated insurgent challenge soon represented such a threat to the stability of the Salvadoran state that a group of junior army officers staged a coup d'etat, deposing the conservative President Carlos Humberto Romero. In the decree announcing the coup, the new civilian-military junta blamed the government for gross violations of human rights and various forms of corruption that had "brought about a veritable economic disaster." It characterized the crisis in El Salvador as "the result of the antiquated economic, social, and political structures . . . that do not offer the majority of the inhabitants the minimum conditions essential for their human fulfillment."[1] Six months after seizing power, the coup leaders announced a three-phase land reform program to begin immediately. They also decreed that elections would be held in 1982 to choose a constituent assembly that would be charged with writing a new democratic constitution to replace the military-dominated authoritarian regime that had governed El Salvador since 1932.

Land reform was intended to restore to peasants some measure of economic security and thereby inoculate them against the appeals of the Salvadoran rebels. In this way, the junta hoped to defeat the growing insurgency by denying the rebels a base of popular support. Over the course of the next ten years, the Salvadoran government redistributed over half a million acres of land to more than 80,000 households. However, instead of declining levels of violence and a restoration of peace and stability, the years during which land reform and democratization were being implemented turned out to be the bloodiest period in a civil war that lasted until 1992. Why did land reform fail to dissipate revolution, restore regime stability, and permit a peaceful transition to democracy? If, as Samuel Huntington (1968: 375) suggests, land reform is supposed to be "a substitute for revolution in the countryside," how do we account for its apparent lack of success in either pre-empting the outbreak of peasant insurrections or diminishing such violence once it was underway?

This chapter and the next explore this question by examining two cases—El Salvador and Peru—in which extensive land reform programs were undertaken largely for the purpose of pre-empting the threat of revolution in the countryside (in the case of Peru) or dissipating an already existing peasant-based insurrection (in the case of El Salvador). In both nations agrarian reform was undertaken to pre-empt a shift in popular support from the regime to the rebels. Yet Sendero Luminoso guerrillas built their armed insurgency twelve years after the initiation of land reform in Peru; and the years immediately following the initiation of agrarian reform in El Salvador turned out to be the most violent period in that nation's civil war. Why did revolutionary violence continue unabated for more than a decade after the initiation of land reform in El Salvador and erupt anew in Peru less than a decade after the completion of agrarian reform there? Why did alleviating the extremes of inequality in land ownership not abate insurgent violence in El Salvador or pre-empt its recurrence in Peru? Why would peasants continue to support guerrilla insurgents even after the incumbent regime has given them the opportunity to acquire land of their own?

Using the framework spelled out in the previous seven chapters, I argue first that growing inequality of income, wealth, and land ownership did erode clientelist mechanisms of subsistence security, confronting peasant households in both nations with an increasing risk of subsistence crisis. Land reform provided some relief from that risk, but not always and certainly not for all classes of peasants. Even for those who did receive land under the terms of the agrarian reform program, the conditions of civil violence—especially the tactics of the state in targeting its counterinsurgent violence—created conditions under which it could still be rational for peasants to support the guerrillas, regardless of whether or not they were beneficiaries of land reform. In both El Salvador and Peru, any remedial effects that land reform might have had on peasant support for the regime were undermined by high levels of repressive violence. When state violence escalated to the point that it became indiscriminately targeted, popular support for the regime eroded in ways that could not be offset by land reform. In Chapter 6 I argued that repressive violence can drive even Huntington's conservative smallholder into the arms of the insurgents if they can offer peasants security not just against the exigencies of weather, markets, and other risks of agriculture but against the indiscriminate, repressive violence of the state. The next two chapters analyze these two cases in an effort to elaborate the relationships between land reform, repression, and the struggle between regimes and revolutionaries for the hearts and minds of peasants.

INEQUALITY AND INSTABILITY

Why has alleviating inequality in land ownership not always pacified the countryside? How do we account for the failure of land reform to pre-empt revolutionary violence? Conventional analyses argue that agrarian reform did not distribute enough land and other benefits to enough peasants to deny the guerrillas a base of peasant supporters sufficient to sustain their insurgency. However, the fact that many marginalized peasants received no reform benefits cannot by itself account for the persistence of civil war in El Salvador or its recurrence in Peru. Joining an insurgency carries extreme risks that most peasants will not take on simply because they were bypassed in the redistribution of land. Less risky everyday forms of peasant resistance are the more likely responses of nonbeneficiaries (Scott 1985). What then is the explanation for the persistence of popular support for guerrilla insurgency in the aftermath of land reform?

Students of civil violence have suggested two alternative answers. First, the relationship between inequality and instability may itself be spurious and, second, the "stick" of repressive violence that accompanies the "carrot" of land reform in most counterinsurgency programs can undermine any remedial effects agrarian reform might have on popular support for the incumbent regime. As noted in chapter 2, analyzing the links between inequality of income and/or land ownership, on the one hand, and revolutionary violence, on the other, has become something of a cottage industry in the social sciences. However, empirical findings on this link have been inconsistent, inconclusive, and at times contradictory. Why has the link between inequality and instability (however measured) not proved more robust?

Although the inequality-instability link has considerable intuitive appeal, when considered historically, its appeal begins to fade. Throughout history, land ownership has been unequally distributed in most nations without rebellion occurring. On the other hand, regimes presiding over far more equitable land tenure systems have nonetheless been torn by peasant revolution (see Magagna 1991). Indeed inequality of land ownership is the norm in premodern societies, while peasant revolts are extremely rare.

If inequality per se is not the proximate cause of revolution in the country-side, what is? For James Scott (1976) it is the erosion of subsistence security that often—but not always—accompanies inequality. Roy Prosterman argues that a high rate of landlessness, not just inequality of land ownership, is what breeds rebellion (Prosterman and Riedinger 1987). Samuel Popkin questions not just the inequality-instability nexus but also the argument that landless-ness breeds rebellion. The "almost universal finding," according to Popkin, is that "agricultural laborers are . . . less likely to protest than are tenants, and that tenants, in turn, are often far less active than landowning middle peas-ants" (Popkin 1979: 250). By contrast, Jeffery Paige (1975) argues that tenants and laborers on certain types of estates are the most revolutionary classes of peasants, not because of their vulnerability to subsistence crisis but because of the ease of organizing them for collective action (compared to other classes of peasants).

Although Paige, Popkin, Scott, Prosterman, and others may disagree on what makes peasants rebellious, there is one point on which they do seem to agree: One must look to factors other than gross levels of inequality for the proximate causes of revolution in the countryside and other forms of rural unrest. Inequality may be correlated with those other factors but not directly with political unrest. Logically, then, redistributing land ownership will not necessarily pre-empt rural unrest unless the state also alleviates those other conditions that are the proximate causes of rebellion.

What factors might intervene to erode the positive effects that land reform is supposed to have on support for the regime? In chapter 6 I argued that proactive violence by the state, targeted on actual or suspected supporters of opposition organizations—organizations whose main purpose is to seek relief for their members from the effects of inequality—narrows the range of be-havioral choices available to peasants by precluding both nonviolent collective action and noninvolvement. In effect, land reform must compete with other counterinsurgency tactics—the most important being repressive violence—in the calculus of peasant political support. Growing inequality places peasant households at risk of subsistence crisis, and this can make them susceptible to the appeals of opposition movements. Land reform can provide some relief from the risk of subsistence crisis for some but not all classes of peasant cul-tivators. Those underserved by land reform will still have a reason to support nonviolent opposition movements. If the state responds to nonviolent oppo-sition with violent repression, opposition leaders will likewise turn to violent tactics of their own. If repressive violence becomes so widespread that it threatens the lives of otherwise neutral peasants, agrarian reform is not likely to have the intended remedial effects that Huntington and others predict, re-gardless of its effects on inequality, subsistence security (Scott), landlessness

(Prosterman), or rural class structure (Paige and Popkin). The loyalty of beneficiaries and nonbeneficiaries alike will erode if they cannot be certain of immunity from state violence so long as they refrain from supporting the rebels. Even Huntington's conservative smallholder may turn to the insurgents in search of security against the risks of state-sanctioned repressive violence. In short, the calculus of consent that is reinforced by agrarian reform can be undermined by the calculus of fear that is induced by repressive violence.

EXPORT AGRICULTURE AND THE BREAKDOWN OF THE CLIENTELIST ORDER IN EL SALVADOR

In the nineteenth and early twentieth centuries, the agrarian social order in both Peru and El Salvador was transformed by those nations' entry into the global economy as exporters of agricultural goods for the industrializing economies of Europe and North America. This process was described in general terms in chapter 3. A dramatic transformation of peasant life resulted from this shift in land use and land tenure. Land ownership became much more concentrated, and land use shifted to the production of export crops. Of more immediate concern for peasants was that these changes also resulted in the erosion of many clientelist mechanisms that had afforded them some security against the risk of subsistence crisis.[2]

What touched off the transformation of El Salvador's agrarian social order was the coffee boom of the last half of the nineteenth century. Up to that point, the nation's agricultural economy had centered around indigo production on large estates. Coexisting alongside these estates was a system of *ejidos,* which were communally owned lands farmed by villages of indigenous peoples and mestizos of mixed European and Indian ancestry. The two production systems could coexist largely because the *ejidos* lands were not suitable for indigo production and therefore were of little interest to the estate owners.

In the 1850s then-president Gerardo Barrios returned from a trip to Europe to proclaim that he would "regenerate" the nation by building infrastructure, promoting industrialization, and expanding communications and education. The key to financing his ambitious development plan was an increase in export earnings (Thiesenhusen 1995: 141). However, world markets for indigo were deteriorating at that time, largely as a result of the development of synthetic dyes. Therefore the agrarian elite needed an alternative crop to generate export earnings. Coffee soon became the favored replacement crop, and the Salvadoran state endorsed this choice with policies that favored coffee over other crops (Browning 1971: 155–57). The shift to coffee production drastically altered the nation's land tenure and land use patterns.

THE COFFEE BOOM AND THE PEASANT

The lands most favorable for the cultivation of coffee happened to be the mountainous, lava-rich soils of El Salvador's western and central provinces. These were the very lands that heretofore had been of little commercial value to the wealthiest landowners. The booming world market for coffee suddenly made the *ejidos* valuable to the landed elite of El Salvador, who also happened to be the only people with the wealth necessary to convert the land to coffee production. How did they do it?

The Salvadoran state intervened. Proclaiming the virtues of freeing up valuable assets for their fullest and most efficient exploitation, the government enacted a series of laws designed to encourage the expansion of coffee production. In 1856 the state decreed that two-thirds of all communal lands had to be planted in coffee, or the lands would revert to the state for sale to those who could and would plant coffee (Montgomery 1995: 30). This posed a grave challenge for *ejidos* residents. Most of them were subsistence farmers who lived from one harvest to the next, growing food for their own consumption and selling their surplus in local markets. Coffee production required a substantial capital investment to acquire the plants and make the necessary improvements in the land. Moreover, coffee plants do not produce a marketable crop for two to three years. Few subsistence farmers could afford to take two-thirds of their land out of food production and devote it to a crop that would produce no cash income (or food) for two or more years.

Still, a number of indigenous communities managed to comply with the decree by pooling resources to plant the mandated proportion of communal lands in coffee. Villages planted coffee on lands that had been devoted to common uses (such as pasture), and individual households continued to farm their own subsistence plots (Browning 1971: 174). In this manner, *ejidos* residents were able to share the costs and the risks of complying with the 1856 decree without eliminating their capacity to produce enough food crops to ensure subsistence. Thus existing patterns of communal cooperation in production afforded *ejidos* residents the means to undertake coffee production by sharing the costs and the risks. Indeed they were more successful at complying with the 1856 decree than the state had ever anticipated (185–89).

When the 1856 decree failed to displace peasants from the *ejidos,* the state raised the bar even higher. President Rafael Zaldivar declared that "the existence of lands under the ownership of *communidades* impedes agricultural development, obstructs the circulation of wealth, and weakens family bonds and the independence of the individual. Their existence is contrary to the economic and social principles that the Republic has accepted" (quoted in Burns 1984: 300). Accordingly Zaldivar enacted further decrees to abolish all forms of communal ownership. In 1881 he decreed that all communal property must be subdivided into individual plots, or the property would revert to the state. The next year, communal ownership of land was abolished altogether (Montgomery 1995: 30; Thiesenhusen 1995: 141). These decrees abolished the *ejidos* system and destroyed the village institutions of cooperation that had provided residents with some insurance against the risks of subsistence crisis. The intended effect of these measures was to displace peasants from the land and free it up for coffee production by an emerging new landed elite. The abolition of the *ejidos* exposed subsistence cultivators to market forces that could be manipulated by those with sufficient market power to drive peasant cultivators into financial insolvency and force them to sell off or abandon their land. The political leadership knew that, as individual smallholders, peasant cultivators would not be able to comply with the mandate that part of their land be planted in coffee. Only those with sufficient capital to finance the shift in land use and with enough cash or credit to remain solvent for the two to three years it took to produce a marketable crop could enter the coffee market. These requirements effectively precluded most peasant smallholders from shifting to coffee production. The protections afforded by communal mechanisms of sharing risks disappeared with the dismantling of the *ejidos*.

Moreover, since *ejidos* had never required registered land titles, it was fairly easy for estate owners to encroach on communal lands and file the necessary papers to claim title to those lands. The affected villages had neither the legal counsel nor the political connections to prevent this (Lindo-Fuentes 1990: 147; Burns 1984: 300). The major credit institutions in El Salvador were controlled by the same landed oligarchy that was pushing the expansion of coffee production (Baloyra 1982: 22–32). They used their control over credit to squeeze peasants financially, force them into insolvency, and then buy up their land. Thousands of peasant households were evicted, as a small group of wealthy families bought up their land, consolidated it into commercial estates, and converted it to coffee production. The displacement of peasants from the land had the further benefit of creating the large pool of cheap labor that coffee estates needed at harvest time. The emerging new landed elite came to be known as the "fourteen families," and they would come to dominate the Salvadoran economy for most of the twentieth century (Montgomery 1995: 30; see also Paige 1993, 1997).

The displacement of peasant cultivators from their lands swelled the ranks of the landless. Despite the boom in export earnings from coffee, very little of the revenue was channeled into industrial investments that would have provided the jobs necessary to absorb the growing landless population. Instead laws were enacted to keep the landless available as a source of cheap labor for the coffee harvest. An 1881 antivagrancy law required the landless to work a

certain number of days on coffee estates or face fines, arrest, and other punishments. The Agrarian Law of 1907 authorized judges to order *campesinos* to
work whenever planters summoned them. The state established a rural con-
stabulary to protect landlords against peasant violence. Local units of the police force were often given salary supplements and other benefits by the landlords, who expected that in return the police would enforce the subordination
of the local peasantry. Peasant uprisings did occur, but they were always
quickly suppressed (Thiesenhusen 1995: 141; Stanley 1996: 47–48; Paige 1997:
106–07).

LA MATANZA AND THE EMERGENCE
OF THE PROTECTION RACKET STATE

The Great Depression hit El Salvador's agricultural economy with devastating
effects. World prices for coffee plummeted. By 1932 they were less than one-
third of their peak in the mid-1920s. As a result, coffee estates cut wages to less
than half the rate that had prevailed during the 1920s. Many planters reduced
their work force and simply let their crops rot on the bushes (Paige 1997: 107).
Male rural unemployment reached 40 percent in 1929 (Thiesenhusen 1995:
142). The resulting crisis of landlessness and unemployment among the Salvadoran peasantry generated pressures in the countryside that eventually
erupted in the uprising of 1932 known as *la matanza* (the massacre).

Late in 1931 growing peasant militancy in the western provinces of El Salvador was causing alarm among both the military and the Salvadoran Communist Party (PCS). The PCS felt that peasants were moving too fast and were
unprepared for a genuine revolution. When the military used fraud to manipulate the results of the January 1932 municipal elections, a rebellion began
to appear all the more imminent. The army managed to capture a number of
rebel leaders before any peasant action occurred. Among their captives was
Augustín Farabundo Marti, the leader of the PCS. Soon the military uncov-
ered evidence that elements of several army units planned to support the rebellion when it occurred. These alleged conspirators were rounded up and
shot, as was Marti. The military leadership became even more convinced that,
if the anticipated peasant rebellion did occur, extreme measures would be required to suppress it and to deter further unrest (Stanley 1996: 53–54). When
the uprising finally did occur, General Maximiliano Hernández Martinez
presided over a slaughter that was unprecedented in Salvadoran history. Estimates of the death toll vary considerably, but at least 8,000 to 10,000 peasants
were killed, and the death toll may have reached as high as 25,000.[3]

The suppression of *la matanza* established what William Stanley (1996)
terms a "protection racket state" in El Salvador for the next half-century: a

military-dominated government enforcing policies designed to enhance the profitability of the agro-export sector while repressing opposition from those marginalized by the expansion of that sector. The agrarian elite feared further insurrections, and the military was more than willing to suppress any hint of peasant unrest in return for the landed elite acceding to the military's control of the state.

NEW EXPORT CROPS AND THE PEASANT

After World War II the advent of new export crops such as cotton, sugarcane, and cattle completed the commercialization of Salvadoran agriculture. Coastal lands previously devoted to subsistence farming were converted to the production of the new export crops. As with coffee, the shift in land use was accomplished by manipulating the terms of trade and distribution of risks between landlord and peasant. Landlords changed tenancy terms from in-kind payments at the end of the growing season (share-cropping) to cash rental at the beginning of the season. This shifted the risks of agriculture onto tenants, compelled them to replace subsistence crops with cash crops, and all but assured their eventual eviction for failure to meet the new payment terms (Williams 1986: 52–59). Smallholders were driven into financial insolvency by the landed elite's manipulation of credit. Between 1961 and 1965, 80 to 90 percent of all commercial agricultural credit went to coffee, sugar, cotton, and cattle growers (Karush 1978: 67). Crowded out of the credit market, many smallholders lapsed into financial insolvency. Their lands were bought up by neighboring commercial estates and converted to export crops. Because cotton production was increasingly mechanized and cattle ranching highly land-intensive, expanding their production reduced the demand for labor and increased the supply of landless workers competing for those jobs. Shifting land from subsistence crops to cotton drastically reduced the number of households being supported on that land. Shifting land to pasture for cattle had even more devastating effects on local peasant populations, because cattle require only one-sixth the amount of labor per acre as cotton, one-seventh as much as sugar, and one-thirteenth the labor required by coffee (Williams 1986: 117).

During the 1960s the Salvadoran state, in a momentary impulse of reformism, extended the minimum wage law to cover permanent workers on agricultural estates. Instead of improving the lot of agricultural laborers, however, the law induced large estates to reduce their demand for labor and to cut out all forms of compensation other than cash wages (Thiesenhusen 1995: 144). Landowners reduced their permanent work force to the minimum needed at the slowest time in the crop cycle and replaced the other permanent workers with temporary labor as needed, and at wages that were depressed by the growing supply of landless laborers. As a consequence, the number of *colonos* (resident workers) declined from 55,000 in 1960 to 17,000 in 1970 (Montgomery 1995: 59; Williams 1986: 59). Landowners ceased hiring women and children as harvest labor. This severely diminished the income earning capacity of landless and land-poor peasant households, who often relied on the entire family being able to earn income as harvest workers on the estates. In-kind payments stopped as well. This included an end to the practice of compensating peasants by allowing them to use small parcels of hacienda land to grow food for their own consumption. Losing access to subsistence plots also undermined many of the means by which peasant women traditionally contributed to household income—by raising pigs, chickens, cows, and vegetables for sale in local markets (Williams 1986: 71). While males could find some work on the estates, women could not. Many were compelled to migrate to the city in search of wage labor positions. As a consequence, the number of female-headed households rose dramatically during the 1960s.[4]

Population growth, which averaged 3.5 percent annually from 1961 to 1971, exacerbated these trends in labor markets. Population density rose from 127 per square mile in 1927 to 325 in 1961. This made El Salvador the most densely populated nation in the Western Hemisphere. In fact, El Salvador's 1976 population density of 190 people per square kilometer exceeded even India's 186 per square kilometer (Durham 1979: 6–7). With labor markets crowded by both the displacement of peasant cultivators and the inexorable growth in population, real agricultural wages fell by 25 percent between 1973 and 1976 and by another 30 percent between 1976 and 1978 (Thiesenhusen 1995: 147). Emigration to Honduras, a traditional escape valve for land-poor Salvadorans, was foreclosed by the Soccer War of 1969. Indeed the Honduran government's expulsion of an estimated 300,000 Salvadorans homesteading on Honduran frontier lands was the spark that began the war. After the war, El Salvador had to absorb most of these refugees back into already crowded markets for land and labor (see Durham 1979). Despite urban migration (San Salvador grew from 128,200 in 1930 to 347,000 in 1960), the number of landless and land-poor persons in the countryside grew by 54 percent, from 211,617 in 1961 to 326,466 in 1971 (Seligson 1995: 60). The industrial boom of the 1960s was not sufficient to absorb the surplus labor. Between 1960 and 1982, the working-age population grew by 1.4 million, while industrial employment increased from 230,000 to 600,000.[5] These trends in population, employment, and land tenure pushed underemployment in El Salvador's agricultural work force to an estimated 47 percent in the 1970s (Brockett 1988: 87).

A further consequence of the shift in land use was inflation in the market for subsistence goods. Peasants who previously had produced their own food became dependent on the market for subsistence goods. Yet the same shifts in land use and land tenure that had forced them into the market for food in the first place also reduced the supply of food available in the market: Food crops were being displaced by export crops, resulting in a decline in per-capita food availability (Durham 1979: 31–32). As a consequence, the consumer price index rose by 182 percent between 1970 and 1977 (Montgomery 1982: 30–31). By the mid-1970s average caloric consumption was only 77 percent of recommended levels, and two-thirds of the children under five years of age were malnourished (Brockett 1988: 76–81).

The shift to export agriculture left El Salvador with one of the most inequitable land tenure systems in all of Latin America (see table 8.1). By 1971 estates larger than 200 hectares constituted only 1.5 percent of farms but controlled 49.5 percent of all farmland. Farms of fewer than 10 hectares accounted for 92.7 percent of all farms but little more than a quarter of all farmland (Brockett 1988: 67–75). By 1971, 38 percent of the economically active agricultural population was landless, compared to 27 percent in 1961 (Seligson 1995: 62).

MOBILIZING THE POOR: THE PROGRESSIVE CHURCH

As land pressures mounted during the 1970s, impoverished peasants found that they now had an alternative between suffering in silence or engaging in the sort of spontaneous uprising that had resulted in *la matanza* of 1932. Following the Medellín conference of Catholic bishops in 1968, Catholic priests and lay catechists, inspired by the doctrines of liberation theology, began instigating a network of grassroots popular organizations—Christian base communities (CEBs, or *communidades eclesiales de base*)—that were intended to empower the poor by organizing projects that would relieve their immediate economic distress.[6] CEBs organized food cooperatives, child care cooperatives, health clinics, and schools, among other things. In some cases, members were able to pool their limited resources to start new businesses that provided them with new sources of income. Thus CEBs overcame collective action problems by first enlisting members in projects that produced direct material benefits for them. In time, participation in such projects imparted a sense of empowerment to the poor, so they were no longer willing to accept poverty and powerlessness as their fate. The teachings of liberation theology—reinforced by the rewards of participation in CEB projects—motivated participants to alter not just their immediate economic circumstances but their worldviews as well, especially their beliefs about what is just and what is unjust, what they were willing to accept and what they felt morally obliged to change through collective action.[7]

Table 8.1 Land Tenure in El Salvador by Size of Unit, 1971

			Number of hectares by form of tenure				
Size[a]	Number (%)	Area (%)	Owned	Cash rent	Mixed[b]	Colonos	Other
<1.0	132,464 (49)	70,287 (5)	17,776	28,125	7,143	6,909	10,334
1.0–1.99	59,063 (22)	81,039 (6)	25,736	24,809	16,222	2,743	11,529
2.0–4.99	43,414 (16)	131,985 (9)	72,661	16,827	28,426	638	13,433
5.0–9.99	15,598 (6)	110,472 (8)	80,788	3,919	18,640	—	7,125
10.0–19.99	9,164 (3)	126,974 (9)	104,842	2,913	14,450	—	4,769
20.0–49.99	6,986 (2)	215,455 (15)	188,633	5,497	15,480	—	5,945
50.0–99.99	2,238 (1)	154,164 (11)	134,801	3,557	9,416	—	6,390
100.0–999.99	1,878 (1)	437,939 (30)	374,745	19,015	20,541	—	23,637
>1,000	63 (—)	123,579 (8)	105,512	—	3,269	—	14,798
Total	270,868	1,451,894	1,105,494	104,662	133,587	10,290	98,090

Source: Strasma (1989: 413), compiled from the 1971 Agricultural Census.

[a]Hectares

[b]Respondents who own some land and also farm some rented land

Accordingly, successful CEBs eventually began to expand their collective action repertoire to include more explicitly political activities. Mobilizing structures that could induce cooperation for self-help projects were readily adapted for mobilizing members in support of nonviolent political activism aimed at influencing the state to undertake reforms to remedy the structural sources of poverty. Soon CEBs came to serve as the support base for reformist political parties, such as the Christian Democratic Party (PDC).

Peterson (1997: 51–52) and Montgomery (1995: 87) both highlight several ways in which CEBs contributed to the political mobilization of the poor. First, they strengthened collective identity among the poor and gave them a new sense of empowerment. For the first time, people were able to participate in decisions that affected their lives, and they came to believe that they could change their lives for the better. They were not simply passive clients forced to comply with the directives of superiors who controlled their livelihood and therefore their lives. The fact that CEBs were small groups (usually twenty or fewer) meant that cooperation was easy to organize; members could readily assure themselves that others would contribute their fair share to the collective endeavor.

The second way in which CEBs contributed to explicitly political mobilization was that their experience with democratic decision making within the CEBs led members to question the legitimacy of the state's authoritarian political institutions. Members came to demand not just economic reform but greater democracy and accountability on the part of the government. Moreover, church sponsorship gave CEBs a degree of moral legitimacy that secular organizations did not enjoy. Initially, at least, this translated into a degree of immunity from repression. Members felt confident about their ability to speak honestly and openly about the need for reform, because they felt that their affiliation with the church and their use of religious symbols in their appeals might give them some immunity from sanctions by landlords, employers, or security forces, at least compared to spokesmen of leftist secular organizations.

Third, involvement in CEBs led members to participate in community projects and then to extend their commitment beyond the village to parties, unions, and peasant associations. These latter organizations, revitalized by the infusion of new support from CEB members, became more aggressive in their efforts to pressure the landed elite and the state to undertake reforms. In short, participation in CEBs became a gateway to political activism aimed at reforming the government and the economy.

Fourth, CEB participants developed skills that enabled them to assume leadership positions in a variety of secular organizations, including peasant associations, labor unions, neighborhood associations, and even political parties. Because the CEBs were small, made up of people from humble backgrounds, and run according to principles of small-group democracy, participants who would have been crowded out of leadership positions in large, bureaucratic, secular organizations could develop the self-confidence and communication skills they needed to eventually move into leadership roles in those secular organizations. In this manner, CEBs energized the grassroots support base for opposition political parties in the 1970s, and CEB participants became active in shaping the programs and platforms of those parties. Indeed the growth in grassroots political activism in the 1970s so dramatically revitalized the electoral fortunes of opposition political parties (especially the PDC) that the military had to resort to blatant fraud in order to prevent a coalition of reformist parties from winning the national elections of 1972 and 1977.

Once mobilized for nonviolent collective action (including opposition politics), how were peasants converted to supporting revolutionary violence? Peterson (1997: 130–34) argues that the changes in consciousness brought about by their participation in CEBs allowed some members to justify supporting revolutionary violence. Differing conceptions of the meaning of martyrdom and the proper response to it allowed some to justify violent opposition. Others felt that violence was precluded by the same teachings of the church, and they eschewed active participation in the guerrilla movement. One factor that distinguished the former from the latter is that many who came to believe that violence was justified had experienced the violence of the war firsthand, through the death of friends, neighbors, and family members. Just as the state's response to new forms of opposition activism influenced whether opposition organizations would remain nonviolent or shift to revolutionary violence, so an individual's experience with state repression also influenced whether that person's beliefs led them to justify violence or reject it.

REPRESSION AND REVOLUTION

The state's initial response to grassroots activism was to engage in repression targeted against the leaders of labor unions, peasant associations, CEBs, and other grassroots organizations. Priests became a special target for Salvadoran death squads. On March 12, 1977, Rutilio Grande, a Jesuit priest, was assassinated along with two peasants who happened to be riding with him at the time. Archbishop Oscar Romero ordered all Catholic schools closed for three days and canceled mass on the second Sunday after the killing as a commemoration to Grande and a way of focusing national attention on the mounting wave of right-wing violence. The killings continued nevertheless. During the summer of 1977 flyers put out by the White Warriors Union (one of the nation's more notorious death squads) began appearing with the slogan, "Be a

Patriot. Kill a Priest" (Peterson 1997: 61–65; see also Byrne 1996: 45–46; Montgomery 1995: 66–67, 98–99). The killings of priests continued through 1978 and 1979. Finally, in 1980, Archbishop Romero himself was gunned down while celebrating mass in San Salvador.

The death squads and their allies within the Salvadoran state by no means confined themselves to the isolated murders of individual priests. All forms of nonviolent activism were met with repression, and individuals who were identified as grassroots leaders (including not just priests and CEB members but students, leaders of labor unions and peasant associations, and PDC activists) were targets for arrest, disappearance, or death. In 1974 peasants in the hamlet of La Cayetana were engaged in a land dispute with a neighboring hacienda. In November units of the national guard and the national police, along with members of ORDEN (Organización Democrática Nacionalista or Democratic Nationalist Organization), surrounded the town and opened fire, killing six peasants. Another thirteen "disappeared," and twenty-five were arrested. In 1975 more than 2,000 students from the University of El Salvador staged a demonstration in San Salvador to protest the exorbitant amount of money being spent by the government on the Miss Universe pageant, which was being held in San Salvador for the first time. Units of the national guard surrounded the demonstrators when they reached the Plaza Libertad. The troops opened fire, resulting in the death of at least thirty-seven demonstrators. Dozens more were "disappeared" (Montgomery 1995: 66–67). In February of 1977 hundreds were wounded or killed and many more arrested by the national guard at a demonstration protesting electoral fraud in the 1977 election that brought General Carlos Humberto Romero to power (Americas Watch 1982: 39).[8]

Over the next few months, some 300 people were arrested and another 130 "disappeared" in what appeared to be a systematic campaign to eliminate the leadership of key opposition organizations. The national May Day rally that year was fired upon by the national guard, resulting in the death of at least eight and the wounding of another sixteen demonstrators. When the military moved in to occupy the town of Aguilares in Chalatenango province, they killed at least fifty and arrested three priests (Stanley 1996: 110). The Archdiocese of San Salvador reported that killings by security forces and death squads averaged fifty-seven a month during 1978 (Stanley 1996: 115). In 1980 at least 200,000 people gathered in San Salvador for what became the largest demonstration in El Salvador's history. The demonstrators were fired upon, leaving forty-nine dead and hundreds more wounded (Leiken 1984: 117).

When nonviolent political opposition was met by violent repression, people then (and usually only then) turned to revolutionary violence. Hugh Byrne (1996: 30–31) captures the sequence by which revolutionary mobilization occurred:

The first step into peasant organizing came through study, reflection, and action within the church's base communities. The next step often involved radical peasant organization and beginning to work collectively for such demands as better wages, improved working conditions, and access to credit. It was the repression almost invariably resulting from this organizing that made the political-military groups—with their ability to provide self-defense, links to other groups, and a society-wide strategy—an appealing option.

The wave of repression reached a crescendo in 1981, the first year of the land reform program.[9] With the escalating repression of nonviolent opposition, more militant insurgent organizations that were committed not to the reform of the existing regime but to its violent overthrow began attracting more followers and even more covert supporters, as they launched their own campaign of retribution against the security forces and the death squads. William Stanley (1996: 131) argues:

> The increasing numbers of militants willing to support the organizations of the left were motivated less by ideological conviction than by personal hatred of the security forces based on experience. Peasant and worker organizations that had avoided violent actions found their members captured, tortured, and killed as if they were guerrillas. The intensity and arbitrariness of violence made it rational to arm oneself in self-defense, which often proved to be the first step toward joining the guerrillas.

James Dunkerly (1985: 116) reports an incident that was typical of this action-reaction cycle. Members of ORDEN arrested a number of leaders of a local peasant association, and the next day one of them was found decapitated. The ORDEN unit was then attacked by peasants, resulting in at least nine more deaths. Four days later, five members of ORDEN were executed by the FPL (the Popular Liberation Forces, one of El Salvador's guerrilla armies). ORDEN then responded by driving villagers out of their homes, and another fifteen people were killed in subsequent clashes.

What these incidents indicate is that, for the first time, peasants were beginning to retaliate against specific incidents of repression. In some cases the retaliation was instigated by one of the several guerrilla armies operating in El Salvador. In other cases the response to death squad violence was instigated by local members of popular organizations, who had begun arming themselves for self defense. The fact that death squad members could no longer be certain of impunity when they perpetrated their violence changed the calculus of conflict for both the left and the right.

In 1980 the Popular Revolutionary Bloc, the Unified Popular Action Front, and the Popular Leagues of the 28th of February formed a coalition as the Faribundo Martí National Liberation Front (FMLN), with the Democratic

Revolutionary Front (FDR) serving as its political wing. The FMLN began with 6,000 to 8,000 active guerrillas, as many as 100,000 part-time militia, and a reported one million sympathizers who provided them with covert support in the form of food, supplies, shelter, intelligence, and sanctuary (Leiken 1984: 118). With the formation of the FMLN, the conflict in El Salvador escalated to a full scale civil war.

LAND REFORM AS A COUNTERINSURGENCY STRATEGY

The failure of repression to contain opposition and the subsequent escalation of revolutionary violence motivated the 1979 coup that brought to power a junta committed to agrarian reform. However, agrarian reform did not end or even diminish revolutionary opposition. The reason is not simply that the reform failed to provide benefits to enough of the rural poor. Rather, revolutionary opposition persisted because agrarian reform was accompanied by a further escalation in repressive violence by right-wing members of the Salvadoran military. That segment of the military had been the beneficiaries of the protection racket arrangement with the landed elite, and they opposed the reforms being carried out by their more progressive junior colleagues who staged the 1979 coup.

Within six months of the October coup, a reconstituted junta proclaimed a three-phase land reform program and elections for a constituent assembly that would write a new democratic constitution. The agrarian reform program was supposed to provide 100,000 to 200,000 households with land, either as smallholders or as members of a cooperative. Phase I of the land reform program expropriated estates larger than 500 hectares and converted them into production cooperatives that would be owned collectively by the former estate's resident workers.[10] The cooperative members were to elect a committee that would have the authority to make decisions concerning cooperative operations, but the government would appoint a co-manager who would be in charge of day-to-day management of the cooperative, including its finances. The appointed manager would also have the authority to veto major decisions by the governing committee (Strasma 1989: 409). By March of 1986, 469 estates had been converted into 317 cooperatives that included a total of 215,167 hectares of land. The lands transferred under Phase I represented about 15 percent of all farmland, 12 percent of all crop land, 14 percent of the coffee acreage, 23 percent of the cotton acreage, and 36 percent of the sugarcane acreage (Thiesenhusen 1995: 154; see table 8.2).

Phase II targeted 1,700 to 1,800 estates of 100 to 500 hectares, which included substantial portions of the land planted in coffee (31 percent), cotton

Table 8.2   **Land Reform Beneficiaries in El Salvador**

	Families benefited	Individuals benefited	Number of hectares	Hectares per family
Phase one[a]	36,697	194,494	215,167	5.86
Phase three	42,183	259,183	69,605	1.63
Voluntary transfers[b]	6,041	36,850	10,922	1.81
Total	85,227	490,527	295,694	3.47

Source: Thiesenhusen (1995: 154).
[a]Figures for Phase I also include all beneficiaries of colonization programs prior to 1980. These are sometimes referred to as Decree 842 properties. Phase I is sometimes referred to as Decree 154.
[b]Voluntary transfers are properties that were offered in voluntary sale beginning in late 1987.

(30 to 41 percent), and sugar (21 percent). Because Phase II affected so much of the lands planted in export crops, its implementation was resisted and successfully delayed by still-powerful agro-export interests. The distribution formula for Phase II (that is, whether the estates would be converted into cooperatives or subdivided into smallholdings) was not specified in the original decree because of the pressures brought to bear on the junta by the agro-export elite. Instead the task of devising a distribution formula for Phase II was left for the new constituent assembly to address after it was elected in 1982.

Despite the reformist Christian Democratic Party (PDC) winning a plurality (40 percent) of the seats in the assembly, a coalition of conservative parties, led by ARENA (30 percent), PCN (Party of National Conciliation, 20 percent) and Democratic Action (AD, 4 percent) managed to gain majority control of the assembly. The coalition named Roberto D'Aubuisson of ARENA as assembly president, despite his implication in death squad violence.[11] With D'Aubuisson as president of the assembly, the right-wing coalition inserted into the 1983 constitution a provision that raised the maximum holdings that Phase II landowners could retain from 100 to 245 hectares and mandated that the excess over 245 hectares could not be expropriated until after December 1986. This gave landowners three years to subdivide or sell off land in order to reduce their holdings below the 245-hectare ceiling. As a result the number of properties subject to Phase II expropriation was reduced from about 1,800 to 400, and the amount of land available for redistribution dropped from over 100,000 hectares to less than 10,000 (Prosterman and Riedinger 1987: 162). None of these estates were ever expropriated, and virtually none of the land originally included in Phase II was ever redistributed to peasant farmers.

With Phase II delayed, the government rushed into law Phase III, the "land to the tiller" program. Under Phase III, tenants and sharecroppers could apply for title to the land they were renting, up to a limit of seven hectares per household (Prosterman and Riedinger 1987: 153–56). Phase III was supposed to have affected some 150,000 to 220,000 hectares of land rented by 130,000 families. These lands comprised 10 to 15 percent of all farm land, but little if any of the acreage in export crops.

By any measure, the Salvadoran land reform was one of the most extensive nonsocialist land reforms in the history of Latin America. It redistributed almost 296,000 hectares of land, amounting to 14 percent of the nation's total land area and 20 percent of its farmland. The number of beneficiaries constituted roughly 21 percent of the nation's economically active population. As a result of land reform, the landless and land-poor population declined from 60.1 percent of the economically active agricultural population in 1971 to 50.7 percent in 1991 (Seligson 1995: 60). By Huntington's logic, an agrarian reform program of this magnitude should have substantially undermined popular support for the FMLN. The fact that it did not leads us to question why.

THE LIMITS OF LAND REFORM

Many critics of the land reform program point to flaws in its design and implementation as the reasons that it did not succeed in dissipating support for the FMLN. One glaring flaw in the Salvadoran land reform was its failure to provide benefits to the most marginalized segment of the population: the landless. Although growth in the landless population had precipitated the crisis of political stability in the first place, landless peasants did not qualify for land, either as members of Phase I cooperatives or as Phase III smallholders. Membership in Phase I cooperatives was restricted to those who were resident workers of the pre-reform estates at the time that Phase I was announced. Given the fact that these estates had been reducing their permanent labor force over the course of the previous two decades, the rules on cooperative membership severely restricted the pool of Phase I beneficiaries. The cooperatives could have absorbed a portion of the landless population by granting membership to some of each estate's nonresident laborers. However, cooperative members developed a preference for hiring wage labor to fulfill the enterprise's labor needs rather than admit new members. While hiring laborers gave members more time to devote to their own subsistence plots, it had the effect of draining the cooperatives' cash reserves, further exacerbating the debt service problem (Strasma 1989). Had the laborers been admitted as members, they could have been compensated with a share of the enterprise's profits at the end of the crop cycle, and this would have reduced the drain that wages imposed on the cooperative's cash flow. However, the legislation did not permit this, and those granted membership were not inclined to admit new members voluntarily. They preferred to minimize the number of claims on the cooperative's profits and on the lands that were allocated to members for use as subsistence plots. Restricting membership minimized the extent to which Phase I contributed to relieving the grievances of the landless.[12]

The landless were likewise excluded from Phase III, because only those who were already renting land could apply for title to it under the law. A frequently heard criticism of Phase III was that its design reflected an ignorance of or insensitivity to the variety of tenancy arrangements that were found among the affected properties. Many Phase III plots were owned by poor farmers who rented out part of their land to equally poor neighbors or relatives (Diskin, 1989: 437; Strasma, 1989: 423). Because size of the property cultivated by the potential beneficiary, and not total size of the owner's holdings, was the criterion for a property's inclusion under Phase III, many poor peasants who happened to be renting out all or part of their meager holdings were subject to expropriation just as much as large landowners who had simply found it more convenient (and profitable) to rent out their land in small plots rather than farm it themselves. In many of these cases, the renter simply declined to apply for title.

Thousands of others who rented their land from large landowners also never applied for title to the land under Phase III, though for a different reason. The transfer of title on over 50,000 parcels of land was fraught with delays that gave landlords the opportunity to evict or intimidate tenants. Late in 1981 the Unión Comunal Salvadoreña (UCS), the nation's largest peasant association, reported that as many as 25,000 potential beneficiaries of Phase III had been evicted before they could apply for title to their plots (Diskin 1989: 439). Not until 1982 was FINATA (the agency created to implement Phase III) able to reverse the effects of intimidation and restore the flow of Phase III applications. Eventually three-fourths of those evicted were reinstated (Strasma 1989: 410–11) .

Phase III beneficiaries were hardly converted into the self-sufficient, conservative yeoman farmers that Huntington and Prosterman envisioned. By 1992 a total of 69,605 hectares of land had been distributed to 42,489 families under Phase III. This represented only 4.5 percent of all farm land in El Salvador and an average of only 1.63 hectares per beneficiary family (Thiesenhusen 1995: 154). A survey of beneficiaries revealed that net earnings from their land accounted for only about one-third of the family's income. The terms of Phase III further magnified the pressure for beneficiaries to find off-farm employment: As tenants, families could compensate the landlord in part through labor services or crop shares, but the land they received under Phase III carried a mortgage that was payable only in cash (Reinhardt 1989: 469). Thus, despite receiving subsistence-size plots or smaller, Phase III beneficiaries were compelled to devote much of their land to cash crops in order to make their mortgage payments.

Despite these limitations, the Salvadoran land reform program did provide benefits to one-fifth of the economically active population engaged in agriculture. Its success led Mitchell Seligson (1995: 66) to conclude that "El Salvador's probability of experiencing an agrarian-based revolution has markedly diminished." Yet revolutionary violence escalated immediately after the reform's initiation and continued unabated for a decade while the land transfers were taking place. Therefore, whatever its success at alleviating inequality of land ownership, one is hard-pressed to attribute the eventual settlement of the Salvadoran civil war to the success of land reform.

REFORM, REPRESSION, AND PEASANT BEHAVIOR

Flaws in program design and implementation cannot fully account for the failure of land reform to quell the revolution in the Salvadoran countryside. Agrarian reforms in other nations were similarly flawed but were not followed by the outbreak of revolution (for example, in Bolivia and Mexico). Those who received land reform benefits in El Salvador were clearly better off than they had been prior to the reform. Even those who received no land were unlikely to take up arms against the state simply because they were still landless or land-poor. Joining the FMLN carried the risk of death, and most peasants would not assume that risk simply because they were bypassed in the distribution of land reform benefits. We must look to other factors to explain the failure of land reform to dissipate revolution.

Land reform was undertaken in El Salvador primarily for political purposes: specifically to build a base of popular support for the newly democratizing regime and to inoculate peasants against the FMLN's call for revolution. If land reform succeeded politically, revolution would atrophy; if it failed, revolution would expand. Constituent assembly elections and the 1984 presidential elections were referenda on the political success of the junta's reform program. For land reform to succeed in its political purpose, it should have generated a high voter turnout and a large share of the votes for the reformist Christian Democratic Party and its 1984 presidential candidate, José Napoleon Duarte. For the opponents of reform to succeed, they had to intimidate peasants into not applying for land reform benefits and not voting for the PDC. The situation in El Salvador was complicated by the fact that there were two forces opposed to land reform and democratization: the rebels of the FMLN and the protection racket coalition of conservative military officers and landed elites. The opponents of reform on the right preferred a return to the status quo ante: a revival of the protection racket state. They used death squad violence and intimidation to deter peasants from applying for land and voting for the PDC. On the left, the FMLN also wanted land reform to fail because its success would preclude the need for the revolutionary overthrow of the incumbent regime. Accordingly the FMLN used insurgent violence to prevent the implementation of land reform and to disrupt elections in the regions they controlled. Peasants were caught in the crossfire between these contending elite groups.

Figure 8.1 depicts the relationships between reform, repression, and support for the regime in the Salvadoran case (see Mason 1986a). The reformers within the regime, led by the PDC, wished to continue the momentum of agrarian reform and democratization. They hoped to use land reform as a device to generate a high level of popular support for the PDC at the polls. This should have been reflected in both a high turnout rate in the 1982 and 1984 elections and a high vote total for the PDC. A high turnout could be interpreted as a popular preference against the option of revolution. By generating a large turnout and a large vote for the PDC, the reformers hoped to pre-empt the right wing's efforts to undermine land reform and democratization. At the same time, the reformers also believed that land reform would win peasant support away from the FMLN and thereby cause the insurgency to atrophy for lack of a civilian support base. In short, the reformers' goal was to defeat the FMLN and the conservatives. Their weapons in this struggle were land reform (as the "carrot" to win popular support away from both the rebels and the conservatives) and democratization (as the institutional means by which to mobilize their supporters against the right wing and prevent a revival of the protection racket state).

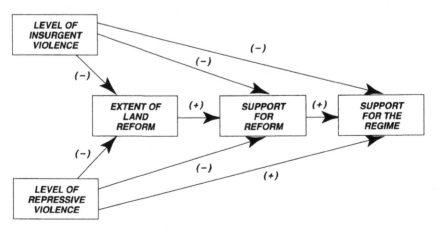

Figure 8.1. Land Reform, Repression, and Support for the Regime in El Salvador. *Source:* Derived from Mason 1985a: 510.

The right-wing opponents of reform within the military and the agrarian elite hoped to reverse the land reform process and defeat the FMLN. Like the reformers, they sought to "drain the sea" of peasant supporters of the FMLN. However, their strategy for doing this was based on violence: They targeted their repressive violence against known or suspected supporters of the FMLN, including anyone who happened to reside in regions that had a substantial guerrilla presence. To defeat the reformers, they also used the threat of violence to intimidate peasants into refraining from applying for land reform benefits. Therefore, as figure 8.1 shows, there should be fewer applications for land reform benefits in those municipalities where the right wing was strong, as indicated by a high rate of death squad violence.

The right wing also shared the PDC's goal of a large election turnout, but they wanted that turnout to reflect a large vote against the PDC. They pursued this goal through the coercion of peasants. A large turnout could be depicted as a rejection of the FMLN, and a large vote against the PDC could be depicted as a rejection of land reform. At the very least a right-wing electoral victory would give them control over the machinery of government and thereby allow them to delay, water down, or dismantle land reform (which they succeeded in doing to Phase II). Therefore, in districts where the right wing was strong, there should be high turnout rates but low vote totals for the PDC. If peasants did not vote, they could expect to be sanctioned by the death squads. While the balloting was secret, El Salvador's history of electoral fraud would make one cautious about voting for reform parties if one's district happened to be one where the right wing presence was strong and the possibility of being identified as a PDC voter, though slim, could not be ruled out. Since the cost of voting for the PDC might be death, one could easily be intimidated into voting for antireform parties, even when one's true preference was for the PDC.

Finally, the FMLN's goal was to achieve revolutionary victory by undermining popular support for the incumbent regime. This required that the FMLN prevent the regime from succeeding in implementing its land reform program. It pursued this goal militarily: to the extent that it could establish control over a region, it could prevent the state's land reform from being implemented there. Second, the FMLN sought to prevent the consolidation of democratic reforms. To achieve this, it called for election boycotts, which it attempted to enforce with violent intimidation of voters and election officials. Therefore, in districts controlled by the FMLN, we would expect low rates of application for land reform benefits, low turnout in the elections, low vote totals for the PDC, and high proportions of the ballots either left blank or defaced. Peasants who supported the FMLN still had to fear for their lives. In the 1982 and 1984 elections, failure to vote was taken by the security forces and the death squads as prima facie evidence of support for the rebels. By casting a vote, an FMLN supporter avoided being marked as a rebel sympathizer. By leaving the ballot blank, however, one could register one's opposition (anonymously) to the status quo and one's preference for the rebels over both the new reformist regime and its right-wing opponents.

FROM REFORMIST COUP TO REVOLUTION

How does this model of the relationships between reform, repression, and revolution conform with events in El Salvador? The campaign of violence that followed the announcement of land reform and democratic elections was intended to undercut the success of both reform projects. As U.S. Ambassador Robert White reported:

> The strategy of the right is clear: (1) destroy the accessible left, those who . . . could potentially be persuaded either to support or at least not violently oppose the junta's reform program; (2) demonstrate the impotence of the junta and the tolerance of the armed forces for savage reprisals by the ultra-right, thereby radicalizing the moderates . . . ; and (3) convince the armed forces that its only hope of survival as an institution is to return to its traditional alliance with the oligarchy, especially those who are bankrolling the right-wing violence. (quoted in Stanley 1996: 199)

Immediately after the proclamation of agrarian reform, the right-wing opponents of the reform mounted a campaign of terror intended to intimidate potential beneficiaries into abandoning their land or foregoing their right to claim title to it. The expropriation of the estates covered under Phase I was even carried out by the military, and in a number of instances they targeted their coercive might not on the estate owners but on the intended beneficiaries. Donald Shulz (1984: 213) quotes a technician from the Salvadoran Institute of Agrarian Transformation (ISTA, the agency charged with implementing Phase I) who witnessed the expropriation of one of the Phase I estates: "The troops came and told the workers the land was theirs now. They could elect their own leaders and run it themselves. The peasants couldn't believe their ears, but they held elections that very night. The next morning the troops came back, and I watched as they shot every one of the elected leaders."

During the first year of land reform, over 500 peasant leaders were assassinated by the security forces and paramilitary death squads (Shulz 1984: 213). Even the Unión Comunal Salvadoreña (UCS), a largely pro-government peasant association, was targeted by the death squads. On July 19, 1980, death squad members accompanied by units of the security forces entered the hacienda Mirador and shot sixty peasants who were UCS members (Shulz 1984:

213). Perhaps the most brazen act of death squad violence intended to disrupt land reform was the 1981 assassination of Adolfo Viera, head of the ISTA, and two USAID workers in the lounge of the Sheraton Hotel in San Salvador.

By 1982 death squad violence had led to the abandonment of seventy-eight Phase I cooperatives. As of 1986 twenty-four of them, representing an estimated 6 percent of national output, were still abandoned (Schwarz 1991: 46–48). The violence that accompanied Phase I was intended, first, to intimidate peasants into abandoning the cooperatives and, second, to prevent organizations on the left from using the cooperatives as a new institutional base of support for their campaign of reform (Stanley 1996: 195). This campaign of terror was conducted by the right wing of the military, with the support of the conservative, land-owning oligarchy. In other words, the traditional protection racket coalition was using repressive violence to undermine the success of land reform and radicalize the left, so that a moderate center (led by the PDC) could not build a coalition for peace, land reform, and democracy. In addition to the violence that accompanied land reform, the antireform elements of the military (and their surrogates in the death squads) also began targeting popular organizations, ranging from CEBs to unions to reformist parties. Hugh Byrne (1996: 64) quotes two FMLN leaders on the early success of this campaign: "The FMLN lost most of its urban network to death squad counter-terrorism in the 1981–1983 period. . . . In a thirty-day period in 1982, the FMLN lost over 100 urban commandos to death squads."

However, the campaign failed to decapitate the FMLN. Instead it compelled the rebel coalition to shift to a protracted war of guerrilla insurgency based in the countryside. And it foreclosed their entry into the electoral process.

The opponents of reform also began targeting Christian Democrats in an effort to undermine their efforts at economic reforms and pre-empt their chances of victory in the elections scheduled for 1982. The Christian Democratic Attorney General, Mario Zamora, was assassinated in his home after Roberto D'Aubuisson appeared on television to accuse him of being a member of one of the guerrilla organizations. A few days earlier, two members of Zamora's staff had been gunned down while driving through the streets of San Salvador in a car with markings that identified it as a government vehicle (Stanley 1996: 191).

Opponents of reform did not confine their violence to opposition leaders. In 1981 alone, 12,501 "extralegal killings of civilians not engaged in combat" (death squad killings) were recorded by Socorro Juridico, the office of the archdiocese of San Salvador that compiled reports on the violence (Simon and Stephens 1982: 61). Although many of these victims were selected because of their political involvement or their determination to apply for land, a bloodbath of this proportion in a nation of less than five million people inevitably included large numbers of peasants who happened to be in the way of the increasingly indiscriminate forces of repression. Massacres at the Sumpul River (May 14–15, 1980), the Lempa River (October 20–29, 1981), and El Mozote (December 1981) were the more gruesome instances of a pattern of right-wing violence that resulted in a civilian death toll of 11,903 in 1980, 16,266 in 1981, and 5,962 in 1982 (Comision de la Verdad 1993: 114–26; see table 8.3). As one Catholic priest lamented, "to be a victim . . . it is enough to be a relative of a militant or to be suspected of having collaborated with the insurgents. The concept of collective responsibility is being progressively extended to the individual, the family, the town, even the province" (quoted in Shulz 1984: 214). The right wing's strategy of indiscriminate repressive violence ensured that civil war would continue, even as the reformist junta was trying to implement a program of democratization. And it ensured that popular support for reform and democratization would be deterred by the calculus of fear induced by the campaign of repression perpetrated by the military and their civilian allies.

In 1984 José Napoleon Duarte of the reformist Christian Democratic Party was elected president. Duarte had run for president in 1972, only to have the election stolen from him by the military. As the first president elected under the new constitution, he did what he could to curb death squad violence. However, the military remained relatively free from civilian control, a condition that was reinforced by U.S. military assistance funds going directly to the military command rather than being funneled through the civilian government. This condition denied reformist civilian leadership discretionary control over the funds, control they could have used to restrain the military's use of repressive violence.

Under Duarte, El Salvador did experience a steady decline in death squad violence (see table 8.3) to the point that the civilian death toll for 1986 was about 10 percent of what it had been five years earlier. However, with U.S. assistance, the Salvadoran army simply shifted from death squad violence to air strikes and helicopter gunship assaults as a means of rapid response to guerrilla operations (Stanley 1996: 229–30). While such firepower did make it difficult for rebels to mass forces for major offensives, it did not discriminate between guerrilla soldiers and local villagers. Instead its use created a situation in which those regions marked by frequent guerrilla operations became free-fire zones, and peasants living there had little choice but to move to refugee camps, to neighboring nations, or to regions firmly under rebel control. Remaining neutral was no longer an option.

When peasants could become victims simply by having a family member or a neighbor come under suspicion of having aided the FMLN, or by living in a village where guerrillas patrolled frequently, they were compelled either to join the insurgents in search of protection or to become refugees. By 1984 an estimated 500,000 Salvadorans, or about 10 percent of the population, had

Table 8.3 Deaths from Repression and Counterinsurgency in El Salvador, 1980–1990

	1980	1981	1982	1983	1984	1985	1986	1987	1988	1989	1990[b]
Targeted deaths[a]	n.a	n.a	3,059	1,259	224	240	123	96	152	40	119
Civilian noncombatant deaths[a]	11,903	16,266	5,962	4,884	2,657	1,656	953	467	718	1,255	971
Disappeared	544	699	692	606	326	151	203	148	183	193	70

Source: Comision de la Verdad para El Salvador (1993); Americas Watch (1984: 3, 41; 1985a: 89; 1987: 7; 1991: 18).
[a]Victims of death squads and government forces.
[b]Includes FMLN victims as well as civilians.

been displaced from their homes but had not left the country. They were categorized as "displaced" rather than as refugees (Lawyers Committee for International Human Rights and Americas Watch 1984: 12). Another 500,000 were believed to have fled the country and settled in the United States, Mexico, or other Central American nations (the United Nations High Commissioner for Refugees puts the figure at 244,000; see Lawyers Committee for International Human Rights and Americas Watch, 31).

FROM STALEMATE TO SETTLEMENT

During the latter half of the 1980s, the civil war settled into a stalemate. The several guerrilla organizations that had formed the FMLN never unified completely into a single combat organization, nor did they ever achieve consensus on strategy and tactics. Hugh Byrne (1996: 40–41) argues that divisions within the FMLN limited their capacity ever to achieve victory on the battlefield.

> Dogmatism, sectarianism, and the struggle for hegemony prevented revolutionary groups from combining certain strategies effectively. . . . Likewise, the complete rejection of electoral approaches left the largest of the revolutionary groups without a meaningful discourse with sectors that had not fully broken with the system. . . . The main weakness of the revolutionary movement was that it was divided among organizations, each of which had its own assessment of the nature of the system and the proper strategies for weakening the regime.

For its part, the government could prevent the FMLN from mounting an effective offensive, but its own tactics continued to alienate and displace large portions of the population. The military's reliance on superior firepower as its primary counterinsurgency device and the persistence of death squad violence by units of the security forces and their paramilitary surrogates prevented Duarte and the PDC from consolidating their control over political power and building a base of popular support for a moderate, reformist center that could have brought the war to an end much sooner and with much less death and destruction. Because of the right's campaign of death squad violence, the initiation of land reform and democratic elections occurred not in an atmosphere of hope for peaceful change but in an environment marked by violence and terror. Suspicions about the sincerity of the reformers were naturally reinforced by this campaign of terror, and the public support that might have coalesced around the reforms instead dissolved in the crossfire between the death squads and the rebels, both of whom shared an interest in the failure of land reform and democratization.

The war also took its toll on the already fragile Salvadoran economy. Estimates of the destruction to infrastructure caused by the war reached $2 billion (Byrne 1996: 159). In 1987 the Central Reserve Bank claimed that 50 percent of the nation's budget was going to the war effort. The gross domestic product had declined 23 percent between 1979 and 1984, and much of the growth after that was attributable to increases in world prices for coffee. Officially recognized unemployment was at 30 percent, and the real income of agricultural workers fell by 30 percent between 1980 and 1984. Foreign debt grew to $1.99 billion, twice the total of export earnings for 1984. The annual debt service burden reached $262.3 million (Montgomery 1995: 190). On top of these conditions, San Salvador was hit by an earthquake on October 10, 1986. The quake, which registered 7.5 on the Richter scale, caused another $2 billion in damages, resulted in 1,500 deaths and 10,000 injuries, and left another 200,000 homeless and destitute (202).

By the end of the 1980s, it was apparent that neither the rebels nor the regime had decisively won the hearts and minds of the population. Schwarz (1991: 13–14) cites a survey indicating that 70 percent of the population were indifferent as to which side won; they simply wanted an end to the violence. The election of ARENA candidate Alfredo Cristiani in 1988 indicated popular disillusionment with the ability of the PDC to implement its reform agenda or to end the violence.

By 1989 a decade of civil war, land reform, and democratic elections had combined to alter the composition of the civilian elite and the structure of the Salvadoran economy in ways that made negotiating a peace agreement and dismantling the protection racket preferable to continuing the war. Land reform had eroded the power of the agro-export elite, and many of them had liquidated their remaining assets and left the country. In their place a new generation of commercial elites emerged to eclipse the landed oligarchy as the strongest influences in ARENA. Based in finance, export processing, and commerce, this new elite had little need to preserve the protection racket that had sustained the old agro-export elite. They had even less interest in continuing a war that threatened the infrastructure and investments that were essential to their own prosperity.[13]

By 1990 the ARENA Party of Alfredo Cristiani was no longer the party of Roberto D'Aubuisson. Tom Gibb (1992: 20–21) characterizes the Cristiani government as "a Salvadoran version of Margaret Thatcher's philosophy," led by "highly capable business people and technocrats" whose "main interest is not in controlling [state] power or government for itself but in creating the best conditions for their own businesses to flourish." Gibb adds that "many business people agree with the left that the military should be brought under civilian control. . . . They are highly critical of the military's performance in the war and believe that it has become a big business for many senior officers." The new elite managed to capture the state from the agro-export elite by transforming ARENA into a viable electoral alternative for a war-weary electorate disillusioned with the ineffectiveness and corruption of the Christian Democratic Party. A peace settlement became feasible because this new elite shared with the FMLN an incentive to dismantle the protection racket.

The critical event in bringing the combatants to the negotiating table was the FMLN offensive of November 1989. After months of secretly stockpiling weapons in the poor neighborhoods of San Salvador, FMLN guerrillas launched attacks throughout the capital city. The Salvadoran military command was caught by surprise. In fact, a number of them were out of the country. President Cristiani himself was at his vacation home when the offensive began. Desperate to prevent a rebel takeover of San Salvador, the Salvadoran military resorted to the one asset it had at its disposal: superior firepower. The military's use of air strikes to root rebel units out of poor neighborhoods in the city caused mounting civilian casualties, further eroding the legitimacy of the regime. When the rebels moved into wealthy neighborhoods, the military refrained from bombing and strafing, a double standard that was not lost on San Salvador's poor (Montgomery 1995: 217). Although the offensive was eventually defeated, the shock of its initial success undermined what was left of the military's claim to dominance in the protection racket state: If they could not protect the capital city against such a coordinated attack, how could they justify their continued dominance of the civilian regime?

During the 1989 offensive the military made another grave error that sealed the doom of its protection racket arrangement with the civilian elite. Frustrated by the rebels' initial success and fearing for the first time the possibility of rebel victory, the top military elite acted on their belief that El Salvador's popular organizations as well as most Catholic priests were nothing more than agents of the FMLN. Accordingly they ordered the assassination Ignacio Ellacuría, Segundo Montes, and several of their Jesuit colleagues at the University of Central America. In the process, the soldiers also murdered Ellacuría'a housekeeper and her daughter. News of this incident caused a storm of international outrage. Thereafter it became increasingly difficult if not impossible for the U.S. Congress to vote for continued funding of the Salvadoran military, especially when it became known that the unit implicated in the murders was the Atlacatl battalion, a unit that had been trained by the United States and touted as the model of a new, professionalized Salvadoran military that was supposed to be immune to corruption and sensitive human rights (Stanley 1996: 245–48).[14]

While the offensive failed to achieve its goal of toppling the government, it did demonstrate that the rebels' capacity to sustain combat operations was at least sufficient to preclude military defeat of the FMLN. The fact that the rebels could mount such an offensive convinced the Cristiani government that it was not going to annihilate the rebels on the battlefield. For the rebels, their failure to achieve victory in the offensive convinced them that some alternative to military victory would be worth pursuing. For the U.S. government, the offensive demonstrated that the U.S. subsidy of the Salvadoran military would never be sufficient for it to achieve victory. Moreover, the final offensive made it politically difficult for the United States to continue subsidizing a war effort that was no closer to victory and that continued to be marked by egregious acts of terror, such as the Jesuit murders. Finally, the failure of the FMLN's November 1989 offensive signaled the unwillingness of most Salvadorans to take up arms against the new administration, even though ARENA was less enthusiastic than the PDC about land reform (Byrne 1996: 152–64; Vickers 1992: 36–37). Thus all the key actors came to the realization that neither the government nor the rebels could achieve military victory. Under such circumstances, to continue fighting was futile.

With UN mediation, Cristiani and the rebels began negotiating a settlement to the war. A number of FDR leaders, including Ruben Zamora and Guillermo Ungo, returned from exile to run for office in the 1991 national assembly elections. On January 16, 1992, Cristiani and the FMLN commanders finally signed a peace accord that mandated reforms of the electoral and judicial systems, demobilization and reintegration into society of FMLN guerrillas, reductions in the size and the jurisdiction of the armed forces, a purge of its officer corps, and the creation of a new civilian police force to replace the old police, the national guard, and the treasury police, all of which were irrevocably tainted by their involvement with death squad activity (Montgomery 1995). Under UN supervision, implementation of the peace accords was slow but ultimately successful, at least in the sense that the process has never deteriorated to the point of armed combat resuming.

CONCLUSION

The Salvadoran case illustrates how difficult it is to implement a land reform program in the midst of an ongoing civil war. Civil war creates a cover for the opponents of reform to subvert reform through violence. Both the revolutionary left and the conservative right had an interest in seeing land reform fail because its success would weaken their claims to popular support. When the political environment is highly polarized and the contending powers are heavily armed, the intended beneficiaries of agrarian reform are too often caught in the crossfire between rebels and regime. No land reform program can restore peasant loyalty to the state if peasants remain subject to violence at the hands of the state. Unless beneficiaries can work their land secure from the threat of violence at the hands of death squads, security forces, or rebels, they will soon abandon the land and the state. If the state is the major perpetrator of violence, then peasants will turn to the rebels for protection. Whatever benefits a regime might provide to peasants, escalating violence will erode the support that those benefits were intended to generate.

NOTES

1. "Proclamation of the Armed Forces of the Republic of El Salvador, 15 October 1979." An English translation of this document appears in Stanley (1996: 267–69).

2. On the transformation of the agrarian society, see Paige 1975; Migdal 1988; and Wolf 1982. On patron-client politics, see Powell 1970; Scott 1972, 1976; Scott and Kerkvliet 1977. On the rational peasant, see Popkin 1979.

3. The definitive work on *la matanza* is Thomas Anderson's (1971) book.

4. See Mason 1992 and Reif 1986 on how this contributed to the remarkable level of participation by women in the guerrilla insurgency, not just as support personnel but as combat soldiers in the guerrilla army.

5. The figures on industrial employment are calculated using 1960 and 1982 figures on total population, percent of the population between fifteen and sixty-four years of age, and the percent of the work force in industry, obtained from Taylor and Jodice 1983 and the World Bank 1984.

6. On the role that the Catholic Church played in mobilizing the poor, see Peterson 1997; Montgomery 1995.

7. The discussion that follows is taken from Mason 1999.

8. The figures cited here are conservative. Stanley (1996: 110) reports that, "witnesses saw about 160 bodies being loaded onto trucks and removed from the plaza; . . . secondhand accounts refer to over 100 corpses seen at a public hospital in the city. Some reports say that the security forces fired for more than four hours."

9. Comision de la Verdad para El Salvador 1993 is the most thorough compilation of information on repression in El Salvador. See also Americas Watch (1984; 1985a,b; 1986).

10. Owners were allowed to retain between 100 and 150 hectares, depending on soil quality. For other details on the terms of the reform, see Diskin 1989; Reinhardt 1989; Strasma 1989; Thiesenhusen 1995; Seligson 1995.

11. D'Aubuisson had held the rank of major in the armed forces before being arrested in 1980 for plotting a countercoup against the reformist junta. Documents found in his quarters when he was arrested demonstrate his extensive involvement in death squad activity and even implicate him in the assassination of Archbishop Romero (Byrne 1996: 59–60).

12. Other problems limited the profitability of the cooperatives. From the start the enterprises were plagued by a substantial debt burden, mainly in the form of the mortgage they assumed to compensate the former landowner. Most of the cooperatives

were able to keep current on their production credit accounts but had little success in meeting their mortgage obligations. The debt burden was relieved to some degree in 1986 when President Duarte used his authority to reduce the interest rate on land debt from 9.5 to 6.0 percent. He also redefined the beginning of the grace period on mortgage payments to the time the cooperative received title to the land rather than when the estate was initially expropriated. Finally Duarte extended the time allowed to pay off the mortgage (Strasma 1989: 420). These steps relieved some of the financial pressures on the cooperatives, but they still fell short of commercial success. Many cooperative members were dissatisfied with the equal pay provisions of the law that created the cooperatives. This policy encouraged free-riding by mandating equal compensation for members on a per diem basis, regardless of their productivity or the skill level required for their assigned job (Theisenhusen 1995: 152). Many members preferred devoting their time to their own plots rather than working as laborers on the cooperatives' commercial production lands. Eventually some cooperatives began ceding or renting larger portions of their land to individual members to farm as smallholders (Strasma: 420).

13. Stanley (1996: 237) argues that remittances from refugees abroad also contributed to the rise of the commercial elite relative to the traditional agro-export elite. He notes that by the end of the 1980s remittances had matched or exceeded all other sources of foreign exchange. Moreover this hard currency was flowing into the hands of peasants and urban nonelites, with the effect of revitalizing the commercial economy: "Remittances increased the income of poorer families, sometimes by as much as a third, . . . [and] domestic buying power generated by remittances helped to buoy the commercial, transportation, and construction sectors." It is from these sectors that the "new" ARENA leadership emerged.

14. The Atlacatl battalion was also implicated in the massacre at El Mozote, one of the most brutal and barbarous acts of the war. Mark Danner (1993) presents a detailed account of El Mozote, and Leigh Binford (1996) puts the massacre in the context of the history of the village and the region in which it lies. Martha Doggett's (1993) account of the 1989 Jesuit murders makes a convincing case for the involvement of the top Salvadoran military leadership in ordering the murders.

Chapter Nine

Peruvian Land Reform and the Rise of Sendero Luminoso

In 1980 the Shining Path guerrillas (Sendero Luminoso) launched an armed insurgency in the department of Ayacucho in Peru's southern sierra. Over the next decade they not only sustained a revolutionary challenge to the Peruvian state but expanded their base to include operations in the capital city of Lima and the coca-growing regions of the Huallaga Valley. What is most puzzling about the rise of the Shining Path insurgency is that it occurred after the Peruvian government had implemented what was to date the most sweeping nonsocialist land reform in the history of Latin America. Between 1968 and 1975 the Peruvian government redistributed over 8.6 million hectares of land to over 370,000 families (Alberts 1983: 141–42). If inequality of land ownership is supposed to be a precursor to revolution in the countryside, then the land reform that Peru undertook between 1968 and 1975 should have made revolt less likely. If, as Huntington (1968) argues, "No social group is more conservative than a landowning peasantry," then why would peasants rise up in support of a revolutionary assault on the state after that state redistributed millions of acres of land to hundreds of thousands of peasants?

Adding to the puzzle of Shining Path is that they chose to launch their armed uprising at the same time that Peru's military government was returning to the barracks to make way for a restoration of civilian democracy. The shift from authoritarian military rule to democratic governance is also supposed to make revolution less likely. Democracies are supposed to be immune to revolution. This was not the case in Peru. In the decade following the completion of land redistribution and the return to civilian democracy, Shining Path grew from an isolated band of between 250 and 500 committed revolutionaries to a broad-based insurgency involving between 5,000 and 15,000 active combatants and hundreds of thousands of civilian supporters. Why did land reform and a return to democracy not preclude the recurrence of revolution in the Peruvian countryside?

The Salvadoran case demonstrates that it is difficult for land reform to succeed when it is implemented in the midst of an ongoing civil war. Civil war provides a convenient cover from which the opponents of agrarian reform can undermine its success through the violent intimidation (or murder) of the proponents of democratization and the beneficiaries of land reform. This is especially true when the regime itself is deeply divided over the question of reform. If a significant faction of the military not only opposes land reform but enjoys sufficient autonomy from the civilian government that they can act on this preference, they can intimidate potential beneficiaries into refraining from applying for reform benefits.

In Peru this was not the case. In 1968 a military coup brought to power a junta headed by General Juan Velasco Alvarado. Recurrent land invasions and regional insurgencies over the course of the previous decade had convinced Velasco and his collaborators that unless the extreme poverty and inequality in the Peruvian countryside were remedied, revolution was likely if not inevitable. Therefore the junta undertook a sweeping land reform program with the explicit goal of pre-empting revolution.

These puzzles surrounding the rise of Shining Path led David Scott Palmer (1986: 127) to conclude that "Sendero Luminoso is fundamentally a sui generis phenomenon" which defies explanation in terms of existing theories of why peasants rebel. While there are aspects of this revolution that mark it as unorthodox (compared to other rural insurgencies), Sendero's ability to build a base of support first among peasants of the southern sierra and later in Lima and the Huallaga Valley can be explained in terms of the same dynamics of revolution in the countryside presented in the first six chapters of this book and applied to the case of El Salvador in chapter 8.

The fact that Shining Path could build a base of civilian support sufficient to sustain its revolution twelve years after Velasco initiated land reform and at the same time that his successor, General Francisco Morales Bermúdez, was restoring civilian democracy suggests that land reform did not succeed in inoculating all segments of Peru's population against the appeals of revolutionaries. Yet we cannot attribute the outbreak of the Peruvian revolution exclusively to shortcomings of Velasco's land reform program. As I argued in chapter 8, participation in revolutionary violence is itself an extremely risky undertaking for peasants, even for those who do not reap the benefits of land reform. If the reform fails to make them better off, they are still not likely to take up arms against the state so long as migration or less risky "everyday forms of peasant resistance" are available. It is only when not supporting the rebels also leaves one at risk of becoming a victim of violence that one has a powerful incentive to support the rebels.

A unique aspect of the Peruvian revolt is that Shining Path never tried to mobilize aggrieved peasants for nonviolent collective action aimed at compelling the state to undertake reforms. Shining Path was committed to revolution from the outset. Therefore, when they undertook the mobilization of peasants displeased with the results of land reform, Sendero adopted tactics designed specifically to induce a repressive response from the state. When the state did respond with repression, Sendero was able to expand its base of support by offering peasants protection from the increasingly widespread and often indiscriminate repression of the Peruvian state. In this manner they were able to build their own revolution in the countryside.

This chapter explores the prereform agrarian status quo in Peru and the ways in which certain classes of peasants were left vulnerable to subsistence crisis by the terms of trade and distribution of risks prevailing between lord and peasant. It then looks at the terms of the Peruvian land reform program and the ways in which agrarian reform affected different classes of peasants. Were some categories of peasants actually worse off than they were before land reform? As with El Salvador, the limits of land reform in and of themselves are not sufficient to spark spontaneous rebellion. Instead we must look to the ways in which the rebels managed to mobilize those underserved by land reform and the ways in which the state's response to Sendero's initial challenge—its counterinsurgent mix of repression and accommodation—affected the distribution of popular support between rebels and regime.

PREREFORM AGRARIAN SOCIAL ORDER IN PERU

If poverty is an antecedent of revolution, then it should be no surprise that Shining Path was able to build its initial base of support primarily in the remote regions of the southern sierra of Peru. The *manchia india* region of the southern Andean highlands (including the departments of Ancash, Apurimac, Ayacucho, Huancavelica, and Puno) differs dramatically from the more commercialized coastal regions in terms of its topography, land use, and land tenure patterns. In addition, the population of the southern sierra is ethnically and culturally distinct from the residents of the coastal region. Isolated from the Latino culture of the coast, communities in the sierra are still populated predominantly by Quechua-speaking descendants of the Incas, and they still retain much of their traditional culture and patterns of social organization.

The poverty that plagued most peasant communities in Peru was exacerbated by both the nation's high agricultural density (the population-to-land ratio) and the highly inequitable distribution of land ownership. As of 1979 there was only one-fifth hectare of arable land per capita in Peru, making it second only to El Salvador (one-sixth hectare per capita) in agricultural density among Latin American nations. In the 1950s a mere 280 families (one-tenth of 1 percent of all farm families) owned about 30 percent of all farmland in Peru, including over half the nation's best-quality crop land (McClintock 1998: 167). In the sierra, the concentration of land ownership was even more extreme. Less that 2 percent of the agricultural units contained some 75 to 80 percent of all arable land. (See table 9.1.) Because many property owners controlled several estates, nearly 75 percent of the land was owned by less than 1 percent of the rural population. In 1960 in Puno there were 68 haciendas that contained over 5,000 hectares each, with the largest containing over 40,000 hectares. In the department of Huancavelica, the 179 largest estates (a mere 0.3 percent of all agricultural units in the department) contained over 72 percent of the usable land, and in Apurimac the largest 119 haciendas (0.3 percent of farm units) controlled a total of 82 percent of all farmland (Handelman 1981: 4–5; 1975: 24–25).

Not surprisingly, Peru's agrarian economy has often been characterized as dualistic. Thomas Ford (1955: 67) describes the difference as follows: "The concentration of land ownership on the coast represents the expansiveness of capitalist enterprise, that of the sierra represents the survival of colonial latifundism." The densely populated coastal region evolved into a center for commercial production of sugar and cotton. It also contained most of Peru's population and almost all of its industry. The Andean highlands (the sierra) retained a traditional hacienda system centered around subsistence production of food crops and livestock. Between the extremes of the two regions lies

Table 9.1.   Land Concentration on the Peruvian Coast and Highlands, 1972

Size of unit[a]	Coast		Sierra	
	Number of units (%)	Area[a] (%)	Number of units (%)	Area[a] (%)
0–5	135,651 (79.9)	176,568 (9.5)	884,209 (81.7)	1,168,998 (6.5)
5–50	31,416 (18.5)	350,657 (19.0)	179,937 (16.6)	2,049,688 (10.6)
50–200	2,271 (1.3)	218,589 (11.8)	11,386 (1.1)	1,086,931 (5.5)
200–2,200	486 (0.3)	245,944 (13.4)	5,741 (0.5)	3,455,042 (17.9)
over 2,500	62 (0.05)	855,513 (46.3)	894 (0.1)	11,530,803 (59.5)
Total	169,886	1,847,271	1,082,167	19,291,462

Source: Handelman (1981: 4).
Note: Handelman (1981: 4) notes that "although the census was conducted three years after the promulgation of the agrarian reform, the data reflect the pre-reform situation, both because the hacienda appropriation had scarcely begun in the highlands, and because those estates already expropriated on both the coast and the sierra were retained as cooperative production units and were not broken up."
[a]Hectares

the *selva,* or jungle regions, of the lower Andean slopes. The low jungle *(selva baja)* is an extension of the Amazon basin. It is sparsely populated and traditionally of little economic importance to the nation. The high jungle *(selva alta)* extends as high as 5,000 feet and is the center of coffee production in Peru (Paige 1975: 126–27). Beginning in the 1970s the *selva alta* also became the center for Peru's illicit coca production.

The Coast: Export Agriculture

Agricultural production on the coastal plain has long been capital-intensive and land-intensive, oriented toward international markets and heavily dependent on irrigation and mechanization (Paige 1975: 127; see also Ford 1955: 57–63). The shift to commercial agriculture on the coast early in the twentieth century dictated a reliance on wage labor rather than smallholding, sharecropping, or other forms of tenancy. By contrast the life of the sierra peasant has long been embedded in a precommercial network of patron-client relationships that bound him, his family, and his community to the informal authority of the local *hacendado,* or hacienda owner (McClintock 1981: 72–83; Ford 1955: 63–67).

Between 1900 and 1930, sugar cultivation on the coastal plain of Peru increased dramatically, at the expense of peasant *minifundistas* (smallholders and tenants). The large haciendas of the region controlled access to irrigation sources that were vital to peasant farmers in the largely desert environment of the coastal plain. By manipulating access to water and other forms of clientelist dependency, the *hacendados* were able to displace peasant *minifundistas* from their land, shift that land to sugar or cotton production, and convert the peasants from subsistence farmers to wage laborers on the estates.

The planting and harvesting of sugar were done largely by hand, and sugarcane could be harvested virtually year-round on the Peruvian coast. This meant that there was always a substantial nonseasonal demand for labor on the sugar estates. As long as the price of sugar on the world market remained relatively high, estate owners had more to fear from a shortage of labor than from acceding to incremental demands for better wages by sugar workers. Indeed *hacendados* offered little resistance to the efforts of APRA (the Alliance Popular Revolutionaria Americana, Peru's socialist party) to unionize sugar workers during the 1950s and 1960s (see Cotler 1969). At times *hacendados* would employ migrant workers from the sierra in an effort to break the unions or weaken their bargaining position. However, sierra migrants usually returned home for planting and harvest time in their own villages, and they were not as skilled at cutting cane as the permanent workers. Consequently migrants could not be relied on as an alternative labor pool to the permanent workers. For these reasons, sugar workers have always enjoyed relatively high wages compared to other segments of the agricultural workforce. Resident workers on a sugar estate earned at least twice the income of the average peasant community resident, and they were usually provided with housing on the estates as a condition of their employment (McClintock 1981: 74).[1] Given their situation, workers on the sugar estates showed little interest in revolution, nationalization of the estates, or even land reform, so long as their wages remained high and their employment steady (Paige 1975: 145–47).

Prior to agrarian reform, cotton was also produced on commercial estates on the coast. Some of these estates used wage labor, while others parceled out their land to sharecroppers (Ford 1955: 61). In neither case, however, did peasants on cotton estates fare nearly as well as sugar estate workers. Cotton estates required a relatively small permanent work force but large amounts of labor at planting and harvest time. Seasonal demand for labor could be met either with migrant workers from the sierra or with peasants from surrounding *minifundias,* many of whom were tenants obligated to provide free labor to the estate as part of their rent. For these reasons, peasants on cotton estates enjoyed a far less favorable bargaining position than their counterparts on the sugar estates. Indeed the relationships between the cotton plantation, its resident workers, and the surrounding *minifundistas* more nearly resembled the clientelist political economy of the traditional subsistence hacienda than the wage-based relationship between peasant workers and the commercial sugar estate (Paige 1975: 150).

The Sierra: Haciendas and Indigenous Communities

In contrast to the coastal region, the southern sierra resembled a traditional clientelist system defined by two distinct agrarian forms: the feudal hacienda and the peasant indigenous community. Haciendas of the sierra were among the largest in Peru, with estates of more than 500 hectares consuming a majority of the crop and livestock land in Ayacucho, Huancavelica, Puno, and Apurimac (Handelman 1981: 4). Unlike the coastal estates, sierra haciendas were not engaged in export crop production. Instead they produced food and livestock for local markets or for the urban markets of Lima and Callao.[2] Despite their large size, however, the sierra haciendas maintained a relatively small permanent work force, because livestock herding requires much less labor per unit of land than row crop production.

In the interstices between the large sierra haciendas were thousands of peasant indigenous communities. Here, land ownership was communal in most cases, with the community allocating subsistence plots to member households and maintaining communal grazing lands that were available for use by all members of the community (Ford 1955: 97–99). The land claimed by the communities was generally of poor quality; the haciendas controlled the rich inter-Andean valleys, and the indigenous communities were confined to lands on the slopes above the valleys. Encroachment by haciendas on the communities' land was a constant source of tension in the region and the cause of intermittent peasant land invasions and uprisings.

This hacienda system divided the peasantry into two classes: *trabajadores*, who were permanent workers on the haciendas, and *comuneros*, who were residents of the surrounding indigenous communities. Although both were bound to the *hacendado* by forms of clientelist dependency, the terms of trade and distribution of risks defining their dependency differed substantialy.

Peasants and the Haciendas

Forty to 75 percent of the land on most haciendas was rented out or granted to the estate's *trabajadores* as part of their compensation (Handelman 1975: 26–28; Paige 1975: 171–73). *Trabajadores* were dependent on the *hacendado* for tools, seeds, emergency loans, and political brokerage with local police and officials of the national government. In return for these services, the *hacendado* extracted from them terms of trade that virtually guaranteed their perpetual poverty. *Trabajadores* were expected to provide as much as 150 to 200 days of free labor to the hacienda in exchange for use of their subsistence plot and limited grazing rights on hacienda pastures. The *hacendado* decided what crops the *trabajadores* would plant and claimed as much as half the crop in rent. *Trabajadores* were not allowed to market surplus crops. Instead they were required to sell their crops to the *hacendado* at prices set by the *hacendado* (Caballero 1981a, 255–72; Handelman 1981: 106; see also Ford 1955: 89–95). The fact that hacienda lands were also devoted to food crops and livestock meant that peak demand for *trabajadores'* labor on the estate coincided with the most critical times in the crop cycle for their own subsistence plots. Often those conflicting demands meant that all members of the peasant household, including children, had to work either on the family's subsistence plot or on the hacienda as partial fulfillment of the family's labor obligation to the *hacendado*.

While *trabajadores* may have enjoyed some security against the risk of subsistence crisis, the *hacendado's* demands on their time and labor as well as his control over their crops guaranteed that *trabajadores* would always exist perilously close to the margins of subsistence and remain totally dependent upon the *hacendado* for security from subsistence crisis. Although there were some prospects for upward mobility available to individual *trabajadores* (such as a salaried position on the hacienda staff or a better subsistence plot), as a class they were not inclined to pursue collective action to alter these exploitative arrangements. Such actions would jeopardize the benefits they received from the *hacendado* and thereby put them at risk of subsistence crisis. As residents on the estates, *trabajadores* could be more easily monitored by the *hacendado*, making organization for any sort of collective action difficult and risky (Handelman 1981: 26–28; Paige 1975: 171–73). Moreover, *hacendados* often played off one *trabajador* against another by manipulating the supply of benefits they provided and the opportunities for upward mobility they alone controlled. Those who resisted the *hacendado's* demands could always be threatened with eviction because the extreme agricultural density of the region meant there was always another peasant family willing to accept the *hacendado's* terms in exchange for access to a subsistence plot (McClintock 1981: 75).

Peasants and the Indigenous Communities

The majority of the sierra peasantry were not *trabajadores* but members of one of the more than 6,000 indigenous communities. *Comuneros* made up 70 to 75 percent of the region's rural population of over three million. *Comuneros* were bound together by kinship patterns and by their Incan heritage (Handelman 1981: 4). These ties, in conjunction with their shared interest in resisting encroachment on their lands by neighboring haciendas, reinforced a strong sense of community among them.

The lands of the indigenous communities were owned communally but cultivated individually. Each household engaged in subsistence cultivation (typically on plots of less than five hectares) and kept some livestock on communal pasture. While some communal lands were set aside for grazing, these lands were the ones that were most vulnerable to encroachment. Moreover, population growth within the communities created additional pressures to shift pasture to subsistence plots (McClintock 1981: 73). Land scarcity was especially acute in the indigenous communities of the southern sierra. The land-to-population ratio in those communities was one of the lowest in Peru. Despite the fact that 75 percent of the rural population in the sierra were *comuneros*, they controlled only 10 to 15 percent of the land. The typical household there had to survive on an average of slightly less than one hectare of crop land, which in most cases was not sufficient for subsistence (see 73–74).

The extreme land pressures facing *comuneros* compelled them to seek ways of supplementing their subsistence farming. The security mechanisms that did evolve often left them dependent on the local *hacendado*. The most readily available hedge against subsistence crisis was part-time or seasonal work on a neighboring hacienda. When land reform was initiated in 1968, seasonal labor was providing as much as 25 to 35 percent of household income for most peasants in the southern sierra (McClintock 1984: 67–68). Another hedge for *comuneros* was to obtain limited grazing rights on hacienda pastures in exchange for labor services, such as tending the hacienda's flocks. The local *hacendado* was also the one person *comuneros* could turn to for seed, credit, emergency loans, marketing services, and mediation with government agencies (Caballero 1981a, 186–88). Thus communities were still dependent on the local *hacendado* for seasonal jobs and for flows of goods and services that would give them some margin of subsistence security. Given these ties of dependency, Paige's (1975: 187) characterization of indigenous communities as "a group of serfs who do not happen to live on the hacienda" is not an exaggeration.

Although *comuneros* did not depend on the *hacendado* for land, they were not immune to his power or that of his allies among the merchants, police, and government officials. *Comuneros*' land was generally of inferior quality and constantly subject to encroachment by the landlords of neighboring estates (Handelman 1981: 4). In many cases the indigenous communities had never filed legal claims to their lands. They neither understood nor were aware of the laws on property titles. They were not aware of the need for such legal proceedings because, after all, their lands had been farmed by the community for centuries, long before the Spanish arrived. Estate owners could take advantage of the ignorance of the *communidades* by simply encroaching on their lands by force. If the *communidades* tried to pursue relief in the courts, the *hacendado* would almost always be at an advantage because of his personal connections with local officials and his access to superior legal representation. In short, estate owners could usually encroach with impunity upon the meager landholdings of neighboring indigenous communities.

Although the indigenous communities were by no means totally independent, politically autonomous, or economically self-sufficient, the relationship of the *comuneros* with the *hacendado* was qualitatively different from that of the *trabajadores*. *Comuneros* had a wider array of options available to them to gain subsistence security. Their land claims were more secure than those of the *trabajadores*. They were free to migrate to the coast or to the coffee *fincas* of the central sierra in search of seasonal wage labor. Although *comuneros* were more likely than *trabajadores* to pursue this option, their ability to do so was constrained by language and other cultural barriers as well as by crowding in the labor market which resulted from rapid population growth throughout the nation.

Comuneros were also better situated than hacienda *trabajadores* to react to perceived injustices with collective action. They had communally owned lands to defend. They were more experienced in cooperative endeavors, through the operation of their own village institutions which governed social relations within the communities. Village institutions organized the community for co-operative endeavors such as building and maintaining roads, bridges, irrigation systems, and other components of the community's physical infrastructure. *Comuneros* were more likely to speak Spanish, to vote, to travel to nearby cities, and to market their crops independently of the local *hacendado* (Handelman 1975: 44, 29–30; see also Ford 1955: 96–102). The risks and opportunities facing *comuneros* left them simultaneously more dependent on outside opportunities for income but more able to migrate in pursuit of a wider array of opportunities than were the hacienda *trabajadores*. And they shared a distinctive heritage and cultural identity which contributed to their willingness and ability to organize for collective action against Hispanic or mestizo estate owners. Thus it should not be surprising that most of the peasant uprisings in Peru in the twentieth century had their origins in the indigenous communities, not among the hacienda *trabajadores* (Paige 1975: 166).

As in El Salvador, it was not inequality per se that led to instability in Peru. After all, land tenure on the coast was highly inequitable, but workers there were not rebellious. Rather, the marginal capacity of the agricultural system in the southern sierra combined with growing land pressures in the indigenous communities to threaten the subsistence security of *comuneros*. Unlike El Salvador, however, patron-client networks centered around the hacienda persisted in the sierra and limited the ability of disaffected peasants to organize politically. Nevertheless spontaneous land invasions became more frequent during the 1960s, escalating to insurgent violence in some departments. This violence inspired the military coup of 1968 that brought to power a junta committed to land reform.

RURAL UNREST AND LAND REFORM

In both Peru and El Salvador, land reform was adopted not just to reduce the extremes of inequality in the countryside but to dampen rural unrest and pre-empt revolutionary challenges to the incumbent regime. In both nations, significant agrarian reform was initiated only after a military coup brought to power a progressive junta that was willing and able to challenge the power of the entrenched landed elite by expropriating their land (with compensation) and redistributing it to peasant cultivators. Yet land reform failed to prevent the recurrence of insurgency in Peru or to quell it in El Salvador, despite these two programs being the most sweeping noncommunist land redistributions in modern Latin American history.

Nevertheless one cannot ignore the success of both programs: Substantial numbers of peasants were better off than they had been before the reform.

Arguably these beneficiaries as well as many who did not benefit directly should have been inoculated against the appeals of insurgents. Why more were not is discussed in the next section. First, I look at the motives for agrarian reform in Peru, the terms of the reform program that was adopted, and the ways in which it affected the economic well-being of different segments of the peasant population.

Land Invasions and Guerrilla Insurgencies of the 1960s

Between 1959 and 1962, a series of land invasions erupted in the central Andean department of Pasco and the coffee-growing valley of La Convención. In Pasco the residents of several villages invaded neighboring haciendas to recover land they claimed had been stolen from them by hacienda encroachments. In La Convención villagers and hacienda sharecroppers, led by Hugo Blanco, formed a union to demand better terms from their landlords. They began by insisting on paying their rent in cash, then refused to pay rent at all, and finally seized the hacienda (Handelman 1981: 6; see also Gott 1970: 373–90). At least fifty-one land invasions occurred between 1960 and the presidential election in 1962. This unrest was brought under control by the time Fernando Belaúnde Terry was elected president in 1962. Belaúnde had actively sought the peasant vote by promising land reform, and peasants were anxious to give him the opportunity to deliver on his pledge. Another sixteen invasions occurred in the months between the election and his inauguration in 1963. However, instead of restoring stability in the countryside, Belaúnde's inauguration was followed by a wave of land seizures by peasants in Pasco, Cuzco, and Junin: ninety-one occurred in the last five months of 1963 and another ninety-five in 1964 (Paige 1975: 165). Instead of initiating land reform, Belaúnde reacted by reversing the land invasions and repressing the peasant organizations that had led them, especially those in the south. In 1965 some members of the targeted peasant federations organized a short-lived guerrilla insurgency, which was quickly suppressed by the military (Handelman 1981: 6; see also Cotler 1970).

Although the military defeated the guerrilla movements, many officers who participated in the operation were shocked by the extreme poverty they witnessed among the residents of the southern sierra. Some in the military leadership became convinced that the highly inequitable distribution of land was the root cause of the Peruvian state's vulnerability to the intermittent peasant uprisings. The land invasions of the early 1960s and the abortive guerrilla insurgencies of the mid-1960s were but early warnings of more serious unrest to come unless the structural inequities that fueled peasant discontent were alleviated. Belaúnde had failed to deliver on his promise of agrarian reform, and proreform officers were soon convinced that an elected president would never be able to assert sufficient autonomy from the landed elite to undertake meaningful land reform. Accordingly in 1968 a group of officers led by Juan Velasco Alvarado staged a coup that installed Velasco as the leader of a junta committed to imposing sweeping agrarian reform. Upon seizing power, the junta sought to break the power of the landed oligarchy (the so-called forty families) by expropriating haciendas and redistributing them to peasants.

THE LAND REFORM PROGRAM

Though committed to agrarian reform, the Velasco regime recognized that preserving the lucrative agro-export estates of the coast as production units was essential to the further development and diversification of the Peruvian economy. These estates generated most of the nation's hard currency earnings, which would be essential to import the capital goods necessary to expand Peru's industrial sector and thereby relieve the severe land pressures in the countryside. Peru's ratio of only 0.18 hectares of crop land per person was so unfavorable that simply redistributing land would not be sufficient to relieve rural poverty. Even if all available land were redistributed to the population engaged in agriculture, they would still be land-poor. Land reform could be only part of the solution. It would have to be accompanied by industrialization that would create occupational alternatives to agriculture for the surplus labor in the countryside. Industrial expansion required hard currency to pay for capital goods imports. If the agro-export estates were subdivided into family plots, they would be converted to subsistence crop production, which would depress export earnings and retard industrialization. Consequently estates were preserved intact as production units by converting them into production cooperatives with the resident workers of each estate as its new collective owners.

To convert estates into cooperatives, the agrarian reform laws created two new corporate forms: the Agricultural Producers' Cooperatives (CAP) and the Agricultural Societies for Social Interest (SAIS). The CAP was the form by which the agro-export estates of the coast were preserved as production units. The SAIS was the mechanism by which the sierra indigenous communities were linked to the cooperatives created from sierra haciendas. The two corporate forms distributed reform benefits quite differently.

Land Reform on the Coast

On coastal CAPs the permanent workers on the prereform estates became the collective owners of the newly created cooperatives, with profit distribution based on either per-capita criteria or the number of days worked. Four categories of estate workers were granted membership in the cooperative: field workers, industrial workers in the estate's sugar processing plants, clerical and service workers, and managerial staff. Each group was given representation on the CAP governing body and a claim to a share of any profits generated by the cooperative. Altogether CAPs received one-third of all the land that was redistributed, even though they included only 2 percent of the agricultural labor force (Handelman 1981: 13). The average value of the property that each cooperative member received amounted to about $1,900 (McClintock 1998: 174). Members also gained access to larger private plots and were relieved of the onerous labor obligations or rental payments that the estate had extracted. Not surprisingly the income of CAP members was the highest in the agricultural labor force. On the three cooperatives Cynthia McClintock studied, real wages doubled between 1973 and 1980 (1982: 142). Shining Path guerrillas had little success mobilizing support among this class of beneficiaries.

Land Reform in the Sierra

Despite the sierra being the source of the unrest that had motivated the land reform program, the Velasco government was slow to expropriate the estates there, probably because most of them were not commercial successes and therefore were less critical to the health of the national economy. The delay gave sierra *hacendados* ample time to decapitalize their estates, sell off their herds, and otherwise liquidate whatever assets they thought might eventually be expropriated (Handelman 1981: 8).

When sierra haciendas were expropriated, they were incorporated into SAISs in order to prevent land invasions by neighboring *comuneros* and the breakup of estate lands into smallholdings. The typical SAIS included the *trabajadores* of one hacienda and the residents of as many as thirty neighboring indigenous communities. Only the former hacienda *trabajadores* were allowed to remain on the estate as resident members of the cooperative. The cooperative was managed by a government-appointed administrator, and the members (the former *trabajodores*) worked for wages, shared in the cooperative's profits, and continued to cultivate the subsistence plots the *hacendado* had granted them as part of their compensation. As shareholding members of the cooperative, however, they were relieved of the onerous *obligaciones* (such as usurious rents, excessive free labor obligations, and monopsonistic control over any surplus crops they might produce on their subsistence plot) that had bound them to the *hacendado*.

Each indigenous community affiliated with a SAIS received an ownership share in the organization. This gave the community representation on the

SAIS governing board and entitled them to a share of any profits the SAIS generated beyond wages, operating expenses, and the investment needs of the cooperative (Matos Mar and Mejia 1980: 141–43).

The Peruvian land reform redistributed more land to more families than any agrarian reform in Latin America: 38.2 percent of all farmland was distributed to 20.9 percent of all farm families. (See table 9.2.) Yet, over a decade after the initiation of agrarian reform, Shining Path guerrillas emerged in the southern sierra and attracted enough peasant support to sustain their operations for over a decade. Why did land reform fail to inoculate Peruvian peasants against the appeals of aspiring insurgents?

LIMITS OF LAND REFORM

As with the Salvadoran program, flaws in the design and implementation of the Peruvian land reform limited the extent to which it benefited those classes of peasant who were most susceptible to insurgent appeals. Reform benefits were unevenly distributed among regions—especially between the coast and the southern sierra—and among classes of peasants within each region. The largest share of redistributed land went to workers on coastal estates (in the form of cooperatives), who were already the highest income earners in the agricultural labor force. The least amount of land went to residents of indigenous communities in the sierra, who were among the lowest income earners in Peru. Not only was less land redistributed to *comuneros;* the number of *comunero* households designated to receive benefits was nearly twice the number of hacienda *trabajadores* designated as beneficiaries. Thus, as table 9.2 reveals, those who were better off before land reform received more land than those who were the most impoverished prior to land reform. Among all classes of beneficiaries, workers on coastal CAPs received an average of 3.8 standardized hectares each, while former *trabajadores* on sierra SAISs received slightly more than half that amount (2.1 hectares each). *Comuneros* received only a little more than one-tenth as much land as the CAP members (0.4 standardized hectares each; see Caballero and Alvarez 1980: 26, 45).

In the sierra the distribution of benefits between residents of the SAIS cooperatives (the former *trabajadores*) and peasants in the affiliated indigenous communities was especially inequitable. First, nearly four times as many *comuneros* as *trabajadores* were designated as beneficiaries, but the *comuneros* received less than one-sixth as much land per family as the former *trabajadores*. Moreover, most of what the communities received was additional grazing lands for the community to share, not crop land to distribute among land-poor *comuneros* households.

Table 9.2. Distribution of Land Reform Benefits in Peru, 1969–1983

Type of unit	Number of units	Number of families (%)	Total hectares (%)	Hectares per family[a]	Standardized hectares per family[b]
CAP	596	100,948 (22.1)	2,350,317 (20.9)	23.3	3.8
SAIS (trabajadores)	58	48,879 (10.7)	2,702,411 (24.0)	55.3	2.1
Native communities[c]	390	12,836 (2.8)	1,352,714 (12.0)	105.4	n.a.
Comuneros	676	162,674 (35.6)	1,515,180 (13.5)	9.3	0.4
Peasant groups	1,024	53,616 (11.7)	1,931,417 (17.2)	36.0	n.a.
Social property	10	1,507 (0.3)	228,665 (2.0)	151.7	n.a.
Other (government agencies)	—	—	125,853 (1.1)	—	n.a.
Individuals	—	73,273 (16.1)	1,052,799 (9.4)	14.4	2.6
Total	2,754	453,733	11,259,356 (100%)	24.8	

Source: Wilkie (1995: 57); Caballero and Alvarez (1980: 26).

[a] In calculating the average hectares per family, land held as state property (123,372 ha.) has been excluded because it was not available for distribution to or use by individual households.

[b] Hectares standardized according to the quality and value of the land.

[c] Category added after official end of land reform in 1980.

Second, the incorporation of hacienda lands into the SAIS effectively resolved long-standing land disputes to the disadvantage of the neighboring indigenous communities. These disputes, the result of hacienda encroachment on community lands, had been the catalyst for the land invasions and insurgencies of the 1960s. After land reform, *comuneros* had no recourse to adjudicate these disputes because the claims of the cooperatives now had the legal backing of the state. Where communities did press their claims with land invasions, the Velasco regime responded by forcibly expelling them. In some cases this occurred on haciendas that had been long abandoned by the *hacendado* and subdivided into tenant plots. As such, they no longer operated as a single production unit. In such cases the forcible expulsion of *comuneros* had the effect of creating a cooperative where a functioning hacienda had long ceased to exist (Berg 1992: 88).

Third, conflicts of interests between cooperative residents and *comuneros* were built into their differing corporate relationship to the SAIS. Indigenous communities' participation in the SAIS was through each community's grant of an ownership share in the SAIS. This gave the community a collective claim to a share of any profits generated by the cooperative. It should be recalled, however, that few haciendas in the southern sierra were commercial successes prior to land reform, and their corporate reorganization into SAISs did little to enhance their profitability. Cooperative workers resented *comuneros* being granted any claim at all to the fruits of their labors. SAIS profit-sharing arrangements created a strong incentive for cooperative workers to devote as much time as possible to cultivating their own household plots and to have as much of the cooperative's revenues as possible devoted to wages, investment, and operating expenses so as to minimize the share of earnings subject to the profit-sharing claims of the indigenous communities. In the first years of their operation, SAIS profits distributed to *comuneros* averaged only about $30 per family (Handelman 1981: 16). Even these meager earnings went not to individual households but to the community for use in community projects. The projects that such small sums could finance did little to enhance the subsistence security of individual households in the communities. Certainly *comuneros* did not view these meager payments as sufficient compensation for abandoning their long-standing land claims against the former hacienda. While the SAIS administrator might have been interested in enhancing the profitability of the cooperative, the affiliated *comuneros* were more interested in gaining access to additional cropland and pasture to relieve the mounting land pressures within their own villages.

Converting haciendas into cooperatives also had the effect of dismantling many of the mechanisms by which *comuneros* had hedged their risk of subsistence crisis. Because land reform replaced the *hacendado* with a professional administrator, the diffuse array of clientelist arrangements between a *hacendado* and neighboring *comuneros* was effectively dismantled by land reform. No longer could individual *comuneros* petition the *hacendado* for emergency loans, seed, tools, credit, or the use of hacienda pastures. The SAIS administrator dealt with *comuneros* not as individual clients but as members of a collective unit that had a limited corporate relationship with the cooperative. His incentive structure mandated that he avoid formal side arrangements with entire communities or informal ones with individual *comuneros* and instead direct as much of the cooperative's resources and revenues as possible to its resident members.

The conversion of haciendas into cooperatives also restricted the *comuneros'* opportunities for seasonal employment. Resident members had a strong incentive to fulfill as much of the cooperative's labor requirements as possible so as to minimize the share of the unit's earnings that flowed to *comuneros* as wages or profit sharing. At best *comuneros* could hope to lease marginal lands from the cooperative or hire on as temporary wage laborers. However, the terms of both arrangements were often no better than what *hacendados* had offered before reform. Coastal sugar and cotton cooperatives replaced labor with capital by mechanizing production, thereby further restricting seasonal employment opportunities for *comuneros*. Prior to land reform, coffee cultivation in the valleys to the north had been so lucrative that even smallholders and tenants often hired *comuneros* to fulfill their labor obligations to the local *hacendado*. Land reform relieved them of these obligations and thus diminished their demand for *comunero* labor. The government's policy of importing grain to keep food prices low for the urban population depressed the prices *comuneros* could get for their surplus food crops. This situation was exacerbated in the mid-1980s by Peru's most serious economic crisis of the century. Wages fell, inflation spiraled, and 60 percent of the nation's industrial capacity was idled, curtailing demand for nonfarm labor and shutting off another income alternative for land-poor *comuneros*.

As in El Salvador, land reform in Peru created a pool of beneficiaries who were better off than they had been prior to land reform. However, the most impoverished and politically volatile segment of Peru's peasantry—sierra *comuneros*—were rendered even more vulnerable to economic crisis by the redistribution of land and income flows on the neighboring haciendas. Land reform may have enhanced the terms of trade available to some classes of cultivators, but it failed to create any institutional mechanisms to reduce the risks of agriculture for those classes of cultivators most susceptible to subsistence crisis. The segment of the rural population that was most vulnerable to subsistence crisis was the least benefited by agrarian reform.

THE RISE OF SHINING PATH

May 17, 1980, marked the eve of Peru's first democratic presidential elections in seventeen years. That night a group of youths broke into the town hall in the Andean town of Chuschi. They seized the ballot boxes and voter lists for the next day's elections and burned them in the town plaza. Shining Path points to that incident as the beginning of the "people's war" in Peru. Over the course of the next several months, Sendero launched a number of small attacks against what it termed "symbols of the fascist state," including police stations, government offices, and infrastructure projects (Degregori 1992: 33–34; McCormick 1990: 15).

Unlike the Salvadoran FMLN, Peru's Shining Path was not driven to insurgency by government repression of peaceful collective action. Cynthia McClintock (1989: 61) observes that, "Without military provocation, Sendero initiated armed struggle in 1980 against an elected government considered democratic by most criteria." From its inception Shining Path was a revolutionary organization. Abimael Guzmán, a professor of philosophy at San Cristóbal de Huamanga University in Ayacucho, had built the membership of the Ayacucho committee of the Peruvian Communist Party (PCP) by recruiting a following among students and faculty at the university. In 1964 the PCP had split into a pro-Soviet faction and a Maoist Red Faction. Guzmán aligned with the latter. The Red Faction was active in community organizing but, soon after the coup of 1968, Guzmán and several other Red Faction leaders were arrested and imprisoned. Factional struggles within the Red Faction led to Guzmán's eventual expulsion from the party. He then decided to reconstitute his Ayacucho organization as its own party: Frente Estudiantil Revolucionario por el Sendero Luminoso de Mariategui, or Shining Path (Degregori 1992: 34–35; McCormick 1990: 4).

Shining Path came into being at precisely the time that Peru was undergoing its land reform program. This was hardly the most propitious time for a revolutionary organization to recruit followers among the peasantry. Peasants were receiving land, and there was no widespread program of repression like that which plagued El Salvador's reform program. Sendero was forced to bide its time during the 1970s, concentrating instead on building a well-organized core of ideologically committed cadres. How, then, were they able to build peasant support for revolution if peasants were not driven to them by indiscriminate repression of nonviolent collective action? More important, how was Shining Path able to mount an insurgency in the aftermath of a sweeping land reform program that was carried out amid relative peace, free from the sort of repressive violence that plagued the Salvadoran program? And why did Shining Path choose the very moment of Peru's return to democracy to launch its insurgency?

Although peasants were being pacified by the promise of land reform, Guzmán found a fertile audience among students and teachers at the University of Huamanga. From the beginning, students and teachers constituted the core of Sendero's membership, and they have continued to make up an unusually large proportion of the membership, especially compared to peasant-based insurgencies elsewhere. By 1990 as many as thirty thousand teachers (15 percent of Peru's teachers) were Senderistas (McClintock 1998: 273). A survey among captured Senderistas indicated that 37 percent had education beyond secondary school and almost 5 percent had training beyond an undergraduate college education (275).

Guzmán's ideological program combined elements of Gang of Four Maoism with the writings of Peruvian Communist José Carlos Mariátegui. Guzmán was committed to political violence as the only way to bring about the transformation of society. For him, both revolutionary victory and the creation of the new social order could be accomplished only by a dedicated, ideologically committed core of revolutionaries. Accordingly Sendero explicitly subordinated the role of the masses in the revolution to the leadership of the party. As Degregori (1992: 37) puts it, "The party decides everything. It rejected the primacy of politics in favor of the primacy of violence; violence is the essence of revolution; war is its principle task." This radical version of Marxism and their unyielding commitment to ideological orthodoxy earned for Shining Path comparisons to Cambodia's Khmer Rouge. Guzmán characterized himself as the "fourth sword of Marxism," the heir to the revolutionary mantle of Marx, Lenin, and Mao.

Guzmán envisioned a five-stage program for revolutionary victory in Peru. The first stage involved building popular support in backward regions. The second called for assaults on symbols of the bourgeois state. The third marked the beginning of the guerrilla war, and the fourth was the expansion of popular support for the armed struggle. The final stage involved the collapse of the cities and final victory (McClintock 1983: 21). Sendero's plan was to begin by securing a base among peasants in the southern Andean region. From this base, it would move to extend its control into the lowlands and the metropolitan areas of the coastal plain. In line with Maoist guerrilla strategy, its plan was to take control of the countryside and surround the cities. The cities of the more-populated coastal plain would eventually be strangled by cutting them off from the interior, which was the source of most of the food supplies and electrical power for the coastal population. Finally, the movement would surround the capital of Lima, and with its fall Sendero would seize power and establish a new revolutionary regime (McCormick 1992: 1–2).

The promise of land reform left peasants unresponsive to Sendero appeals for revolutionary violence. Consequently Sendero's strategy during the 1970s involved integrating its members socially and culturally into the peasant communities of the southern sierra in preparation for mobilizing peasants when they became disillusioned with land reform. A rigorous screening process and intense ideological training assured the loyalty and unswerving obedience of the movement's early recruits. They were then sent out into the countryside to build the movement's base of popular support among the peasants of the southern sierra. Senderistas fanned out into the villages of Ayacucho and took up jobs, many as teachers. They married into village families and learned to speak the Quechua language if they did not already speak it (McClintock 1983: 26; Palmer 1986: 137). The Senderistas endeavored to make themselves valuable members of the indigenous communities of the sierra. As they gained acceptance in peasant communities, they began to assume a role similar to that of the priests and lay catechists who had organized the Christian base communities in El Salvador. Shining Path began providing local services to the communities, and individual Senderistas began organizing collective action among residents. Many young Senderistas with college training served as teachers in remote villages, using that position to spread Sendero's message among the young while earning the gratitude of parents for giving their children the literacy skills that might allow them to escape the grinding poverty of the isolated communities.

The indigenous communities of the southern Andes proved to be the most fertile ground for Sendero's efforts at mobilization. For many of these communities, land reform had left them worse off economically than they had been prior to land reform. Population growth continued to intensify already severe land pressures within the communities. Population density in Ayacucho had increased by over 25 percent between 1961 and 1980 and by almost 50 percent since 1940 (McClintock 1984: 63). Cynthia McClintock (1983: 26) highlights the hardship of life there:

> Life expectancy was forty-four years in the southern highlands versus fifty-four on the coast; literacy 47 percent, versus 84 percent on the coast; each highlands physician had to serve 21,650 people, versus 1,822 on the coast; farm family incomes were only about one-third those in coastal Peru. . . . Malnutrition, rare in Peru until recent years, became prevalent. Average caloric intakes in the highlands in 1980 were down to approximately 72 percent of UN Food and Agriculture Organzation (FAO) daily requirements.

Agrarian reform had done little or nothing to relieve those hardships for residents of indigenous communities.

Sendero's initial forays into violence were carefully targeted to win the allegiance of peasants. They targeted thieves, corrupt local officials, landlords, and merchants, who were viewed by local residents as "bad people" for their mistreatment and exploitation of villagers. Sendero would first gather intelli-gence on wrongdoers who had earned the enmity of a community, threaten them with sanctions unless they changed their ways, and finally punish or kill them if they failed to heed Sendero's warnings (McClintock 1998: 291). Thus Sendero earned the respect and gratitude of villagers and created a local power vacuum into which they could assert their own authority. In the absence of effective government programs to relieve the distress of sierra *comuneros,* Sendero filled the institutional void by providing paramedical, farming, liter-acy, and other services to disaffected *comuneros.* They also contributed labor to communal projects, something that the local agents of the Peruvian govern-ment had rarely if ever taken it upon themselves to do (McClintock, 1989: 78).

The coincidence of Sendero's strategy with the absence of an effective gov-ernment presence in the southern sierra created a situation where, in David Palmer's (1986: 137) words, "the points of greatest contact between the peas-antry and Sendero tended to be those of least contact between the peasantry and the government." Land reform itself often brought indigenous communi-ties into confrontation with the Peruvian state. Sendero was able to capitalize on the frustration that *comuneros* felt with land reform by providing services that restored some measure of subsistence security to marginalized *comuneros* (at least more than the land reform program had) (McCormick 1990: 18–19).

The SAISs created by the agrarian reform program had become the symbol of *comuneros'* frustration with the state's land reform program. Not surpris-ingly, they became a favorite target for Sendero action. To peasants the SAIS symbolized the land the indigenous communities did not receive in the land reform. The promise of income for the communities from their SAIS affilia-tion never amounted to much, and this intensified *comuneros'* frustration. To exploit this frustration Sendero would come in and drive out the SAIS man-agers, take control of the cooperative, and redistribute its land and livestock to peasants (McClintock 1998: 292). By reversing the expropriation of a ha-cienda and distributing its land and livestock among *comuneros,* Shining Path could win the gratitude and support of those communities and enlist their residents as part of a civilian support base for their insurgency. At the very least, Shining Path could count on those communities to refrain from in-forming on Sendero to the army and the police.

By targeting former landlords, shopkeepers, cooperative administrators, and others who held some claim on the income, time, and loyalty of local peasants, Sendero violence eventually drove out most government officials and landowners in Ayacucho. In their place, Sendero units assumed the role of de facto local government. Once they seized control in a town or region, they canceled peasant debts, broke up cooperatives, redistributed land, and drove out or executed criminals, moneylenders, shopkeepers, and others accused of exploiting local peasants.[3] Thus Sendero violence initially produced direct material benefits and debt relief for *comuneros* who had been denied agrarian reform benefits and had been forcibly repulsed when they attempted to seize hacienda lands. McClintock's (1989: 63) interviews with peasants in Ayacucho indicated that most were unwilling to report on Senderista activity and in fact willingly supplied them with food and shelter.

THE STATE'S RESPONSE: REPRESSION

The response of the Belaundé government to Sendero's initial successes was to match violence with violence. Late in 1982 the government declared a state of emergency in Ayacucho and sent in a force of 1,500 specially trained paramilitaries known as Sinchis. However, Sinchi tactics further eroded peasant loyalty to the state. Sinchis were unfamiliar with the region, did not speak Quechua, and generally held the local population in contempt. Their counterinsurgency tactics often involved brutal sanctions against known or suspected Sendero supporters. However, their intelligence was often faulty because the population did not trust them and feared reprisals at the hand of Shining Path if they were found to be informing on the rebels. In some cases, peasants would tell the Sinchis that a neighbor against whom they had some long-standing personal grievance was a supporter of Shining Path, and the Sinchis would eliminate that neighbor. When intelligence was lacking, Sinchis would undertake large-scale search-and-destroy missions in areas thought to be occupied by Shining Path. Indiscriminate searches of peasant homes, arbitrary arrests, and brutal interrogations of people suspected of having information on Shining Path were typical of these sweeps. When troops entered a community, they often killed or detained schoolteachers, leaders of peasant associations, high school students, and leftist political leaders who were deemed likely Senderistas simply by virtue of their age, occupation, or level of education (McClintock 1989: 89; 1998: 295). When Shining Path proved to be elusive, the Peruvian military, like its counterpart in El Salvador, resorted to air strikes, resulting in virtual massacres in some villages. In 1983 the village of Huancasancos was the target of an air strike, and in 1984 Chapi was hit with one. The death toll from these two incidents alone was estimated to be as high as 3,000 (1989: 89).

Inevitably, neutral peasants were victimized by counterinsurgency sweeps and air strikes. These operations did little but raise the death toll among the civilian population, victimize more neutral peasants than active supporters of Shining Path, and thereby increase the pool of Sendero sympathizers. The death toll surpassed 700 in the first five months of 1983 and totaled 3,028 for the year (Palmer 1986: 139). More than fifty mass graves have been located in the emergency zone, and the number of "disappeared" reached 1,325 by 1985. By the end of 1988, civilian deaths had mounted to 5,134, while the military and police had suffered 827 killed (Hazleton and Woy-Hazleton 1988: 480). (See table 9.3.) Peasants came to fear the Sinchis more than Shining Path. Despite claims that the government had killed some 5,384 alleged Senderistas and arrested another 3,000 between 1980 and 1988, the counterinsurgency program seems to have had no effect on the ability of Shining Path to conduct operations in the sierra. Indeed the frequency of Sendero operations actually increased during this period. The 400 armed attacks recorded in April of 1985 alone were more than twice the total for the first three months of that year. Instead of reducing Sendero's strength and restricting the frequency and range of its operations, Sinchi tactics actually contributed to a diffusion of Sendero operations into neighboring provinces. This provoked the government to expand the emergency zone to include twenty-nine provinces in six of the twenty-four departments and to send in another 7,000 troops (McClintock, 1989: 63–64).

By the mid-1980s the Senderistas had moved into the coca producing region of the Huallaga Valley. This gave them access to unprecedented flows of revenues, as they were able to extract payments from peasant coca growers and traffickers in return for protection from the army and police. Coca revenues allowed them to begin paying full-time Senderistas salaries of $250 to $500 a month, or about three to eight times the salaries of most teachers in Peru (McClintock 1998: 292). By the late 1980s Sendero had moved into the central highland department of Junin, which gave it access to the source of Lima's electricity and much of its food supply (86). And, it had established a substantial underground presence in Lima itself (McCormick 1992). Shining

Table 9.3. Deaths from Political Violence in Peru, 1980–1990

	Military and police	Civilians	Insurgents	Total
1980	0	3	9	12
1981	6	5	71	82
1982	32	52	109	193
1983	59	692	1,226	1,977
1984	81	1,785	1,721	3,587
1985	76	770	630	1,476
1986	119	448	884	1,451
1987	188	593	335	1,116
1988	266	786	399	1,451
1989	348	1,450	2,400	4,198
1990	258	1,652	1,542	3,452

Source: Hazleton and Woy-Hazleton (1988: 480); Americas Watch (1992: 13–18).

Path's numerical strength grew with its geographic expansion. By 1991 its ranks numbered between 3,000 and 15,000 combatants, depending on whose estimate one believes.[4] Its recruiting base also expanded. Beginning as a movement largely of young students from the University of Huamanga, the rank-and-file membership soon diversified to include people from a wider range of age categories, occupations, and regions (McClintock, 1989: 63).

Another indicator of the diffusion of Shining Path's support was the increase in the number of blank or null ballots in regions where they were active. In the 1989 municipal elections, absenteeism was 36 percent nationwide, and 22 percent of all ballots were blank or invalid. However, in Ayacucho, Sendero's initial base, absenteeism was 85 percent, and 70 percent of the ballots cast were blank or defaced. In Huanuco the figures were 59 and 45 percent. In Junin absenteeism was 68 percent, and 35 percent of ballots cast were blank or null, a significant increase over the previous election cycle in that department (McClintock 1998: 79).

However, because of its own ideological rigidity and tactical brutality, Shining Path failed to capitalize on government repression and the economic crisis that crippled Peru in the late 1980s. In towns that came under its control, Shining Path enforced its own brand of ideological orthodoxy by such measures as closing down bars, expelling prostitutes, forcibly drafting youth into their units, and dealing harshly with anyone suspected of disloyalty to their cause or collaboration with the government (Gonzáles 1987: 70; Americas Watch 1992: 62–64). Enforcement of Shining Path's authority even extended to assaults on local peasant organizations that posed the slightest organizational alternative to Shining Path. Their economic warfare against the regime included attacks on rural development projects that were viewed favorably by peasants. Shining Path imposed planting quotas on peasants, restricted the marketing of surplus crops, and destroyed many roads and bridges that were used by peasants to transport crops to market. Shining Path justified these actions on the grounds that such commerce was not only capitalistic (and therefore exploitative) but sustained a regime they were dedicated to overthrowing (McCormick 1990: 19). For a peasant household, the sale of surplus crops is a vital part of its subsistence strategy, and any guerrilla organization that forcibly prevents such activity will not hold peasant loyalty for long.[5]

One disturbing indicator of Shining Path's strategy of control was the rise in deaths among peasants in the regions it controlled or contested. In 1989, 76 percent of Shining Path's victims were peasants or poor urban dwellers. Indeed only 17 percent of Sendero's victims were members of the army or the police. Most were unarmed civilians who either violated Sendero directives, informed on them, or were otherwise disloyal to the cause. Shining Path also targeted local leaders of various stripes who refused to join them. Between

1980 and 1992 Sendero killed at least 8 priests, 9 foreign development workers, 44 grassroots leaders, 203 businessmen, 244 teachers, 303 students, 424 workers, 502 political officials, 1,100 urban residents, and 2,196 peasants (McClintock 1998: 68). In one instance Senderistas assassinated the popular mayor of a town in Puno. The citizens were so outraged by this act that they withdrew support for Shining Path, and the guerrillas' advance in the entire department came to a halt (McClintock 1998: 69). The rebels continued to target government officials as well, killing 166 in 1989, as compared to 261 over the course of the previous eight years. Among their victims were 52 mayors. Another 263 mayors resigned in the face of death threats. At one point, 123 out of 435 districts in Peru had no registered candidates for local elections (McCormick 1990: 11–12). By the end of 1989 some 80 districts in four provinces had no municipal authorities left at all. By mid-1989, 70 percent of the public works projects in the central sierra had been abandoned due to Shining Path attacks on the engineers and administrators in charge of them (Hazleton and Woy-Hazleton 1992: 64–73). For peasants in the sierra, the targeting of local officials meant the virtual disappearance of government authority from the region, leaving a political void that Shining Path sought to fill.

The only way that peasants could avoid sanctions by Shining Path was by complying with its directives. Resistance to Shining Path was dealt with swiftly and harshly, even if the rebels were scrupulously selective in the application of sanctions (at least compared to government forces). For these reasons, Shining Path's support was based at least in part on intimidation. Therefore it could be reversed by counterinsurgency strategies that targeted Senderistas exclusively and avoid punishing local peasants.

By the mid-1980s peasant support for Shining Path had begun to diminish in Ayacucho, Apurímac, and Huancavelica, as indicated by the decline in the number of abstentions and blank or defaced ballots in these departments from 1980 to 1986.[6] The decline in the number of Sendero attacks in Ayacucho, from 1,226 in 1983 to 495 in 1986, also indicates a waning of peasant support for its operations. The erosion of peasant support for Sendero can be attributed in part to Shining Path's own harshness and in part to changes in the government's counterinsurgency strategy. In 1985 President Alan García began restraining the use of repression in the government's counterinsurgency mix, resulting in a steady decline in the number of civilians and "assumed terrorists" killed or disappeared (see table 9.3). He also took steps to relieve the economic distress of those classes of cultivators who had not benefited from land reform. More credit was funneled to the southern sierra. Prices for agricultural inputs were cut, and farmers were guaranteed better prices for their crops. Agricultural development projects that would benefit the rural poor received a higher priority in the government budget. A public employment program provided jobs for over a quarter million people, nearly 30 percent of whom lived in the Andean region. In 1986–1987 some 750,000 hectares of land were redistributed to 400 peasant communities, benefiting some 150,000 people. While these steps showed initial positive results as counterinsurgency tactics, they soon foundered on the growing crisis in the Peruvian economy, the sheer magnitude of the problems they were designed to address, and widespread mismanagement and corruption.

THE COCA CONNECTION

García's efforts were also thwarted by a shift in Sendero strategy. The rebels began cultivating links to the coca economy in the mid-1980s. These links provided them with an extremely lucrative source of funding for their operations and a new source of leverage to attract supporters among a new class of peasants: coca cultivators.

Coca is unique among export crops with respect to its impact on peasant cultivators. First, unlike most legal export crops introduced in the past, coca production did not displace peasant cultivators from their land. Of those involved in the Peruvian coca economy, an estimated two-thirds to three-quarters were coca farmers. Estimates of the number of peasant families engaged in growing coca ranged from 60,000 to 300,000 in the upper Huallaga Valley alone. Subsequently production expanded beyond the Huallaga Valley, especially into the "three rivers" area in the vicinity of the Ene, Perene, and Tambo rivers in Satipo province of Junin department. By the late 1980s the coca trade was providing employment for an estimated 300,000 to 500,000 Peruvians, which amounted to approximately 5 percent of the workforce (Gonzales 1992: 120).

Second, coca does not compete with other export crops for land. The Huallaga Valley and other coca growing regions were not heavily cultivated in legal crops in the past, at least not in export crops. The jungles on the Andean slopes where coca is grown are not suitable for other export crops (besides being difficult to patrol by antidrug units). Therefore engaging in coca production did not bring a peasant into conflict with existing (and often powerful) agricultural interests.

Finally, unlike other export crops, peasants' earnings from coca cultivation are substantial, even if they represent only a tiny fraction of the total earnings generated by the cocaine industry. Most growers plant one or two hectares of coca, and estimates of the net income they could earn range from $1,000 to $10,000 or more annually, depending upon the prevailing price for raw leaf (which fluctuates considerably) and the amount of land one could plant in coca. According to the *Andean Report,* a coca grower in the upper Huallaga

Valley could earn as much as $12,350 a year from each hectare of coca (at 1985 leaf prices), with approximately 60 percent of this sum being clear profit. Other estimates place the earning potential as high as $50,000 a year for a peasant household (McClintock, 1989: 128). This earnings potential is between four and ten times what one could earn from cultivating cacao, thirty-four times what one could earn from growing corn, and ninety-one times what one could earn from rice (Lee 1989, 26–27; Palmer 1992, 68). As such, coca is the first crop that offers peasants an opportunity to escape the risks of subsistence crisis and enjoy a decent standard of living.

While coca cultivation offered peasants unprecedented earnings potential, it also carried substantial risk. Because coca farming is illegal, growers risk arrest, incarceration, destruction of their crops, and loss of their land and other property. At one time, five different agencies of the Peruvian government had anti-drug-law enforcement responsibilities: the Guardia Civil, or the regular police; the Guardia Republicana del Peru (GRP), the equivalent of the National Guard; the Policia de Investigaciones del Peru (PIP), the Peruvian equivalent of the FBI; the Unidad Móvil de Patrullaje Rural (UMOPAR), a new agency created specifically for coca eradication; and the Sinchis. The duties, responsibilities, and tactics of these agencies differed considerably, and there was little coordination of activities among them (Morales 1989: 93–94, 122–23). Each earned a reputation among peasants for extortion and other forms of corruption and for arbitrariness and brutality in their treatment of suspected growers. Because law enforcement officials could also be persuaded to grant virtual immunity to traffickers in exchange for bribes, growers were often at the mercy of coca traffickers as well. Colombian traffickers used their own paramilitary forces to threaten peasants with violent sanctions (including death) if they failed to deliver coca leaf on time at a price set by the traffickers (Tarazona-Sevillano 1990: 112).

Shining Path stepped into this void in the mid-1980s to offer growers protection from the army, the police, coca eradication units, and Colombian smugglers. However, Sendero's presence in the Huallaga Valley made that region a target of government counterinsurgency efforts. This posed a new risk for coca growers: Involvement in the coca economy could mark one as a supporter of Shining Path and therefore subject one to the counterinsurgent violence directed against known, alleged, and suspected Senderistas. Thus cocaine economics became politicized by insurgent politics, with peasant cultivators caught in the crossfire between Senderista guerrillas, government counterinsurgency forces, and Colombian traffickers. To the extent that peasants turned to Shining Path for protection from these deadly cross pressures, they became part of the support base for that movement's efforts to overthrow the government of Peru (Mason and Campany 1995).

THE DEMISE OF SHINING PATH

By the end of 1991 Shining Path had established a base of support that allowed it to operate throughout most of the Huallaga Valley. It retained enough of its original base in Ayacucho to remain a presence in the southern sierra. It had built an underground organization in Lima and other cities to the point that some analysts felt that Sendero was preparing to embark upon the final phase of its five-stage plan to seize power in Peru.[7]

The growing threat posed by Shining Path was one of the motivations for President Alberto Fujimori's *autogolpe* of April 5, 1992. He suspended the 1979 constitution, arrested several opposition leaders, dissolved the legislature and the judiciary, and assumed virtual dictatorial powers. Shining Path responded by increasing the frequency of its attacks. In June and July of 1992, guerrillas staged 293 attacks nationwide, resulting in at least 179 deaths. It appeared that, amid the continuing crisis of the economy and the instability accompanying the coup, Shining Path was poised to launch an offensive that might topple the regime and bring the rebels to power.

Then on September 12, 1992, Abimael Guzmán, Shining Path's founder and leader, was captured in Lima, along with two other members of Sendero's central committee. Within weeks police arrested another thousand suspected Senderistas, including twelve of the nineteen central committee members. The threat of a Shining Path victory, which had been looming ominously when the year began, had waned by the end of 1992 (McClintock 1998). The capture of Guzmán and other Shining Path leaders severely diminished the threat that Sendero posed to the Peruvian government. However, Sendero's tight cell-based structure and rigorous discipline allowed units in the field to be relatively self-sufficient in providing for their own survival. Their Huallaga Valley organization did not dissolve with the arrest of Guzmán. Units there continued to conduct operations, generating enough revenues from the coca trade to sustain them as an insurgent organization. Although the threat it posed to the Peruvian government diminished severely, Shining Path retained the capacity to cause human and material damage through intermittent strikes.

CONCLUSION

Conventional analyses of the failure of land reform to pre-empt revolution focus on structural constraints confronting the reformers and technical flaws in the design and implementation of the reform program itself. In Peru, as in El Salvador, land reform was constrained by the fact that not enough land was available to relieve the economic distress of any more than a minority of the rural poor. With respect to design and implementation, the priority that the Velasco government attached to preserving agro-export estates imposed severe limitations on the pool of people eligible for reform benefits. In Peru the coastal CAPs could have absorbed more of the landless, and the distribution of SAIS benefits between the cooperatives and the affiliated *comunidades* could have been more equitable without jeopardizing the economic viability of the cooperatives or the economic security of its members. Land reform failed to target reform benefits to the most impoverished and most volatile sectors of the peasantry. Although the sierra *comuneros* were the source of earlier land invasions in Peru, they received the least amount of land reform benefits. Not surprisingly Shining Path found its most fertile source of support initially among the sierra *comuneros,* the very segment of the peasantry that was the most politically volatile, the most economically marginalized, and the least served by land reform.

However, as with El Salvador, structural constraints and design flaws cannot by themselves account for the eruption of insurgent violence in the aftermath of agrarian reform in Peru. Instead we must look to the level of violence—especially state-sanctioned violence—against beneficiaries and nonbeneficiaries alike as an explanation for the failure of reform to preserve stability. What is unusual about the Peruvian case is that Shining Path initiated the violence; it did not wait for the state to repress nonviolent opposition. By launching its own campaign of violence Shining Path induced the state to respond with repression which served Sendero's interest more than the state's. Land reform could not restore peasant loyalty to the state once beneficiaries became subject to violence at the hands of the state. Peasants turned to the rebels for protection from state-sanctioned violence. Whatever benefits a regime might provide to peasants, escalating violence will erode the support that those benefits were intended to generate. The second remarkable feature of the Peruvian case concerns its outcome. Shining Path rebels are subject to the same dilemma as the state: If they (and not the state) are seen as the perpetrators of violence, then peasants will turn away from them and to the state for protection. Rebel violence against civilian supporters can erode their base of support, just as government violence erodes popular support for the government. Sendero's near defeat was as much a function of its own harsh treatment of peasants as the government's tactical agility.

NOTES

1. On prereform Peruvian agriculture, see Matos Mar and Mejía 1980: 16–50 and Caballero 1981b: 26–29. On sugar haciendas and the status of their workers, see Kay 1983: 186–9; Paige 1975: 141–47; Lastarria-Cornhiel 1989: 128–31.

2. Some haciendas did produce wool and alpaca for export. This often worked to the disadvantage of peasant herdsmen (*huacchilleros*) because landlords worried that the quality of their own flocks would be diminished by interbreeding with the inferior stock of the *huacchilleros*. See Lastarria-Cornhiel 1989: 131 and Kay 1983: 190–91.

3. See Isbell 1992 and Berg 1992 on Sendero's tactics in two villages in Ayacucho. On their strategy for building a base of peasant support include McCormick 1990: 15–18; McClintock 1983; 1984; 1989: 78–79; Palmer 1985; 1986; Mason and Swartz-fager 1989.

4. See McCormick 1992. Any estimate of Sendero strength is largely guesswork. Because of the secretive cell-based organizational structure used by Sendero, any one active member probably knows the identity of only a handful of other members.

5. See also Isbell 1992: 66 on peasant reaction to planting quotas and other re-strictions Sendero imposed on them.

6. The share of ballots that are left blank or defaced can be taken as an indicator of support for an insurgent opposition. Abstention marks one as a possible supporter of the rebels and, therefore, marks one for possible retribution by the state. Casting a blank ballot avoids that risk without providing any support for any of the legal par-ties. McClintock (1984: 55) uses this figure as a measure of support for Shining Path in Peru.

7. McCormick (1992) presents an especially rigorous analysis of Sendero's strate-gic progression of taking the war from the countryside to the cities. He also points out the vulnerability of Lima to attacks on a few key infrastructure targets, most of which had become vulnerable by 1992 because of Sendero's expanded range of operational capabilities.

Chapter Ten

The Future of Revolutions in the Countryside: Globalization, Democratization, and Peacekeeping

This book began with the observation that in the last half of the twentieth century civil war replaced interstate war as the dominant mode of armed conflict in the world. In the previous nine chapters, I have endeavored to integrate a number of research traditions into a reasonably coherent theoretical explanation for why civil wars have become so frequent and so deadly, and what would make peasants and other nonelites willing to participate in them, especially when the risks are so grave and the prospects for victory so remote. In this chapter I conclude by speculating on what trends, if any, we might expect to see in patterns of civil war in the new century. Has the end of the Cold War made revolution in the countryside less likely? Or will the relaxation of Cold War bipolarity unleash tensions that were held in check by the major powers' concern with preserving the fragile balance of power? Will the conditions of rural poverty and state repression that fuel revolutionary violence become less pervasive? Or will poverty and repression continue to stoke the flames of revolution in Asia, Africa, and Latin America?

A few authors have considered this question, and opinion is divided on what the future holds. Some point to globalization and democratization as trends that promise to diminish the frequency of revolutions in the Third World by alleviating some of the conditions that are conducive to political violence. Jeff Goodwin (2001: 274) asserts that "revolutionary movements are less likely to arise and revolutions are less likely to occur during the contemporary period than during the cold war era." He points to globalization and the collapse of the Soviet Union as "two possible keys to our nonrevolutionary times." Globalization will presumably relieve much of the poverty that fuels popular support for revolutionary movements. The collapse of the Soviet Union will presumably deny aspiring revolutionaries the logistic and financial support that, according to Goodwin, sustained many Third World revolutionary organizations during the Cold War. For Goodwin, the most critical deterrent to revolution in the post–Cold War era is the spread of democracy to the Third World: *"No popular revolutionary movement, it bears emphasizing, has ever overthrown a consolidated democratic regime"* (Goodwin 2001: 276; emphasis in original). In a similar vein Richard Snyder draws on Francis Fukuyama's (1989) "end of history" thesis to argue that "revolutions were time-bound phenomena that were a major part of a distinct period of state-led modernization and international conflict." They occurred "only in a few particular types of states that are rapidly becoming obsolete" (1999: 5–6). For Snyder, revolution, like war among major powers, is becoming obsolete with the spread of liberal democracy and market-based economics. "Four particular factors—democracy, markets, middle classes, and transnationalism—make revolution less likely" (14).

Countering this optimistic perspective, a second group of scholars argues that the persistence of widespread poverty and repression in the Third World ensures that revolutionary violence will remain a feature of the political landscape in Asia, Africa, and Latin America for the foreseeable future (Selbin 2001; Foran 1997). Even if, as Snyder contends, globalization means that more citizens in the Third World will enjoy a middle-class standard of living, high rates of population growth in impoverished regions of Asia, Africa, and Latin America mean that the absolute number of people living in poverty will not diminished substantially. Indeed Eric Selbin (289–90) points out that in Latin America there are more people living in poverty today than twenty years ago: "Nearly half of the region's 460 million people are poor—an increase of 60 million in one decade." The growing number of poor will provide fertile recruiting grounds for opposition movements that can depict the incumbent regime—even a democratic one—as more responsive to the imperatives of global capital markets than to the needs of their own impoverished citizens. Selbin (286–87) concludes that "revolution is as likely, perhaps even more likely, than ever before. As global gaps between the haves and the have-nots increase and neo-liberalism fails to deliver on its promise, revolution will become more likely." For Selbin, globalization will not be a cure for revolution but instead "will likely offer more space for such activities rather than diminish their likelihood due to a lack of funds and support from the now defunct communist bloc."

Samuel Huntington's (1996) "clash of civilizations" thesis raises doubts about the remedial effects of democracy on armed conflict in the Third World. He cautions that democracy will not make conflicts less likely because democracy, as an institutional regime grounded in Western Christian culture, will not readily take root in non-Western civilizations. This implies that revolutions are likely to occur where the institutions of Western democracy are imposed in nations populated by peoples whose cultures are grounded in the values of one of the non-Western civilizations he identifies. While Goodwin and others may argue that no revolution has ever overthrown a consolidated democracy, Huntington foresees fundamental cultural barriers to the consolidation of democracy in many regions of the Third World. If democracy fails in non-Western societies, then those nations will be highly susceptible to violent revolution as a reaction against the perceived imposition of institutions that are antithetical to that people's culture. For Huntington, democracy and markets are not the panacea for revolution, because democracy and capitalism are not compatible with the fundamental values of many non-Western civilizations. He predicts that armed conflicts will continue to occur at the geopolitical fault lines where major civilizations meet. In some cases those fault lines might be boundaries between nation states from different civilizations (for instance, China versus Russia, India versus Pakistan, Israel versus surrounding Arab states). In other cases, those fault lines occur as divisions within nations divided between conflicting ethno-cultural enclaves (for instance, Sudan, Nigeria, Sri Lanka, Russia, and Yugoslavia). In Huntington's view, democracy and capitalism cannot prevent the clash of civilizations from erupting into war between bordering nations from different civilizations. Nor can they prevent civil wars from erupting within nations divided between two or more civilizations.

How do we resolve these competing perspectives on the prospects for revolution in the post–Cold War era? Any assessment of the prospects for revolution must begin with the observation that there has been no significant abatement in the frequency or the deadliness of civil wars since the end of the Cold War. A number of protracted conflicts were brought to a peaceful conclusion once they were disentangled from Cold War politics. Nevertheless, new conflicts have erupted in the aftermath of the Cold War. The most disturbing feature of the post–Cold War era has been the spread of civil war to the states of the former Soviet Union. Since 1991 ethnic separatist wars have broken out in Azerbaijan, Georgia, Moldova, and Russia (the Chechnya secession), and a civil war occurred in Tajikistan. Public attention to these conflicts has sometimes obscured the grim legacy of new conflicts in the Third World. The near genocidal violence in Rwanda in 1994 stands out as the most shocking of these events. But Rwanda represents only one among many new conflicts that have occurred in the Third World during the last decade of the twentieth century.

According to Wallensteen and Sollenberg (2000), the 1990s began with forty-six civil wars underway, and the decade ended with thirty-five still underway. Of those thirty-five, eighteen were new conflicts that began during the 1990s and were still ongoing at decade's end. These included the Chechen rebellion in Russia, the Islamic uprising in Algeria, and the civil war in Sierra

Leone. About forty civil wars began and ended during the 1990s. Among those were conflicts in Bosnia, Croatia, Georgia, Yemen, and Tajikistan. Sixteen conflicts that were underway in 1989 continued to rage more than a decade after the Cold War's end. The New People's Army and the Islamic Moro National Liberation Front were still active in the Philippines. FARC (Fuerzas Armadas Revolucionarias de Colombia) and ELN (Ejército de Liberación Nacional) guerrillas continued to control large portions of Colombia's countryside.[1] Tamil guerrillas continued to wage their separatist war in Sri Lanka. And Sudan remained torn by civil war between the Muslim north and non-Muslim populations in the south. Thus the empirical record suggests little cause for optimism concerning the possible abatement in the frequency or destructiveness of civil wars in the new millennium.

Predicting the future involves more than simply extrapolating from current trend lines. It involves the application of theory to the analysis of those trends. This book presents a theory of why and under what conditions revolutions in the countryside are likely to occur. That theory suggests a set of factors that should influence future trends in the incidence of civil war. Based on empirical evidence, a simple linear extrapolation from recent trends would lead us to expect little change in the incidence of civil war. However, the theory presented in this book suggests a set of factors that might lead to a different trend.

Do the causal dynamics of Third World revolutions, as outlined in this book, lead us to expect their frequency and destructiveness to decline, increase, or stay the same? There is no simple answer to this question. What we can say is that theory presented in this book provides some insight into what conditions and dynamics should be monitored to anticipate trends in the incidence of civil war. Likewise, theory gives some clues as to why, how, and under what conditions a given nation might become susceptible to revolution in the countryside.

In particular, the theory of this book suggests three trends in the post–Cold War era that hold the possibility (but not the certainty) of moderating the conditions that fuel civil war in the Third World. These are (1) the globalization of national economies, (2) the "third wave" of democratization, and (3) the increased reliance on United Nations mediation of peace settlements to civil wars. Globalization promises to bring new investments to Third World nations, diversifying their economies and stimulating growth. Economic development could alleviate the harsh deprivation that has often fueled support for revolutionary movements. The spread of democracy will mean that Third World regimes faced with opposition challenges will be far less likely to respond with the level of repression that has often turned peaceful opposition into revolutionary movements. And the expanded use of United Nations peacekeeping operations suggests that, when revolutions do occur, the international community is more likely to intervene early in the conflict to negotiate a peaceful settlement. Even when civil wars do occur, there is reason to believe that they will be less destructive than in the past because UN mediation will shorten their duration.

Will globalization bring prosperity to peasants and, in so doing, make them less inclined to support revolutionary movements? Will the trend toward democratization diminish the tendency of Third World states to respond to opposition movements with violent repression? And, when these remedies fail, will the international community demonstrate the political will and capacity to intervene early in conflicts so as to prevent them from escalating into protracted and deadly civil wars of the sort we have witnessed all too often over the course of the last half century?

GLOBALIZATION AND REVOLUTION

The end of the Cold War has unleashed a trend toward integration of national economies—including the Third World—into a truly global economy. No longer is the international economy divided between the market economies of the capitalist West and the state socialist economies of the Leninist East. The dismantling of the economic wall between East and West has encouraged the globalization of industrial production and finance. This phenomenon is expected to alter the dynamics of national economic development in fundamental ways. Can these trends create enough opportunity for enough of the population to pre-empt revolution in the countryside?

Optimists predict that globalization will result in higher rates of investment and economic growth in the Third World, as those nations become full partners in a global system of production, consumption, and finance. The diffusion of industrial production to the Third World will diversify those economies, making them less dependent on raw materials exports and less vulnerable to market fluctuations in the price of those exports. Expansion in the industrial and service sectors of Third World economies is expected to create occupational alternatives to agriculture that promise to absorb much of the surplus rural labor that traditionally has provided the civilian support for revolutionary insurgencies. By expanding economic opportunity and increasing incomes, globalization promises to remedy the grievances that fuel popular support for revolutionary movements. In nations where this occurs, revolution in the countryside should become less likely; as these effects diffuse to more nations, the frequency of peasant-based revolutions should decline throughout the Third World.

On the other hand, critics of globalization acknowledge that the integration of the Third World into a global system of production and finance may well shift some low-wage manufacturing jobs to the Third World. However, they contend that the local benefits of this trend will be limited and temporary. Benefits will be limited because the jobs will be low-skill and low-wage positions. As such, they promise little improvement in the standard of living of workers there. Nor do they promise to alleviate the extremes of income inequality that most deprived actor models of revolution depict as the source of popular grievances. Moreover, high population growth rates in the Third World mean that the absolute number of people living in poverty will remain large, even if the anticipated benefits of globalization do lift some out of poverty. Whatever benefits flow from globalization will be temporary, because those are precisely the kinds of jobs that are targeted for eventual elimination through automation. The only industries that will relocate to the Third World are those that pay low wages and generate the kinds of environmental problems that publics in wealthier nations will no longer tolerate. Indeed part of the reason that those industries relocate to the Third World in the first place is that social movements in advanced industrial democracies have succeeded in enacting "green" legislation compelling manufacturers to make expensive investments in environmental cleanup. They can avoid these costs by relocating to the Third World, where environmental movements are as yet politically weak if not nonexistent. Firms often find that the promise of job-creating investments overwhelms environmental concerns in the political calculus of government elites in many Third World states. Thus, critics argue, globalization will have little if any effect on the economic grievances that fuel support for revolutionary movements. There will still be an ample supply of impoverished individuals and communities to build and sustain revolutionary movements.

How do we reconcile these contending views on globalization and its impact on the Third World? Does globalization promise to alleviate those economic conditions that are conducive to revolution in the countryside? The simple answer is there is no simple answer. Yes, globalization will result in increased capital flows to many (but not all) Third World nations, and those investments will fuel economic growth and diversification, absorbing part of the surplus rural labor force that traditionally has served as the support base for revolutionary movements. On the other hand, globalization of industrial production and capital markets is not the panacea that will bring the Third World into economic parity with the post-industrial north. To assess its impact on the future of revolution, we must inventory some of its specific effects on grievances among the rural poor, on mobilization of aggrieved populations, and on state responses to opposition social movements.

Globalization and Economic Development

In many ways, the arguments on globalization, both critical and optimistic, closely parallel earlier debates in the field of comparative politics over the concepts of "modernization" and "development." Globalization can mean almost anything. It encompasses everything and, as such, explains nothing. There is nothing new about its core notion: the penetration into the most remote corners of national economies—including the rural economy of Third World nations—of the principles of exchange and production that govern a global economy. This notion was also at the core of world systems theory's critique of the modernization paradigm.

Half a century ago, modernization theorists extrapolated from the experience of Western Europe and North America to predict that the commercialization of agriculture in the Third World would transform the surplus rural population of those nations into an urban labor force that would fuel an industrial revolution in those same nations (Lewis 1954, cited in McMichael 2000: 274; see also Rostow 1990). Dependency and world systems theorists observed the same phenomena but saw their outcome as quite different. They saw the commercialization of agriculture leading to high rates of landlessness, over-urbanization, environmental deterioration, and the impoverishment of large portions of the urban and rural populations. The much-anticipated industrial revolution did not occur in most nations of the Third World, especially those that were integrated into the global economy as exporters of agricultural commodities.

If the modernization paradigm envisioned Third World nations replicating the developmental path that Western Europe and North America had experienced in the nineteenth century, globalization represents an abandonment of that goal. Instead nations seek niches of specialization in a global economy whose dynamics are determined more by capital markets than by states. "Nation-states no longer 'develop'; rather, they position themselves in the global economy" (McMichael, 2000: 275). Different nations or even regions within nations specialize in some phase of a globalized production process. In so doing, they hope to make themselves indispensable partners in a global production and distribution network. To the extent that they succeed, capital flows into their economy, fueling the growth and prosperity that allows them to become full partners in the global consumer market.

Critics counter that this vision of globalization is simply the old wine of modernization in a new bottle. For the critics, globalization arguments sound remarkably similar to the "comparative advantage" solution that modernization theory prescribed for Asia, Africa, and Latin America. Comparative advantage implied that these regions' economic development was best served by specializing in the production of raw materials for export to European industrial economies. Critics point out that the actual outcome was something far less than the replication of the growth, development, and prosperity that Europe and North America experienced. To the contrary, the result was the marginalization and immiserization of increasing portions of the rural populations in these countries. If the prescription of comparative advantage failed to replicate Europe's industrial revolution, is there any reason to believe that the postmodern prescription of globalization will be any more of a panacea for Third World underdevelopment? If not, why should we expect any substantial decline in the frequency with which revolutionary situations emerge in the Third World?

Globalization and the State

Both optimists and critics of globalization agree on one primary difference between the changes resulting from globalization and those predicted by modernization theorists: The influence of the state on national economic development will be substantially diminished. Indeed, Arrighi (1994) links the shift from "development" to "globalization" to the onset of "financialization" of the global economy: a preference on the part of investors for liquid rather than fixed capital. The heightened mobility of capital has privileged financial speculation at the expense of fixed investment. It has also privileged international financial and corporate elites (as well as the managers of international economic agencies such as the World Bank, the International Monetary Fund, and the World Trade Organization) at the expense of government officials in the nations penetrated by the global trade and financial system (McMichael 2000: 279). This too can be good or bad for a nation's development.

Under globalization, "boosting export production and offering attractive conditions for foreign investment became the new priorities for governments in the Third World, alongside an extraordinary roll-back of public investment" (McMichael 2000: 281). In order to make their nation attractive to global financial elites, state leaders in the Third World are compelled to reduce taxes, devalue their currency, and cut public spending, whether it be for social welfare benefits or investment in infrastructure. It also requires the privatization of state assets, auctioning them off to these same global financial elites at prices dictated by global financial markets. McMichael notes that privatization increased tenfold over the course of the 1980s.

Critics argue that structural adjustments of these sorts undermine the coherence and sovereignty of national economies. Lowering wages in order to attract foreign direct investment reduces purchasing power in the domestic economy. Privatizing public enterprises reduces the capacity of states to influence domestic economic development and to cushion their constituents against shocks emanating from the global economy. The promise of low-wage manufacturing jobs today can disappear tomorrow with shifts in global currency or capital markets, innovations in production technology, or changes in consumer demand. State elites who enact policies designed to attract those investments often find that global market forces are far more critical than their own policies in determining the flow of investment into and out of their nation's own economy. Generally, compliance with the rules of the global economy results in the shrinking of state capacity. Shrinking the state reduces its capacity to allocate and redistribute resources in response to the demands of popular sectors, including workers and peasants. States must give up some of the very policy instruments with which they could accommodate the demands of mobilized publics within their own polity and thereby defuse tensions that otherwise might fuel political violence.

Some argue that such changes will be good for the development of national economies. The fear of driving away foreign investment will make states less likely (and less able) to intervene in the economy in ways that disrupt markets. In the past, such interventions were justified on the grounds of protecting vulnerable domestic constituencies, such as urban workers or peasant farmers. However, such policies often produced more in the way of political payoff for state elites than economic protections for targeted sectors of the labor force. Brazil's failed experiments in import substitution industrialization and Argentina's populist policies under Peron are illustrative of the long-term economic consequences that can accrue to politically motivated interventions in markets. Moreover, state interventions in the economy often fail to protect the very constituencies in whose name the interventions were undertaken. Globalization makes such interventions less likely by raising the costs to states—in terms of international investment—of intervening in the market. As such, the reduction in state capacity can be good for national economic development.

Indeed, Richard Snyder (1999: 13) argues that shrinking the state will make revolution less likely, because the diminished role of the state in the economy will make it less of a target for popular discontent. Jeff Goodwin (2001: 275) adds that, by this reasoning, "State power—the traditional prize of revolutionaries—has been dramatically eroded by the growing power of multinational corporations and by the increasingly rapid and uncontrollable movements of capital, commodities, and people." Accordingly, as globalization hollows out the state, it is no longer a prize worth the costs and risks of revolutionary action.

Moreover, the globalization imperative suggests that, when popular discontent is mobilized, states will be far less likely to respond with repression for fear of scaring off international investment. Multinational corporations are .

notoriously risk averse. The political risks that accompany state repression can deter foreign direct investment, especially when capital is as mobile as it is today. Thus the imperatives of globalization may make states in the Third World less repressive than they were during the Cold War, when the prospects of large fixed capital investments could induce state elites to repress social movements. The Mexican government's response to the Zapatista uprising on the day that the North American Free Trade Agreement went into effect is illustrative. During the Cold War, an armed uprising of the sort that occurred on January 1, 1994, would likely have provoked a harsh military response, no doubt with the active support of the United States. Instead the Mexican government (at the urging of the United States) restrained its military response for fear of driving off the investors who were poised to pour capital into the Mexican economy as soon as the free trade agreement went into effect.

On the other hand, critics point out that popular discontent can become politicized over state impotence in the face of economic grievances just as well as over state intervention in markets to redistribute the benefits and costs of economic development. Within the state, globalization has privileged the financial and trade ministries at the expense of ministries whose clients include factory workers, peasants, the urban poor, and other marginal social groups. State agencies that support and regulate sectors of the economy that affect the lives of the majority of the citizenry have lost resources to agencies concerned with and connected to global interests (McMichael 2000: 281). States are no longer in a position to enter joint ventures with private firms, nor can they use such investments to "pick winners" in the domestic economy, so as to shape the nation's developmental trajectory in ways that state leaders believe are best for the long-term health of the national economy or the short-term stability of the political system. If globalization diminishes the state's capacity to address the grievances of mobilized publics, how will the state respond to new social movements arising within the polity? This question leads us to consider the impact of globalization and democratization on mobilization processes in the Third World: Will these two trends make it easier for peasants and other nonelites to mobilize for contentious political action, and will these trends make the state more or less likely to respond to such challenges with repression rather than reform?

Globalization and Social Movements

Regardless of its effects on state capacity and economic development (and therefore on grievances), globalization also affects the ability of aggrieved populations to mobilize for collective action. The same global communications networks, including the Internet and wireless communications, that make possible the instantaneous movement of capital around the globe also facilitate the coordination of social movement activities and the diffusion of social movement technologies to the most remote corners of the world. Globalization gives Third World social movement organizations access to supporters and resources exogenous to their own nation. Globalization means that repertoires of contention are more easily diffused from one nation to another. And the coordination of supporters' behavior by Third World social movements is facilitated by the same processes of globalization that supposedly make revolution less likely by diminishing grievances. If, as Tilly (1978), McCarthy and Zald (1977), and others have argued, the emergence of dissident social movements is less a function of grievances and more a function of social movement organization, then globalization might not necessarily diminish the frequency of revolution, because it will certainly facilitate the mobilization of a wider variety of constituencies in Third World nations. The more social movements there are, the more likely it is that at least one of them will escalate into a revolutionary movement.

At the very least, any assessment of the prospects for civil violence in the Third World must consider how changes in the global economy—and in the domestic political economy of those nations—affect the prospects for grassroots mobilization of peasants and the urban poor in the Third World. There is no reason to expect globalization processes to act as a deterrent to grassroots mobilization in the Third World. Indeed there is every reason to believe that mobilizing the poor for collective action will be facilitated by the trends toward globalization and democratization. Democratization reduces the costs and the risks associated with collective action generally and social movements specifically. And globalization builds links between communities, social organizations, and identity groups in the Third World and their counterparts in the North. If, as McCarthy and Zald (1977) argue, prosperity makes it possible for a society to sustain a class of professional social movement activists, the very trends that globalization optimists point to as making revolution less likely in the Third World should make the proliferation of social movements all the more robust. The diffusion of social movement organizations, the emergence of transnational social movements, and the expansion of links between Third World social movements and their counterparts or sympathizers in wealthier nations to the north suggest that activists in the Third World will find the tasks of building a social movement organization and mobilizing the resources necessary to sustain the movement easier in the era of globalization than they were during the era of Cold War conflicts.

The question then becomes how globalization and democratization will affect the willingness of individual peasants and urban nonelites to support and participate in social movements. What matters to an impoverished individual is not the "big" issues of global integration or political democratization but how these trends affect the immediate conditions of his or her daily existence. "Globalization tends to be understood as a process of economic integration— observed through local prisms, or 'grounded' in local terms, giving a local face to processes of globalization" (McMichael 2000: 275). Although globalization is, first and foremost, a matter of integrating national economies into the global economy, the effects of globalization are felt locally and are defined for people in local terms. For example, neoliberal reforms of the Salinas administration in Mexico had profound effects on peasant farmers in that nation. The elimination of guaranteed crop prices, reductions in state-subsidized credit, and the dismantling of trade barriers under the banner of NAFTA exposed Mexican farmers to competition from American agribusiness conglomerates, and this competition threatened their very livelihood (Harvey 1998: 170). Some of Salinas's proposals on land tenure were perceived by indigenous communities in Chiapas as threatening, not just to their control of the *ejidos* but to a way of life based around communal lands (Wager and Shulz 1995: 5–7). With NAFTA the prospects for expanded beef exports to the United States drove up the value of land that could be used as pasture. This increased the incentives for neighboring haciendas to encroach on *ejidos* lands that indigenous peoples in Chiapas had farmed communally for centuries. The encroachments and the prospect of the Mexican government enacting legislation that would compel the privatization of communal lands threatened the way of life of peasants in Chiapas. These threats became real precisely because of the local incentives created by NAFTA. Communities threatened by globalization were able to turn their own community institutions into mobilizing devices to mount organized opposition to NAFTA and to the Mexican government as the champion of NAFTA. Thus the Zapatista movement was born: the Ejército Zapatista de Liberación Nacional or EZLN.

Movements such as the Zapatistas are more likely to emerge today precisely because the last two decades of the twentieth century were marked by the spread of democratic governments to a number of Third World nations. Under democracy, aggrieved citizens are more able to organize for collective action, because the basic rules of democratic governance guarantee citizens the right to organize. They are freer to form social movement organizations without fear of repression than they would be in a more authoritarian regime.

The same trend toward democratization could also make it less likely that movements such as the EZLN will escalate to revolutionary violence. When the Zapatistas surprised the Mexican government and the world with their carefully timed uprising, the government resisted the reflexive response of retaliating with massive military firepower. Within two weeks after the EZLN's opening offensive, the government had declared a cease-fire and initiated settlement talks. Within six months, the government had poured over $220 million into social development projects in the region, a 44 percent increase over what had been budgeted, in an effort to win over civilian supporters and sympathizers of the EZLN cause (Wager and Shulz 1995: 29). Had the government tried to crush the movement militarily, relying on its overwhelming advantage in troops and firepower, the surviving Zapatista combatants would likely have concentrated on building their own military capabilities. Some portion of their civilian support base would have committed to supporting guerrilla operations. While the chances of a Zapatista victory would still have been remote, the likelihood of protracted guerrilla conflict that would destabilize an already fragile Mexican economy would have increased. The fact that Salinas did not pursue the military response as aggressively as he could have is due in part to external pressure (from the United States and global financial interests) but also in part to the democratic pressures that his own government faced as a result of the political reforms undertaken by Salinas and his successors.

Despite the intrusion of global issues into the local political economy and despite the growth in the number of transnational social movement organizations, it appears that "most political challengers continue to operate within fairly traditional, nationally focused political arenas" (Smith 2000: 3; see also Imig and Tarrow 2000, 2001a,b). Globalization of national economies has not yet resulted in truly transnational social movements. Third World social movement organizations may have counterparts and colleagues in the wealthier nations of Europe and North America. However, to date, the emergence of transnational social movements has not kept pace with the globalization of national economies. Imig and Tarrow (2000) point to the higher costs of transnational activism and the greater obstacles of mobilizing voluntary support and labor through impersonal, long-distance communications. Their research—and most research on transnational social movements—is focused on the European Union. If transnational social movements have a difficult time achieving success there— with well-educated and prosperous publics and few barriers to the flow of people, capital, or information across national boundaries—it is unrealistic to expect transnational social movements to emerge either within the Third World or between Third World movements and their counterparts in the north.

Smith (2000: 9) notes that only 23 percent of transnational social movement organizations are based in the south. Even these are largely associations of people who, by local standards, would be considered elites. In short, the transnational social movements headquartered in the south rarely consist of associations of the poor. Nor are they likely to involve heavy participation from the impoverished rural populations that are most likely to support a revolutionary social movement. Activists in the Third World may receive moral support, publicity for their cause and their activities, and even some financial support from their counterparts in the north. However, their northern colleagues are not likely to relocate in large numbers to serve as foot soldiers in Third World social movements. They may stage demonstrations in Seattle to raise public consciousness about land and poverty issues in the Third World, but they are not likely to show up in large numbers to participate in land invasions in rural areas of Asia, Africa, or Latin America. Therefore Third World activists can expect to receive only marginal amounts of assistance from their counterparts in the north. Transnational links between social movements are not likely to become so substantial as to determine the success of those movements in Third World nations.

Whether local activists succeed in mobilizing a following will be determined primarily by local conditions. Whether local movements remain nonviolent or transform into revolutionary movements depends in large part on how the state responds to nonviolent social movements. This brings us to a consideration of how the trends toward democratization in the Third World will affect the probability of revolution in any one nation and the frequency of revolutions across the Third World.

DEMOCRATIZATION: THE "COFFIN OF REVOLUTION"?

The third post–Cold War trend that should affect the frequency and destructiveness of revolution is what Samuel Huntington (1991) has labeled the "third wave of democracy." Over the last quarter of the twentieth century, we witnessed the transition from authoritarianism to democracy in over fifty nations, many of them in the Third World (Diamond 1997: xiii–xiv). Democratization is directly relevant to the future of revolutionary conflict, because stable democracies do appear to be relatively immune to civil war. In part this is because democracies are far less likely to engage in the sort of repressive violence that transforms nonviolent political opposition into revolutionary movements. The prospects for revolution in the Third World hinge in part on trends in the repressive tendencies of Third World states. If democracies are less likely to repress opposition movements, then the diffusion of democracy to more Third World nations should make revolution less likely to occur.

Larry Diamond (1997: xiii) observes that, at the beginning of 1975, there were only forty democracies in the world, and almost all were found among the wealthy industrialized nations of Western Europe and North America (plus Japan). Leninist regimes prevailed in Eastern Europe and the Soviet Union as well as in the People's Republic of China. The Third World—where most of the revolutionary violence was occurring—was populated by a variety of neopatrimonial dictatorships, bureaucratic authoritarian states, corporatist regimes of various stripes, and Leninist regimes. In this context it is not surprising to find "intellectual fashions dismissing democracy as an artifice, a cultural construct of the West, or a 'luxury' that poor states could not afford."

Then came the third wave of democracy. First, in southern Europe, democratic regimes replaced long-standing authoritarian states in Portugal, Greece, and Spain. In 1983 Turkey made the transition to an elected civilian regime. In the late 1970s and early 1980s a number of Latin American regimes made the transition from authoritarian rule to democracy. In 1986 the "people power" movement in the Philippines brought down the regime of Ferdinand Marcos. In 1987 student demonstrations in South Korea sparked a movement that compelled the authoritarian state there to allow democratic reforms. The crest of the wave occurred with the collapse of Leninist regimes in Eastern Europe in the autumn of 1989. This was followed by the disintegration of the Soviet Union as a sovereign entity in 1991 and the transition to some form of democracy in most of the fifteen newly independent states of the former Soviet Union. In the 1990s students of African politics began speaking of a "second liberation" of Africa (the first being the end of colonialism) marked by democratic transitions in a number of nations there. By 1994 thirty-eight of the forty-seven states in sub-Saharan Africa had held competitive multiparty elections for the legislature, and the number of fully democratic states had gone from three in 1988 to eighteen in 1994 (Diamond 1997).

If, as Goodwin and Skocpol (1989: 495) argue, "the ballot box . . . has proven to be the coffin of revolutionary movements," then the spread of democracy throughout the Third World should make revolutions and other forms of civil war less likely in the future. Indeed a number of scholars have found empirical support for this domestic corollary of the "democratic peace" proposition on interstate war. The democratic peace thesis holds that, while democracies are no less likely than nondemocracies to go to war, they do not go to war against other democracies. Democratic institutions and processes impose constraints on leaders' ability to choose war as an option in foreign policy. The public's role in foreign policy decision making, though certainly indirect, nonetheless constrains leaders' willingness to undertake large-scale violence without first building public support for the effort. Failure to do so can have grave repercussions for the elected leader and his or her party. They know that voters have to bear the calamities of war: They are the ones who do the fighting and the dying. Voters have to pay the financial costs of war in the form of taxes. And voters have to repair the devastation that war leaves behind. Given this, democratically elected leaders can expect to bear the political costs of voter discontent over unpopular wars. Therefore political leaders in democratic societies will be more cautious than their authoritarian counterparts in choosing the war option.

Russett (1993) adds that there are also international constraints on democratic leaders' willingness to go to war. Democracies are accommodative internally, and they project those beliefs onto the leaders of other democracies. Leaders of other states perceive leaders of democracies to be constrained and therefore less likely to choose the conflict option in a crisis situation. Democracies are less likely to instigate a surprise attack that precipitates war. Because of institutional constraints and democratic norms that guide leaders' behavior, democratic states are better equipped than other types of states to defuse conflict situations at an early stage before they escalate to armed conflict (Dixon 1994: 14). If this is true—and there is a rather substantial body of empirical evidence to support this proposition—then the spread of democracy to Eastern Europe and the Third World should make interstate wars increasingly unlikely in the international system.

The domestic corollary of the democratic peace holds that democratic norms and institutions allow domestic constituencies to resolve their differences peacefully, without resort to violent political conflict. Empirical support for this proposition is found in the frequently cited "inverted U-curve" relationship between repression and civil violence:[2] "[T]he relationship between degrees of democracy and civil war assumes the shape of an inverted U-curve. Neither democracies nor autocracies are very likely to experience civil conflict. Democratic government opens up a variety of ways for addressing conflict without resorting to violence, while autocracy represses any possibility of mobilizing for violent conflict" (Hegre et al. 1999: 4–5).

The inverted U suggests that established democracies and harshly autocratic regimes are less susceptible to civil war than weak authoritarian regimes (Hegre et al. 1999; Mueller and Weede 1990). Democratic regimes defuse revolutionary violence by diverting popular discontent into institutionalized channels of electoral competition and nonviolent protest. Dissident movements can seek the redress of their grievances through electoral means and other forms of nonviolent collective action. Democratic states are less likely to repress nonviolent protest. Hence opposition social movements are not compelled by state repression to choose between withdrawing from politics to avoid repression or shifting to violent tactics of their own to combat it. In a democracy the benefits of peaceful negotiations exceed the benefits of violent conflict. Conversely, harshly autocratic regimes pre-empt revolutionary violence by crushing opposition movements before they develop the capacity to mount a serious challenge to the state. In this circumstance, rebellion is irrational, because the costs are prohibitively high, and the likelihood of success is remote. It is weak authoritarian states that are the most susceptible to civil war. On the one hand, they lack the institutional capacity to accommodate opposition grievances through electoral mechanisms. On the other hand, they lack the coercive capacity to crush opposition movements pre-emptively. When organized opposition movements emerge, the weak authoritarian state attempts to repress them but fails. In so doing, the state converts nonviolent opposition into a revolutionary movement.

Thus there are well-developed theoretical arguments and ample empirical evidence to support the notion that Huntington's third wave of democracy will result in a decline in the incidence of civil war. However, there are several rather strong arguments for caution on this proposition. First, in a number of cases the transition to democracy took place while a civil war was already underway, and democratization did not bring about an end to that civil war. In the Philippines, the "people power" movement may have brought democracy to that nation, but the ongoing guerrilla insurgency of the New People's Army has not abated, nor has the secessionist movement of the Islamic Moro National Liberation Front subsided. After more than a decade of democracy, the government of the Philippines has not been able to defeat either group. Nor has it been able to negotiate them into the democratic fold by convincing them that the grievances that fuel support for their movements can be resolved peacefully through democratic processes. Likewise, twenty years of democracy has not brought an end to the Shining Path insurgency in Peru. Nor has the transition to democracy in Colombia brought an end to the civil war there. Thus the transition to democracy does not automatically mean an end to revolutionary movements whose existence predates the transition. A well-established revolutionary movement may not be willing to compromise its demands if its leaders believe they still have a chance of achieving military victory, or if they believe that the best compromise they can hope to achieve through democratic processes is less than they can achieve through a continuation of violence.

Second, the domestic version of the democratic peace applies most clearly to well-established democracies, and most of the new democracies of the Third World have not yet achieved democratic consolidation. Where democratic consolidation has not yet been achieved, "universalistic limits on the state cannot be sustained.... Violence and intimidation may be commonplace and major political parties may advocate the overthrow of the government" (Weingast 1997: 260). The risk of reversion to nondemocratic forms of government cannot be discounted in many new democracies in the Third World. Huntington (1968, 1991) warns that new democracies can decay. Indeed he argues that each of the three waves of democracy was followed by a period of reversal, in which some newly democratic regimes reverted to nondemocratic forms of governance.

Adam Przeworski and his collaborators document fifty transitions to democracy that occurred between 1950 and 1990, but they also identify forty transitions from democracy to some nondemocratic form of government during the same period (Przeworski et al. 1997: 295). Their study details a number of conditions that are statistically related to the likelihood of democracy's demise. Among these are economic stagnation, poverty, and high rates of inflation. Democracies in which per capita income is less than $1,000 have a life expectancy of less than nine years, and those in the $1,000-to-2,000 range can expect to survive only about sixteen years. In addition, certain institutional configurations are less likely to survive than others. For instance, presidential systems with highly fragmented legislative party systems are less likely to than parliamentary systems with less fragmented party systems.

The newly democratic regime in the Philippines has been threatened numerous times by attempted military coups. The inability of that regime to resolve the land issues that fuel popular support for the New People's Army has allowed the NPA to continue to thrive under democratic rule. The NPA's persistence has in turn fed frustrations among hard-liner elements within the Philippine military, inciting them to attempt several coups to remove a regime that they saw as ineffectual in dealing with a critical national security threat. So far those military elements have not succeeded. However, that is not to say they will not in the future. Pakistan, for instance, has seen the demise of its democracy. The October 1999 military coup removed a democratically elected prime minister, and few Pakistanis opposed the coup. This suggests that democracy is far from the only game in town in Pakistan.

While the transition to democracy may make revolution in the countryside less likely, the failure of new democracies to achieve consolidation—and the subsequent reversion to authoritarian governance—should make revolution more likely. Typically the authoritarian juntas that seize power from failed democracies announce their rule by demobilizing popular sectors through violent repression. When that occurs, we can expect some of the targeted social movement organizations to reconstitute themselves as revolutionary insurgencies. Just as the transition to democracy makes revolution less likely, the reversion to authoritarian rule makes it more likely. Given the history of the first two waves of democracy, and given the findings that Przeworski and his colleagues report, we should expect some proportion of the third-wave democracies to fail, and in some portion of those cases revolution is likely to occur.

Third, when democracy is installed in ethnically divided societies, it often fails to have the intended remedial effects on civil conflict. Indeed democratic competition can, under some circumstances, exacerbate ethnic conflict. Donald Horowitz (1985) points out that, in ethnically divided democracies, parties tend to form along ethnic lines, and this makes the consolidation of democracy problematic. When parties form along ethnic lines, elections reduce to little more than an ethnic census, and ethnic minorities come to see themselves as relegated to the status of permanent opposition parties. While democratic consolidation requires that losers in elections accept defeat, it also requires that they have a reasonable expectation of winning control of the government at some point in the foreseeable future. Ethnic minority parties may conclude that the latter condition is not true. Doomed to permanent opposition status, they are subject to the tyranny of an ethnic majority. In Sri Lanka the Tamil minority found itself victimized by democratically enacted legislation designed to confer advantages on the Sinhalese majority at the expense of the Tamil community. Under those circumstances, the legitimacy of Sri Lanka's democracy eroded in the eyes of the Tamil minority, and Tamil youth became increasingly susceptible to the appeals of radicals calling for violent secession from Sri Lanka.

In ethnically divided democracies, any effort on the part of leaders to form coalitions across ethnic lines or to forge multiethnic parties leaves them vulnerable to challenges within their own ethnic group. The votes they hope to gain by making appeals across ethnic lines are fewer in number than the votes they stand to lose to challengers from within their own ethnic group who appeal to ethnic solidarity. In these circumstances it is difficult to build support for democracy across ethnic lines. Minority groups have strong motives to challenge the legitimacy of democratic rules that relegate them to permanent opposition status. If they resort to extra-constitutional means to challenge the dominance of ethnic majorities, the majority may feel justified in repressing that movement. An escalating cycle of repression and violence that culminates in revolution or secessionist violence may ensue. Not surprisingly, most of the post–Cold War civil wars that have erupted have been ethnically based conflicts, and many of them have occurred in new democracies that were deeply divided along ethnic lines.

Finally, the consolidation of democracy is, to some extent, dependent upon newly elected leaders' ability to resolve the economic problems that plague the rural and urban poor in their nation. Democracy empowers those segments of the population, at least in the sense that they are granted the right to vote. Because the poor are more numerous than their more prosperous fellow citizens, their votes can be decisive in elections. As a consequence, elected politicians in new democracies face what Barbara Geddes (1994) has termed "the politician's dilemma." On the one hand, the imperatives of getting elected and staying in office dictate that elected leaders enact policies that distribute economic resources according to patronage criteria. In short, government budgetary priorities are dictated by the goal of maximizing electoral payoffs for incumbents. On the other hand, the long-term consolidation of democracy depends on elected leaders' ability to build a strong and stable economy, which requires fiscal responsibility and, in the era of globalization, conformity to global standards of financial rectitude. Those standards often require elected leaders to impose austerity measures on their constituents. Fiscally responsible elected leaders are vulnerable to being outbid at the polls by populist rivals who promise to end austerity and reinstitute social welfare spending. This dilemma confronts all democratically elected leaders. However, in new democracies, where democracy is not yet viewed as "the only game in town" (to borrow Linz and Stepan's [1996] phrase), the policy conflicts that arise from this dilemma can embolden nondemocratic segments of the national elite to stage a coup or otherwise sacrifice democracy in the name of economic stability and austerity. This was the dynamic that gave rise to the spread of bureaucratic authoritarian regimes in Latin America in the 1960s and 1970s. We cannot discount the possibility of similar antidemocratic reversions occurring among the new democracies of Asia, Africa, and Latin America. The relevant lesson from that earlier era (the second wave of democracy) is that when democratic regimes are forcibly dismantled by authoritarian recidivists, hard-liners use the coercive power of the state to demobilize society by repressing dissent and crushing social movement organizations. In those circumstances, the arguments presented in chapter 5 would suggest that a revival of revolution in the countryside would not only be possible but likely.

PEACEKEEPING AND PEACEMAKING

I close on an optimistic note with the observation that, since the end of the Cold War, the international community has become increasingly active in intervening in Third World conflicts for the purpose of bringing them to swift and peaceful conclusions. This was all but foreclosed during the Cold War, when rival superpower blocs treated Third World conflicts as battlegrounds in the East-West geopolitical struggle. They viewed the outcomes of these conflicts in zero-sum terms: A victory for one superpower's client was treated as a geopolitical gain for that power and a corresponding loss for the rival bloc. Accordingly it was rare that the UN Security Council, divided between the Soviet Union and the United States, could achieve the consensus required to authorize UN mediation of Third World civil wars. The disastrous intervention in the Congolese civil war of 1960–1964 no doubt reinforced this reluctance. When UN forces were sent in to help the government of the newly independent Congo establish civil order, they were drawn into a civil war when rebels in Katanga province launched a secessionist war. UN forces ended up taking sides in the conflict and, in the process, lost their credibility as an impartial keeper of peace (Karns and Mingst 1998: 207; Diehl 1993: 49–53). As a consequence, a number of subsequent conflicts that threatened regional security never found their way onto the agenda of the Security Council. Among these were the conflicts in Vietnam, Cambodia, and Laos, as well as the civil wars in Angola, Mozambique, and Zimbabwe/Rhodesia and separatist revolts in Ethiopia and Sudan.

Besides Cold War politics, it was far more problematic for the UN to provide peacekeeping or mediation services in civil wars as opposed to interstate wars. The introduction of peacekeeping forces in any conflict requires (1) the consent of the parties involved in the conflict, (2) the consent of any major power with the capacity to veto the operation, either formally in the Security Council or practically by intervening militarily in the conflict, and (3) the agreement of donor nations who contribute the forces and funding to sustain the operation. In a civil war, securing the consent of both parties in the conflict is difficult, especially for the UN. At least one of the combatant parties (the rebels) is not a sovereign state. Therefore it has no legal standing in the UN, while its rival (the incumbent state) does. This presents the UN with a diplomatic quandary. On the one hand, the UN will have a difficult time convincing the rebels that it can be a neutral mediator between them and one of its own members. On the other hand, for the UN to approach the rebels about peace negotiations can be interpreted by the involved state as a de facto grant of diplomatic recognition to the rebels and, by implication, a challenge to the sovereignty of that state. Thus UN intervention in civil wars was often opposed on the grounds that it represented an intrusion on the principle of national sovereignty.

Practically speaking, peacekeeping operations are difficult to implement in a civil war. Peacekeepers perform their function by establishing a buffer zone between the warring parties and policing a truce while settlement talks take place. Establishing a territorial buffer is difficult if not impossible in a civil war where the rebels employ guerrilla tactics. Under these circumstances it is all but impossible to establish a buffer between warring parties because those factions are not confined to separate territorial enclaves. Civilians in any region of the nation can be covert participants in guerrilla war. With these constraints, it should not be surprising that UN peacekeeping was rare during the Cold War, and when such interventions were employed, they were almost exclusively used in interstate wars, not civil wars.

The end of the Cold War dismantled some of the constraints on peacekeeping and other forms of mediation. The first step in this process involved a change in the major powers' willingness to sanction such operations or, more precisely, to refrain from vetoing them in the Security Council. In 1987 Mikhail Gorbachev reversed the long-standing Soviet position of skepticism toward UN peacekeeping when he publicly declared that UN military observers and peacekeeping forces played a valuable role in promoting international peace and security (Karns and Mingst 1998: 208). His declaration forced the Reagan administration to moderate its own antagonism toward UN peacekeeping. The result was a dramatic increase in UN activism in mediating conflicts generally and civil wars specifically. In 1988 UN observers were employed to oversee the withdrawal of Soviet military forces from Afghanistan. Later in 1988 the UN supervised a cease-fire that ended the eight-year-old war between Iran and Iraq. At the same time, the UN brokered an agreement between Cuba and South Africa to recognize the independence of Namibia. Subsequently UN forces supervised a cease-fire between SWAPO guerrillas (the Southwest African People's Organization) and Republic of South Africa (RSA) forces, monitored the withdrawal of RSA forces from Namibia, and eventually presided over the first democratic elections in the newly independent state of Namibia. With the collapse of Leninist states in Eastern Europe in 1989, the UN became even more active in peacekeeping and peacemaking operations. Between 1989 and 1993, thirteen new peacekeeping operations were initiated by the UN. This equaled the total number of such operations the UN had undertaken in the previous forty years of its existence (Karns and Mingst 1998: 210). Following the Gulf War, the UN launched seventeen additional peacekeeping operations, all of which involved civil wars.

In the post–Cold War era UN peacekeeping operations have gone beyond mere truce supervision to include postwar state building and more. UNTAG (UN Transition Assistance Group) supervised the withdrawal of South African forces from Namibia. It also supervised the establishment of a civilian police force, secured the repeal of discriminatory legislation, and oversaw the conduct of that nation's first free and fair elections (Karns and Mingst 1998: 209). In October of 1991 peace agreements ending the civil war in Cambodia endowed the UN with the authority to demobilize combatant forces, repatriate refugees, train and monitor local police forces, and organize that nation's first elections under the new democratic regime. This represented the first instance ever of the international community charging the UN with the political and economic restructuring of a member state (212). In Central America, ONUCA (UN Observer Group in Central America) oversaw the disarming and demobilization of combatants on both sides of civil wars in El Salvador and Nicaragua. ONUSAL (the United Nations Observers in El Salvador) took on the unprecedented task of documenting human rights violations that had occurred in El Salvador during more than a decade of civil war.

In the aftermath of the Cold War, it is clear that the international community is more willing to intervene in civil wars for the purpose of bringing them to a quick and peaceful solution. The UN is no longer hobbled into inaction by the Cold War bipolarity that prevented the Security Council from authorizing interventions. Nor does the doctrine of national sovereignty preclude the UN's intervention in civil wars, even when those wars involve separatist movements that, if successful, would alter the membership of the UN itself (by adding the new secessionist state) and the territorial makeup of one of its sovereign members. Nor do the tactical and logistical dilemmas of peacekeeping in civil war (as opposed to interstate war) any longer preclude UN action. Finally, the dramatic increase in the number of peacekeeping operations over the last decade of the twentieth century has, if nothing else, given the militaries of a number of nations considerable experience in the mechanics of peacekeeping, as opposed to war fighting. The success of most of these operations has made the UN as an institution, the major powers with veto rights on the Security Council, and nations that donate troops and equipment to such operations more confident in the likelihood of their success, and therefore more willing to contribute to them.

CONCLUSION

One general conclusion that emerges from this analysis is that the patterns of revolution and civil war are likely to be different from what they were during the Cold War era. First, it is probably safe to conclude that democratization and globalization will have a moderating effect on the occurrence of revolution, at least in one sense. Some nations will experience domestic political and economic crises that in all likelihood would have escalated to civil war during the Cold War. But because those nations have made the transition to democratic governance and are actively pursuing integration in the global economy, the crisis may not escalate to civil war. Mexico's response to the Zapatista uprising is illustrative of this dynamic. Faced with a similar crisis during the height of the Cold War, the Mexican government would likely have reacted much more aggressively. And, in all likelihood, the Mexican government would have felt pressure from the United States and other external actors to respond more harshly. The absence of Cold War politics and the presence of global economic interests instead generated pressures on the Mexican government to restrain its response. To the extent that democratically elected governments do refrain from repressing opposition social movements, and to the extent that global economic interests exert pressure on those regimes to do so in order to remain attractive to foreign direct investment, then revolutions will be less likely to occur than they would have been during the Cold War, when international pressures were, in many cases, supportive of the sort of repression that transformed nonviolent movements into revolutions.

On the other hand, we should not forget that it was globalization that provided the Zapatistas with the motive for their uprising. The rebels framed the issues confronting peasants in Chiapas in terms of the intrusion of global market forces into their lives. Moreover, democratic reforms open the political space in which opposition movements can arise, facilitating their emergence, their organization, and their ability to mobilize human and material resources, precisely because they are relatively free from state repression. Therefore the same forces that optimists argue make revolution less likely also make the mobilization of opposition social movements easier. To borrow Huntington's argument, this expansion of social movements may strain the capacity of a newly established democratic regime and embolden antidemocratic forces to justify a coup against democratic institutions, on the grounds that preserving domestic stability by repressing domestic opposition is essential to attracting foreign investment. That repression can transform democratic opposition movements into revolutionary insurgencies.

Moreover, despite the potential for economic development that globalization promises, we must keep in mind the overwhelming demographic pressures that face most Third World regimes. In most nations that would otherwise be prime candidates for the sorts of revolutionary dynamics discussed in this book, it is unlikely that globalization will lift enough of the population out of the grip of poverty to render that nation immune to political discontent. Whatever the benefits of globalization, those benefits will not be sufficient to eradicate poverty in the Third World. There will continue to be an ample supply of impoverished people available for activists to mobilize in social movements that challenge the state to take actions to address their grievances. Indeed globalization and democratization should actually facilitate the mobilization of political discontent in the Third World. Given this, the critical question becomes whether states respond with the sort of repression that converts nonviolent social movements into revolutionary movements. As Eric Selbin (2001: 286) puts it, "Real people in the real world will continue to struggle for justice and dignity regardless of whether we choose to recognize it as such, whether we define it as revolution. The question that remains is whether it is still useful to define these struggles for justice as revolutions, not whether we will continue to encounter them."

More precisely, the question is whether newly democratic regimes, when confronted with these movements, will be able to resist the antidemocratic forces in and around the state who view these movements as a threat to the nation and the democratic regime as incapable of adequately dealing with the threat. If the institutions of democracy—including democratic political culture—are not fully consolidated when these social movements arise, then those newly democratic regimes are vulnerable to overthrow by antidemocratic forces who view repression as the only remedy to mobilized political opposition. Under those circumstances, revolutions remain likely.

Finally, even if revolutions continue to recur, we can take hope in the willingness and ability of the international community to intervene in civil wars for the purpose of bringing about peaceful settlements. Civil war is costly, not just to the nation in which it occurs but to the international community. Where those costs threaten the territory or other vital interests of major powers, there is a greater likelihood now than during the Cold War that the international community will take action to resolve the conflict. The conflicts in the Balkans threatened Europe with a refugee crisis at a minimum. Accordingly the European Union and the United States acted to resolve the conflict in Bosnia and contain the conflict in Kosovo. However, where no such interests are jeopardized, we should not expect international action to resolve civil wars in the Third World. A number of conflicts in Africa and Asia (for example, Congo, Sudan, Sri Lanka) threaten no vital interests of major powers and, accordingly, no coalition of nations has emerged to sponsor UN intervention to resolve those conflicts. Thus, to the extent that civil wars continue to occur in the Third World, there is reason to believe that at least some of them will be brought to an earlier and less destructive conclusion, but only if those conflicts threaten vital interests of major powers in the global community.

Revolutions and other forms of civil war have dominated the patterns of conflict during the Cold War era. But this does not mean that these forms of conflict will disappear with the end of the Cold War. Civil war is not a historically anomalous phenomenon, confined to some limited set of regime types that have been rendered obsolete by the end of the Cold War. Nor is it the product of unique historical circumstances whose passing will render civil war no longer in vogue, to borrow Forrest Colburn's (1994) phrase. The end of the Cold War, the emergence of a more thoroughly global economy, and the spread of democracy to nations previously subject to various forms of authoritarian rule may render civil war unlikely to occur in nations that previously were ripe for revolt. However, we should recall that revolutions have always been a rare phenomenon, but that is not to say they will become extinct. Moreover, revolutions are made by small minorities. Nothing in the current global scene suggests that poverty and repression will cease to exist, or that communities that are victims of these circumstances will forever cease to mobilize to remedy those conditions. There will still be a small minority of nations in which a small minority of the population manages to organize a challenge to the state, and in a small minority of those cases the state's response will compel them to resort to revolutionary violence or die at the hands of the state.

NOTES

1. The English translations of these two guerrilla armies' names are, respectively, the Revolutionary Armed Forces (FARC) and the National Liberation Army (ELN).

2. Studies supplying theoretical arguments and empirical evidence in support of the inverted-U relationship between state repression and civil violence include Muller 1985; Muller and Seligson 1987; DeNardo 1985; and Francisco 1995.

References

Alberts, Thomas. 1983. *Agrarian Reform and Rural Poverty: A Case Study of Peru.* Boulder, Colo.: Westview.

Americas Watch. 1982. *Report on Human Rights in El Salvador.* New York: Vintage.

———. 1984. *Free Fire: A Report on Human Rights in El Salvador.* New York: Americas Watch.

———. 1985a. *The Continuing Terror: Seventh Supplement to the Report on Human Rights in El Salvador.* New York: Americas Watch.

———. 1985b. *Draining the Sea: Sixth Supplement to the Report on Human Rights in El Salvador.* New York: Americas Watch.

———. 1986. *Settling into Routine: Human Rights Abuses in Duarte's Second Year.* New York: Americas Watch.

———. 1987. *The Civilian Toll, 1986–1987.* New York: Americas Watch.

———. 1988. *Human Rights in El Salvador on the Eve of Elections.* New York: Americas Watch.

———. 1991. *El Salvador's Decade of Terror: Human Rights since the Assassination of Archbishop Romero.* New York: Americas Watch.

———. 1992. *Peru Under Fire: Human Rights Since the Return to Democracy.* New Haven: Yale University Press.

Anderson, Thomas. 1971. *Matanza: El Salvador's Communist Revolt of 1921.* Lincoln: University of Nebraska Press.

Arrighi, Giovanni. 1994. *The Long Twentieth Century: Money, Power, and the Origins of Our Times.* London: Verso.

Austin, Dennis. 1995. *Democracy and Violence in India and Sri Lanka.* New York: Council on Foreign Relations.

Aya, Roderick. 1979. "Theories of Revolution Reconsidered: Contrasting Models of Collective Violence." *Theory and Society* 8 (July): 39–98.

———. 1984. "Popular Intervention in Revolutionary Situations." In *State Making and Social Movements: Essays in History and Theory,* edited by Charles Bright and Susan Harding. Ann Arbor: University of Michigan Press.

Ayoob, Mohammed. 1992. "The Security Predicament of the Third World State: Reflections on State Making in a Comparative Perspective." In *The Insecurity Dilemma: National Security in Third World States,* edited by Brian L. Job. Boulder, Colo.: Lynne Rienner.

———. 1995. *The Third World Security Predicament: State Making, Regional Conflict, and the International System.* Boulder, Colo.: Lynne Rienner.

Ball, Patrick, Paul Kobrak, and Herbert F. Spirer. 1999. *State Violence in Guatemala, 1960–1996: A Quantitative Reflection.* Washington: American Association for the Advancement of Science, Science and Human Rights Program.

Baloyra, Enrique. 1982. *El Salvador in Transition.* Chapel Hill: University of North Carolina Press.

Barraclough, Solon L., and Arthur L. Domike. 1970. "Agrarian Structure in Seven Latin American Countries." In *Agrarian Problems and Peasant Movements in Latin America,* edited by Rodolfo Stavenhagen. Garden City, N.Y.: Anchor.

Bennett, D. Scott, and Allan C. Stam III. 1996. "The Duration of Interstate Wars, 1816–1985." *American Political Science Review* 90: 239–57.

———. 1998. "The Declining Advantages of Democracy: A Combined Model of War Outcomes and Duration." *Journal of Conflict Resolution* 42: 344–66.

Berejikian, Jeffrey. 1992. "Revolutionary Collective Action and the Agent-Structure Problem." *American Political Science Review* 86: 647–57.

Berg, Ronald H. 1992. "Peasant Responses to Shining Path in Andahuaylas." In *Shining Path of Peru,* edited by David Scott Palmer. New York: St. Martin's.

Binford, Leigh. 1996. *The El Mozote Massacre.* Tucson: University of Arizona Press.

Booth, John A. 1985. *The End and the Beginning: The Nicaraguan Revolution.* 2d ed. Boulder, Colo.: Westview.

———. 1991. "Socioeconomic and Political Roots of National Revolts in Central America." *Latin American Research Review.* 26: 33–73.

Bratton, Michael. 1990. "Ten Years After: Land Redistribution in Zimbabwe, 1980–1990." In *Agrarian Reform and Grassroots Development: Ten Case Studies,* edited by Roy L. Prosterman, Mary N. Temple, and Timothy M. Hanstad. Boulder, Colo.: Lynne Rienner.

Bratton, Michael, and Nicolas Van De Walle. 1992. "Popular Protest and Political Reform in Africa." *Comparative Politics* 24: 419–42.

———. 1994. "Neopatrimonial Regimes and Political Transitions in Africa." *World Politics* 46 (July): 453–89.

———. 1997. *Democratic Experiments in Africa: Regime Transitions in Comparative Perspective.* New York: Cambridge University Press.

Brewer, Toy Helena. 1983. "Women in El Salvador." In *Revolution in Central America,* edited by Stanford Central America Action Network. Boulder, Colo.: Westview.

Brinton, Crane. 1965. *The Anatomy of Revolution.* Rev. ed. New York: Vantage.

Brockett, Charles D. 1988. *Land, Power, and Poverty: Agrarian Transformation and Political Conflict in Central America.* Boulder, Colo.: Westview.

Brogan, Patrick. 1990. *The Fighting Never Stopped: A Comprehensive Guide to World Conflict Since 1945.* New York: Vintage.

Browning, David. 1971. *El Salvador: Landscape and Society.* Oxford, U.K.: Clarendon Press.

Brush, Stephen G. 1996. "Dynamics of Theory Change in the Social Sciences: Relative Deprivation and Collective Violence." *Journal of Conflict Resolution* 40: 523–45.

Burns, E. Bradford. 1984. "The Modernization of Underdevelopment: El Salvador, 1858–1931." *Journal of Developing Areas* 18: 293–316.

Buzan, Barry. 1983. *People, States, and Fear: The National Security Problem in International Relations.* Aldershot, U.K.: Wheatsheaf Books.

———. 1991. *People, States, and Fear: An Agenda for International Security Studies in the Post-Cold War Era.* London: Harvester Wheatsheaf.

Byrne, Hugh. 1996. *El Salvador's Civil War: A Study of Revolution.* Boulder, Colo.: Lynne Rienner.

Caballero, José María. 1981a. *Economía Agraria de la Sierra Peruana Antes de la Reforma Agraria de 1969.* Lima: Instituto de Estudios Peruanos.

———. 1981b. *From Belaundé to Belaundé: Peru's Military Experiment in Third Roadism.* Cambridge, U.K.: Centre of Latin American Studies, Cambridge University.

Caballero, José María, and Elena Alvarez. 1980. *Aspectos Cuantitativos de la Reforma Agraria, 1969–1979.* Lima: Instituto de Estudios Peruanos.

Cardoso, Fernando, and E. Faletto. 1979. *Dependency and Development in Latin America.* Berkeley: University of California Press.

Chehabi, H. E., and Juan J. Linz, eds. 1998a. *Sultanistic Regimes.* Baltimore: Johns Hopkins University Press.

———. 1998b. "A Theory of Sultanism 1: A Type of Nondemocratic Rule." In *Sultanistic Regimes,* edited by H. E. Chehabi and Juan J. Linz. Baltimore: Johns Hopkins University Press.

———. 1998c. "A Theory of Sultanism 2: Genesis and Demise of Sultanistic Rule." In *Sultanistic Regimes,* edited by H. E. Chehabi and Juan J. Linz. Baltimore: Johns Hopkins University Press.

Chong, Dennis. 1991. *Collective Action and the Civil Rights Movement.* Chicago: University of Chicago Press.

Clapham, Christopher. 1998. "Rwanda: Perils of Peacemaking." *Journal of Peace Research* 35 (2): 193–210.

Colburn, Forrest D., ed. 1989. *Everyday Forms of Peasant Resistance.* Armonk, N.Y.: M. E. Sharpe.

———. 1994. *The Vogue of Revolution in Poor Countries.* Princeton: Princeton University Press.

Collier, David, ed. 1979. *The New Authoritarianism in Latin America.* Princeton: Princeton University Press.

Comision de la Verdad para El Salvador. 1993. *De Locura a la Esperanza: La Guerra de 12 Anos en El Salvador.* New York: United Nations.

Cotler, Julio. 1969. "Peru: Peasant Organizations." In *Latin American Peasant Movements,* edited by Henry Landsberger. Ithaca: Cornell University Press.

———. 1970. "Traditional Haciendas and Communities in a Context of Political Mobilization in Peru." In *Agrarian Problems and Peasant Movements in Latin America,* edited by Roberto Stavenhagen. New York: Doubleday.

Crosby, Faye. 1979. "Relative Deprivation Revisited: A Response to Miller, Bolce, and Halligan." *American Political Science Review* 73: 103–12.

Damrosch, Lori Fisher, ed. 1993. *Enforcing Restraint: Collective Intervention in Internal Conflicts.* New York: Council on Foreign Relations.

Danner, Mark. 1993. *The El Mozote Massacre.* New York: Vintage.

Davies, James C. 1962. "Toward a Theory of Revolution." *American Sociological Review* 27: 5–19.

Deeb, Marius. 1980. *The Lebanese Civil War.* New York: Praeger.

DeFronzo, James. 1996. *Revolutions and Revolutionary Movements.* 2d ed. Boulder, Colo.: Westview.

Degregori, Carlos Iván. 1992. "Return to the Past." In *Shining Path of Peru,* edited by David Scott Palmer. New York: St. Martin's.

Deitchman, Seymour J. 1964. *Limited War and American Defense Policy.* Cambridge: Massachusetts Institute of Technology Press.

DeNardo, James. 1985. *Power in Numbers: The Political Strategy of Protest and Rebellion.* Princeton: Princeton University Press.

Desai, Raj, and Harry Eckstein. 1990. "Insurgency: The Transformation of Peasant Rebellion." *World Politics* 42 (July): 441–65.

de Soto, Hernando. 1989. *The Other Path: The Invisible Revolution in the Third World.* New York: Harper and Row.

Diamond, Larry. 1997. "Introduction: In Search of Consolidation." In *Consolidating Third Wave Democracies,* edited by Larry Diamond et al. Baltimore: Johns Hopkins University Press.

Diehl, Paul F. 1993. *International Peacekeeping.* Baltimore: Johns Hopkins University Press.

Diskin, Martin. 1989. "El Salvador: Reform Prevents Change." In *Searching for Agrarian Reform in Latin America,* edited by William C. Thiesenhusen. Boston: Unwin Hyman.

Dix, Robert H. 1983. "Varieties of Revolution." *Comparative Politics* 15: 281–94.

———. 1984. "Why Revolutions Succeed and Fail." *Polity* 16 (Spring): 423–66.

Dixon, William J. 1994. "Democracy and the Peaceful Settlement of International Conflict." *American Political Science Review* 88 (March): 14–32.

Doggett, Martha. 1993. *Death Foretold: The Jesuit Murders in El Salvador.* Washington: Lawyers Committee for Human Rights and Georgetown University Press.

Dollard, John, L. W. Doob, N. E. Miller, O. H. Mowrer, and R. R. Sears. 1939. *Frustration and Aggression.* New Haven: Yale University Press.

Dos Santos, T. 1983. "The Structure of Dependence." In *The Struggle for Economic Development: Readings in Problems and Policies,* edited by Michal P. Todaro. New York: Longman.

Dunkerly, James. 1985. *The Long War: Dictatorship and Revolution in El Salvador.* London: Verso.

Durham, William H. 1979. *Scarcity and Survival in Central America: Ecological Origins of the Soccer War.* Stanford: Stanford University Press.

Eckstein, Harry. 1965. "On the Etiology of Internal Wars." *History and Theory* 4: 133–63.

Eisinger, Peter K. 1973. "The Conditions of Protest Behavior in American Cities." *American Political Science Review* 67: 11–28.

Eisenstadt, Sergei N., and René LeMarchand, eds. 1981. *Political Clientelism, Patronage, and Development.* Beverly Hills, Calif.: Sage.

Feierabend, Ivo, and Rosalind Feierabend. 1966. "Aggressive Behavior within Polities, 1948–1962: A Cross-National Study." *Journal of Conflict Resolution* 10: 249–71.

———. 1972. "Systemic Conditions of Political Aggression: An Application of Frustration-Aggression Theory." In *Anger, Violence, and Politics,* edited by Ivo Feierabend et al. Englewood Cliffs, N.J.: Prentice Hall.

Foran, John. 1997. "The Future of Revolutions at the *Fin-de-siecle.*" *Third World Quarterly* 18 (December): 791–820.

Ford, Thomas. 1955. *Man and Land in Peru.* Gainesville: University of Florida Press.

Foster, George M. 1965. "Peasant Society and the Image of Limited Good." *American Anthropologist* 67 (April): 293–315.

Francisco, Ronald A. 1995. "Coercion and Protest in Three Coercive States." *Journal of Conflict Resolution* 39: 263–82.

Frohlich, Norman, and Joe A. Oppenheimer. 1973. "Governmental Violence and Tax Revenue." In *Violence as Politics,* edited by H. Hirsch and D. Perry. New York: Harper.

———. 1974. "The Carrot and the Stick: Optimal Program Mixes for Entrepreneurial Political Leaders." *Public Choice* 19 (Fall): 43–61.

Frohlich, Norman O., Joe A. Oppenheimer, and Oran Young. 1971. *Political Leadership and Collective Goods.* Princeton: Princeton University Press.

Fukuyama, Francis. 1989. "The End of History?" *National Interest* 16: 3–18.

Furtado, Celso. 1964. *Development and Underdevelopment: A Structural View of the Problems of Developed and Underdeveloped Countries.* Berkeley: University of California Press.

Gaddis, John Lewis. 1987. *The Long Peace: Inquiries Into the History of the Cold War.* Oxford, U.K.: Oxford University Press.

Geddes, Barbara. 1994. *The Politician's Dilemma: Building State Capacity in Latin America.* Berkeley: University of California Press.

Geller, Daniel S., and J. David Singer. 1998. *Nations at War: A Scientific Study of International Conflict.* Cambridge, U.K.: Cambridge University Press.

Gendell, Murray. 1986. "Population Growth and Labor Absorption in Latin America, 1970–2000." In *Population Growth in Latin America and U.S. National Security,* edited by John Saunders. New York: Allen and Unwin.

Gibb, Tom. 1992. "Elections and the Road to Peace." In *Is There A Transition to Democracy in El Salvador?,* edited by Joseph S. Tulchin with Gary Bland. Boulder, Colo.: Lynne Rienner.

Giddens, Anthony. 1987. *The Nation State and Violence.* Berkeley: University of California Press.

Goldfrank, Walter. 1986. "The Mexican Revolution." In *Revolutions: Theoretical, Comparative, and Historical Studies,* edited by Jack Goldstone. San Diego: Harcourt Brace Jovanovich.

Goldstone, Jack A. 1980. "Theories of Revolution: The Third Generation." *World Politics* 32: 425–53.

————, ed. 1986. *Revolutions: Theoretical, Comparative, and Historical Studies*. New York: Harcourt Brace Jovanovich.

————. 1991. *Revolution and Rebellion in the Early Modern World*. Berkeley: University of California Press.

————. 1994. "Is Revolution Individually Rational? Groups and Individuals in Revolutionary Collective Action." *Rationality and Society* 6 (1): 139–66.

————. 1997. "Population Growth and Revolutionary Crises." In *Theorizing Revolution*, edited by John Foran. New York: Routledge.

Gonzales, José. 1992. "Guerrillas and Coca in the Upper Huallaga Valley." In *Shining Path of Peru*, edited by David Scott Palmer. New York: St. Martin's.

Gonzáles, Raúl. 1987. "Coca y Subversion en el Huallaga." *Quehacer* 48: 59–72.

Goodwin, Jeff. 1997. "State-Centered Approaches to Social Revolutions: Strengths and Limitations of a Theoretical Tradition." In *Theorizing Revolutions*, edited by John Foran. London: Routledge.

————. 2001. "Is the Age of Revolution Over?" In *Revolution: International Dimensions*, edited by Mark N. Katz. Washington: CQ Press.

Goodwin, Jeff and Theda Skocpol. 1989. "Explaining Revolutions in the Contemporary World." *Politics and Society* 17 (December): 489–509.

Graham, Douglas H. 1984. "Economic Dimensions of Instability and Decline in Central America and the Caribbean." In *Revolution and Counterrevolution in Central America and the Caribbean*, edited by Donald Schulz and Douglas H. Graham. Boulder, Colo.: Westview.

Grofman, Bernard N., and Edward N. Muller. 1973. "The Strange Case of Relative Gratification and Potential for Political Violence: The V-Curve Hypothesis." *American Political Science Review* 67: 514–39.

Grossman, Herschel I. 1991. "A General Equilibrium Model of Insurrections." *American Economic Review* 81: 912–21.

Gugler, Josef. 1982. "The Urban Character of Contemporary Revolutions." *Studies in Comparative International Development* 17: 60–73.

Gupta, Dipak K. 1990. *The Economics of Political Violence: The Effect of Political Stability on Economic Growth*. New York: Praeger.

Gurney, Joan Neff, and Kathleen J. Tierney. 1982. "Relative Deprivation and Social Movements: A Critical Look at Twenty Years of Theory and Research." *Sociological Quarterly* 23: 33–47.

Gurr, Ted Robert. 1970. *Why Men Rebel*. Princeton: Princeton University Press.

————. 1986. "The Political Origins of State Violence and Terror: A Theoretical Analysis." In *Government Violence and Repression: An Agenda for Research*, edited by Michael Stohl and George A. Lopez. Westport, Conn.: Greenwood Press.

Handelman, Howard. 1975. *Struggle in the Andes: Peasant Political Mobilization in Peru*. Austin: University of Texas Press.

————. 1981. *Peasants, Landlords and Bureaucrats: The Politics of Agrarian Reform in Peru*. American Universities Field Staff Report 1. Hanover, N.H.: American Universities Field Staff.

Handy, Jim. 1994. *Revolution in the Countryside: Rural Conflict and Agrarian Reform in Guatemala, 1944–1954*. Chapel Hill: University of North Carolina Press.

Hardin, Russell. 1971. "Collective Action as an Agreeable *n*-Person Prisoner's Dilemma." *Behavioral Science* 16: 472–81.

———. 1982. *Collective Action.* Baltimore: Johns Hopkins University Press.

———. 1995. *One For All: The Logic of Group Conflict.* Princeton: Princeton University Press.

Harvey, Neil. 1998. *The Chiapas Rebellion: The Struggle for Land and Democracy.* Durham, N.C.: Duke University Press.

Hawes, Gary. 1990. "Theories of Peasant Revolution: A Critique and Contribution from the Philippines." *World Politics* 42: 261–98.

Hazleton, William A., and Sandra Woy-Hazleton. 1988. "Terrorism and the Marxist Left: Peru's Struggle against Sendero Luminoso." *Terrorism* 11: 471–90.

———. 1992. "Shining Path and the Marxist Left." In *Shining Path of Peru,* edited by David Scott Palmer. New York: St. Martin's.

Hegre, Håvard, Tanja Ellingsen, Nils Petter Gleditsch, and Scott Gates. 1999. "Towards a Democratic Civil Peace? Opportunity, Grievance, and Civil War, 1816–1992." Washington: World Bank.

Hirschman, Albert. 1982. *Shifting Involvements: Private Interest and Public Action.* Princeton: Princeton University Press.

Hobsbawm, Eric. 1973. "Peasants and Politics." *Journal of Peasant Studies* 1 (1): 3–22.

———. 1974. "Peasant Land Occupations." *Past and Present* 62: 120–52.

Holl, Jane. 1993. "When War Doesn't Work: Understanding the Relationship between the Battlefield and the Negotiating Table." In *Stop the Killing: How Civil Wars End,* edited by Roy Licklider. New York: New York University Press.

Holsti, K. J. 1992. "International Theory and War in the Third World." In *The Insecurity Dilemma: National Security in Third World States,* edited by Brian L. Job. Boulder, Colo.: Lynne Rienner.

———. 1996. *The State, War, and the State of War.* Cambridge, U.K.: Cambridge University Press.

Horowitz, Donald L. 1981. "Patterns of Ethnic Separatism." *Comparative Studies in Society and History* 23: 165–95.

———. 1985. *Ethnic Groups in Conflict.* Berkeley: University of California Press.

Human Rights Watch. 1995. *Slaughter Among Neighbors: The Political Origins of Communal Violence.* New Haven: Yale University Press.

Huntington, Samuel P. 1968. *Political Order in Changing Societies.* New Haven: Yale University Press.

———. 1991. *The Third Wave: Democratization in the Late Twentieth Century.* Norman: University of Oklahoma Press.

———. 1996. *The Clash of Civilizations and the Remaking of World Order.* New York: Touchstone.

Iklé, Fred C. 1971. *Every War Must End.* New York: Columbia University Press.

Imig, Doug and Sidney Tarrow. 2000. "Processing Contention in a Europeanised Polity." *Western European Politics* 23 (4): 73–93.

———. 2001a. "Mapping the Europeanization of Contentious Politics." In *Contentious Europeans: Protest and Politics in an Integrating Europe,* edited by Doug Imig and Sidney Tarrow. Boulder, Colo.: Rowman and Littlefield.

———. 2001b. "Studying Contention in an Emerging Polity." In *Contentious Europeans: Protest and Politics in an Integrating Europe,* edited by Doug Imig and Sidney Tarrow. Boulder, Colo.: Rowman and Littlefield.

Isbell, Billie Jean. 1992. "Shining Path and Peasant Responses in Rural Ayacucho." In *Shining Path of Peru,* edited by David Scott Palmer. New York: St. Martin's.

Jackson, Robert. 1987. "Quasi States, Dual Regimes, and Neoclassical Theory: International Jurisprudence and the Third World." *International Organization* 41 (Autumn): 519–49.

Jackson, Robert H., and Carl G. Rosberg. 1982. "Why Africa's Weak States Persist: The Empirical and the Juridical in Statehood." *World Politics* 35: 1–24.

Jenkins, J. Craig. 1983a. "Resource Mobilization Theory and the Study of Social Movements." *Annual Review of Sociology* 9: 527–53.

———. 1983b. "Why Do Peasants Rebel? Structural and Historical Theories of Modern Peasant Rebellions." *American Journal of Sociology* 88 (November): 487–514.

Jenkins, J. Craig, and Charles Perrow. 1977. "Insurgency of the Powerless: Farm Worker Movements (1946–1972)." *American Sociological Review* 42: 249–68.

Job, Brian L. 1992. "The Insecurity Dilemma: National, Regime, and State Securities in the Third World." In *The Insecurity Dilemma: National Security in Third World States,* edited by Brian L. Job. Boulder, Colo.: Lynne Rienner.

Johnson, Chalmers. 1962. "Civilian Loyalties and Guerrilla Conflict." *World Politics* 14 (July): 646–61.

———. 1982. *Revolutionary Change.* 2d ed. Stanford: Stanford University Press.

Karnow, Stanley. 1983. *Vietnam: A History.* New York: Viking Press.

Karns, Margaret P., and Karen A. Mingst. 1998. "The Evolution of United Nations Peacekeeping." In *World Security,* 3d ed., edited by Michael T. Klare and Yogesh Chandrani. New York: St. Martin's

Karush, Gerald E. 1978. "Plantation, Population, and Poverty: The Roots of the Demographic Crisis in El Salvador." *Studies in Comparative International Development* 8: 59–75.

Kaufman, Stuart J. 1996. "Spiraling to Ethnic War: Elites, Masses and Moscow in Moldova's Civil War." *International Security* 21 (2): 108–38.

Kaufmann, Chaim. 1996. "Possible and Impossible Solutions to Ethnic Civil Wars." *International Security* 20 (4): 136–75.

Kay, Cristóbal. 1983. "The Agrarian Reform in Peru: An Assessment." In *Agrarian Reform in Contemporary Developing Countries,* edited by Ajit Kumar Ghose. New York: St. Martin's.

Kerkvliet, Benedict J. 1977. *The Huk Rebellion: A Study of Peasant Revolts in the Philippines.* Berkeley: University of California Press.

Khong, Yuen Foong. 1992. *Analogies of War: Korea, Munich, Dien Bien Phu, and the Vietnam Decisions of 1965.* Princeton: Princeton University Press.

Kitschelt, Herbert P. 1986. "Political Opportunity Structures and Political Protest: Anti-Nuclear Protests in Four Democracies." *British Journal of Political Science* 16: 57–85.

Klare, Michael T., and Peter Kornbluh, eds. 1988. *Low Intensity Warfare: Counterinsurgency, Proinsurgency, and Antiterrorism in the Eighties.* New York: Pantheon.

Korpi, Walter. 1974. "Conflict, Power, and Relative Deprivation." *American Political Science Review* 68: 1569–78.

Krain, Matthew, and Marissa Edson Myers. 1997. "Democracy and Civil War: A Note on the Democratic Peace Proposition." *International Interactions* 23: 109–18.

Kuran, Timur. 1989. "Sparks and Prairie Fires: A Theory of Unanticipated Political Revolution." *Public Choice* 61: 41–74.

———. 1991. "Now Out of Never: The Element of Surprise in the East European Revolutions of 1989." *World Politics* 44: 7–48.

———. 1995. *Private Truths, Public Lies: The Social Consequences of Preference Falsification.* Cambridge: Harvard University Press.

Lamberg, Robert F. 1970. "Che in Bolivia: The 'Revolution' That Failed." *Problems of Communism.* 19 (July-August).

Lastarria-Cornhiel, Susanna. 1989. "Agrarian Reforms of the 1960s and 1970s in Peru." In *Searching for Agrarian Reform in Latin America,* edited by William C. Thiesenhusen. Boston: Unwin Hyman.

Lawyers Committee for International Human Rights and Americas Watch. 1984. *El Salvador's Other Victims: The War on the Displaced.* New York: Lawyers Committee for International Human Rights and Americas Watch.

Lee, Rensselaer W. 1989. *The White Labyrinth: Cocaine and Political Power.* New Brunswick, N.J.: Transaction.

Leiken, Robert. 1984. "The Salvadoran Left." In *Central America: Anatomy of a Conflict,* edited by Robert L. Leiken. Elmsford, N.Y.: Pergamon.

Leites, N., and C. Wolf, Jr. 1970. *Rebellion and Authority.* Santa Monica, Calif.: Rand.

LeMarchand, René. 1972. "Political Clientelism and Ethnicity in Tropical Africa: Competing Solidarities in Nation Building." *American Political Science Review* 66: 68–90.

———. 1994. "Managing Transition Anarchies: Rwanda, Burundi, and South Africa in Comparative Perspective." *Journal of Modern African Studies* 32 (4): 581–604.

Levy, Jack. 1983. *War in the Modern Great Power System, 1495–1975.* Lexington: University of Kentucky Press.

Lewis, W. Arthur. 1954. "Economic Development with Unlimited Supplies of Labor." *Manchester School of Economics and Social Studies* 22: 139–91.

Lichbach, Mark Irving. 1984. "An Economic Theory of Governability: Choosing Policy and Optimizing Performance." *Public Choice* 44: 307–37.

———. 1987. "Deterrence or Escalation in Repression and Dissent." *Journal of Conflict Resolution* 31: 266–97.

———. 1989. "An Evaluation of 'Does Economic Inequality Breed Political Conflict?' Studies." *World Politics* 41: 431–70.

———. 1990. "Will Rational People Rebel Against Inequality? Samson's Choice." *American Journal of Political Science* 34: 1049–76.

———. 1992. "Nobody Cites Nobody Else: Mathematical Models of Domestic Political Conflict." *Defence Economics* 3: 341–57.

———. 1994a. "Rethinking Rationality and Rebellion: Theories of Collective Action and the Problems of Collective Dissent." *Rationality and Society* 6 (1): 8–39.

———. 1994b. "What Makes Rational Peasants Revolutionary?" *World Politics* 46: 383–418.

———. 1995. *The Rebel's Dilemma*. Ann Arbor: University of Michigan Press.

———. 1997. "Contentious Maps of Contentious Politics." *Mobilization: An International Journal* 2 (1): 87–98.

Licklider, Roy. 1992. "How Civil Wars End: Preliminary Results from a Comparative Project." In *Controlling and Ending Conflict: Issues Before and After the Cold War*, edited by Stephen J. Cimbala and Sidney R. Waldman. New York: Greenwood Press.

———. 1993a. "How Civil Wars End: Questions and Methods." In *Stop the Killing: How Civil Wars End*, edited by Roy Licklider. New York: New York University Press.

———, ed. 1993b. *Stop the Killing: How Civil Wars End*. New York: New York University Press.

———. 1995. "The Consequences of Negotiated Settlements in Civil Wars, 1945–1993." *American Political Science Review* 89: 681–91.

Lijphart, Arend. 1969. "Consociational Democracy." *World Politics* 21 (January): 207–25.

Lindo-Fuentes, Hector. 1990. *Weak Foundations: The Economy of El Salvador in the Nineteenth Century, 1821–1998*. Berkeley: University of California Press.

Linz, Juan. 1975. "Totalitarian and Authoritarian Regimes." In *Handbook of Political Science*, vol. 3, edited by Nelson Polsby. Reading, Mass.: Addison-Wesley.

Linz, Juan J., and Alfred Stepan. 1996. *Problems of Democratic Transition and Consolidation: Southern Europe, South America, and Post-Communist Europe*. Baltimore: Johns Hopkins University Press.

Lipsky, Michael. 1968. "Protest as a Political Resource." *American Political Science Review* 62: 1144–58.

Lopez, George A. 1986. "National Security Ideology as an Impetus to State Violence and Terror." In *Government Violence and Repression: An Agenda for Research*, edited by Michael Stohl and George A. Lopez. Westport, Conn.: Greenwood Press.

Magagna, Victor. 1991. *Communities of Grain: Rural Rebellion in Comparative Perspective*. Ithaca: Cornell University Press.

Malloy, James, ed. 1977. *Authoritarianism and Corporatism in Latin America*. Pittsburgh: University of Pittsburgh Press.

Maranto, Robert. 1988. "Better to Fight Another Day: A Pre-Theory of Insurgent Coalitions." *Journal of Peace Research* 25 (2): 137–48.

Marwell, Gerald, and Pamela E. Oliver. 1984. "Collective Action Theory and Social Movements." *Research in Social Movements, Conflict and Change* 7: 1–27.

———. 1993. *The Critical Mass in Collective Action: A Micro-Social Theory*. New York: Cambridge University Press.

Marwell, Gerald, Pamela E. Oliver, and Ralph Prahl. 1988. "Social Networks and Collective Action: A Theory of the Critical Mass, III." *American Journal of Sociology* 94: 502–34.

Mason, T. David. 1984. "Individual Participation in Collective Racial Violence: A Rational Choice Synthesis." *American Political Science Review.* 78: 1040–56.

———. 1986a. "Land Reform and the Breakdown of Clientelist Politics in El Salvador." *Comparative Political Studies* 19: 487–516.

———. 1986b. "Population Growth and the 'Struggle for the Hearts and Minds' of the Rural Population in Central America." In *Population Growth in Latin America and U.S. National Security*, edited by John Saunders. New York: Allen and Unwin.

———. 1989. "Nonelite Response to State-Sanctioned Terror." *Western Political Quarterly* 42: 467–92.

———. 1990. "Dynamics of Revolutionary Change: Indigenous Factors." In *Revolution and Political Change in the Third World,* edited by Barry M. Shutz and Robert O. Slater. Boulder, Colo.: Lynne Rienner.

———. 1992. "Women's Participation in Central American Revolutions: A Theoretical Perspective." *Comparative Political Studies* 25: 63–89.

———. 1994. "Modernization and Its Discontents Revisited: The Political Economy of Urban Unrest in the People's Republic of China." *Journal of Politics* 56 (May): 400–24.

———. 1996. "Insurgency, Counterinsurgency, and the Rational Peasant." *Public Choice.* 86: 63–83.

———. 1998. "Take Two Acres and Call Me in the Morning: Is Land Reform a Remedy for Peasant Unrest?" *Journal of Politics* 60: 199–230.

———. 1999. "The Civil War in El Salvador: A Retrospective Analysis." *Latin American Research Review* 34 (3): 179–96.

Mason, T. David, and Christopher Campany. 1995. "Guerrillas, Drugs, and Peasants: The Rational Peasant and the War on Drugs in Peru." *Terrorism and Political Violence* 7 (Winter): 140–70.

Mason, T. David, and Patrick J. Fett. 1996. "How Civil Wars End: A Rational Choice Approach." *Journal of Conflict Resolution* 40: 546–68.

Mason, T. David, and Dale A. Krane. 1989. "The Political Economy of Death Squads." *International Studies Quarterly* 33: 175–98.

Mason, T. David, and Janet Schwartzfager. 1989. "Land Reform and the Rise of Sendero Luminoso in Peru." *Terrorism and Political Violence* 1 (October): 482–516.

Mason, T. David, Joseph P. Weingarten, and Patrick J. Fett. 1999. "Win, Lose, or Draw: Predicting the Outcome of Civil Wars." *Political Research Quarterly* 52 (2): 239–68.

Matthews, Bruce 1989. "Seeds of the Accord." *Asian Survey* 24 (February): 229–34.

Matos Mar, José, and José Manuel Mejía. 1980. *La Reforma Agraria en el Peru.* Lima: Instituto de Estudios Peruanos.

McAdam, Doug. 1982. *Political Process and the Development of Black Insurgency, 1930–1970.* Chicago: University of Chicago Press.

———. 1986. "Recruitment to High-Risk Activism: The Case of Freedom Summer." *American Journal of Sociology* 92: 64–90.

———. 1996. "Conceptual Origins, Current Problems, Future Directions." In *Comparative Perspectives on Social Movements: Political Opportunities, Mobilizing Structures, and Cultural Framings,* edited by Doug McAdam, John D. McCarthy, and Mayer N. Zald. Cambridge, U.K.: Cambridge University Press.

McAdam, Doug, John D. McCarthy, and Mayer N. Zald, eds. 1996. *Comparative Perspectives on Social Movements: Political Opportunities, Mobilizing Structures, and Cultural Framings.* Cambridge, U.K.: Cambridge University Press.

McAdam, Doug, and Ronnelle Paulsen. 1993. "Specifying the Relationship between Social Ties and Activism." *American Journal of Sociology* 99: 640–67.

McAdam, Doug, and David A. Snow, eds. 1997. *Social Movements: Readings on Their Emergence, Mobilization and Dynamics.* Los Angeles: Roxbury.

McAdam, Doug, Sidney Tarrow, and Charles Tilly. 1996. "To Map Contentious Politics." *Mobilization: An International Journal* 1 (1): 17–34.

———. 1997. "Toward an Integrated Perspective on Social Movements and Revolution." In *Comparative Politics: Rationality, Culture, and Structure,* edited by Mark Irving Lichbach and Alan S. Zuckerman. Cambridge, U.K.: Cambridge University Press.

McCarthy, John D. 1996. "Constraints and Opportunities in Adopting, Adapting, and Inventing," In *Comparative Perspectives on Social Movements,* edited by Doug McAdam, John D. McCarthy, and Mayer N. Zald. Cambridge, U.K.: Cambridge University Press.

McCarthy, John D., and Mayer N. Zald. 1973. *The Trend of Social Movements in America: Professionalization and Resource Mobilization.* Morristown, N.J.: General Learning Press.

———. 1977. "Resource Mobilization and Social Movements: A Partial Theory." *American Journal of Sociology* 82: 1212–41.

McClintock, Cynthia. 1981. *Peasant Cooperatives and Political Change in Peru.* Princeton: Princeton University Press.

———. 1982. "Post-Revolutionary Agrarian Politics in Peru." In *Post-Revolutionary Peru: The Politics of Transformation,* edited by Stephen Gorman. Boulder, Colo.: Westview.

———. 1983. "Sendero Luminoso: Peru's Maoist Guerrillas." *Problems of Communism* 32: 19–34.

———. 1984. "Why Peasants Rebel: The Case of Peru's Sendero Luminoso." *World Politics* 37: 48–84.

———. 1989. "Peru's Sendero Luminoso: Origins and Trajectory." In *Power and Popular Protest: Latin American Social Movements,* edited by Susan Eckstein. Berkeley: University of California Press.

———. 1993. "Peru's Fujimori: A Caudillo Derails Democracy." *Current History* 95: 112–19.

———. 1998. *Revolutionary Movements in Latin America: El Salvador's FMLN and Peru's Shining Path.* Washington: U.S. Institute of Peace.

McCormick, Gordon. 1990. *The Shining Path and the Future of Peru.* Santa Monica, Calif.: Rand.

———. 1992. *From the Sierra to the Cities: The Urban Campaign of the Shining Path.* Santa Monica, Calif.: Rand.

McCuen, John J. 1965. *The Art of Counter-Revolutionary War.* Harrisburg, Pa.: Stackpole Books.

McMichael, Philip. 2000. "Globalization: Myths and Realities." In *From Modernization to Globalization: Perspectives on Development and Social Change,* edited by Roberts Timmons and Amy Hite. Malden, Mass.: Blackwell.

Midlarsky, Manus I. 1982. "Scarcity and Inequality: Prologue to the Onset of Mass Revolution." *Journal of Conflict Resolution* 26: 3–38.

———. 1988. "Rulers and Ruled: Patterned Inequality and the Onset of Mass Political Violence." *American Political Science Review* 82: 491–509.

Midlarsky, Manus I., and Kenneth Roberts. 1985. "Class, State, and Revolution in Central America: Nicaragua and El Salvador Compared." *Journal of Conflict Resolution* 29: 163–95.

Migdal, Joel S. 1974. *Peasants, Politics, and Revolution: Pressures Towards Political and Social Change in the Third World.* Princeton: Princeton University Press.

———. 1988. *Strong Societies and Weak States: State-Society Relations and State Capabilities in the Third World.* Princeton: Princeton University Press.

Miller, Abraham, Louis Bolce, and Mark Halligan. 1977. "The J-Curve Theory and the Black Urban Riots: An Empirical Test of Progressive Relative Deprivation." *American Political Science Review* 71: 864–82.

Mitchell, Edward J. 1968. "Inequality and Insurgency: A Statistical Study of South Vietnam." *World Politics* 10: 421–53.

Montgomery, Tommie Sue. 1982. *Revolution in El Salvador: Origins and Evolution.* Boulder, Colo.: Westview.

———. 1995. *Revolution In El Salvador: From Civil Strife to Civil Peace,* 2d ed. Boulder, Colo.: Westview.

Moore, Barrington. 1966. *Social Origins of Dictatorship and Democracy.* Boston: Beacon Press.

———. 1978. *Injustice: The Social Bases of Obedience and Revolt.* White Plains, N.Y.: M. E. Sharpe.

Moore, Will H. 1995. "Rational Rebels: Overcoming the Free Rider Problem." *Political Research Quarterly* 48: 417–54.

Moore, Will H., Ronnie Lindström, and Valerie O'Regan. 1996. "Land Reform, Political Violence, and the Economic Inequality-Political Conflict Nexus: A Longitudinal Analysis." *International Interactions* 21: 335–63.

Morales, Edmundo. 1989. *Cocaine: White Gold Rush in Peru.* Tucson: University of Arizona Press.

Mueller, John, and Erich Weede. 1990. "Cross-National Variations in Political Violence: A Rational Action Approach." *Journal of Conflict Resolution* 34: 624–51.

Muller, Edward N. 1985. "Income Inequality, Regime Repressiveness, and Political Violence." *American Journal of Sociology* 50: 47–61.

Muller, Edward N., and Mitchell Seligson. 1987. "Inequality and Insurgency." *American Political Science Review* 81: 425–51.

National Bipartisan Commission on Central America. 1984. *Report of the President's National Bipartisan Commission on Central America.* New York: Macmillan.

Oberschall, Anthony. 1973. *Social Conflict and Social Movements.* Englewood Cliffs, N.J.: Prentice Hall.

———. 1993. *Social Movements: Ideologies, Interests, and Identities.* New Brunswick, N.J.: Transaction.

O'Donnell, Guillermo. 1973. *Modernization and the Bureaucratic Authoritarianism: Studies in South American Politics.* Berkeley: Institute for International Studies, University of California.

———. 1979. "Tensions in the Bureaucratic-Authoritarian State and the Question of Democracy." In *The New Authoritarianism in Latin America,* edited by David Collier. 1979. Princeton: Princeton University Press.

―――. 1988. *Bureaucratic Authoritarianism: Argentina, 1966–1973, in Comparative Perspective.* Berkeley: University of California Press.

Oi, Jean C. 1989. *State and Peasantry in Contemporary China: The Political Economy of Village Government.* Berkeley: University of California Press.

Oliver, Pamela E. 1980. "Rewards and Punishments as Selective Incentives for Collective Action: Theoretical Investigations." *American Journal of Sociology* 85: 1356–75.

―――. 1984. "'If You Don't Do It, Nobody Else Will': Active and Token Contributors to Local Collective Action." *American Sociological Review* 49: 601–10.

―――. 1993. "Formal Models of Collective Action." *Annual Review of Sociology* 19: 271–300.

Oliver, Pamela E., and Gerald Marwell. 1988. "The Paradox of Group Size in Collective Action: A Theory of the Critical Mass, II." *American Sociological Review* 53: 1–8.

―――. 1992. "Mobilizing Technologies for Collective Action." In *Frontiers in Social Movement Theory,* edited by Aldon D. Morris and Carol McClurg Mueller. New Haven: Yale University Press.

Olson, Mancur. 1965. *The Logic of Collective Action: Public Goods and the Theory of Groups.* Cambridge: Harvard University Press.

Opp, Karl-Dieter. 1986. "Soft Incentives and Collective Action: Participation in the Anti-Nuclear Movement." *British Journal of Political Science* 16: 87–112.

Opp, Karl-Dieter, and Wolfgang Roehl. 1990. "Repression, Micromobilization, and Political Protest." *Social Forces* 69: 521–47.

Osanka, Franklin Mark. 1962. *Modern Guerrilla Warfare: Fighting Communist Guerrilla Movements, 1941–1961.* New York: Free Press.

Paige, Jeffery M. 1970. "Inequality and Insurgency in Vietnam: A Re-analysis." *World Politics* 23: 24–37.

―――. 1975. *Agrarian Revolution: Social Movements and Export Agriculture in the Underdeveloped World.* New York: Free Press.

―――. 1993. "Coffee and Power in El Salvador." *Latin American Research Review* 28 (3): 7–40.

―――. 1996. "Land Reform and Agrarian Revolution in El Salvador: Comment on Seligson and Diskin." *Latin American Research Review* 31: 127–39.

―――. 1997. *Coffee and Power: Revolution and the Rise of Democracy in Central America.* Cambridge: Harvard University Press.

Palmer, David Scott. 1985. "The Sendero Luminoso Rebellion in Peru." In *Latin American Insurgencies,* edited by George Fauriol. Washington: Georgetown Center for Strategic and International Studies and National Defense University.

―――. 1986. "Rebellion in Rural Peru: The Origins and Evolution of Sendero Luminoso." *Comparative Politics* 18 (January): 127–46.

―――, ed. 1992. *Shining Path of Peru.* New York: St. Martin's.

Panning, William H. 1983. "Inequality, Social Comparison, and Relative Deprivation." *American Political Science Review* 77: 323–29.

Paranzino, Dennis. 1972. "Inequality and Insurgency in Vietnam: A Further Reanalysis." *World Politics* 24: 565–78.

Park, Han S., and T. David Mason. 1986. "The Developmental Parameters of Relative Deprivation Theory." *Studies in Comparative International Development* 21 (Fall): 85–117.

Peterson, Anna L. 1997. *Martyrdom and the Politics of Religion: Progressive Catholicism in El Salvador's Civil War.* Albany: State University of New York Press.

Pfaffenberger, Bryan. 1988. "Sri Lanka in 1987: Indian Intervention and Resurgence of the JVP." *Asian Survey* 28 (February): 137–47.

Pillar, Paul R. 1983. *Negotiating Peace: War Termination as a Bargaining Process.* Princeton: Princeton University Press.

Pion-Berlin, David. 1989. *The Ideology of State Terror: Economic Doctrine and Political Repression in Argentina and Peru.* Boulder, Colo.: Lynne Rienner.

Piven, Frances Fox, and Richard A. Cloward. 1977. *Poor People's Movements: Why They Succeed, How They Fail.* New York: Vintage.

Popkin, Samuel L. 1979. *The Rational Peasant: The Political Economy of Rural Society in Vietnam.* Berkeley: University of California Press.

———. 1988. "Political Entrepreneurs and Peasant Movements in Vietnam." In *Rationality and Revolution,* edited by Michael Taylor. New York: Cambridge University Press.

Powell, John Duncan. 1970. "Peasant Society and Clientelist Politics." *American Political Science Review* 64: 411–25.

Prebisch, Raul. 1950. *The Economic Development of Latin America and its Principal Problems.* New York: United Nations.

———. 1959. "Commercial Policy in the Underdeveloped Countries." *American Economic Review* 49 (2): 251–73.

———. 1964. *Towards a New Trade Policy for Development.* Report by the Secretary General of UNCTAD. New York: United Nations.

Prosterman, Roy L. 1981. "El Salvador's Land Reform: The Real Facts and the True Alternatives." *Food Monitor* 22 (July–August): 13–19.

Prosterman, Roy L., and Jeffrey M. Riedinger. 1987. *Land Reform and Democratic Development.* Baltimore: Johns Hopkins University Press.

Prosterman, Roy L., Jeffrey M. Riedinger, and Mary N. Temple. 1981. "Land Reform and the El Salvador Crisis." *International Security* 6 (Summer): 50–74.

Prosterman, Roy L., Mary N. Temple, and Timothy M. Hanstad, eds. 1990. *Agrarian Reform and Grassroots Development: Ten Case Studies.* Boulder, Colo.: Lynne Rienner.

Prunier, Gérard. 1995. *The Rwanda Crisis: History of a Genocide.* New York: Columbia University Press.

Przeworski, Adam, Michael Alvarez, José Antonio Cheibub, and Fernando Limongi. 1997. "What Makes Democracies Endure?" In *Consolidating Third Wave Democracies,* edited by Larry Diamond et al. Baltimore: Johns Hopkins University Press.

Race, Jeffrey. 1972. *War Comes to Long An.* Berkeley: University of California Press.

Redfield, Robert. 1960. *Peasant Society and Culture.* Chicago: University of Chicago Press.

Regan, Patrick. 1996. "Conditions of Successful Third Party Intervention in Intrastate Wars." *Journal of Conflict Resolution* 40: 336–59.

———. 2000. *Civil Wars and Foreign Powers: Outside Intervention in Intrastate Conflict.* Ann Arbor: University of Michigan Press.

Reif, Linda L. 1986. "Women in Latin American Guerrilla Movements: A Comparative Perspective." *Comparative Politics* 18: 147–69.

Reinhardt, Nola. 1989. "Contrast and Congruence in the Agrarian Reforms of El Salvador and Nicaragua." In *Searching for Agrarian Reform in Latin America*, edited by William C. Thiesenhusen. Boston: Unwin Hyman.

Riedinger, Jeffrey M. 1995. *Agrarian Reform in the Philippines: Democratic Transitions and Redistributive Reform*. Stanford: Stanford University Press.

Rokkan, Stein. 1975. "Dimensions of State Formation and Nation-Building: A Possible Paradigm for Research on Variations Within Europe." In *Formation of National States in Western Europe*, edited by Charles Tilly. Princeton: Princeton University Press.

Ronfeldt, David. 1986. "The Modern Mexican Military." In *Armies and Politics in Latin America*, rev. ed., edited by Abraham F. Lowenthal and J. Samuel Fitch. New York: Holmes and Meier.

Rostow, W. W. 1990. *The Stages of Economic Growth*. 3d ed. New York: Cambridge University Press.

Rothchild, Donald, and Caroline Hartzell. 1995. "Interstate and Intrastate Negotiations in Angola." In *Elusive Peace: Negotiating an End to Civil Wars*, edited by William Zartman. Washington: Brookings.

Rueschemeyer, Dietrich, Evelyne Huber Stephens, and John D. Stephens. 1992. *Capitalist Development and Democracy*. Chicago: University of Chicago Press.

Rule, James B. 1988. *Theories of Civil Violence*. Berkeley: University of California Press.

Rummel, Rudolph J. 1994. "Power, Genocide, and Mass Murder." *Journal of Peace Research* 31 (1): 1–10.

———. 1995. "Democracy, Power, Genocide, and Mass Murder" *Journal of Conflict Resolution* 49: 3–26.

Rupesinghe, Kumar. 1988. "Ethnic Conflicts in South Asia: The Case of Sri Lanka and the Indian Peace-Keeping Force (IPKF)." *Journal of Peace Research* 25 (4): 338–50.

Russett, Bruce M. 1964. "Inequality and Insurgency: The Relation of Land Tenure to Politics." *World Politics* 16: 442–54.

———. 1993. *Grasping the Democratic Peace: Principles for the Post–Cold War World*. Princeton: Princeton University Press.

Ryan, Stephen. 1988. "Emerging Ethnic Conflict: The Neglected International Dimension." *Review of International Studies* 14: 161–77.

Sandler, Todd. 1992. *Collective Action: Theory and Applications*. Ann Arbor: University of Michigan Press.

Saunders, John, ed. 1986. *Population Growth in Latin America and U.S. National Security*. New York: Allen and Unwin.

Scarritt, James R. 1991. "Zimbabwe: Revolutionary Violence Resulting in Reform." In *Revolutions of the Late Twentieth Century*, edited by Jack Goldstone, Ted Robert Gurr, and Farrokh Moshiri. Boulder, Colo.: Westview Press.

———. 1993. "Communal Conflict and Contention for Power in Africa South of the Sahara." In *Minorities at Risk: A Global View of Ethnopolitical Conflicts*, edited by Ted R. Gurr. Washington: United States Institute of Peace.

Scarritt, James R., and Susan McMillan. 1995. "Protest and Rebellion in Africa: Explaining Conflicts between Ethnic Minorities and the State in the 1980s." *Comparative Political Studies* 28: 323–49.

Schlesinger, Stephen, and Stephen Kinzer. 1983. *Bitter Fruit: The Untold Story of the American Coup in Guatemala.* New York: Doubleday.

Schmidt, Steffan W., L. Guasti, Carl H. Landé, and James C. Scott, eds. 1977. *Friends, Followers, and Factions: A Reader in Political Clientelism.* Berkeley: University of California Press.

Schwarz, Benjamin C. 1991. *American Counterinsurgency Doctrine and El Salvador: The Frustrations of Reform and the Illusions of Nation Building.* Santa Monica, Calif.: Rand.

Scott, James C. 1972. "Patron-Client Politics and Political Change in Southeast Asia." *American Political Science Review* 66: 91–113.

———. 1976. *The Moral Economy of the Peasant: Rebellion and Subsistence in Southeast Asia.* New Haven: Yale University Press.

———. 1977. "Hegemony and the Peasantry." *Politics and Society* 7 (3): 267–96.

———. 1985. *Weapons of the Weak: Everyday Forms of Peasant Resistance.* New Haven: Yale University Press.

———. 1986. "Everyday Forms of Peasant Resistance." *Journal of Peasant Studies* 13 (January): 5–35.

Scott, James C., and Ben Kerkvliet. 1977. "How Traditional Rural Patrons Lose Legitimacy." In *Friends, Followers and Factions: A Reader in Political Clientelism,* edited by S. W. Schmidt et al. Berkeley: University of California Press.

Selbin, Eric. 2001. "Same As It Ever Was: The Future of Revolution at the End of the Century." In *Revolution: International Dimensions,* edited by Mark N. Katz. Washington: CQ Press.

Seligson, Mitchell A. 1966. "Agrarian Inequality and the Theory of Peasant Rebellion." *Latin American Research Review* 31: 140–57.

———. 1987. "Democratization in Latin America: The Current Cycle." In *Authoritarians and Democrats: Regime Transition in Latin America,* edited by James M. Malloy and Mitchell A. Seligson. Pittsburgh: University of Pittsburgh Press.

———. 1995. "Thirty Years of Transformation in the Agrarian Structure of El Salvador, 1961–1991." *Latin American Research Review* 30: 43–76.

———. 1996. "Agrarian Inequality and the Theory of Peasant Rebellion." *Latin American Research Review* 31: 141–57.

Shafer, D. Michael. 1988. *Deadly Paradigms: The Failure of U.S. Counterinsurgency Policy.* Princeton: Princeton University Press.

Shorter, Edward, and Charles Tilly. 1974. *Strikes in France, 1830–1968.* Cambridge, U.K.: Cambridge University Press.

Shulz, Donald E. 1984. "El Salvador: Revolution and Counterrevolution in the Living Museum." In *Revolution and Counterrevolution in Central America and the Caribbean,* edited by Donald E. Shulz and Douglas H. Graham. Boulder, Colo.: Westview.

Simon, L. R., and J. C. Stephens. 1982. *El Salvador Land Reform 1980–1981: Impact Audit.* 2d ed. Boston: Oxfam America.

Singer, J. David. 1988. "Reconstructing the Correlates of War Data Set on Material Capabilities of States, 1816–1985," *International Interactions* 14: 115–132.

Singer, J. David, and Melvin Small, producers. 1993. *Correlates of War Project: International and Civil War Data, 1816–1992.* Computer file. Ann Arbor, Mich.: Inter-university Consortium for Political and Social Research.

Sivard, Ruth. 1991. *World Military and Social Expenditures, 1991.* Leesburg, Va.: World Priorities.

Skocpol, Theda. 1976. "France, Russia, and China: A Structural Analysis of Social Revolutions." *Comparative Studies in Society and History* 18: 175–209.

———. 1979. *States and Social Revolutions: A Comparative Analysis of France, Russia, and China.* Cambridge, U.K.: Cambridge University Press.

———. 1982. "What Makes Peasants Revolutionary?" *Comparative Politics* 14: 351–75.

———. 1994. *Social Revolutions in the Modern World.* Cambridge: Harvard University Press.

Small, Melvin, and J. David Singer. 1973. "The Diplomatic Importance of States, 1916–1970: An Extension and Refinement of the Indicator." *World Politics* 25: 577–99.

———. 1982. *Resort to Arms: International and Civil Wars, 1816–1980.* Beverly Hills, Calif.: Sage.

Smelser, Neil. 1963. *Theory of Collective Behavior.* New York: Free Press.

Smith, Anthony. 1981. "War and Ethnicity: The Role of Warfare in the Formation, Self-Images and Cohesion of Ethnic Communities." *Ethnic and Racial Studies* 4: 373–96.

———. 1983. *State and Nation in the Third World.* Aldershot, U.K.: Wheatsheaf Books.

Smith, Jackie. 2000. "Globalization and Political Contention: Brokering Roles of Transnational Social Movement Organizations." Paper prepared for the annual meeting of the American Sociological Association.

Snow, David A., and Robert D. Benford. 1992. "Master Frames and Cycles of Protest." In *Frontiers in Social Movement Theory,* edited by Aldon Morris and Carol M. Mueller. New Haven: Yale University Press.

Snow, David A., E. Burke Rochford, Jr., Steven K. Worden, and Robert D. Benford. 1986. "Frame Alignment Processes, Micromobilization, and Movement Participation." *American Sociological Review* 51: 464–81.

Snyder, David, and Charles Tilly. 1972. "Hardship and Collective Violence in France." *American Sociological Review* 37: 520–32.

Snyder, Richard. 1992. "Explaining Transitions from Neopatrimonial Dictatorships." *Comparative Politics* 24: 379–400.

———. 1999. "The End of Revolution?" *Review of Politics* 61 (Winter): 5–28.

Sollenberg, Margareta, and Peter Wallensteen. 1995. "Major Armed Conflicts." *SIPRI Yearbook 1995.* Oxford, U.K.: Oxford University Press.

———. 1996. "Major Armed Conflicts." *SIPRI Yearbook 1996.* Oxford: Oxford University Press.

Stam, Allan C., III. 1996. *Win, Lose, or Draw: Domestic Politics and the Crucible of War.* Ann Arbor: University of Michigan Press.

Stanley, William. 1996. *The Protection Racket State: Elite Politics, Military Extortion, and Civil War in El Salvador.* Philadelphia: Temple University Press.

Stedman, Stephan. J. 1991. *Peacemaking in Civil War: International Mediation in Zimbabwe, 1974–1980.* Boulder, Colo.: Lynne Rienner.

Stinchcombe, Arthur. 1961. "Agricultural Enterprise and Rural Class Relations." *American Journal of Sociology* 67: 165–76.

Strasma, John. 1989. "Unfinished Business: Consolidating Land Reform in El Salvador." In *Searching for Agrarian Reform in Latin America,* edited by William C. Thiesenhusen. Boston: Unwin Hyman.

Tanham, George K. 1961. *Communist Revolutionary Warfare: The Vietminh in Indochina.* New York: Praeger.

Tarazona-Sevillano, Gabriela. 1990. *Sendero Luminoso and the Threat of Narcoterrorism.* New York: Praeger.

Tarrow, Sidney. 1988. "National Politics and Collective Action: Recent Theory and Research in Western Europe and the United States." *Annual Review of Sociology* 14: 421–40.

———. 1994. *Power in Movement: Social Movements, Collective Action and Politics.* New York: Cambridge University Press.

———. 1995. "Cycles of Collective Action: Between Moments of Madness and the Repertoires of Contention." In *Repertoires and Cycles of Collective Action,* edited by Mark Traugott. Durham, N.C.: Duke University Press.

———. 1996a. "Social Movements in Contentious Politics: A Review Article." *American Political Science Review* 90: 874–83.

———. 1996b. "States and Opportunities: The Political Structuring of Social Movements." In *Comparative Perspectives on Social Movements: Political Opportunities, Mobilizing Structures, and Cultural Framings,* edited by Doug McAdam, John D. McCarthy, and Mayer N. Zald. Cambridge, U.K.: Cambridge University Press.

———. 1998. *Power in Movement: Social Movements and Contentious Politics.* 2d ed. New York: Cambridge University Press.

Taylor, Charles L. and David A. Jodice. 1983. *World Handbook of Political and Social Indicators.* 3d ed. New Haven: Yale University Press.

Taylor, Michael, ed. 1988a. *Rationality and Revolution.* New York: Cambridge University Press.

———. 1988b. "Rationality and Revolutionary Collective Action." In *Rationality and Revolution,* edited by Michael Taylor. New York: Cambridge University Press.

Theobold, Robin. 1982. "Patrimonialism." *World Politics* 34 (July): 548–59.

Thiesenhusen, William C. 1995. *Broken Promises: Agrarian Reform and the Latin American Campesino.* Boulder, Colo.: Westview.

Thompson, Robert. 1966. *Defeating Communist Insurgency: The Lessons of Malaya and Vietnam.* London: Chatto and Windus.

Tilly, Charles. 1978. *From Mobilization to Revolution.* Reading, Mass.: Addison Wesley.

———. 1985. "War Making and State Making as Organized Crime." In *Bringing the State Back In,* edited by Peter B. Evans, Dietrich Rueschemeyer, and Theda Skocpol. New York: Cambridge University Press.

———. 1990. *Coercion, Capital, and European States,* A.D. 900–1990. Cambridge, Mass.: Basil Blackwell.

———. 1993. *European Revolutions, 1492–1992.* Oxford, U.K.: Basil Blackwell.

———. 1995a. "Contentious Repertoires in Great Britain, 1758–1834." In *Repertoires and Cycles of Collective Action,* edited by Mark Traugott. Durham, N.C.: Duke University Press.

———. 1995b. *Popular Contention in Great Britain, 1758–1834.* Cambridge: Harvard University Press.

Traugott, Mark. 1995a. "Barricades as Repertoire: Continuities and Discontinuities in the History of French Contention." In *Repertoires and Cycles of Collective Action,* edited by Mark Traugott. Durham, N.C.: Duke University Press.

————, ed. 1995b. *Repertoires and Cycles of Collective Action.* Durham, N.C.: Duke University Press.

Trimberger, Ellen Kay. 1972. "A Theory of Elite Revolutions." *Studies in Comparative International Development* 7: 191–207.

————. 1978. *Revolution From Above: Military Bureaucrats and Development in Japan, Turkey, Egypt, and Peru.* New Brunswick, N.J.: Transaction.

Tsebelis, George. 1989. "The Abuse of Probability in Political Analysis: The Robinson Crusoe Fallacy." *American Political Science Review* 83: 77–91.

Tullock, Gordon. 1971. "The Paradox of Revolution." *Public Choice* 11 (Fall): 89–99.

Turner, R. N., and L. Killian. 1972. *Collective Behavior.* 2d ed. Englewood Cliffs, N.J.: Prentice-Hall.

Valeriano, Napoleon D., and Charles T. R. Bohannan. 1962. *Counter-Guerrilla Operations: The Philippine Experience.* New York: Praeger.

Van Belle, Douglas A. 1996. "Leadership and Collective Action: The Case of Revolution." *International Studies Quarterly* 40: 107–32.

Vasquez, John A. 1993. *The War Puzzle.* New York: Cambridge University Press.

Vickers, George R. 1992. "The Political Reality After Eleven Years of War." In *Is There a Transition to Democracy in El Salvador?* edited by Joseph S. Tulchin with Gary Bland. Boulder, Colo.: Lynne Rienner.

Vilas, Carlos M. 1995. *Between Earthquakes and Volcanoes: Market, State, and the Revolutions in Central America.* Translated by Ted Kuster. New York: Monthly Review Press.

Wager, Stephen J., and Donald E. Shulz. 1995. "Civil-Military Relations in Mexico: The Zapatista Revolt and Its Implications." *Journal of Interamerican Studies and World Affairs* 37 (1): 1–42.

Wagner, R. Harrison. 1993. "The Causes of Peace." In *Stop the Killing: How Civil Wars End,* edited by Roy Licklider. New York: New York University Press.

Walder, Andrew G. 1998. "Collective Protest and the Waning of the Communist State in China." In *Challenging Authority: The Historical Study of Contentious Politics,* edited by Michael P. Hanagan, Leslie Page Moch, and Wayne te Brake. Minneapolis: University of Minnesota Press.

Wallensteen, Peter, and Karin Axell. 1994. "Major Armed Conflicts." *SIPRI Yearbook 1994.* Oxford, U.K.: Oxford University Press.

Wallensteen, Peter, and Margareta Sollenberg. 1995. "After the Cold War: Emerging Patterns of Armed Conflict, 1989–94," *Journal of Peace Research* 32 (3): 345–60.

————. 1997. "Armed Conflicts, Conflict Termination and Peace Agreements, 1989–96." *Journal of Peace Research* 34 (3): 339–58.

————. 1998. "Armed Conflict and Regional Conflict Complexes, 1989–1997," *Journal of Peace Research* 35 (5): 621–34.

————. 2000. "Armed Conflict, 1989–1999." *Journal of Peace Research* 37 (5): 635–49.

Walter, Barbara F. 1997. "The Critical Barrier to Civil War Settlement." *International Organization* 51: 335–64.

Walton, John. 1984. *Reluctant Rebels: Comparative Studies of Revolution and Underdevelopment.* New York: Columbia University Press.

Weingast, Barry R. 1997. "The Political Foundations of Democracy and the Rule of Law." *American Political Science Review* 91: 245–63.

White, Christine Pelzer. 1974. "The Vietnamese Revolutionary Alliance: Intellectuals, Workers, and Peasants." In *Peasant Revolution and Communist Revolution in Asia,* edited by John Wilson Lewis. Stanford: Stanford University Press.

White, Richard. 1984. *The Morass: United States Intervention in Central America.* New York: Columbia University Press.

Wickham-Crowley, Timothy P. 1987. "The Rise (and Sometimes Fall) of Guerrilla Governments in Latin America." *Sociological Forum* 2: 472–99.

———. 1989. "Understanding Failed Revolution in El Salvador: A Comparative Analysis of Regime Types and Social Structures." *Politics and Society* 17: 511–37.

———. 1990. "Terror and Guerrilla Warfare in Latin America, 1956–1970." *Studies in Comparative International Development* 32: 201–37.

———. 1992. *Guerrillas and Revolution in Latin America: A Comparative Study of Insurgents and Regimes Since 1956.* Princeton: Princeton University Press.

———. 1997. "Structural Theories of Revolution." In *Theorizing Revolutions,* edited by John Foran. New York: Routledge.

Wilkie, James W. 1995. *Statistical Abstract of Latin America.* Vol. 31. Los Angeles: UCLA Latin American Center Publications.

Williams, Robert G. 1986. *Export Agriculture and the Crisis in Central America.* Chapel Hill: University of North Carolina Press.

Wittman, Donald. 1979. "How a War Ends: A Rational Model Approach." *Journal of Conflict Resolution* 23: 743–63.

Wolf, Eric. 1969. *Peasant Revolts of the Twentieth Century.* New York: Harper and Row.

———. 1982. *Europe and the People without History.* Berkeley: University of California Press.

Wolf, Eric, and Sidney W. Mintz. 1957. "Haciendas and Plantations in Middle America and the Antilles." *Social and Economic Studies* 6: 380–412.

World Bank. 1984. *World Development Report, 1984.* New York: Oxford University Press.

Young, Crawford. 1988. "The African Colonial State and Its Political Legacy." In *The Precarious Balance: State and Society in Africa,* edited by Donald Rothchild and Naomi Chazan. Boulder, Colo.: Westview.

———. 1994. *The African Colonial State in Comparative Perspective.* New Haven: Yale University Press.

Zartman, William. 1989. *Ripe for Resolution: Conflict and Intervention in Africa.* 2d ed. New York: Oxford University Press.

———. 1993. "The Unfinished Agenda: Negotiating Internal Conflict." In *Stop the Killing: How Civil Wars End,* edited by Roy Licklider. New York: New York University Press.

———, ed. 1995. *Elusive Peace: Negotiating an End to Civil Wars.* Washington: Brookings.

Zhao, Dingxin. 1998. "Ecologies of Social Movement: Student Mobilization during the 1989 Prodemocracy Movement in Beijing." *American Journal of Sociology* 103 (6): 1493–530.

Index

Index

About the Author

T. David Mason is professor of political science at the University of North Texas, Denton.